Information Tasks
Toward a User-Centered Approach to Information Systems

Library and Information Science

Consulting Editor: *Harold Borko*
Graduate School of Library and Information Science
University of California, Los Angeles

Harold Borko and Charles L. Bernier
Abstracting Concepts and Methods

F. W. Lancaster
Toward Paperless Information Systems

H. S. Heaps
Information Retrieval: Computational and Theoretical Aspects

Harold Borko and Charles L. Bernier
Indexing Concepts and Methods

Gerald Jahoda and Judith Schiek Braunagel
The Librarian and Reference Queries: A Systematic Approach

Charles H. Busha and Stephen P. Harter
Research Methods in Librarianship: Techniques and Interpretation

Diana M. Thomas, Ann T. Hinckley, and Elizabeth R. Eisenbach
The Effective Reference Librarian

G. Edward Evans
Management Techniques for Librarians, Second Edition

Jessica L. Milstead
Subject Access Systems: Alternatives in Design

Dagobert Soergel
Information Storage and Retrieval: A Systems Approach

Stephen P. Harter
Online Information Retrieval: Concepts, Principles, and Techniques

Timothy C. Craven
String Indexing

The list of books continues at the end of the volume.

Information Tasks
Toward a User-Centered Approach to Information Systems

Bryce L. Allen
School of Library and Informational Science
University of Missouri
Columbia, Missouri

Academic Press
San Diego   London   Boston   New York   Sydney   Tokyo   Toronto

Copyright © 1996 by ACADEMIC PRESS

Academic Press, Inc.
525 B Street, Suite 1900, San Diego, California 92101-4495, USA
http://www.apnet.com

Academic Press Limited
24-28 Oval Road, London NW1 7DX, UK
http://www.hbuk.co.uk/ap/

Library of Congress Cataloging-in-Publication Data

Allen, Bryce.
    Information tasks : toward a user-centered approach to information
systems / by Bryce L. Allen.
           p.   cm. -- (Library and information science series)
    Includes index.
    ISBN 0-12-051040-5 (alk. paper)
    1. User interfaces (Computer systems)   2. System design.
3. Information storage and retrieval systems.   I. Title.
II. Series: Library and information science (New York, N.Y.)
QA76.9.U83A5   1996
025.04--dc20   96-28239
                                                         CIP

PRINTED IN THE UNITED STATES OF AMERICA
96 97 98 99 00 01 BC 9 8 7 6 5 4 3 2 1

Contents

Preface   xi

1
Introduction

Information: Some Definitions   2
Information Systems: Some Definitions   4
Information Systems as Communication Systems   5
Information Systems: A General Systems Approach   6
The Problem-Solving Perspective   11
User-Centered versus Data-Centered Design   14
Systems, Services, and Institutions   19
Conclusion   21
References   22

2
An Introduction to User-Centered Information-System Design

Needs Analysis   26
Task Analysis   29
Resource Analysis   35
    Knowledge   35
    Individual Differences   39
User Models   41
Designing for Usability   43
    Enabling States   44
    Usability   45
User-Centered Design: A Practical Guide I   48
References   50

3

Information Needs

Introduction	55
Information Needs: A Cognitive Model	58
Cognition and Behavior	61
Information Needs as Knowledge Gaps	62
Information Needs: A Social Model	73
Social Influences and Individual Behavior	74
Perception and Social Influence	75
Identification of Alternative Actions	77
Selection of Alternative Courses of Action	77
Social Cognition and the Collective Nature of Information Needs	78
Perception and Group Knowledge	79
Identification of Alternative Actions	82
Selection of Alternative Courses of Action	83
Information Needs: The Organizational Perspective	85
Social Influences and Collective Behavior	85
Collective Perception and Social Influence	86
Identification of Alternative Actions	87
Selection of Alternative Courses of Action	87
The Person-in-Situation Model	88
Example 1: Health Information Needs	90
Example 2: Consumer Information Needs	94
Example 3: Political Information Needs	96
Example 4: Newcomer Information Needs	98
Example 5: Managerial Decision Making	100
Summary	103
References	103

4

Information Needs and Information Design

Introduction	108
Design Directions: Some Initial Hints	108
Failures of Perception	110
Alternative Identification	114
Alternative Selection	116
Bounded Rationality	118
Conclusion	121
User-Centered Design: A Practical Guide II	122
References	125

5

Expressing Information Needs

Introduction   126
Individual Expressions of Information Need   127
    Questions and Question Answering   129
    Expressing Failure of Perception   130
    Expressing Needs for Slot Filling and Alternative Identification 136
    Expressing Needs for Evaluation of Alternatives   138
    Informant Selection and Statements of Need   140
    The Social Nature of Statements of Information Need 143
    Intermediaries and Need Expressions   144
Group Expressions of Information Need   145
References   150

6

Designing Systems to Meet Expressed Information Needs

Introduction   152
    General Design Principle   152
    Specific Design Implications   152
Designing for World Knowledge   154
Designing for Knowledge of a Language   155
Designing for Source Selection   156
Designing for Social Understanding   157
Designing for Failure of Perception   158
    Browsing: Classification   159
    Browsing: Interfaces   161
    Experts and Failures of Perception   163
    Definition of and Explanation for Failures of Perception 164
Designing for Alternative Identification   167
Designing for Evaluation   172
Designing for Group Information   176
Summary   181
User-Centered Design: A Practical Guide III   182
References   185

7

Information Tasks: Interacting with Information Systems

Scanning   190
    Scanning Text   191
    Scanning Documents   194

Scanning Electronic Documents 195
Reviewing and Evaluating 197
Evaluating Text 198
Evaluating Documents 199
Evaluating Electronic Documents 199
Learning 200
Learning from Text 202
Learning from Documents 203
Learning from Electronic Documents 205
Learning from People and Media 206
Planning 208
Cognitive Load 209
Collective Interaction with Information Systems 210
Conclusions 212
References 213

8

Design Details for Information Systems

Introduction 218
General Design Principle 219
Specific Design Implications 219
Designing for Scanning 221
Designing for Evaluation 225
Designing for Learning 228
Designing for Planning 231
Designing for Group Information Tasks 232
Refocusing Information-System Design 234
Information Selection 235
Organization of and Access to Information 236
Interface Selection 237
Conclusion 238
User-Centered Design: A Practical Guide IV 239
References 243

9

Information Services from the User's Perspective

Introduction 245
Partnership Model of Service Interaction 246
Designing Services 250
Expressing Statements of Information Need 250
Scanning, Evaluating, and Learning from Information 252

Balancing Devices and Intermediaries 253
Intermediaries and Group Information Activities 254
Instruction 255
Contacting Users 257
Conclusion: A User-Centered Approach to Information Services 259
References 261

10

Information Institutions

Introduction 262
A Market Focus 263
Identifying Markets 264
Service Development 265
Customer Relations 267
Strategic Planning 268
The Short-Range Focus 269
Technology and People 271
Interinstitution Integration 272
Value and Pricing 274
Private or Public? 276
Resource Management 280
Personnel for Service 281
Organizational Structure 282
Program Budgets 283
Conclusions 284
User-Centered Design: A Practical Guide V 285
References 289

11

Conclusion: User-Centered Design and Evaluation

Introduction 290
Evaluating Information Systems 292
Evaluating Information Services 295
Evaluating Information Institutions 297
Conclusion 299
References 300

Index 303

Preface

The ideas that form the foundation of this book were developed during 25 years of working in libraries. In libraries, I worked on a daily basis with information systems and their users, and repeatedly wondered, "Why aren't these information systems more usable?" Now, as I wander through the campus of a major research university, I see students lining up to use automated teller machines (ATMs). They use ATMs easily, almost automatically, without thinking about it. Then I see the same students laboring over the online public access catalog (OPAC) in the University Library, every mark of agony and frustration indicating their lack of success in using the OPAC. To its credit, the library offers regular, hour-long instruction in how to use the library catalog, including both beginner and advanced sessions. But I wonder, "If a bank had to have its customers attend two hour-long evening sessions to enable them to use the ATM, wouldn't that be a terrible admission of failure in the design of their system?" And I am reminded of the objective articulated by the designers of Xerox copiers: "If we could make the experience of using a Xerox photocopier as simple and straightforward as the experience of walking through a door, then we will have made a truly usable copier" [Rheinfrank, J. J., Hartman, W. R., & Wasserman, A. (1992). Designing for usability: Crafting a strategy for the design of a new generation of Xerox copiers. In P. S. Adler & T. A. Winograd (Eds.), *Usability: Turning technologies into tools* (pp. 15–40). New York: Oxford Univ. Press].

The apparent difference in usability between ATMs and online catalogs may at first appear to derive from an inappropriate comparison. After all, OPACs are general-purpose search systems, while ATMs are special-purpose machines designed for limited tasks. Yet it is precisely the difference in the design of the two systems that produces the differences in their usability. Banks have thought out the tasks that their customers need to accomplish and have assigned some of those tasks to a system that has limited objectives but accomplishes those objectives in a reasonably straightforward way. Libraries, on the other hand, seem neither to have thought through the needs of their users and the tasks they are accomplishing nor to have developed appropriate systems to address those needs and tasks.

This first example compared a library information system with a commercial information system. In this book, there are a number of library examples, but for the most part the discussion is kept at a reasonably high level of generality. It is intended that this general discussion about the design of information systems, services, and institutions will cover principles and approaches that can be applied in a wide variety of design settings. The literature of system design suggests that information systems that support and manage business information, scientific data, and government files are as much in need of the user-centered approach as are library information systems.

The term "user-centered" in the sense used in this book can be traced back to 1974 [Walther, G. H., & O'Neil, H. F. J. (1974). The user–computer interface in an information utility delivery system: An empirical approach to user-centered design. In P. Zunde (Ed.), *Information utilities: Proceedings of the 37th ASIS annual meeting* (pp. 114–119). Washington, DC: ASIS], and perhaps further; the bibliographic tools do not really allow detailed searches of earlier materials. The term "user-centered" and the concepts driving its use are encountered today in an increasing number of domains. A recent scan of the literature showed this term being applied to specific design decisions, such as creating voice mail systems, vehicles for highway use, or computer-aided manufacturing systems. But the main focus of user-centered approaches seems to cluster around the design of information systems of various kinds. So, for example, we find the term being applied to databases, interfaces, and information architectures such as hypermedia. At the level of a specific information institution, user-centered redesign has been proposed for many functions of libraries, such as user-centered catalog design, indexing, and interlibrary loan.

This book brings together a great deal of the literature that is relevant to user-centered information systems and services in an integrated discussion that chronicles the revolutionary impact of user-centered approaches on the way information systems, information work, and information institutions are envisioned. But this book does not simply describe the changes that are occurring or that might occur in the future. The approach is frankly one of advocacy, and throughout the book there is a continuing argument that user-centered approaches are needed to achieve successful and usable information systems, services, and institutions. The terribly simplistic conviction that provides the conceptual foundation for this book is that much information-system design emphasizes the data contained in the system rather than the users of the system and what they want to do, and that is why there are so many bad information systems. Throughout the book I will try to convince the reader that user-centered design is possible and that, when applied to information systems, user-centered design will produce usable, effective information systems.

Ideas that lead to the creation of successful and usable information systems, services, and institutions form the core of library and information science. But the approach to library and information science taken here is not parochial. Rather, it is driven by an understanding that the ideas and concepts of library and information science can be found under different labels in many academic disciplines, ranging from the social sciences to engineering. One of the objectives of this book is to bring together from many disciplines a wide range of literature relevant to user-centered design. Of course, completing this task in any comprehensive manner is impossible, and the continued evolution of the literature makes such an endeavor as difficult as jumping onto a moving train. Readers may find that the literature cited in this book is representative of a large corpus of research that is relevant and important to scholars and students in library and information science. This representative sample can form a starting point from which they can delve more deeply into this research, as they seek to understand users and to use this understanding to create usable information systems and services.

The contents of this book have been used as text materials in courses taught in three different schools of library and information science. The detailed discussion of users and their information needs, tasks, and resources is suitable for use in a course in information organization and access. The consideration of design principles and design alternatives can be used in courses on information-system design and information technology. The final chapters, on information services and institutions, could be applied to courses in user services and in management, respectively.

In addition to its academic audience, this book should be of interest to those who are responsible for designing information systems. Each chapter of the book discusses one step in the process of analyzing the users of information systems and designing elements of the information infrastructure to respond directly to those users' needs. It is anticipated that designers will adapt each of these general discussions to their specific domains and develop detailed approaches to the design of specific information systems, services, and institutions. At the same time, the general outline of information systems and information work presented here may be used by information professionals to understand the tools they are using and how they can influence the development of more usable information systems and services. To facilitate the use of this book by designers and professionals, a summary of the practical design implications developed in the detailed discussions is provided at the end of each of the even-numbered chapters.

This book was written in many interesting places, including Kilcrohane, County Cork (thanks to Betsy Hearne), and Pivot Lake, Ontario (thanks to my parents). But the bulk of the writing occurred during a semisabbatical from the University of Illinois during which I was invited to be a visiting scholar at the I. D. Weeks Library of the University of South Dakota. I particularly express my appreciation to the librarians and staff of that library, and I give a special thanks to Imre Meszaros and Heidi Nickisch for their hospitality in providing an environment in which I could write in peace.

Many colleagues will recognize ideas we have discussed over the years. To them, I can only express my gratitude for their willingness to debate and brainstorm. I am also indebted to four anonymous reviewers for their helpful comments. To my wife, Gillian, who helped me over many difficult spots with her constructive editing and suggestions, I owe more than gratitude.

1

Introduction

This book is about user-centered design of information systems, services, and institutions. Progress toward sound, user-centered design principles for information systems has been uneven. In more traditional information systems, such as databases, research focuses on interface design, usability analysis and testing, and user modeling. However, there has been little progress in the investigation of how human factors influence the use of large bibliographic systems, full-text databases, or the financial records of companies. Usability testing of these types of large, general-purpose information systems, when it happens at all, tends to occur after the design process is substantially complete. Postdesign usability testing is essentially a trial-and-error approach, unless the complete design process has been informed by a clear understanding of users' information needs, the tasks they accomplish to meet those needs, and the resources they employ as they work through those tasks.

Throughout this book, user-centered design of information systems is contrasted with data-centered design of such systems. This is a convenient way to show that the user-centered approach has been much neglected and has much to offer to the design process. Of course, it is an overly simplistic dichotomy. Information-system designers can be influenced by the nature of the data contained in their information devices, by the technology used to store and retrieve that data, or by the information needs of users. In reality, the design process always takes all of these factors into account, and the difference between the user-centered, the data-centered, or the technology-centered approaches to design is the emphasis given to one influence over the others. In this book, the preference for user-centered information-system design over data-centered approaches should be understood as a recommendation that the information needs of users play a more influential role in design than data or technology.

Information systems are the building blocks of information services and information institutions. The qualms and concerns previously expressed about information systems can be extended to the services that use them and the institutions that contain them. Most contemporary information services seem to be created on the "If you build it, he will come" principle, where "he" is the imagined user. Of

1

course, there is no guarantee that users will be willing or able to employ services that are assembled without serious attention to their needs. At the same time, information institutions resemble vast hierarchical bureaucracies where responsibility to the user falls far behind responsibility to the data, to the institution, or even to one's own professional priorities. This critique applies as much to management information systems (MIS) departments and database vendors as to libraries. In the chapters that follow, the approach to user-centered information-system design will be extended to cover the creation and maintenance of information services and institutions. Again, the argument presented in this book is that user-centered approaches will produce better services and institutions than traditional bureaucratic approaches.

This dichotomy between user-centered and bureaucratic approaches to the organization of information institutions can be regarded as a necessary oversimplification. It is essential to consider the demands of the market, the needs of the institution for structural stability and continuity, and the nature of the technological infrastructure in organizing an information institution. The difference between the user-centered, bureaucratic, and technology-based approaches to the organization of information institutions is really a question of the emphasis given to each of these influences. The strong preference for user-centered institutions over bureaucratic institutions expressed in this book is really a recommendation that market demand play a more influential role in designing information institutions.

To lay the foundation for the discussions that will follow, this chapter will first consider what is meant by information and then will focus briefly on a few preliminary ideas about information systems, information services, and information institutions.

Information: Some Definitions

"Information" is understood here as the nominalization of the verb "to inform." This is an active verb, which indicates that information involves both an activity accomplished by someone and a process experienced by someone. From the perspective of the informant, information is an activity that is accomplished. From the perspective of the user, information is a process: something that happens to the user. This process perspective is one emphasis found in discussions of information. As Buckland (1991a, 1991b) has so helpfully observed, the word "information" is used to refer to things, knowledge, or a process. The position taken here is that it is the process that is the truly essential aspect of information. People inform themselves or are informed. In doing so, they may make use of things such as books or databases, and they may acquire knowledge, but the things they use are information things precisely because they are used in the process of informing or becoming informed. It is the underlying process that distinguishes an information thing from all other things.

Information as knowledge is more difficult to understand. The noun "knowledge" is one of those words that, like information, represents a nominalization of a verb. The crucial aspect of knowledge is that it is known, so the emphasis is placed on the process of knowing and coming to know (or learning). This consideration seems to blur the distinction between information-as-knowledge and information-as-process. I know, because I have learned. I have learned, frequently, because I have been informed. At the same time, I am able to inform someone, because I know something. The processes of knowing, learning, informing, and being informed are inextricably bound up with each other.

If knowledge is essentially a process, how can information-as-knowledge be distinguished from information-as-process? It seems clear that there is a tendency, described by Dervin (1977) and associated with Popper's (1972) philosophy of science, to reify knowledge: to consider knowledge as something with an independent existence in the world. The idea of knowledge as something that has a separate existence, independent of any individual knower, seems to be based on the phenomenon of social knowledge. There are ideas that are reasonably common in any social group: things that "everybody knows." These serve as the basis for a socially constructed reality that is real and important to the social group. In the American legal system, for example, certain kinds of knowledge can be accepted without requiring evidence to be presented; these are considered "notorious common knowledge."[1] This socially constructed knowledge makes sense of Buckland's "information as knowledge," Dervin's "Information$_1$," and Popper's "Third World." In other words, information-as-knowledge is the socially constructed collective experience of the informing process.

The focus on information-as-process adopted in this book must be distinguished from a very different focus that presents information as a collection of recorded messages, to be distinguished from data, knowledge, understanding, and wisdom (Kochen, 1974). This traditional definition focuses on information-as-thing rather than information-as-process. As Ingwersen (1992) points out, the concept of information must include the processes in which the informant's knowledge is transformed by the act of communication and the processes of perception, evaluation, interpretation, and learning, in which the information seeker's knowledge is transformed. Therefore, our definition of information is:

> The process in which an informant's cognitive structures are encoded and transmitted to an information seeker, who perceives the coded messages, interprets them, and learns from them.

This definition of information will be carried forward throughout this book. Information is a process that happens to people. Through information (although

---

[1] I am indebted to a student, Vivian Bliss, for pointing out this concept of "judicial notice" to me.

not solely through it), people learn and so have knowledge. Knowledge shared in a social group takes on an external reality as a social construct. People who have been informed are able to inform others. To do this, people may use things, which consequently can be defined as information things. Accordingly, in this book the term "information" will be used to refer to the informing process, to the knowledge that is communicated and achieved, or to the messages that encode that knowledge.

Information Systems: Some Definitions

Any system may be characterized as a number of components that have relationships with each other. Such systems may be either physical or social in nature. The cardiovascular system, as an example of a physical system, has components such as the heart, the arteries, and the veins. The relationships between these components define the collective purpose and function of the system. An electoral system, as an example of a social system, consists of components such as voters, electors, candidates, and legislatures. The relationships between the components define the function of the system, although social systems may be more complex than physical systems. In defining information systems, Buckland's three-part approach to information can be used to identify the components of information systems and their relationships with each other. From the perspective of information as thing, an information system is a linked network of information things: computers, pieces of paper with black squiggles on them, etc. For the sake of clarity, this kind of thing, or network of things, can be referred to as an **"information device**." Examples of information devices are books (viewed as separable from authors and readers), and electronic database systems (viewed apart from their authors, creators, programmers, intermediaries, and users).

From the perspective of information-as-knowledge, an information system is a linked network of knowledge. It will be recalled that the only meaningful distinction that can be made between information-as-knowledge and information-as-process is to accept that there is a socially constructed reality of common knowledge that records the collective experiences of being informed. So, from the information-as-knowledge perspective, an information system can be understood as organizing public knowledge. Ordinarily, it would be tempting to define a network of public knowledge as a "knowledge base." This term has already been appropriated by the designers of expert systems, who use it to refer to the encoded knowledge and expertise of their systems. Perhaps the best term to use for a network of public knowledge is **"body of knowledge**." If the "thing-ness" of an encyclopedia is ignored, the contents of the encyclopedia can be considered to be an example of this kind of body of knowledge. Other examples of bodies of knowledge are the law or the sciences.

The information-as-thing and information-as-knowledge perspectives iden-tify some of the components of information systems. The information-as-process perspective identifies the remaining components and also the relationships between the components that define the purpose and function of the information system. From the perspective of information-as-process, an information system must be defined as a linked and related set of entities that play a role in the process of being or becoming informed. This definition adds a group of users to the components of information systems, as well as mechanisms (such as interfaces) and people (such as intermediaries) that facilitate the process. A more important contribution, how-ever, is the purpose and function of the system conveyed by the information-as-process perspective. With the purpose of an information system defined as "playing a role in the process of being, or becoming, informed," the interrelationships of the components of the information system can be functionally defined.

An **information system** is a linked and related system of entities (including one or more information devices) that provides access to one or more bodies of knowledge and acts as a mechanism through which individuals can inform other people or become informed. Typically, people inform other people by communi-cating with them. Accordingly, the mechanisms that enable people to inform each other can be seen as media of communication.

Information Systems as Communication Systems

An important concept in the development of the field of information sci-ence and in the education of information professionals is that an information sys-tem is, at least to some extent, a communication system. An informant, or source of information, communicates that information through media of communication (which may include information devices such as books, images, or databases) to a user. The entire information interaction can be seen as a dialog in which the in-formant and the user communicate with each other.

The idea that information systems resemble communication systems relates to the definitions offered previously. Communication models do not play a major role in this book, but the idea of information being intimately linked with com-munication underlies many of the detailed analyses of information systems. The question that must be asked is, "To what extent is the process of information a communication process?" Does informing always require an informant? The looseness of language is a problem here. Some people will say they are informed by clouds that it will rain or by trees that it is windy. Certainly, people *learn* by per-ception. The communication model of information, however, maintains that this learning is not being informed. The term "being informed" is reserved for what is learned through acts of communication with other beings. (Note the deliberate choice of the term "beings" here. This allows for those who communicate with their dogs or horses. However, most information or communication processes presume that the informant is human!)

The standard, stereotypical case of information is being informed by communication with someone else. I may stop by the road to ask directions. I may consult the knowledge of individuals embodied in publications. I may post a note and receive a number of answers on an electronic bulletin board or listserver. The important feature of all of these exchanges is the collective process, instead of just an individual one. The information system is, therefore, a system designed to create collective processes for informing and being informed. This is a quick and partial view of communication models as applied to information systems. Budd (1992) presents a thorough discussion of the library as a communication system, and Meadow (1987) and Dervin (1977) provide a broad approach to information systems as communication systems. The definition proposed here for the term "information system" consists of all of the components of the communication process, including the informant, the searcher for information, and any other people that are involved in the information process. This definition of information system is therefore broad or general.

Information Systems: A General Systems Approach

An information system is a linked and related system of entities that acts as a mechanism through which individuals can inform other people or become informed. An understanding of any system must include knowing the entities that are part of the system and how they relate to each other in performing a function. This section (a general systems approach) examines more closely the entities that are components of information systems, and the following section (the problem-solving perspective) considers the functional relationships that define the way information systems work.

A simple example may be the best way to begin a consideration of the components of information systems. Perhaps the simplest information system is typified by a driver stopping to ask someone for directions to a certain place. If the respondent knows the answer, can communicate it clearly, and is willing to communicate it clearly, and the answer is understood by the driver, then the information system will work. Note the complexity of even this simple information system. A great deal of understanding of the knowledge of the respondent and the communication abilities of both the inquirer and the respondent is required to assess the effectiveness of the information interaction.

Complexity increases when the informant is represented by an information device. Here the knowledge and the communication abilities of the informant are circumscribed by the technical characteristics of the device. This device may be a book or other printed matter, an electronic information-retrieval device, or any other form of external memory. To extend the previous example, the driver in this more complex case may consult the expertise of someone who is not present, but whose knowledge has been encapsulated in the form of a map. Here complexity is added by the requirement that the driver understand the conventions by which the knowledge of the mapmaker has been encoded and be able to convert those codes to a form of understanding that will determine which road to take. If the example is expanded to include other forms of information technology, then the complexity would increase again. A driver consulting a computerized map has to understand not only the conventions by which the knowledge of the mapmaker is encoded, but needs to know how to retrieve the required display. In other words, an understanding of the information system includes an understanding of the coding and representation of knowledge in the body of knowledge, an understanding of the mechanics of the information device, and of course, an understanding of the information need being resolved.

Complexity is further increased when other individuals are included in the information system. In the previous examples, complexity increases when the informant and the driver are joined as parts of the information interaction by the mapmaker (encoding the body of knowledge) and the system designer (creating the information device). Other individuals can be added to the information system and with them comes more complexity. There may be an indexer who provides "metadata," or descriptions of the information contained in the information system. These metadata may be a separate database and may also be used to organize the body of knowledge. There may be an intermediary to accomplish the actual retrieval or to interpret the results to the user. An elaboration of this understanding of human intermediaries reveals that they are engaged in complex social interactions that impinge on the informing process. This means that both individual and social variables influencing the information behavior of the human participants are essential elements of an understanding of the information system. Clearly, systems incorporating all of these sources of expert knowledge are more complex than those that incorporate fewer sources. In this discussion, the term "information system" is intended to include all levels of complexity. In some of the examples, it will be necessary to begin with relatively simple models and to add complexity to achieve a more complete understanding of the system. "Information system" does not refer simply to a technology or to a family of technologies, but includes humans in several different capacities.

Because people tend to think of an information device (particularly a computer-based device) when they hear the term "information system," it is important to emphasize again that any information technology is only one fragment of an information system. A full understanding of information-retrieval devices requires that they be examined in a systems context. Figure 1 may help to clarify this.

Figure 1 has two time axes. The user's life begins at the top and extends to the bottom. The information device's existence begins at the left and extends to the right. At some point and for some duration, the two existences overlap. This is the

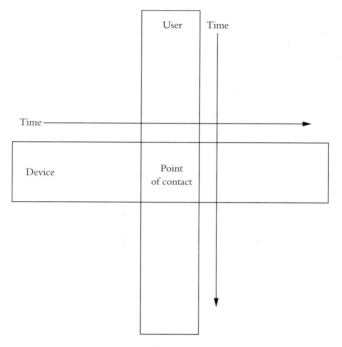

Figure 1
The user–device interaction.

point of contact between the user and the information device. Much information-science research focuses on the device. For example, Dalrymple and Roderer (1994) survey research on databases, and O'Brien (1994) does the same for research on online catalogs. In more specific focuses on the device, Newby (1993) surveys the hardware and software associated with virtual-reality techniques in information retrieval, while Lange (1993) considers the possibility of adding speech synthesis and recognition to information devices. In terms of evaluation, the performance of information devices has been viewed as an end in itself and is measured against abstract standards of excellence. Kantor (1994) reviews developments in information-retrieval techniques, most of which have been evaluated using such abstract standards. It seems clear from the discussion of the complexities of information systems that this focus on the device has certain shortcomings. The crucial focal point shown in the diagram is the point of contact between the user and the device, when it is possible to measure performance in a much more realistic manner. At that point in time, both the user and the device are in play; the performance of the device in terms of the efficiency of its data structures for storing information can be measured, and the effectiveness of its interface and the satisfaction of the user with the retrieved results can be assessed. The evaluation thus becomes much more balanced.

It is true, however, that the performance of the information device, even measured in this more complete and balanced manner at the point of contact, is determined by the state of the device and what has happened to the user in previous periods. In other words, both the device and the user bring a history to the point of encounter. In the case of the device, this history includes design decisions made during the creation of the device, value-added processes that occurred when the data was entered into the device, and previous assessments of its usability and effectiveness by other users. In the case of the user, the history includes the life situation that gave rise to the information problem and the cumulative experience of the searcher that gave rise to his or her cognitive structures. The natures of the device and the user are clearly determined by their respective backgrounds.

It follows that understanding the point of contact involves thinking backward along both axes of the diagram, considering the background of the information device and the cognitive structures and social situation of the user. At the same time, it is possible to see the point of contact as being important for the continued evolution of both the user and the information device. Just as the present state of the information device is the product of evaluations of its past performance, the future state of the information device can be affected by the point of contact. Similarly, the outcome of the contact with the information retrieval device can transform the user. Solving one problem can reveal additional problems, and the contact with the information device becomes cyclical in nature. The point of contact, represented in the diagram as a simple quadrilateral, can be seen as a kind of loop or Möbius strip, returning on itself. Alternatively, as may be the case, failing to resolve the problem may affect future approaches to information retrieval in general or the particular information device specifically.

Accordingly, there is a large constellation of effects that will facilitate an understanding of the information-retrieval system. The point of contact, within which there is a complex interaction between an information device and its user, provides a starting place for analyzing information systems. Tracing both of these agents back in time provides an understanding of the elements that went into the design and creation of the information device and its evolution, not only to its present point of development, but in the future. It can be noted that machine learning, never applied with great success to information retrieval, would make the continuous development of information devices a matter of fact, not just of speculation.

The institutional context in which the information device operates is also important in understanding the information system. The way the device is set up to operate, the expectations of it, and the use to which it is put may vary from institution to institution. In this sense, the machine has a social embeddedness that influences its operation and thus is central to understanding how the device works. Of course, users also have their own institutional contexts, more broadly defined as social and organizational contexts. The expectations that they bring to contact with the device are also conditioned by the social situations in which they are embedded. For example, the motivations of the user who approaches the information device, the expectations that determine behavior, and the ways in which the user will assess the effectiveness of the interaction with the device must be considered. At the same time, the abilities of the user and the knowledge and skills that are brought to the encounter with the information device are important factors in how the user interacts with the device. Further, the point of contact can only be understood from the user's perspective if how the information is used and its impact on the individual user as well as the social situations in which he or she is embedded are considered. These situations, as outlined by Taylor (1982), represent the information environment in which the interaction between the user and the device takes place. Variables from that environment that can influence the way information seeking occurs are the demographic situation of the user, the organization in which the user is found, and the social, intellectual, and cultural background of the user. Any or all of these factors can affect the informing process and the impact that communication will have on the user. To further complicate matters, it is possible for the user, represented until this point as an individual, to be a group of people, acting in a single, coherent, and collective manner, bringing a social and organizational context that is unique to the group to the encounter with the device.

The definitions previously presented maintain that an information system is a communication system. The simple diagram presented in Fig. 1 is rather a lonely reality. The user is the only person represented. However, tracing back along the existence of the information device reveals that there are a multitude of other individuals assembled just off the edge of the diagram. These are the individuals who create the messages that are incorporated into the system, and of course, incorporating any message means that one must also encode a set of cognitive structures associated with the individuals who are the informants. These knowledgeable individuals, who have contributed the body of knowledge contained in the device, have structured that knowledge in a way consistent with how their knowledge is structured. Superimposed on these cognitive structures, which may be called authorial structures, are those of individuals who have restructured the knowledge using metadata, including subject classifications and controlled vocabulary indexing. The cognitive content of the information system arises from a variety of human communication activities: the activities of writing or otherwise creating informative material and the activities of structuring and organizing collections of such materials. These structures, added to those built into the device itself by its designers and creators, are brought to the point of contact.

An information device may bring with it a set of interpreters and guides: those individuals identified as information specialists or intermediaries. Such individuals add to the cognitive content of the information device their own understanding, not only of the device, but of the user. The cognitive structures, abilities, and attitudes of these intermediaries can also be traced back in time to their origin and can be projected ahead to see how they may develop in the future. At the point of contact, however, intermediaries' cognitive structures, abilities, and attitudes can be of central importance to the success of the information contact. Accordingly, a true systems view of information systems must take these cognitive effects into account.

This section began with a promise to consider information systems from a broad and general systems perspective. The meaning of this may now be clearer. The point of contact between user and device is the point where the operation of the device is assessed most accurately and completely. Generating that intersection are a variety of antecedents, ranging from design decisions to the training of intermediaries, and from personal knowledge previously obtained by users to their ability to reason logically. All of these elements form the larger system, which must be understood in order to approach information devices in a thorough manner. Similarly, there is an ongoing developmental process that must be understood and that encompasses all of the actors present at the intersection. The systems approach at the foundation of this book is a way to understand information systems through these important influences on how they perform their functions.

The Problem-Solving Perspective

The above discussion considers the components of information systems and outlines the complexity of the interactions between the various components. The following discussion reduces that complexity somewhat. This book takes a problem-solving approach to the process of being informed. In other words, it considers the functional interactions of the components of the information system as defining a single function: problem solving. This restriction of the discussion is necessary to narrow the topic sufficiently to permit adequate depth and detail in considering information systems. To try to include all possible information and communication processes requires an analysis of an impossibly varied and diverse set of activities. A few examples illustrate activities that are included in and excluded from the discussion of information system function.

First, it is possible to distinguish between an individual who seeks out information and one who is informed in passing by communication that is present in the environment. For example, an individual who is planning a trip may turn on the television in the morning to obtain a weather forecast. While waiting for the forecast, the individual may learn that a certain type of automobile is available at a discount, that a specific breakfast cereal appeals to children, and that there has been a coup in an African nation. The problem-solving perspective relates to the first example of information activities (information seeking) and not the second (information received in passing).

Similarly, it is possible to distinguish between someone who seeks information for some specific purpose (as in the traveler mentioned previously) and someone who seeks information for its intrinsic value. Some people watch television news, not to find out any particular fact, but rather out of a general desire to be well informed. Other people are "information junkies" in certain areas. For example, people may keep informed about politics as a hobby. They do not need political information for any particular purpose, but they find the antics of the candidates and the electorate endlessly entertaining. Again, the problem-solving perspective focuses on the first type of information activity (purposive use of information) and not on the second type (gratification through information).

Finally, there is a distinction between people who seek information as a means of making sense of their lives and those who avoid information for the same purpose. There is frequently a tacit assumption that the former behavior is acceptable and the latter somewhat irrational, but no individual can seek information in a complete and purposive way on all topics that affect his or her life. Most people engage in a combination of information-seeking and information-avoiding behaviors. The problem-solving perspective is broad enough to include both information-seeking and information-avoiding activities. However, it is probably fair to say that this book concentrates more on the former than the latter.

The problem-solving perspective narrows the scope of the discussion considerably. This book will, of course, make reference to some of the other types of information activities where relevant. However, for the most part, it concentrates on a subset of the information activities in which people engage. Accordingly, the assumption is that someone wants to be informed because he or she has a problem to be solved. It is important to recognize, however, that although all information seeking is problem solving, not all problem solving is information seeking. In other words, being informed is only one aspect of problem solving. The problem-solving approach taken here has been influenced by a number of other researchers in the area of information systems. Mason and Mitroff (1973) propose the following focus for management information systems:

> [There must be] at least one person of a certain psychological type who faces a problem within some organizational context for which he needs evidence to arrive at a solution (i.e., to select some course of action) and that evidence is made available to him through some mode of presentation (p. 475).

Each of the elements of this definition is important. The first is the focus on the individual person, although it is sometimes true that the individual is part of a group that has its own information activity. The second is the psychological type of the individual, but this element is subsequently modified in the definition by noting that the individual is working within an organizational context. It follows that both individual and social characteristics may influence the information activities. The next elements are probably the most central. The individual who seeks information does so because of a problem that can be resolved by evidence that will allow him or her to select a course of action. The information device is the technology that presents this evidence. This approach was subsequently elaborated upon by van Gigch, Le Moigne, and Frischknecht (1989), who show how the problem-solving idea can be incorporated into a complete paradigm for research and development on information systems.

Of course, the study of problem solving is itself quite complex, and the approach taken here is a rather simplistic one compared to those taken in some disciplines. This book treats problem solving as requiring three steps:

1. recognition of the problem,
2. identification of alternative courses of action, and
3. evaluation of the alternatives in order to select a course of action.

This approach is similar to those taken in texts on problem solving, such as Hoffman (1979), Bransford and Stein (1984), and Mayer (1992).

Hoffman (1979), in dealing with group problem solving, comes up with a model for the stages or steps involved in problem solving:

1. define the problem,
2. specify the nature of the problem,
3. generate possible solutions,
4. evaluate the solutions, and
5. implement the selected solution.

Bransford and Stein (1984) identify the steps in problem solving as:

1. identify the problem,
2. define and represent the problem,
3. explore possible strategies,
4. act on the strategies, and
5. look back and evaluate.

Similarly, Mayer (1992), thinking particularly of solving word problems in arithmetic, identifies the steps as:

1. problem translation,
2. problem integration,
3. solution planning, and
4. solution execution.

The approach to problem solving taken in this book also owes a debt of intellectual gratitude to some of the work of Sam Neill (1985). Neill was an esteemed and respected teacher, and something of a maverick and gadfly in the field of information science. His approach, borrowed from Popper's philosophy of science, was of recursive problem solving. A user's initial conception of a problem gives rise to a tentative theory, which is tested by scientific investigation to (theoretically) remove errors. The result is a reformulated theory, which gives rise to a new problem. One does not have to accept the entire Popperian philosophy to realize that there is a truth there. Problems are not one-time events, and cycling neatly through a sequence of steps, such as those outlined previously, is unlikely to be the end of any problem-solving process. In information seeking, conceptualized as problem solving, the resolution of one information need can create a host of additional information needs. Neill's thinking is a salutary reminder that all step-wise models are suspect and information seeking is cyclical and ongoing in nature. This point is further supported by Vosniadou (1992), who argues that the knowledge structures of an individual at any one time can be regarded as a set of theories that are constantly being tested by experience and reformulated as a result of problem-solving activities.

These general approaches to problem solving are to be contrasted with the more detailed approaches found, for example, in studies of crises in international relations or in more complex organizational problems such as labor-management difficulties. These more complex situations, explored in texts such as Rubin, Pruitt, and Kim (1994), require additional problem-solving strategies, such as compromise, negotiation, or the exercise of various kinds of power. While it is possible that more complex approaches to problem solving are also applicable to information seeking and to the definition of information systems, the simple approach taken here is seen as more appropriate, at least for beginning the analysis of information activities. More complex aspects of problem solving will be considered in the discussion of group information activities.

Although the problem-solving perspective deliberately limits the discussion of information activities, it is possible to minimize that limitation somewhat by adopting a liberal definition of a problem. Not all problems are crucial, life-threatening situations. Some problems may be simple or even trivial. But the problem-solving perspective assumes that some level of problem underlies information seeking or other kinds of purposive information behavior. The nature of these problems and how they are interpreted as information needs is discussed in Chapter 3.

The problem-solving perspective on information systems requires a user-centered rather than a data-centered approach to information-system design, for the simple reason that users have problems but data do not. This distinction is crucial to the approach to system design and institutional implications discussed in this book. A more detailed exploration of the differences between the two approaches to information-system design can now be presented.

User-Centered versus Data-Centered Design

This book is about user-centered design of information systems. Earlier in this chapter, there was a suggestion that the opposite of user-centered design is data-centered design. This suggestion derives from the competing definitions of information discussed previously. Data-centered design focuses on information-as-thing. It considers the recorded messages to be the most important aspect of information systems. User-centered design focuses on information-as-process, particularly on the ways that information systems meet the information needs of users.

The difference between user-centered and data-centered design is identical to the difference between the skills-based and technology-based design approaches discussed by Salzman (1992). User-centered design focuses on the skills that users possess, along with other user characteristics, while data-centered design focuses on information technology, including its data structures and formats.

A thorough reading of the literature of information-system design suggests that most existing general-purpose information-retrieval systems have been designed using a data-centered approach. In this approach, the first step is to obtain or create a set of data. This data set is then organized for access, retrieval, and use. Finally, recognizing that data sets and their associated organization are seldom self-explanatory, an interface is created to instruct the user in how to search and (possibly) how to interpret the results obtained.

The data-centered approach designs the data structures and user interfaces around the data. The nature of the data dictates to a large extent how the data can be arranged for access and retrieval. Bibliographic retrieval devices exemplify this type of design. The data consist of records, divided into fields. The organization of the data is accomplished by indexing those fields. If the data happen to include a title field, title access will likely be included in the retrieval device. In a full-text retrieval device, one has data structures (perhaps originally indicated through a markup system such as Standard Generalized Markup Language) that are derived from text components. If the device is a book, it will have data elements such as chapter, paragraph, illustration, caption, and heading. If the device is a database of newspaper articles, it will have data elements such as byline, data, headline, and paragraph. It is noteworthy that none of these data elements or structures makes any reference to a user and the information he or she might want to obtain. Nor does any data element refer to the problems that users might wish to solve or to the characteristics of the communication that will allow them to become informed. Such devices are essentially blind to users, except insofar as users are somehow embodied in the file format.

It is possible, although not particularly plausible, to argue that a book has a particular data structure (which then gets mirrored in the metadata structure) because that data structure reflects the way users understand and think about topics. There is an element of truth here. Textlinguistic structures are in fact used by people who read and understand documents. They have a real purpose and foundation in the ways people use text. This purpose, however, coexists with many other purposes. The book exists as an instrument of the author, trying to persuade the reader as to a particular perspective or point of view. It exists as an artifact produced by a publisher, designed to meet the production standards of the editors and the publishing firm. And, as van Dijk (1989) suggests, the structures of the artifact may in fact be power structures, designed to force agreement to specific points of view. So the user focus in the organization of the text and its representation in bibliographic retrieval devices is at least submerged in a number of other foci. Some may question the extent to which a real user focus exists here. Certainly the data

structure cannot anticipate any and all problems that may be solved by the communication mechanism of the book. At most it can only represent in a generic and
vague way the problem situation facing the user. A book may have a specific audience in mind and may tailor its content to that audience, but the structure is likely
to be more generic than the topic, and so may miss even that generic user focus.

The data-driven approach also dominates the value-added processes involved
in information systems. Indexing and classification devices, for example, are almost
inevitably created using "literary warrant" rather than "user warrant." In a sense,
this is a function of feasibility. Trying to develop a classification scheme that allows
individuals to solve particular problems in their work is a great deal more difficult
than simply analyzing texts to determine the topics covered. All data can be put to
multiple uses, and these uses cannot be anticipated when the value-added process
is accomplished. The closest information devices have come to a user focus is to
allow users the freedom and flexibility to select and combine the existing data
elements in such a way as to meet their information needs. This approach (post-
coordinate indexing, for example) has limited effectiveness and can only begin to
resolve the problems that users face.

The result of data-centered design, recognized by Brown (1986), is information systems that are opaque to the user. They are complex, because of built-in
functional complexity and because they are designed to accommodate multiple
agents: authors, value-added information professionals, and (perhaps least of all)
users. Data-centered information systems have no causal metaphors that will explain what goes wrong in any particular search, and the underlying ambiguity of
the system's functioning makes interpretation of results difficult.

The alternative approach, user-centered design, begins with the user rather
than the data. User-centered design emphasizes the process by which users become
informed, rather than the information things that are used in the process. The
background of user-centered design can be traced to Norman and Draper (1986).
In a chapter on cognitive engineering, Norman (1986) suggests that system design
should focus on the goals of the users and the action sequences that they employ
to achieve those goals. Chapter 2 discusses in detail what this may mean for information-system design. The first step is to assess the types of problems that users
may wish to resolve. These problems are analyzed in terms of the goals of the user,
the tasks that must be accomplished before the goals can be achieved, and the resources that the user brings to those tasks. An information device is then created
that takes advantage of the resources that users have and augments them when necessary, so that users can complete the necessary tasks and thus meet their goals and
satisfy their needs. In other words, the data, its organization, and the retrieval mechanisms and interfaces are all directed toward enabling users to solve specific information problems.

Reformulating information-system design to a user-centered approach is the
focus of the first eight chapters of this book, in which the ways that information
systems can be designed from the user-centered perspective are examined. Before

proceeding with this in-depth investigation of the user-centered approach, it should be noted that Dervin (1989) has raised some very significant objections to the traditional user categories that have dominated communication-system design. Her point is that a balanced and complete approach to users is necessary if system design is to be successful. This book attempts to balance views of users from several perspectives: cognitive, social, individual, group, and organizational.

The clear superiority of the user-centered over the data-centered approach to information-system design seems self-evident to some, but what is obvious to one may be obscure to another. Perhaps an analogy will clarify the advantages of the user-centered approach. Suppose someone has the task of designing a saw to cut wood. The data-centered approach is analogous to having that designer go and wander through a lumberyard, noting the various sizes, shapes, and densities of the wood. The designer may find large floor beams, hefty pieces of furniture-grade hardwood, and a wide variety of smaller materials. With this observation as input, the designer may very well create a saw with a 16-inch circular blade, attached by a belt drive to a 35-hp electric motor. This would certainly handle everything in the lumberyard, but it also might be so powerful and dangerous that it would require two weeks of training before people could be trusted to use it.

The user-centered approach first identifies some group of users, for example, ordinary householders. It then considers what goals they have for a wood saw, in this case, doing a bit of home repair or minor construction. If the tasks that will accomplish these goals are analyzed, it becomes clear that the saw will not have to handle anything more substantial than spruce 2×4's and half-inch plywood. So the saw can have a 7-inch blade and a small electric motor. The designer may also note that the average householder is not strong or physically well-coordinated. So the saw will have to be light and easy to handle, with enough safety features to prevent the user from cutting off some portion of his or her anatomy along with the wood. The result is a usable tool. Starting with the users rather than the raw materials is the only way to create truly usable systems.

The lumberyard example is a case of what Vicente (1990) calls a correspondence-driven domain. By this he means that there is an external reality (the raw materials that are found in the lumberyard) that must be incorporated into the design process. In designing any system in this kind of domain, one must balance an understanding of the users with an understanding of the raw materials to create usable systems.

On the other hand, there are situations in which the raw materials are intangible and mutable: things like ideas. An idea may mean different things to different people. It would be like having a lumberyard in which the size, shape, and density of the wood changes as different people walk through it. Vicente (1990) calls this type of situation a coherence-driven domain. Information systems are good examples of tools developed in coherence-driven domains.

Another way of expressing this idea is to say that information cannot be described independently of its users. A philosophical underpinning for this statement is cogently argued by Budd (1995a, 1995b). He proposes a phenomenological/ hermeneutic approach as the basis for library and information science, replacing a positivistic view. This philosophical approach is entirely compatible with the user-centered focus. For the author or generator of any information there may be one understanding of the topic, for the indexer there may be a second, and for each subsequent reader there may be a different interpretation. The only way one can treat information as raw material is to do violence to its true nature by labeling it once and for all as pertaining to a specific topic. If the true nature of information differs from one user to another, a user-centered approach becomes imperative. In summary, in correspondence-driven domains (such as designing a saw), user-centered design is a sensible approach to developing usable systems. In coherence-driven domains (such as designing an information system), user-centered design is the only viable approach.

After a more detailed introduction to user-centered design (Chapter 2), this book draws attention to the information needs that people have (Chapter 3), the tasks and processes that occur when people search for information (Chapters 5 and 7), and the kinds of design approaches that may lead to user-centered information-system design (Chapters, 4, 6, and 8). It then considers some of the professional and organizational consequences of adopting such an approach (Chapters 9 and 10).

The system-design chapters (Chapters 4, 6, and 8) sketch out the general characteristics of information systems that may be designed employing the user-centered approach. For the present, it is possible to consider how an information device would work if it were designed from the user in rather than from the data out. A user may well wish to solve a particular problem. A faculty member in engineering may wish to find an illustration of a particular physical principle for use in a class on fluid dynamics. A student may need to find an example of a particular research technique that can be used in a specific area of investigation. A child may need to find out how to create a science fair project. All of these are clearly problem-solving situations in which there is an information need to be met. To design a device that allows users to express their needs, to progress through the information search, and to resolve those needs through the information presented by the device is the objective of user-centered information design.

Designing an information device with problem solving in mind presents many challenges. There are, however, examples of information systems that have at least some attributes of a problem-solving information device. A student who uses an electronic encyclopedia to obtain information about the history of the Baltic states in the twentieth century is using an information device organized to optimize the resolution of certain problems. So too is the travel agent who dials into an airline reservation system to determine the cheapest rate from Chicago to Los Angeles (and, typically, that there are no seats available at that rate). Similarly, problem-solving information-retrieval devices allow people to obtain account balances for their bank accounts or to ask questions of colleagues during a networked discussion of specified topics.

The research base that allows the creation of such (somewhat) user-centered systems draws from a variety of areas. In information science, there is a long and distinguished research tradition that supports the data-centered approach. This includes the discussions of databases, data models, knowledge organization, and retrieval techniques. However, there is also a long and productive research tradition that supports the user-centered approach to information systems. Here much of the research centers on interface design, usability analysis and testing, and user modeling.

Systems, Services, and Institutions

In this book, the term "information system" is used a bit more broadly than is usual in the literature of information science. Although the term usually incorporates the data, indexes, retrieval engines, interfaces, and postprocessing software associated with an electronic information device, in this book these features are considered only as part of the system conceived as a whole. The systems approach outlined in this chapter means that the information system must be taken to include the users who interact with the system, the designers who create the system, and the information specialists who select and organize the data and who interact with the users as intermediaries.

Information services are collections of information systems. Thinking about what this means leads to an understanding that the devices collected together in a service may be quite different from each other. The data that these systems contain may differ. In fact, all aspects of the information systems, except the users and the intermediaries, may differ from each other in any information service. It follows that the factors that define an information service are precisely the users and the intermediaries. Accordingly, the definition of an information service is a collection of information systems brought together to meet the needs of a specified group of users and employing a staff of human intermediaries in meeting that objective. The function of the information service is to provide a consistent basis for interaction between the user and the information systems, including providing instruction for users about how to use the information systems and the information they obtain from the systems.

This discussion leads to a consideration of information institutions. Such institutions are collections of information services. There may be different groups of users served by an institution, and the institution may employ separate groups of intermediaries to interact with those different groups of users. On the other hand, an institution normally has some superordinate goal that defines it with respect to its environment. An information institution will typically have a mission statement that can be viewed as a statement of selectivity. It specifies the kinds of information needs that the institution's services (and their constituent systems) will try to meet.

In other words, the institution acts as a kind of filter: attracting users with certain types of information needs and repelling other users. The filter can make operational the information needs that it attracts on the basis of a variety of criteria. For example, it may use topic covered, level of information provided, or type of user served as a basis for selecting information needs. This function is, in general terms, the marketing function of the institution. There are, however, many other kinds of managerial functions besides the marketing function that are accomplished in institutions. Individual information systems or services may not be appropriate organizational units in which to employ financial management, personnel management, or a variety of other managerial techniques. At the broader level of the institution, however, such management is not only possible, but essential. So the institution provides a managerial framework that supports the information functions provided by the constituent information services and systems.

An example may serve to illustrate the distinctions made previously. A good example of an information institution is a public library. This institution has a financial base and is usually managed by a central administration that takes care of marketing, financial control, personnel, and relations between the library and its environment. Within the library, there may be a number of information services. For example, there may be an adult reference service and a children's reference service, each of which employs a variety of information systems. An adult reference service may include an information system such as an index to periodical literature with instructional resources to help people use the index. Included in each system is one or more information devices, in this case the printed volumes or computer system that stores the information and permits its retrieval. This multiple embedding of information devices within the human context of information systems and services and within the organizational context of the library means that the capabilities of the device are constrained by its larger context. It does not make sense, for example, to think of the capabilities of the device as separable from that broader context.

One additional example may help to illustrate the complex nature of institutional considerations: the Educational Resources Information Center (ERIC) database as presented on a CD-ROM disc by a company such as Wilson or Silver-Platter. To describe the information system that creates and uses the database requires an analysis of more than the workstation. The system includes the data, the people who generate the data at the ERIC clearinghouses, and the people at the CD-ROM company who add value by generating indexes and coupling them with retrieval engines and postprocessing software. However, this is an incomplete description of the system, which can be made more complete by an understanding of the users. Suppose they are undergraduates in education, engaged primarily in the task of completing term papers for their classes. This view of the system remains incomplete. The intermediaries who work with the students to help them find information are also an essential component of the system. For example, they may be graduate students in education and therefore bring to the information interaction a number of cognitive structures and socially constructed perceptions that influence how users find information. At this point, a reasonably complete picture of the information system has emerged.

To expand this picture to visualize the information service, other information systems that may be used to accomplish the users' objectives must be included. Perhaps there are other CD-ROM information devices that are also being used. Possibly there is a print collection of books and journals. One may assume that there is also a microfiche collection of ERIC documents. A picture emerges of an information service that may be called an education library or possibly an undergraduate library. This service brings together a group of information systems, designed to serve the needs of the specified user group and employing personnel as intermediaries and advisors. The ERIC information system may be used differently in this information service than in a variety of other services. For example, if it is installed in a setting in which the primary user group is composed of teachers whose primary goal, purpose, or objective is professional upgrading, the information system will be used differently. Similarly, if there are other information devices in the immediate context, the system will be used differently. It is possible to imagine an ERIC system set up in a school that does not have the collection of printed books and journals that the education library may have. Clearly, this will constrain the use of the system. It is also possible that other types of intermediaries will be available in the different setting, and their characteristics will influence the kind of use made of the system.

There are, additionally, several different institutions that must be considered in this example. The first is the ERIC clearinghouse. This institution, funded by taxpayers through the Department of Education, supports the collection of data, its analysis and enhancement through indexing and abstracting, and its further enhancement by associated products and services. The second institution is the CD-ROM firm, which adopts a marketing strategy that includes pricing, promotion, and (to some extent) an influence on the nature of the product being sold. The third institution is the library, which invites some users while excluding others and presents a support structure that values certain kinds of use while devaluing or de-emphasizing other aspects of use. Decisions made by each of these institutions affect and constrain the nature of the information system and how users will interact with it.

Conclusion

Taking the user-centered approach means that the data-centered set of information-science research (data structures, databases, and knowledge organization) must be considered *after* the user-centered set of information-science research (interfaces, usability, and user models). No database question can be resolved independently of the interface. No data model can stand without a user model. Those devices (and they constitute a majority) that are designed from the data out (or even worse, from the computer out) work only in general and problematic ways. The fact that they work at all is a tribute, not to system design, but to the infinite flexibility of users in adapting to bad devices. In this book, the position is taken that information systems are first and foremost communication devices devoted to solving user problems. This is the approach elaborated in the following chapters.

References

Bransford, J. D., & Stein, B. S. (1984). *The ideal problem solver: A guide for improving thinking, learning, and creativity.* New York: W.H. Freeman.

Brown, J. S. (1986). From cognitive to social ergonomics and beyond. In D. A. Norman & S. W. Draper (Eds.), *User centered system design: New perspectives on human-computer interaction* (pp. 457–486). Hillsdale, NJ: Lawrence Erlbaum Assoc.

Buckland, M. K. (1991a). *Information and information systems.* New York: Praeger.

Buckland, M. K. (1991b). Information as thing. *Journal of the American Society for Information Science, 42*, 351–360.

Budd, J. M. (1992). *The library and its users: The communication process.* New York: Greenwood Press.

Budd, J. M. (1995a). An epistemological framework for library and information science. *Library Quarterly, 65*(3), 295–318.

Budd, J. M. (1995b). User-centered thinking: Lessons from reader-centered theory. *RQ, 34*(4), 487–496.

Dalrymple, P. W., & Roderer, N. K. (1994). Database access systems. *Annual Review of Information Science and Technology, 29*, 137–178.

Dervin, B. (1977). Useful theory for librarianship: Communication, not information. *Drexel Library Quarterly, 13*(3), 16–32.

Dervin, B. (1989). Users as research inventions: How research categories perpetuate inequities. *Journal of Communication, 39*(3), 216–232.

Hoffman, L. R. (1979). *The group problem solving process: Studies of a valence model.* New York: Praeger.

Ingwersen, P. (1992). Information retrieval interaction. London: Taylor Graham.

Kantor, P. B. (1994). Information retrieval techniques. *Annual Review of Information Science and Technology, 29*, 53–90.

Kochen, M. (1974). *Principles of information retrieval.* Los Angeles: Melville.

Lange, H. R. (1993). Speech synthesis and speech recognition: Tomorrow's human–computer interfaces? *Annual Review of Information Science and Technology, 28*, 153–185.

Mason, R. O., & Mitroff, I. I. (1973). A program for research on management information systems. *Management Science, 19*(5), 475–487.

Mayer, R. E. (1992). *Thinking, problem solving, cognition.* New York: W. H. Freeman.

Meadow, C. T. (1987). Communication in library and information science. *Canadian Journal of Information Science, 12*(1), 1–9.

Neill, S. D. (1985). The reference process and the philosophy of Karl Popper. *RQ, 24*(3), 309–319.

Newby, G. B. (1993). Virtual reality. *Annual Review of Information Science and Technology, 28*, 187–229.

Norman, D. A. (1986). Cognitive engineering. In D. A. Norman & S. W. Draper (Eds.), *User centered system design: New perspectives on human-computer interaction* (pp. 31–61). Hillsdale, NJ: Lawrence Erlbaum Assoc.

Norman, D. A., & Draper, S. W. (1986). *User centered system design: New perspectives on human-computer interaction.* Hillsdale, NJ: Lawrence Erlbaum Assoc.

O'Brien, A. (1994). Online catalogs: Enhancements and development. *Annual Review of Information Science and Technology, 29*, 219–242.

Popper, K. R. (1972). *Objective knowledge: An evolutionary approach*. Oxford: Clarendon.

Rubin, J. Z., Pruitt, D. G., & Kim, S. H. (1994). *Social conflict: Escalation, stalemate, and settlement*. New York: McGraw-Hill.

Salzman, H. (1992). Skill-based design: Productivity, learning and organizational effectiveness. In P. S. Adler & T. A. Winograd (Eds.), *Usability: Turning technologies into tools* (pp. 66–95). New York: Oxford University Press.

Taylor, R. S. (1982). Value-added process in the information life cycle. *Journal of the American Society for Information Science, 33*(5), 341–346.

van Dijk, T. A. (1989). Structures of discourse and structures of power. *Communication Yearbook, 12,* 18–59.

van Gigch, J. P., Le Moigne, J. L., & Frischknecht, F. (1989). A paradigmatic approach to the discipline of information systems. *Behavioral Science, 34*(2), 128–147.

Vicente, K. J. (1990). Coherence- and correspondence-driven work domains: Implications for systems design. *Behaviour and Information Technology, 9*(6), 493–502.

Vosniadou, S. (1992). Knowledge acquisition and conceptual change. *Applied Psychology: An International Review, 41*(4), 347–357.

2

An Introduction to User-Centered Information-System Design

In the introductory chapter, a plea for user-centered design is expressed. The contention there, which will be explored in the rest of this book, is that user-centered design provides an avenue toward the design of usable information systems. It should be noted that research into user-centered aspects of information-system design is one of the most active fields of information-science research. At the same time, it must be admitted that the research has not advanced far. Despite the amount of excellent and solid research, the state of the art in user-centered information-system design is fairly primitive. To lay the foundation for in-depth consideration of user-centered information-system design that begins in the next chapter, this chapter will briefly survey the state of this research. In part, this survey will set the context for subsequent chapters by showing the vitality and variability of the research that has been accomplished in support of user-centered design. The literature review will present a model of user-centered design that will be followed throughout the first section of this book. This model organizes ongoing research and can help to structure thinking about the challenge of user-based information-system design. This model has five components:

1. **Needs analysis:** determining user goals, purposes, and objectives
2. **Task analysis:** determining the tasks and activities that users accomplish in meeting their needs
3. **Resource analysis:** investigating the resources (both cognitive and social) that are used in completing the tasks
4. **User modeling:** synthesizing needs, tasks, and resources
5. **Designing for usability:** assessing how users' needs, tasks, and resources interact with system characteristics to create usable systems

It is important that the relationship between this design model and the problem-solving approach discussed in the last chapter be understood. In Chapter 1, it was assumed that information needs are driven by problems that people want to solve. Since problems give rise to information needs, the first step of this model, needs analysis, derives directly from the problem-solving perspective. The remaining components of the model (task analysis, resource analysis, user modeling, and system design) all depend on the needs revealed by the needs analysis. Chapter 3, which considers information needs in detail, shows how the problem-solving approach defines different kinds of information needs.

This five-step model for user-centered design has a number of elements in common with Dillon's (1994) thorough approach to the user-centered design of electronic texts. His model of the design process also contains five elements:

1. stakeholder identification,
2. user analysis,
3. task analysis,
4. specification, and
5. prototype.

Dillon's approach works well for a constrained design task; the main difference between his model and the one presented here is that Dillon proceeds farther into the actual design process than does this book. To compensate, the model presented here goes into greater depth in user analysis and task analysis. Dillon's approach, however, provides a specific example of user-centered design.

Another related approach to user-centered design is presented by Olson and Olson (1991). Specifically focused on the design of technology to facilitate collaboration between individuals, they developed the following ten questions for user-centered design:

1. Analyze the goal: what is the purpose of this activity?
2. How should the activity be done, ideally?
3. What potential problems are there with doing it the way it is typically done?
4. How do current technologies or processes support this activity?
5. What are the limits to these?
6. What are the requirements for new aids?
7. How can information technology meet these requirements?
8. What costs may be incurred by new technology aids?
9. What special characteristics of the specific domain must be taken into account?
10. What are the potential differences from groups with various natures and size?

It seems clear that the first two steps in this schema are needs and task analysis. Rather than considering resource analysis as a separate step, these authors move directly to systems analysis and design. Again, because of their rather narrow design focus, this approach can be justified, but their final points (numbers 9 and 10) present a vital perspective. They emphasize that both the domain (the problem area) and the nature of the group are important factors in user-centered design. These concerns are considered but are not included as separate steps in the model adopted in this book. Obviously, the domain and the group context must be considered systematically whenever approaching design from the user-centered perspective.

Finally, the model suggested in this book can be compared with that of Mahling (1994), who defines the six steps of cognitive systems engineering:

1. goal analysis,
2. domain/task analysis,
3. user/group analysis,
4. model formation,
5. system design and implementation, and
6. usability testing.

The first five steps are identical in content, if not in emphasis, to the five-step approach to user-centered design espoused in this book. The final step, usability testing, is important, but the emphasis here is to focus on usability before and during the design process, rather than after the fact.

Needs Analysis

Understanding what users want to accomplish when they seek information has been one of the foci of research in information science, as is well documented in a series of Annual Review of Information Science and Technology (ARIST) chapters, of which two relatively recent chapters (Dervin & Nilan, 1986; Hewins, 1990) are good examples. Representative studies have investigated the needs for and uses of information by medical professionals as important indicators for how medical information systems should be designed. Other approaches consider information provision and user modeling in business with implications for the development of management information systems. Finally, a number of studies have investigated how information seeking is influenced by the individual cognitive processes of users. Some of the best library and information science research regarding users has investigated less prestigious groups. For example, Chatman (1987) found that low-skilled workers lack access to information that may meet their information needs. This study and others like it make it clear that the social embeddedness of information needs and information behavior must be investigated as part of user-centered system design.

Chapter 3 is entirely devoted to an analysis of information needs. It should be noted here that studies of information needs are also found in many cognate disciplines. The literature of psychology provides many interesting and illuminating studies. For example, Ball-Rokeach (1973) shows how information seeking is a necessary component of making sense of an ambiguous social situation. In this investigation, students who expected to be participating in a research project were placed in a virtually empty room and made to wait for a lengthy period. The students were strangers to each other and had no idea why they were in the room or how long they might have to wait there. Meanwhile, the researchers were observing carefully how the students reacted to each other and coped with this highly ambiguous situation. Most people alternated between information-seeking behavior (for example, asking each other what was going on) and tension-reducing behavior (for example, joking and teasing) as they worked with other people to achieve a consensus about the situation and thus make sense of it. Generalizing from this research indicates that people need information in many of the ambiguous or problematic situations in which they find themselves. Information is central to making sense of the events of daily life.

The literature of clinical psychology illustrates that the social context in which people are found can place constraints on how they obtain and process the information they need to make sense of their lives. Dodge, Bates, and Pettit (1990) report that, in their study, abused children were less competent in social information processing than other children. For example, they were more likely to attribute hostile intent to others. This is just one example of the types of influence that arise from individual differences and social contexts that impact on how people use information in their lives.

Sociology provides many additional examples of how important information is to people living in communities and how those communities influence the ways that their members process information. For example, Stamm and Guest (1991) examined the information needs of newcomers to a community and found that an important need was to develop ties to the community and to local institutions. Unfortunately, the most frequently consulted information source (the local newspaper) was not well adapted to providing the information that these newcomers needed to make sense of their situation and develop links to their new community. Also typical of individual information needs were the concerns of elderly people assessed by Jones, Morrow, Morris, and Ries (1992). By examining letters sent by elderly individuals and extracting statements of information need, Jones *et al.* identified three basic types of information needs: how to improve the quality of life, questions related to health issues, and aids to understanding individual and societal responsibilities.

Members of professions and occupations represent a different way of understanding communities. Clark (1979) assessed the information needs of psychologists and sociologists and found that these professionals experienced pressure to find information to improve their job performance. This pressure was also associated with high levels of information overload. Interestingly, no association was found between information use and the effectiveness of the performance of the professionals. This research provides additional evidence both that information needs are real and that people may experience needs that will lead to further problems if satisfied.

Research from political studies focuses on information needed for decision making and reveals that decision makers frequently have a kind of ambivalence about the information they need. Caplan (1976) interviewed federal government policy makers to assess what impact information of various kinds had on policy making. The results showed that the highest frequency of information use was in bureaucratic management and that there was an attitude of parochialism: policy makers tended to place the highest value on information created within their own agencies. Information is necessary for decision making, but it is also carefully filtered. Too much information can be just as bad as too little information. This point also emerged from Mooney's (1993) examination of the information needs of state legislative decision makers. This research found that legislators searched for information only when it would do them the most good: for example, if they were sponsoring a bill or serving as a leader or member of a committee that was considering a particular topic or issue.

Some of the most revealing research into information needs can be found in the literature of social and cultural anthropology. For example, Clarke (1973) studied high school students and how they sought information about pop music. One finding was that an awareness of how their peers felt about musical groups was the primary factor in explaining the information needs of these teenagers. It seems clear that these needs were generated by the social situation in which the students found themselves.

The literature of business administration also emphasizes the importance of social and cultural influences on information seeking and use. Salancik and Pfeffer (1978) introduce an influential model for explaining job attitudes that shows how social information processing influences those attitudes. They found that workers' attitudes, behaviors, and beliefs were based on information they acquired about past work behaviors and about what their peers thought about the appropriateness of those behaviors. In other words, people need information to establish the norms for work behavior. These norms, as derived from interaction with their coworkers, determine how people will behave in work situations. Note how this model resembles the findings about the students in the empty room. Neither students nor workers can make sense of their situations unless they obtain information from each other.

The preceding example illustrates how information needs occur in the work environment. Rasmussen, Pejtersen, and Goodstein (1994) recognize the importance of the work environment in designing information systems. Their approach to cognitive systems engineering includes analyses of the work domain and the task space of the work environment. The work domain is the area within which work is being accomplished and is modeled in terms of the purposes of the work, the constraints placed upon the work; the general, abstract, and physical functions that are being accomplished; and the physical configuration of the workplace. The task space is what is actually being done in the work domain: the general activities that are being accomplished that may give rise to information needs. Although these concepts generally apply to all kinds of work, within a job context or not, they seem particularly applicable to the workplace.

This summary of examples of research into the objectives, goals, and purposes of information seekers demonstrates first how pervasive information needs are. Secondly, it illustrates the variability of information needs. People seek information to integrate themselves into a community or workplace or into a social group of peers. They need information to ensure that they act in the ways others expect. They may feel they need information to improve their work performance or to develop policy that will direct the ways in which government agencies interact with citizens. The variability of information needs is discussed in slightly different terms by Bystrom and Jarvelin (1995), who contrast the information required for various kinds of decision making with information needs associated with information processing.

Analyzing the information needs of a user population is the first step of user-centered information-system design. This analysis can be conceptualized in terms of finding out from information users their goals, purposes, and objectives (or to use the language of the problem-solving perspective, the problems they need to solve). Do they wish to become integrated into a community? Or to demonstrate the extent of their integration? Are they solving work-related problems? Making policy decisions? The implication of this discussion of information needs is that information systems that function well in resolving one kind of need may be less appropriate, or unusable, for meeting a different need. The work of Stamm and Guest (1991) criticizes local newspapers for not meeting the primary information needs of newcomers to a community. As information-system designers approach each information need, they must ensure the systems they design are appropriate for the needs of their users. That is why needs assessment is the first and most crucial step of user-centered information-system design. Chapter 3 presents a detailed analysis of information needs seen from cognitive, social, and organizational perspectives and provides several examples of types of information needs that users might experience. Chapter 4 begins the task of extracting principles for designing workable and usable information systems based on the study of information needs.

Task Analysis

The second element of this model of effective user-centered design is task analysis. One approach to task analysis is to determine what tasks are accomplished by users as they attempt to meet their information needs and how those tasks are performed. A second approach to task analysis identifies and analyzes the tasks associated with using information devices. These two approaches are to be carefully distinguished. Hoppe and Schiele (1992) call tasks accomplished by users as they meet their information needs external tasks, differentiating them from internal tasks, which are accomplished using information devices. External tasks are device-independent. The tasks accomplished are general in nature and are derived from the information need and characteristics of the user and his or her social environment. In fact, these general tasks may be considered to be subgoals, each of which is important to the accomplishment of the broader goal and to meeting the information need. In this book, the main emphasis is on external tasks; Chapters 5 and 7 are devoted to a detailed examination of some of the tasks that are associated with meeting information needs. However, internal tasks are also important. Information devices are part of the technological environment in which individuals are found, and the tasks accomplished while using the devices are part of any realistic task assessment. In addition, it is unlikely that system design will occur *ex nihilo*. Although existing information devices have many shortcomings, they constitute the starting points for new approaches to system design. Accordingly, the tasks associated with using current devices are relevant to task analysis. At the same time, it must be acknowledged that the internal tasks required by current information devices may change considerably as technology changes. As a result, focusing too closely on device-dependent tasks can act as a barrier to innovative system design. As Hoppe and Schiele (1992) point out, system design should consider internal tasks, but should recognize that these internal tasks depend on external tasks. In other words, consideration of device-dependent tasks should be subordinated to a consideration of more general, device-independent tasks.

Probably the most researched and best documented task model in information science is that developed by Kuhlthau (1988, 1993), initially used in the context of students writing term papers and subsequently applied more generally. This six-step information-search process identifies not only the tasks that are involved, but also how the students felt while completing each of the tasks:

1. Task initiation: to recognize the information need
2. Topic selection: to identify the general topic
3. Prefocus exploration: to investigate information on a general topic
4. Focus formulation: to decide on a narrower topic
5. Information collection: to gather information on the narrower topic
6. Search closure: to complete the information search

A task model such as Kuhlthau's does not, of course, imply that all users proceed in a step-wise fashion through each of the tasks in turn, but it does point out that meeting an information need is a complex process, in which a number of different tasks can occur. For example, the kind of information system that may work well during topic selection may perform poorly during focus formulation. Designing an information system from the user's perspective must focus not only on the different needs that users experience, but also on the different processes that they accomplish as they meet those needs.

Marchionini (1992) suggests that for information-seeking tasks such as those found in end-user searching of text or bibliographic databases, there are five tasks that can drive interface design:

1. defining the problem,
2. selecting the source,
3. articulating the problem,
4. examining the results, and
5. extracting the information.

Clearly, these are not discrete tasks, but rather complex constructs that incorporate a variety of subsidiary tasks. However, if this task model were elaborated thoroughly, it could be useful in creating an information system that would respond to the needs of users.

An entertaining example of a task model is Stern's (1992) analysis of the tasks involved in managing information during an international crisis (the Swedish "Whisky on the Rocks" crisis[2]). The tasks identified are:

1. Search: collection of data about the operational environment
2. Processing: development of the data into politically relevant statements about the situation
3. Communication: interaction between the parties that distributes the statements and produces meaning from the data

These are clearly external tasks, and of course, each of them entails a number of internal tasks for their completion.

The area of medical information science has produced a number of task analyses. For example, Sheng, Wei, Ozeki, Ovitt, and Ishida (1992) examine how radiologists make use of images. They found that one task involved in extracting information from radiological images is to compare older images with current images. They were therefore able to suggest that an information device for radiologists should automatically fetch older images for quick comparison with current images. Ramey, Rowberg, and Robinson (1992) used ethnographic interviews to elicit similar information about the tasks accomplished by radiologists. Frascina and Steele (1992) identified information-based tasks on hospital wards and used these tasks as the basis for the design of a hospital information system.

Internal tasks, those associated with specific types of communication media or information devices, are also important. For example, Gillan (1994) investigated the tasks involved in deciphering the information from graphs. The tasks identified were:

1. searching for indicators,
2. encoding the value of indicators,
3. performing arithmetical operations on the values, and
4. making spatial comparisons among indicators.

This is clearly a set of internal tasks used in interacting with a particular device that presents information in graphic form. Gillan (1994) found that the type of

---

[2] This crisis occurred when a Soviet submarine (NATO code named "Whisky") was discovered grounded within Swedish territorial waters. The information tasks centered on managing the crisis in international relations that ensued.

graph used and the goal the user had for the graph (or the external tasks associated with that goal) determined the sequence and combination of these internal tasks.

Processing information in numerical form requires a different set of internal tasks. Goh and Coury (1994) collected verbal (i.e., thinking aloud) protocols from people who were processing information. The tasks they identified were get, divide, compare, add, select, evaluate, multiply, difference, round, and respond. However, this specialized set of tasks contains a more general subset. If the tasks that relate to processing numbers (add, subtract, multiply, divide, compare, round) are omitted, the tasks that may be accomplished in any information system remain: get, select, evaluate, and respond. These can be considered basic tasks in information behavior.

In related research, Kirby (1994) assesses two different approaches to understanding cartographic information. The first approach considers maps as concrete objects and deals with them spatially. The second approach deals with maps as text (i.e., verbally and abstractly). The task of extracting information from maps seems to combine both of these approaches with different weights, depending on the objective being accomplished.

Duchastel (1990) suggests that four cognitive tasks are central to searching for information using hypermedia. These are:

1. browsing,
2. searching,
3. integrating, and
4. angling (establishing multiple perspectives).

This article suggests that these four tasks are central to hypermedia usage, while acknowledging that the purpose of the use and the context in which the use occurs put constraints on the accomplishment of the tasks. In other words, depending on the information need and the external task being accomplished, the tasks may be accomplished differently or in different sequences.

Each task can contain subordinate tasks, as is demonstrated by the observations that Duchastel (1990) includes browsing as one of the hypermedia tasks and Peck and John (1992) subsequently identify the tasks involved in browsing in general. These were:

1. find appropriate help,
2. define search criteria,
3. define evaluation criteria, and
4. browse.

These tasks are fairly obvious. Browsing does not make much sense unless one has at least a general idea of what one is looking for (and how one will know it when one sees it). However, even such obvious task components can be important in the task of user-centered system design. Helping someone to define evaluation criteria dynamically while browsing will presumably be a worthwhile component of any hypermedia information device.

At a more basic level of analysis, there is a variety of tasks used in becoming informed that are also used more generally in human thinking. These tasks are cognitive processes, which include mental activities such as learning, remembering, reasoning, and judging. These basic cognitive processes, although clearly essential to an understanding of information systems and services, have not been as thoroughly studied in information science as one might wish. Winn (1994) examines the role of cognitive processes in tasks that contribute to the comprehension of graphics. The first process identified is associative linking; a type of learning. Associative learning creates links between symbols and the objects those symbols represent. The second process identified is interpretation, in which spatial relationships among symbols are identified with relationships among the objects represented by the symbols. Interpretation is the same type of cognitive process that is used in learning by analogy or in interpreting a new situation using knowledge of an existing situation. This research identifies learning processes as being central to understanding graphics, and it is possible to generalize beyond this context to consider learning as the central cognitive process in all information seeking. Chen and Dhar (1991) investigated the cognitive processes involved in online document retrieval and developed models of the various cognitive processes, which were subsequently incorporated into the design of an experimental "intelligent" information device. This new device seems to produce better retrieval than the original device, which did not utilize the cognitive process model. Allen (1991) surveyed the information-science research on cognitive processes, including learning, memory, problem solving, and comprehension. One point made in that review is that it may be more difficult to investigate cognitive processes than to study the knowledge resources that are created by and used in those processes. The difference here is between studying the processes of remembering and studying the knowledge that is contained in memory.

There are a number of standard techniques that can be used for task analysis. Smith, Normore, and Denning (1991) used three methods simultaneously to assess the tasks involved in editing a record for *Chemical Abstracts*. They found that concurrent verbal reports (i.e., thinking-aloud protocols), quality-control reviews, and performance monitoring together resulted in a cognitive task analysis that proposed design solutions for the information device used by the editors. Similarly, Thordsen (1991) compares two tools for task analysis: concept mapping and the critical decision method. Concept mapping provides an overview of the user's image of the tasks, including information about the clustering of and flow between concepts. This is similar to techniques for assessing the cognitive structures used in completing tasks, discussed in following sections. Thordsen also found that the critical decision method is an effective tool for identifying decision strategies, critical cues, situation assessment, goals and intent, expectancies, mental simulation strategies, and improvisation that are used in defining and completing tasks. The combination of the two methods was found to be particularly effective in task analysis.

The tasks discussed thus far are generally individual tasks, which (to anticipate the next section of this chapter) use individual resources or cognitive resources.

For this reason, the kinds of task analysis discussed previously are usually called "cognitive task analysis." There are, however, many instances in which the tasks involved in becoming informed are not individual, but are social or collective. In these situations, there are other tasks that are as important as the cognitive tasks, and research has investigated some of these as well. As Kukla, Clemens, Morse, and Cash (1992) emphasize, it is important to understand the users of information systems, but it is equally important to observe the organization in which users are working. For example, Berger, Norman, Balkwell, and Smith (1992) point out that, when working on any task within a group, there may be inconsistent cues about the status of oneself and of other members of the group. For the group to function cohesively, this status inconsistency must be resolved. In a group information-processing situation, there is social information processing going on as well as individual information processing; the members of the group are assessing each other's status as they try to reach a consensus.

Individual status in a group is important, as demonstrated experimentally by Sev'er (1989) in a mock jury situation. This research found that the confidence portrayed by one member of the group in discussing a resolution of the jury deliberations had a significant influence on the judgment finally adopted by the jury. Other research in jury decision making suggests that a central task in coming to a decision is continually adjusting one's opinion as each member of the jury speaks (Boster, Hunter, & Hale, 1991). In business decision making, social location and social influence also must be processed by groups, and how well this social information processing occurs can affect the quality of the decisions being made (Tushman & Romanelli, 1983). This research clearly shows that group information processing includes tasks that are associated with the dynamics of the group and the interrelationship between its members, as well as tasks that are involved with comprehending and assimilating information from outside the group.

Another social task that can accompany collective information retrieval is group processing (Johnson, Johnson, Stanne, & Garibaldi, 1990), in which groups review their collective performance, describe and diagnose individual contributions, and then direct the way the group will function in the future. Developing a group memory, in which group members share a common information structure and common information habits, can also be crucial to group information seeking (Berlin, Jeffries, O'Day, Paepcke, & Wharton, 1993).

In the organizational context, Rasmussen, Pejtersen, and Goodstein (1994) recognized that the tasks required to meet information needs and objectives can be analyzed in a number of different ways. For example, they considered the ways that tasks may be divided up and coordinated between different workers: essentially the social organization of the workplace. At the same time, they recognized that some information tasks can have several applications; their completion may impact the work that is being done or decisions that must be made. The information processes, which are complex in themselves, have a complex set of organizational antecedents and outcomes that make task analysis of the sort discussed here more difficult. But again, the point is clear: if information systems are to be designed from the user's perspective, they must take into account the organizational context in which the users are embedded.

Task analysis as part of user-centered information-system design must take into account both the cognitive and social tasks that are necessary to achieve a user's goal, purpose, or objective. Task analysis of this sort serves to indicate ways in which information systems can be designed to bring users to the point that they can accomplish the tasks and so meet their information needs. This approach, the enabling-states approach, is described in more detail in the section "Designing for Usability."

Resource Analysis

Having analyzed the tasks involved in meeting the purpose, objective, and goal of the user, the next aspect of the model of user-centered design is to determine what resources are required by and used in each task. In this discussion, the focus will remain firmly on cognitive and social resources employed in completing information tasks, because these seem most central to the successful completion of the tasks and thus the eventual meeting of the information need embodied in the goals, purposes, and objectives of the user. It is worth noting at the beginning that there are other less-known resources that also may be important. For example, Tenopir, Nahl-Jakobovits, and Howard (1991) report on the completion of information tasks by novice users of an information-retrieval device. They note that affective behavior and cognitive activities occur. This finding leads to the conclusion that emotional resources as well as cognitive resources can be considered as part of user-centered system design.

The resources used to complete information-related tasks can be conveniently categorized into two groups: the knowledge (including both individual and social knowledge) required to complete a task and the abilities that make a task easier to accomplish. These resources will be considered in more detail in Chapters 5 and 7, but the following summary serves to introduce them to the reader.

Knowledge

Individual Knowledge
What people know determines what they need to know, so knowledge resources are critical in delineating information needs. As people perform information tasks, they must have knowledge of how those tasks are to be accomplished. Because knowledge resources are so central to the process of becoming informed, information-science research has paid a great deal of attention to the knowledge

structures that are employed in information-seeking tasks. There have been attempts to build information devices that employ knowledge bases; Richardson (1995) provides a good summary of such systems. Similarly, Guida and Tasso (1994), in a thorough manual for designing knowledge-based systems, provide an outline of the type of conceptual modeling and knowledge acquisition that occurs in this kind of system design. From the user-centered perspective, the problem with knowledge-based or expert systems is that by definition they encode the knowledge of experts. This knowledge may be in-depth knowledge of a subject domain, comparable to what was described in Chapter 1 as a body of knowledge. Alternatively, it may be the procedural knowledge of information-retrieval experts about how to complete information tasks. The fact that most users do not have in-depth knowledge of the topic about which they need to be informed and are not expert searchers may reduce the usefulness of the encoded expert knowledge. An information system that makes effective use of expert knowledge must find a way to link the knowledge structures of inexpert users with those of experts. This link allows users to pose questions using the knowledge they have and to retrieve information they need to meet their information needs.

By definition, seekers for information tend to have less than complete knowledge of the topic, which is why they are seeking information. Latta and Swigger (1992) demonstrate that users' knowledge structures are different from those of experts. The authors suggest that users' knowledge structures can be used in intelligent front-end interfaces for information retrieval. In a totally different area, Kirschenbaum (1992) examines the differences between the strategies of experts and novices in gathering information in the field of submarine warfare. Again, substantial differences between the groups in terms of information-seeking behaviors, understanding of the situation, and decision accuracy can be attributed to previous experience, which gave the experts better knowledge of the domain and also better tactics for dealing with problems as they occurred.

It seems clear that different levels of knowledge in users will result in different approaches to completing information-retrieval tasks. For example, Patel and Groen (1992) analyze how individuals with different levels of expertise in medicine approach medical information devices. They found that experts have knowledge structures defined as clinically based schemata, which allow them to filter irrelevant hypotheses and information better than novices or even searchers with an intermediate knowledge of the field. They suggest that medical information devices, particularly those that employ knowledge bases, should employ knowledge representations that allow differences in knowledge to be accommodated within the devices.

One example of identifying the knowledge resources of users is presented by Todd, Parker, and Yerbury (1994). They used focus group discussions to define concept clusters of users of a multimedia information device. These knowledge structures were then used in the system design, as were navigational devices based on the way experts navigate from one topic to another. Similarly, Case (1991) studied historians to see how they categorize and organize knowledge and found that spatial configuration and document type are important ways of organizing knowledge for these users. Case suggests that user knowledge categories can be useful in information-system design, particularly in interface development. Coll, Coll, and Nandavar (1993) show how the conceptual structures of users can be used to structure menus. Their work emphasizes that system designers should pay attention to research in perception and memory and should clearly present menus with an appropriate number of choices on each screen. Even more important is the conceptual organization of the menus. Menus can be perfectly designed in terms of screen layout, but if the menu items are not associated with each other in a logical sequence, the menu system will not be usable. As a result, understanding the logic of how users associate processes and choices in their minds is essential for designing usable menu systems.

In related research, Garber and Grunes (1992) investigated how art directors use knowledge about art and images to search for specific images. They then designed a search interface based on this knowledge. Johnson and Briggs (1994) studied how managers associate goals and causes with outcomes and then developed an experimental information device in which documents are selected by traversing networks of causes and goals. Kuncheva (1993) uses an understanding of the physician's decision-making process to design an expert medical decision support device. All of these examples show how the specialized knowledge of users can be important in creating new approaches to information retrieval.

The technique of system design known as "soft systems methodology" (Lewis, 1993) contains techniques for identifying and representing cognitive categories of users and the associations between those categories. This representation of user knowledge can be associated with the tasks that users are accomplishing and forms a basis for designing the information system. For example, the data structures used in the information device can be modeled after the cognitive categories of users. Wildemuth and O'Neill (1995) study the knowledge that users employ in finding known bibliographic items and conclude that such knowledge provides a solid basis for building a retrieval system. This research represents the beginning of a serious attempt at user-centered information-system design.

At this point a different type of knowledge that is in the domain of metacognition can be noted. This is the knowledge (or feeling) of knowing. In one investigation, Allen (1994) found that actual knowledge has less impact on users' information-seeking behavior than perceived knowledge. In other words, actual knowledge, of the type investigated and modeled in the research cited previously, may be less important in certain information-retrieval situations than perceived knowledge. To the extent to which metaknowledge can influence information-related behavior, this kind of knowledge modeling represents an important addition to research into user knowledge.

The preceding discussion is concerned primarily with knowledge of topics or domains (factual knowledge) and knowledge of information-related tasks (procedural knowledge). Procedural knowledge can be understood more generally to refer to external tasks, such as how to decide on a focus for a paper one has to write. It can also refer to general cognitive processes, such as skills in reading or tactics for learning certain kinds of facts. Finally, as noted previously, procedural knowledge can refer to internal tasks, such as browsing in an online catalog or combining terms using Boolean operators. It should be clear that, although all of these kinds of how-to knowledge are important, knowledge of methods for completing internal tasks is secondary to the more general knowledge of tactics for completing external tasks and strategies for effective completion of basic cognitive processes. The contention that knowledge of internal tasks is secondary to knowledge of external tasks is supported by the findings of Dimitroff and Wolfram (1995). They investigated searchers using a hypertext retrieval system and found that knowledge of the hypertext model or experience with information-retrieval systems had no effect on search processes. It is possible that technological change may lead to the development of information systems in which internal tasks are transparent to the user. This possibility carries with it an understanding that external tasks and the knowledge required to complete them will be much more important in determining user behavior and system usability.

Social Knowledge

Social knowledge structures that are applied to information tasks should also be considered in user-centered information-system design. Social knowledge goes beyond an individual's knowledge of how to behave in society (Bye & Jussim, 1993) and considers ideas that are jointly created and used by members of a community (Morgan & Schwalbe, 1990). An example of social knowledge that can impact on information seeking and information processing is the stereotype. Hamilton, Sherman, and Ruvolo (1990) surveyed a substantial body of research on how stereotypes influence information seeking. Rahn (1993) considered partisan stereotypes and their influence on how people process information about political candidates. This research found that stereotypes have a strong impact on people's judgments about candidates.

Consideration of the social resources that may help individuals or groups complete information-related tasks is an area of research that is just developing. Social cognition research considers primarily cognitive processes in social settings. This research has been reviewed by Sherman, Judd, and Park (1989) and by Schneider (1991). As Augoustinos and Innes (1990) point out, this research is conducted primarily within an individualistic framework. However, social cognition involves social groups that develop collectively-shared social knowledge representations that originate and develop within social interaction and communication. In other words, it is possible to think in terms of cognitive resources that are group resources or cognitive structures that are found as group rather than individual knowledge.

Larson and Christensen (1993) express this point of view in their discussion of group problem solving. They see problem-solving tasks (problem identification, conceptualization, information seeking, etc.) as group tasks, to which group cognitive resources are directed. In problem identification, the group becomes aware of the problem when the individual members are aware that other members of the group also perceive the problem. In storing and retrieving information that is pertinent to the problem, the group has collective access to the information collected by its members, who are delegated to accomplish the information-seeking task. This approach makes it clear that user-centered information-system design should focus not only on individual resources, but also on group resources that are available in the social setting and that can be applied to completing the tasks of information seeking. One example of such social resources is identified by Birkel and Reppucci (1983). They studied the information-seeking behavior of low-income mothers involved in parent education. Mothers involved in high-density social networks of friends and family sought less information than those in loosely structured social networks. The clear implication is that the social network of friends and family acts either to diminish the perceived need for information or to decrease the incentive people have to obtain information about parenting. In either case, the social resource is clearly relevant to information-seeking behavior.

Other resources for social knowledge that are important to information behavior can be found in organizations. Rasmussen, Pejtersen, and Goodstein (1994) emphasize that some of the knowledge applied to completing information tasks is found in the organization. Some of this knowledge may be identified as mental strategies used to complete tasks, while other knowledge may be described as cognitive resources or subjective preferences. In any case, these resources are tied closely to the work domain from which the information need emanates. In other words, there are ways that organizations have of doing things, and members of an organization can adopt those ways of doing things as their own knowledge of how to complete their work. There is, accordingly, an association between individual and organizational knowledge.

Individual Differences

In addition to knowledge structures, user-centered design must take into account the abilities, styles, and preferences of users. These individual differences influence searches for information and thus are relevant input to the design of systems. In particular, these abilities, styles, and preferences serve as resources that are used by individuals as they complete the tasks that lead them to become informed. Andersen (1987) surveyed research that investigates the role of individual differences in interpersonal communication. This review particularly is to be recommended because of the conclusions drawn by the author. Andersen maintains that the only way one can account for differences in communication behavior is by looking at the interactions between individual and social factors. In effect, this review proposes a person-in-situation model such as that outlined in Chapter 3 of this book. There has been a certain amount of investigation into the effects of individual differences on information behaviors. Allen (1992) investigated the effects of cognitive abilities such as vocabulary comprehension, logical reasoning, spatial orientation, and perceptual speed, and found that all of them influence the way people interact with end-user bibliographic information-retrieval devices. In particular, vocabulary comprehension influences the willingness of people to express their information needs in alternative forms, and logical reasoning affects the selectiveness of individuals, both in terms of their vocabulary selection in statements of information need and in terms of the number of useful items selected as being informative. Perceptual speed and spatial orientation seem to influence how people scan information presented to them by an information device and how they learn from what they scan. These different scanning strategies, based at least in part on differences in cognitive abilities, influence how well people find information from devices such as those currently in use in many information settings. Bell and Perfetti (1994) found that verbal abilities and language comprehension skills were central to reading skill. This conclusion will come as no surprise, but it is important to recognize that not all users can absorb information with the same facility using information devices that require reading. Just as some people read better than others, some people learn better than others. Kozminsky and Kaufman (1992) explore some of the individual characteristics that can influence learning abilities. Because learning is an important component and outcome of information retrieval, individual differences between users in terms of their learning abilities can be important in determining how well they will be able to interact with information systems.

Additional research has focused on other kinds of individual differences. Ellis, Ford, and Wood (1993) assessed the effects of differences in the cognitive styles of field dependence/independence and holism/serialism on how people use hypertext information devices. They found that these cognitive styles help to determine individual behavior in using hypertext. They concluded that alternative ways of using the tools must be designed into hypertext systems so that users with different cognitive styles can make optimal use of the systems. Related research of specialist searching using more traditional information-retrieval devices has found that the ability to conduct effective online searches is associated with differences in learning styles (see, for example, Logan, 1990; Saracevic, 1991; Wood, Ford, & Walsh, 1994).

Sometimes age differences can influence information-searching abilities. Gaylord (1989) summarizes research findings that show slower information processing, less learning, and lower levels of memory in older people. In particular, research has documented that increasing age is associated with decreasing perceptual speed. As indicated previously, perceptual speed is an important resource used in at least one strategy for learning from information systems. Information-system design should take into account that there are other learning strategies that can be equally successful, but that emphasize other cognitive abilities; these can be used in information retrieval by those who have lower levels of perceptual speed. Giving users the option of selecting systems that allow them to employ these alternative strategies or that are optimized for these alternative strategies seems to be a reasonable approach to system design.

Other examples of individual differences have been found in more specialized fields of information seeking. Ferguson and Valenti (1991) found that risk-taking strategies influence not only the motivation of people to find out about health issues, but also the approach to information seeking that they subsequently adopt. Interestingly, differences in risk-taking preferences also filter the information they receive. Some information sources give rise to greater levels of concern about health issues than other information sources. They conclude that different types of information provision should be employed for people with different risk strategies.

In summary, there are differences in knowledge and in skills, preferences, and abilities that impact how people complete information-related tasks. This body of research shows that each individual has a different level of resources that he or she needs to accomplish information tasks. Further, people with varying levels of knowledge or cognitive abilities adopt different strategies for finding information. These results indicate that a one-size-fits-all approach to information-system design will be less than successful in achieving usability. On the other hand, it is far from clear (initially) how these various differences in resources can be accommodated within the context of a multi-user information device. The next section considers this conundrum.

User Models

To achieve user-centered design, it seems inevitable that the understanding of the user achieved through needs analysis, task analysis, and resource analysis should be embodied in the information system in a user model. This model will incorporate the different purposes, goals, or objectives of the user, the tasks that may be used to achieve those goals, and the resources that are important in accomplishing those goals. This model or set of models of system users should be central to the design process and ultimately should influence how the information system functions. Probably the most thorough design for incorporating user information in an information system is described by Barnard and May (1993). They include families of task models and methods for representing both semantic and procedural knowledge. The idea is that, with this information about the user represented within the system, user requirements can be interpreted, and the system can meet the needs of users more effectively. Other user models are less sophisticated, relying on stereotypes of users. For example, Ford and Ford (1993), in a study in which interactions between users and a knowledge-based information device were logged, identify four information-accessing strategies, which they suggest may be used to design improved information systems. These four styles (deep-enders, midshallow-enders, shallow-enders, consolidators) may be useful in a general sense, but it is hard to see how they alone could capture the variety of objectives, tasks, and resources that information seekers may have in any realistic sense. Similarly, Tan, Smith, and Pegman (1990) describe a system that incorporates enough information about the user to enable the retrieval of documents at an appropriate intellectual level. This is, however, a rather limited approach, because a difference in intellectual level is just one of many characteristics of the information provided by information systems that can be adjusted in accordance with user characteristics.

As one considers more detailed or sophisticated user models, the question becomes "What elements should be incorporated into the model?" Daniels (1986) addresses this question in her review of cognitive models. It seems undeniable that one element that must be included is what Howes and Young (1991) call a task–action grammar. Actually, in the terms used in this chapter, this grammar should be called a need–task grammar, or a set of links that suggests that, whenever a specific objective is being met, a particular series of tasks (usually in a prescribed order) should be accomplished. Howes and Young (1991) suggest that such a grammar will allow information systems to interact dynamically with users, drawing guidance from the interaction itself, rather than having its interaction with the user programmed in advance.

In systems that make use of user stereotypes as part of their user modeling function, systems can be made to assess user behavior and assign users to categories. Chiu, Norcio, and Petrucci (1991) and Chiu, Norcio, and Hsu (1994) suggest that a neural network can be used to recognize users' behavior patterns, assign them to stereotypes dynamically, and so solve retrieval problems. Although implemented in a constrained field (i.e., helping users create UNIX file security commands), their system was able to infer domain knowledge from dialog behavior. Fischer and Stevens (1991) suggest that a user's individual preferences and the content of the messages deemed interesting by the user can be monitored to generate suggestions about how best to complete an information-retrieval task. Of course, matching individual users to stereotypes can only be approximate. Mitchell, Woodbury, and Norcio (1994) describe a way of creating fuzzy user classes that can be used to develop adaptive user interfaces. These fuzzy classes assign a person to a stereotype with a certain "grade of membership." If these user-stereotype assignments are updated on a continual basis, the information device can adapt to the user as the user changes his or her objective, task, or approach. For example, the approach proposed by Brajnik, Guida, and Tasso (1990) begins with classifying a user into a stereotype, but then uses a dynamic reclassification scheme to update the user model.

Allen (1990) emphasizes that user models can predict users' preferences in a general way, but that they can break down when they are employed at too specific a level. This result is a salutary reminder that models are just that: simplified versions of a complex reality. Forcing users to fit stereotypes is a recipe for information-retrieval disaster. It follows that user models can be used to recognize genuine differences between groups of users, but that they must not be used to restrict the flexibility of information system operation. The user model can provide a starting place, but individual users must be able to customize information systems to meet their specific needs, tasks, and resources.

One aspect of users that seems particularly difficult to model is the resources that they bring to their search for information. It is possible to produce stereotypes of users with different needs and to model their behavior as they progress from one task to another in meeting their needs, but the variability of knowledge resources, abilities, styles, and preferences in any user population must defeat any attempt to include these resources in a user model in any realistic manner. At the same time, the research cited previously shows how crucial these resources are to the completion of information tasks. It seems likely that the somewhat fuzzy boundary between tasks and resources delineates the characteristics that can usefully be included in user models.

The area of user modeling is dynamic, and there seems to be a great deal of skepticism about user models in the minds of some system designers. If system design is to be truly user-centered, it seems inevitable that there must be some mechanism for incorporating an understanding of the user population into the information system. Subsequent chapters will consider approaches that may allow effective modeling of users as preference sets. Given the current technology, this may be the most practical approach to building information devices that incorporate knowledge about users. However, as technology changes, other options may be developed. The body of research briefly reviewed here offers some clues as to how user models can now be incorporated into more effective information systems.

Designing for Usability

The discussion thus far has identified a variety of user characteristics that seem relevant to how users search for information. The users' goals, purposes, and objectives (their information needs) are clearly relevant, as are the tasks they accomplish in meeting those needs. The resources they bring to bear on completing tasks are also important in influencing how the tasks will be completed. It was suggested that these user characteristics should be incorporated into user models that reside in the information device, thereby allowing the device to adapt to users and their situations. These user characteristics are also the focus of other kinds of analysis that are relevant to this discussion. For example, Jirotka and Goguen (1994) edited a volume that describes the techniques of requirements engineering. These techniques, which are described in considerable detail, can be used to develop precisely the kind of picture of user characteristics that is recommended in this chapter. Similarly, MacLean, Bellotti, and Shum (1993) describe an analytical technique called "design space analysis" that illuminates many of the user characteristics discussed here. In this technique, questions posed to users, options offered to users, and criteria for selecting options are explored in an iterative process to analyze user requirements. Now the design process must be considered. Exactly how can an understanding of all of these user characteristics affect the way information systems are designed? Two kinds of answers are discussed in the following sections. The first is a global approach to system design called "enabling-states" design; the second is an approach to specific design choices that ties these design decisions directly to user characteristics in order to create usable products.

Enabling States

The enabling-states model (May et al., 1993) is one approach to system design that synthesizes this discussion and presents a persuasive model for how user-centered and usable information systems can be created. This model provides a detailed design approach that can only be summarized here. The objective of information-system design is to bring users to a point where they are able to meet their goals. Given a specific goal (for example, writing a five-page paper on dinosaurs), the system should enable the users to attain a state where they can complete the tasks that will contribute to the achievement of the goal. This implies first that there is a recognition mechanism that will allow the user to specify a goal or (more fancifully) that will allow the system to diagnose a goal from its examination of user behavior. Secondly, it implies that there exists a goal–task grammar that provides a sequence of tasks that can be employed in achieving the recognized goal. One of the tasks to be completed in writing the dinosaur paper may be selecting an approach to be taken in the paper. Another may be reviewing literature about dinosaurs. Kuhlthau's work (1993) has helped to identify some of the tasks that may be associated with this type of goal. In any case, the first step in enabling is to suggest (or at least recognize) the tasks that must be accomplished.

For any particular task, the resources required to complete the task must also be modeled. The user may or may not have access to those resources. For example, in reviewing the literature about dinosaurs, a knowledge of technical vocabulary (geological and biological labels, for example) may be required. The information system must have at least enough awareness of user characteristics to be able to offer augmentation of user resources. In other words, the system provides enough resources to enable the user to complete the tasks and so achieve the goals. Through these steps, the system brings the user to a state of enablement. For example, if a user lacks the knowledge of technical vocabulary required to review the literature about dinosaurs, the system should incorporate a word list or similar vocabulary-suggestion device that can augment the user's knowledge enough that he or she can complete the task.

Usability

Of course, the objective of all of this analysis is to produce usable information systems. It is therefore appropriate to spend some time at this point discussing the concept of usability. Most of the literature on usability relates to usability testing: something that typically occurs after a system has been substantially designed. For example, Treu (1994) presents a textbook on interface evaluation that includes a number of methods of usability testing, such as heuristic evaluation, comparison against guidelines, and cognitive walkthroughs. Similarly, Bias and Mayhew (1994), in a text that focuses on the costs and benefits of usability testing, provide an excellent overview of usability testing methods to date. A detailed comparison of four usability testing techniques applied to interface design is provided by Jeffries, Miller, Wharton, and Uyeda (1991). Interface design is a primary focus of much of the literature on usability testing. In traditional, data-centered approaches to information-system design, other aspects of the design process are determined, not by user considerations, but by the nature of the data or technology that manipulates the data. For example, design decisions that relate to data structures or search mechanisms are not typically determined by the same type of user considerations that drive interface design. As the user focus is extended to all aspects of the design process, it will be increasingly important to expand usability testing to address the entire information system, not just the user interface.

The approach proposed here is that usability should be built into the design process from the beginning, rather than treating it as a somewhat awkward appendage of the design process. The key to understanding this approach is that, as Richards (1987) maintains, the sociotechnical variables that influence how an information system works fail to provide an adequate explanation of usability. Rather the individual, social, and technological variables should be considered simultaneously. This basic understanding drives the development of a componential approach to usability analysis for design. In other words, having analyzed the users' goals, needs, tasks, and resources according to the outline presented previously, the designers of an information system will have a typology of relevant user characteristics. This typology may be incorporated into a user model. Now a similar analysis of information-system components can be considered: the information contained; how it is organized, accessed, and searched; and how the user interacts with the system through the user interface. These system components may be derived from components currently in use in information systems or from the many novel approaches to interfaces and retrieval techniques that are being produced in research laboratories on a continuous basis. Having identified the relevant components of user behavior and the system components, usability analysis can begin by testing each user component against each system component.

A simplified model for this kind of usability testing begins with a single user characteristic. As noted in the previous chapter, logical reasoning is a cognitive

		Order of presentation	
		Ranked	Traditional
Logical reasoning	High	A	B
	Low	C	D

Figure 2
Matrix for usability testing.

ability that seems to be relevant to evaluating information the system presents to users. For the sake of simplicity, users can be divided into two groups: those who have high levels of this ability and those who have low levels of this ability. Now an element of system design is added. In this example, that design feature is the order in which elements of information (i.e., texts, images, or document surrogates) are presented to users. Again, for the sake of simplicity, it is assumed that there are only two orders of presentation being considered. One of them is the order of calculated relevance. This is an order of presentation familiar to users of vector-space-based information systems, those based on probabilistic retrieval, and even some Boolean-based systems that use postprocessing to assess the similarity between a statement of information need and a unit of information. The alternative order of presentation will be the reverse of the sequence in which information units have been added to the information system. Most of the time, this means that newer information will be presented before older information.

Usability testing sets up a two-by-two matrix for this simple example, illustrated in Fig. 2. If a researcher assumes that all other variables remain constant and tests the four different groups of users A, B, C, and D, he or she will obtain a basis for deciding whether to use ranked order of presentation or traditional order of presentation in the system. If A and C complete consistently better[3] information retrieval than B and D, this indicates that the ranked order of presentation should be adopted. If the reverse occurs, this indicates that the traditional order of presentation should be implemented. Suppose that A and B perform consistently better (or worse) than C and D. There is nothing that can be done at this stage to improve the retrieval of the group that does not do as well in finding information, because the system does not appear to make a difference in this matter. But there is a final and most interesting case. Suppose that A does better than C, and D does better than B (or vice versa). This is an instance in which there is a strong interaction between the system design feature and the user characteristic. In this case, both orders of presentation should be included in system design and be made available to the users. This will allow users to select the order of presentation that they prefer. It is also possible that there will be a weak interaction between the user

[3] This type of testing requires that there be an operational definition of "better" in this context. Without limiting the generality of this discussion, a variety of user-based evaluation measures can be suggested, including satisfaction, user-assessed relevance, and speed of satisfactory completion.

characteristic and the system feature. Suppose A does better than C, but B and D perform about equally. In this case, because the ranked order or presentation ·benefits half of the user population and does not handicap the other half of the user population, this order of presentation should be selected for the information system. It is only in the case of strong interaction that both system features should be included and user-based customizing of the information system permitted. This type of strong interaction between user characteristics and system-design features has been found in a number of different investigations, typical of which is that reported by Meadow, Wang, and Yuan (1995). A strong interaction between the knowledgability of users about the topic being searched and the different types of interface is found to affect important retrieval variables such as the time spent reading the material presented by the information system. This kind of result can be indicative of the need to build into an information system the ability for the user to select the kind of interface that he or she prefers.

It should be noted that the phrase "user-based customizing" conceals two rather different approaches. One is the approach advocated previously: that both options be made available and users be given the choice of setting up the information system according to their own preferences. This approach is similar to the kinds of preference settings that occur in word processors or spreadsheets. The other approach is to diagnose what kind of user is presenting itself to the system and to set the appropriate system choice for the user. This latter approach does away with the possibility of a user making an inappropriate choice of system setting, but at the cost of the possibility of the system making an inappropriate choice.

In all probability, the best approach to user-centered system customizing is a combination of both alternatives. The vision presented here is of a system with minimal diagnostic capabilities and a number of preset preferences. In other words, there can be a number of user models, each with a set of preferences attached to them. On the basis of initial interaction with the user (perhaps through a series of questions or through observation of user behavior), the system will assign the user to one particular user model and select the preset preference cluster that is associated with that user model. Then the user will be free to (and might be advised to) try out and select other preferences as he or she employs the system. This is an important criterion for usability proposed by Adler and Winograd (1992). They maintain that the key criterion for usability is the extent to which a system supports the potential for users who work with it to understand, to learn, and to make changes. Each time the user returns to the system and is identified by it, the previous set of preferences is automatically loaded, unless the user specifies a desire to set up a new set of preferences for this interaction. Opperman (1994) provides a more detailed approach to "automatically adaptable software" that is slightly different than the one used here, but provides additional insights on how software can adapt to support different users as they meet their goals and accomplish tasks.

There appear to be a number of difficulties with the componential approach to usability testing previously outlined. First, there are a large number of potentially relevant user goals, tasks, and resources, and a large number of system-design choices. To conduct a systematic analysis of every possible combination of user characteristics and system-design features would be an impossibly huge task. In all probability, technology will evolve faster than research, and new system capabilities will have to be added and obsolete ones subtracted from the set of possible user–system combinations. Fortunately, user-based system design does not occur in a vacuum, and the task of usability testing can be informed by research in related fields. There already exists a substantial body of research in psychology, sociology, education, management, and other cognate fields that suggests that certain system features may be particularly likely to interact with certain user characteristics. For example, the tasks of information seeking are related to the tasks involved in learning from reading. There is also a large body of research that shows how different user characteristics (and different text characteristics) influence how well people learn from reading.

A more serious objection to the componential approach is that it looks at all of the bits and pieces, but never at the whole. It is quite possible, for example, that one system feature may be much better for all users in accomplishing one specific task, but that it will be much worse for all users in accomplishing a different task. If both tasks are part of the information-search process, componential analysis will not resolve the issue of whether or not to incorporate the system feature. After all the components have been put together, postdesign usability testing will still be necessary to make sure that the parts fit together as they should. Freundschuh and Gould (1991) show how cognitive experimentation can validate the design of geographical information systems, and their approach fits into the model of designing for usability presented here. Predesign componential analysis and postdesign usability testing are both necessary parts of the usability equation.

User-Centered Design: A Practical Guide I

Note: At the end of each even-numbered chapter of this book, a brief guide to the practical aspects of design is provided. This guide summarizes discussions in preceding chapters as they relate to the practical aspects of conducting user-centered design.

1. Identify a user population. The first and obvious step in user-centered design is to find a user, or more appropriately, a user population. Sometimes user identification is dictated by the mission of the organization where the designer works. In other cases, users may be selected by the designer. The identification of the user population is such an obvious step that it is sometimes omitted. This omission results in systems that are not particularly usable for any set of users.

2. Investigate the information needs of your user group. The users identified in step 1 have a number of information needs. These can be investigated using a wide range of research methods, which are easily accessible in manuals on social science research or market research [e.g., Miller (1991) or Babbie (1992) discuss social science research, while Worcester and Downham (1986) present market research techniques]. The key element of this step is to talk to users and find out what kinds of information they need to resolve the problems they encounter. No information system can meet all of the information needs of a user group. Once the full range of information needs has been identified, system designers must select those that their information system will be designed to meet.

3. Discover the tasks that users accomplish as they meet these information needs. Again, research methods from social science and market research are useful in this step. The key element is to talk to users and observe them as they work on meeting their information needs. Identify the tasks that users employ as they meet their information needs and how they accomplish these tasks. Note the sequential ordering of the tasks. Try to distinguish between the tasks that are essential and those that are optional. The result will be one or more task models for each information need.

4. Investigate the resources that users require to complete these tasks. Each task completed by a user who is meeting an information need requires a variety of resources: background knowledge, procedural knowledge, and abilities. List the resources required for each task and identify the level of the resources required. For example, expert knowledge or high levels of verbal ability may be required to complete a task involving vocabulary selection. At the same time, it is important to note the levels of these resources that users possess. Some users, for example, may have less expert topic knowledge or lower levels of verbal abilities, and gaps between resources required and resources possessed are obvious areas of concern. Research methods to investigate the resources possessed by users can be found in any text on psychometrics (e.g., Kline, 1993).

5. Summarize the preceding steps in user models. For each distinct user group to be served by the information system, there will be a number of information needs that the system is designed to meet. For each of these information needs, there will be a number of tasks that must be accomplished. For each of the tasks, there will be a list of resources that are necessary. Integrating these elements together results in a user model that can be used to guide design decisions or that can be implemented as part of the information system to direct how the system will respond to users. For example, user models can form the basis for the preset options for how the information system will work, but users will be able to change the options to make the system conform to their own preferences.

6. Consider each design decision in the light of resource augmentation and enabling. The goal of system design is to allow users to complete the tasks that will meet their information needs. With this in mind, system features that will augment the resources of users when necessary will enable them to complete the tasks. Some of these features will be required by all users, while others will be required by only a portion of the user group. In the latter case, system features are best implemented as user-selectable options. Experimental research to identify interactions between user resources and design options can be used to select system features that should be implemented as user-selectable options. Experimental research techniques are discussed in considerable detail by Atkinson, Herrnstein, Lindzey, and Luce (1988).

References

Adler, P. S., & Winograd, T. A. (1992). The usability challenge. In P. S. Adler & T. A. Winograd (Eds.), *Usability: Turning technologies into tools* (pp. 3–14). New York: Oxford University Press.

Allen, B. L. (1991). Cognitive research in information science: Implications for design. *Annual Review of Information Science and Technology, 26*, 3–37.

Allen, B. L. (1992). Cognitive differences in end-user searching of a CD-ROM index. In *15th International Conference on Research and Development in Information Retrieval Proceedings.* Baltimore: ACM.

Allen, B. L. (1994). Cognitive abilities and information system usability. *Information Processing & Management, 30*, 177–191.

Allen, R. B. (1990). User models: Theory, method, and practice. *International Journal of Man Machine Studies, 32*(5), 511–543.

Andersen, P. A. (1987). The trait debate: A critical examination of the individual differences paradigm in interpersonal communication. *Progress in Communication Sciences, 8*, 47–82.

Atkinson, R. C., Herrnstein, R. J., Lindzey, G., & Luce, R. D. (Eds.) (1988). *Steven's handbook of experimental psychology.* New York: Wiley.

Augoustinos, M., & Innes, J. M. (1990). Towards an integration of social representations and social schema theory. *British Journal of Social Psychology, 29*(3), 213–231.

Babbie, E. (1992). *The practice of social research.* Belmont, CA: International Thompson.

Ball-Rokeach, S. J. (1973). From pervasive ambiguity to a definition of the situation. *Sociometry, 36*(3), 378–389.

Barnard, P. J., & May, J. (1993). Cognitive modelling for user requirements. In P. F. Byerley, P. J. Barnard, & J. May (Eds.), *Computers, communication and usability: Design issues, research and methods for integrated services* (pp. 101–145). Amsterdam: North-Holland.

Bell, C., & Perfetti, C. A. (1994). Reading skill: Some adult comparisons. *Journal of Educational Psychology, 86*(2), 244–255.

Berger, J., Norman, R. Z., Balkwell, J. W., & Smith, R. F. (1992). Status inconsistency in task situations: A test of four status processing principles. *American Sociological Review, 57*(6), 843–855.

Berlin, L. M., Jeffries, R., O'Day, V. L., Paepcke, A., & Wharton, C. (1993). Where did you put it? Issues in the design and use of a group memory. In S. Ashlund, K. Mullet, A. Henderson, E. Hollnagel, & T. White (Eds.), *INTERCHI '93 conference proceedings: Conference on human factors in computing systems INTERACT '93 and CHI '93: Bridges between the worlds* (pp. 23–30). New York: Association for Computing Machinery.

Bias, R. G., & Mayhew, D. J. (Eds.) (1994). *Cost-justifying usability.* Boston: Academic Press.

Birkel, R. C., & Reppucci, N. D. (1983). Social networks, information seeking, and the utilization of services. *American Journal of Community Psychology, 11*(2), 185–205.

Boster, F. J., Hunter, J. E., & Hale, J. L. (1991). An information processing model of jury decision making. *Communication Research, 18*(4), 524–547.

Brajnik, G., Guida, G., & Tasso, C. (1990). User modeling in expert man machine interfaces: A case study in intelligent information retrieval. *IEEE Transactions on Systems, Man, and Cybernetics, 20*(1), 166–185.

Bye, L., & Jussim, L. (1993). A proposed model for the acquisition of social knowledge and social competence. *Psychology in the Schools, 30*(2), 143–161.

Bystrom, K., & Jarvelin, K. (1995). Task complexity affects information seeking and use. *Information Processing & Management, 31*(2), 191–213.

Caplan, N. (1976). Social research and national policy: What gets used, by whom, for what purposes, and with what effects? *International Social Science Journal, 28*(1), 187–194.

Case, D. O. (1991). Conceptual organisation and retrieval of text by historians: The role of memory and metaphor. *Journal of the American Society for Information Science, 42*(9), 657–668.

Chatman, E. A. (1987). The information world of low skilled workers. *Library and Information Science Research, 9*(4), 265–283.

Chen, H., & Dhar, V. (1991). Cognitive process as a basis for intelligent retrieval system design. *Information Processing & Management, 27*(5), 405–432.

Chiu, C., Norcio, A. F., & Hsu, C.-I. (1994). Reasoning on domain knowledge level in human–computer interaction. *Information Sciences, 1*, 31–46.

Chiu, C., Norcio, A. F., & Petrucci, K. E. (1991). Using neural networks and expert systems to model users in an object-oriented environment. In *Conference Proceedings of the 1991 IEEE International Conference on Systems, Man, and Cybernetics* (pp. 1943–1948). Piscataway, NJ: IEEE.

Clark, A. W. (1979). Information use: A professional strategy. *Human Relations, 32*(6), 503–522.

Clarke, P. (1973). Teenagers' coorientation and information seeking about pop music. *American Behavioral Scientist, 16*(4), 551–566.

Coll, J. H., Coll, R., & Nandavar, R. (1993). Attending to cognitive organization in the design of computer menus: A two-experiment study. *Journal of the American Society for Information Science, 44*(7), 393–397.

Daniels, P. J. (1986). Cognitive models in information retrieval: An evaluative review. *Journal of Documentation, 42*(4), 272–304.

Dervin, B., & Nilan, M. (1986). Information needs and uses. *Annual Review of Information Science and Technology, 21*, 3–33.

Dillon, A. (1994). *Designing usable electronic text: Ergonomic aspects of human information usage.* London: Taylor and Francis.

Dimitroff, A., & Wolfram, D. (1995). Searcher response in a hypertext-based bibliographic information retrieval system. *Journal of the American Society for Information Science, 46*(1), 22–29.

Dodge, K. A., Bates, J. E., & Pettit, G. S. (1990). Mechanisms in the cycle of violence. *Science, 250* (4988), 1678–1683.

Duchastel, P. C. (1990). Examining cognitive processing in hypermedia usage. *Hypermedia, 2*(3), 212–233.

Ellis, D., Ford, N., & Wood, F. (1993). Hypertext and learning styles. *Electronic Library, 11*(1), 13–18.

Ferguson, M. A., & Valenti, J. M. (1991). Communicating with environmental health risk takers: An individual differences perspective. *Health Education Quarterly, 18*(3), 303–318.

Fischer, G., & Stevens, C. (1991). Information access in complex, poorly structured information spaces. In S. P. Robertson, G. M. Olson, & J. S. Olson (Eds.), *Human factors in computing systems. Reaching through technology. CHI '91 Conference Proceedings* (pp. 63–70). New York: Association for Computing Machinery.

Ford, N., & Ford, R. (1993). Towards a cognitive theory of information accessing: An empirical study. *Information Processing & Management, 29*(5), 569–585.

Frascina, T., & Steele, R. A. (1992). The integration of hospital information systems through user centered design. In K. C. Lun, P. Degoulet, T. E. Piemme, & O. Reinhoff (Eds.), *Medinfo 92: Proceedings of the seventh world congress on medical informatics* (Vol. 2, pp. 1274–1279). Amsterdam: North-Holland.

Freundschuh, S. M., & Gould, M. D. (1991). Empirical user testing for validation of GIS design. In *GIS/ LIS '91 Proceedings* (pp. 922–931). Bethesda, MD: American Congress on Surveying and Mapping.

Garber, S. R., & Grunes, M. B. (1992). The art of search: A study of art directors. In P. Bauersfeld, J. Bennett, & G. Lynch (Eds.), *CHI '92 conference proceedings: ACM conference on human factors in computing systems: Striking a balance* (pp. 157–163). New York: Association for Computing Machinery.

Gaylord, S. (1989). Women and aging: A psychological perspective. *Journal of Women and Aging, 1*(1), 69–93.

Gillan, D. J. (1994). A componential model of human interaction with graphs: 1. Linear regression modelling. *Human Factors, 36*(3), 419–440.

Goh, S. K., & Coury, B. G. (1994). Incorporating the effect of display formats in cognitive modelling. *Ergonomics, 37*(4), 725–745.

Guida, G., & Tasso, C. (1994). *Design and development of knowledge-based systems: From life cycle to methodology.* Chichester: Wiley.

Hamilton, D. L., Sherman, S. J., & Ruvolo, C. M. (1990). Stereotype based expectancies: Effects on information processing and social behavior. *Journal of Social Issues, 46*(2), 35–60.

Hewins, E. T. (1990). Information need and use studies. *Annual Review of Information Science and Technology, 25*, 145–172.

Hoppe, H. U., & Schiele, F. (1992). Toward task models for embedded information retrieval. In P. Bauersfeld, J. Bennett, & G. Lynch (Eds.), *CHI '92 conference proceedings: ACM conference on human factors in computing systems: Striking a balance* (pp. 173–180). New York: Association for Computing Machinery.

Howes, A., & Young, R. M. (1991). Predicting the learnability of task-action mappings. In S. P. Robertson, G. M. Olson, & J. S. Olson (Eds.), *Human factors in computing systems. Reaching through technology. CHI '91 Conference Proceedings* (pp. 113–118). New York: Association for Computing Machinery.

Jeffries, R., Miller, J. R., Wharton, C., & Uyeda, K. M. (1991). User interface evaluation in the real world: A comparison of four technologies. In S. P. Robertson, G. M. Olson, & J. S. Olson (Eds.), *Human factors in computing systems. Reaching through technology. CHI '91 Conference Proceedings* (pp. 119–124). New York: Association for Computing Machinery.

Jirotka, M., & Goguen, J. A. (1994). *Requirements engineering: Social and technical issues.* London: Academic Press.

Johnson, D. W., Johnson, R. T., Stanne, M. B., & Garibaldi, A. (1990). Impact of group processing on achievement in cooperative groups. *Journal of Social Psychology, 130*(4), 507–516.

Johnson, R. J., & Briggs, R. O. (1994). A model of cognitive information retrieval for ill-structured managerial problems and its benefits for knowledge acquisition. In J. F. Nunamaker & R. H. Sprague (Eds.), *Proceedings of the 27th Annual Hawaii International Conference on System Sciences.* Piscataway, NJ: IEEE.

Jones, R. A., Morrow, G. D., Morris, B. R., & Ries, J. B. (1992). Self perceived information needs and concerns of elderly persons. *Perceptual and Motor Skills, 74*(1), 227–238.

Kirby, J. R. (1994). Comprehending and using maps: Are there two modes of map processing? In W. Schnotz & R. Kulhavy (Eds.), *Comprehension of graphics* (pp. 63–76). Amsterdam: North-Holland.

Kirschenbaum, S. S. (1992). Influence of experience on information gathering strategies. *Journal of Applied Psychology, 77*(3), 343–352.

Kline, P. (1993). *Handbook of psychological testing.* London: Routledge.

Kozminsky, E., & Kaufman, G. (1992). Academic achievement and individual differences in the learning processes of Israeli high school students. *Learning and Individual Differences, 4*(4), 335–345.

Kuhlthau, C. C. (1988). Developing a model of the library search process: Cognitive and affective aspects. *RQ, 28*(2), 232–242.

Kuhlthau, C. C. (1993). *Seeking meaning: A process approach to library and information services.* Norwood, NJ: Ablex.

Kukla, C. D., Clemens, E. A., Morse, R. S., & Cash, D. (1992). Designing effective systems: A tool approach. In P. S. Adler & T. A. Winograd (Eds.), *Usability: Turning technologies into tools* (pp. 41–65). New York: Oxford University Press.

Kuncheva, L. (1993). An aggregation of pro and con evidence for medical decision support systems. *Computers in Biology and Medicine, 23*(6), 417–424.

Larson, J. R., Jr., & Christensen, C. (1993). Groups as problem-solving units: Toward a new meaning of social cognition. *British Journal of Social Psychology, 32*, 5–30.

Latta, G. F., & Swigger, K. (1992). Validation of the repertory grid for use in modeling knowledge. *Journal of the American Society for Information Science, 43*(2), 115–129.

Lewis, P. J. (1993). Identifying cognitive categories: The basis for interpretative data analysis within soft systems methodology. *International Journal of Information Management, 13*(5), 373–386.

Logan, E. (1990). Cognitive styles and online behavior of novice searchers. *Information Processing & Management, 26*(4), 503–510.

MacLean, A., Bellotti, V., & Shum, S. (1993). Developing the design space with design space analysis. In P. F. Byerley, P. J. Barnard, & J. May (Eds.), *Computers, communication and usability: Design issues, research and methods for integrated services* (pp. 197–219). Amsterdam: North-Holland.

Mahling, D. E. (1994). Cognitive systems engineering for visualization. In M. J. Tauber, D. E. Mahling, & F. Arefi (Eds.), *Cognitive aspects of visual languages and visual interfaces* (pp. 41–75). Amsterdam: North-Holland.

Marchionini, G. (1992). Interfaces for end-user information seeking. *Journal of the American Society for Information Science, 43*(2), 156–163.

May, J., Byerley, P. F., Denley, I., Hill, B., Adamson, S., Patterson, P., & Hedman, L. (1993). The enabling states method. In P. F. Byerley, P. J. Barnard, & J. May (Eds.), *Computers, communication and usability: Design issues, research and methods for integrated services* (pp. 247–290). Amsterdam: North-Holland.

Meadow, C. T., Wang, J., & Yuan, W. (1995). A study of user performance and attitudes with information retrieval interfaces. *Journal of the American Society of Information Science, 46*(7), 490–505.

Miller, D. C. (1991). *Handbook of research design and social measurement.* Newbury Park, CA: Sage.

Mitchell, K. C., Woodbury, M. A., & Norcio, A. F. (1994). Individualizing user interfaces: Application of the grade of membership (GoM) model for development of fuzzy user classes. *Information Sciences, 1*, 9–29.

Mooney, C. Z. (1993). Strategic information search in state legislative decision making. *Social Science Quarterly, 74*(1), 185–198.

Morgan, D. L., & Schwalbe, M. L. (1990). Mind and self in society: linking social structure and social cognition. *Social Psychology Quarterly, 53*(2), 148–164.

Olson, G. M., & Olson, J. S. (1991). User-centered design of collaboration technology. *Journal of Organizational Computing, 1*(1), 61–83.

Opperman, R. (Ed.) (1994). *Adaptive user support: Ergonomic design of manually and automatically adaptable software.* Hillsdale, NJ: Lawrence Erlbaum.

Patel, V. L., & Groen, G. J. (1992). The representation of medical information in novices, intermediates, and experts. In K. C. Lun, P. Degoulet, T. E. Piemme, & O. Reinhoff (Eds.), *Medinfo 92: Proceedings of the seventh world congress on medical informatics* (Vol. 2, pp. 1344–1349). Amsterdam: North-Holland.

Peck, V. A., & John, B. E. (1992). Browser-Soar: A computational model of a highly interactive task. In P. Bauersfeld, J. Bennett, & G. Lynch (Eds.), *CHI '92 conference proceedings: ACM conference on human factors in computing systems: Striking a balance* (pp. 165–172). New York: Association for Computing Machinery.

Rahn, W. M. (1993). The role of partisan stereotypes in information processing about political candidates. *American Journal of Political Science, 37*, 472–496.

Ramey, J., Rowberg, A. H., & Robinson, C. (1992). Adaptation of an ethnographic method for investigation of the task domain in diagnostic radiology. In R. G. Jost (Ed.), *Medical imaging VI: PACS design and evaluation* (pp. 325–334). Bellingham, WA: Society of Photo-Optical Instrumentation Engineers.

Rasmussen, J., Pejtersen, A. M., & Goodstein, L. P. (1994). *Cognitive systems engineering.* New York: Wiley.

Richards, C. E. (1987). Roles: A strategy to avoid information overload. *Central Issues in Anthropology,* 7(1), 9–12.

Richardson, J. V., Jr. (1995). Knowledge-based systems for general reference work: Applications, problems, and progress. San Diego: Academic Press.

Salancik, G. R., & Pfeffer, J. (1978). A social information processing approach to job attitudes and task design. *Administrative Science Quarterly,* 23(2), 224–253.

Saracevic, T. (1991). Individual differences in organizing, searching and retrieving information. In J. Griffiths (Ed.), *ASIS '91. Systems understanding people. Proceedings of the 54th Annual Meeting of the American Society for Information Science* (Vol. 28, pp. 82–86). Medford, NJ: Learned Information.

Schneider, D. J. (1991). Social cognition. *Annual Review of Psychology,* 42, 527–561.

Sev'er, A. (1989). Simultaneous effects of status and task cues: Combining, eliminating, or buffering? *Social Psychology Quarterly,* 52(4), 327–335.

Sheng, O. R. L., Wei, C. P., Ozeki, T., Ovitt, T., & Ishida, J. (1992). Design of knowledge-based image retrieval system: Implications for radiologists' cognitive processes. In R. G. Jost (Ed.), *Medical imaging VI: PACS design and evaluation* (pp. 243–254). Bellingham, WA: Society of Photo-Optical Instrumentation Engineers.

Sherman, S. J., Judd, C. M., & Park, B. (1989). Social cognition. *Annual Review of Psychology,* 40, 281–326.

Smith, P. J., Normore, L. F., & Denning, R. (1991). Knowledge acquisition techniques: A case study in the design of a reference materials access tool. In *Proceedings of the Human Factors Society 35th Annual Meeting* (Vol. 1, pp. 273–277). Santa Monica, CA: Human Factors Society.

Stamm, K. R., & Guest, A. M. (1991). Communication and community integration: An analysis of the communication behavior of newcomers. *Journalism Quarterly,* 68(4), 644–656.

Stern, E. (1992). Information management and the whiskey on the rocks crisis. *Cooperation and Conflict,* 27(1), 45–96.

Tan, T. C., Smith P., & Pegman, M. (1990). RADA: A research and development advisor incorporating artificial intelligence techniques and expert system approaches. *Expert Systems with Applications,* 1(2), 171–178.

Tenopir, C., Nahl-Jakobovits, D., & Howard, D. L. (1991). Strategies and assessments online: Novices' experience. *Library and Information Science Research,* 13(3), 237–266.

Thordsen, M. L. (1991). A comparison of two tools for cognitive task analysis: Concept mapping and the critical decision method. In *Proceedings of the Human Factors Society 35th Annual Meeting* (Vol. 1, pp. 283–285). Santa Monica, CA: Human Factors Society.

Todd, R. J., Parker, J., & Yerbury, H. (1994). Knowledge representation and multimedia knowledge base design: A methodology for alignment. In *Proceedings of the 2nd International Interactive Multimedia Symposium 1994* (pp. 543–548). Perth, Australia: Curtin University of Technology.

Treu, S. (1994). *User interface evaluation: A structured approach.* New York: Plenum.

Tushman, M. L., & Romanelli, E. (1983). Uncertainty, social location and influence in decision making: A sociometric analysis. *Management Science,* 29(1), 12–23.

Wildemuth, B. M., & O'Neill, A. L. (1995). The "known" in known-item searches: Empirical support for user-centered design. *College & Research Libraries,* 56(3), 265–281.

Winn, W. (1994). Contributions of perceptual and cognitive processes to the comprehension of graphics. In W. Schnotz & R. Kulhavy (Eds.), *Comprehension of graphics* (pp. 3–27). Amsterdam: North-Holland.

Wood, F., Ford, N., & Walsh, C. (1994). The effect of postings information on searching behaviour. *Journal of Information Science,* 20(1), 29–40.

Worcester, R. M., & Downham, J. (Eds.) (1986). *Consumer market research handbook.* Amsterdam: North-Holland.

3

Information Needs

Introduction

The previous chapter presents a general model for user-centered information system design. The first element of this model is needs analysis, which requires that the designer develop an understanding of the goals, purposes, and objectives of the potential users of information systems being designed. A few examples were given of the variety of goals, purposes, and objectives that can lead people to look for information; enough were provided to make it clear that it is foolhardy to try to enumerate them all. The specific goals, purposes, and objectives of any group of information users must be determined by talking to them, analyzing their needs, and finding out what they wish to do. The primary purpose of this chapter is to provide a framework that can guide designers of information systems in their task of discovering user information needs.

Information-system designers are not the only people who may need to understand information needs, however. Academic researchers have been very active in investigating information needs of users in different contexts. The purpose of the outline developed in this chapter is to unify this large body of research and to point toward a research agenda that will influence the future course of studies of information needs. In addition, information-service providers are vitally interested in understanding information needs so they can render more effective services. The model developed in this chapter is intended to facilitate a balanced understanding of the needs encountered and met by information-service providers.

In this chapter, information goals, purposes, and objectives are presented as information needs within the problem-solving perspective outlined in Chapter 1. To recapitulate, the three steps of the problem-solving approach are:

1. recognition of the problem,
2. identification of alternative courses of action, and
3. evaluation of the alternatives in order to select a course of action.

This use of a narrower focus has already been explained, but it is appropriate to repeat it here. This focus assumes that people search for information because they need information (i.e., their goal, purpose, or objective is to satisfy an information need). Further, it assumes that this search for information is purposive and thus can be analyzed as a kind of problem solving. These narrow assumptions exclude a range of information behaviors that are not associated with information needs and do not appear to fit the problem-solving perspective. It is quite possible for someone to search for information, not because of an information need, but for some other motivation. People who watch television programs may do so because they need to know what is going on in the world, or they may just want to be entertained and diverted. They may just have the television on because they want to have the companionship of a resonant voice while they do something else (perhaps eat their dinner). The same may be true for other types of information-related goals, purposes, and objectives. There may be a variety of gratifications that are provided by the information-seeking process that cannot be considered meeting a specific information need or solving a particular problem. Another way of looking at these information activities is that they meet needs (such as the need for entertainment or companionship) that are not classified as information needs. It is the contention here that, in most cases, it is purposive information behavior that leads people to interact with information systems, and accordingly that information needs are central to the design of such systems. The domain of nonpurposive information behaviors may have implications for information system design as well, but discussion of that domain is not within the scope of this book.

One thing noted in the discussion of information needs in Chapter 2 was the extreme variety of such needs. It would be impossible to enumerate them all, and no such treatment will be attempted here. Rather, a general model drawn from a variety of theoretical perspectives is presented. This general model can be applied to each user population. In each case, the general categories of needs that are discussed here can be made quite specific. For example, this chapter deals with information needs that result from failures of perception. In a specific user population (say, for example, a group of students), one example of a failure of perception may be an inability to perceive what is required to complete a successful term paper. The expectation is that the general model or template provided in this chapter can be used to guide the information-needs analysis activities of system designers working with specific user groups. At the end of the chapter, a few examples of concrete information needs are presented, which should put the general model in a practical perspective.

People who need, seek, and use information are the raison d'être of information systems. Information needs set the context in which users employ information systems and services, and they provide the criteria against which the performance of those information systems and services can be evaluated. Information seeking is the behavior that is the directly observable evidence of information needs and the only basis upon which to judge both the nature of the need and its satisfaction. The position taken here is that needs are explanatory constructs that help in understanding behavior. This discussion does not posit the reality of mental entities, but explains why people act the way they do. If this explanation helps information professionals to design more effective information systems, the utility of the explanatory construct will be sufficiently supported.

People who need, seek, and use information can be understood from a variety of perspectives. For example, consider the driver who is asking for directions. This person and his or her information need can be examined in many ways. Why does the driver need directions? Perhaps because his or her knowledge of the area is incomplete. This is the cognitive perspective. Perhaps because the driver is a foreigner, a member of an outside group. This is the sociological perspective. Perhaps because he or she is traveling for an employer to meet prospective customers. This is the organizational perspective. Perhaps because the driver is a member of a disadvantaged group and has never traveled before. This is the economic perspective. The level of complexity introduced by these varied and somewhat complementary perspectives is so great that it may occlude understanding.

To provide an outline that will simplify this, it is necessary to understand that people are simultaneously individuals and members of groups. It seems clear that some behaviors are individual in nature; that different people placed in the same situation will act differently. At the same time, it seems clear that some behaviors are social or collective in nature. People behave differently when together than they do when they are alone. Their group behavior is different from any one member's individual behavior. This collective behavior can be seen as group action toward meeting a common goal. Examples include group learning, group problem solving, and group decision making as they occur in organizations. This dichotomy between individual and social behavior constitutes the first element in the models of information needs developed here.

There are many influences on people's behavior. When one is behaving individually, both individual and social influences determine behavior. For example, in searching for information as an individual, a person may be guided both by his or her level of existing knowledge (an individual influence) and by the accepted practices of his or her profession (a social influence). Similarly, when a group is behaving collectively (i.e., engaging in social behavior), there can be individual or social influences on that behavior. An individual influence may come from the consensus of the group as to their purposes. Social influences come from the external situation in which the group is embedded. This dichotomy between individual and social influences on behavior or between internal and external factors that can determine behavior constitutes the second element in the models of information needs.

This discussion presents an outline for beginning to understand the behavior that surrounds meeting information needs. Figure 3 presents this outline in graphical form. In this chapter, the four arrows in this diagram will be considered in turn. The first arrow, linking individual influences to individual behaviors, is the cognitive model. The second arrow, linking social influences to individual behavior, is the social model. The third arrow, linking individual influences to social behavior,

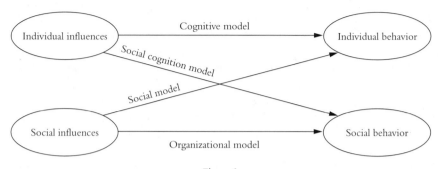

Figure 3
Four models of information behavior.

is the social cognition model. The fourth arrow, linking social influences to social behavior, is the organizational model.

Information Needs: A Cognitive Model

This section discusses information needs from the cognitive perspective, emphasizing the role of knowledge structures and the cognitive processes of learning and interpretation in defining and meeting information needs. As indicated in a review of this body of theory and research (Allen, 1991), the term "cognitive" has been used in so many ways that its meaning is sometimes obscure. For the purpose of this discussion, the cognitive perspective is defined (in overly simplistic terms) as an attempt to explain behavior by reference to what people think and know. In the particular context of this chapter, the cognitive model seeks to explain information needs and how information systems and services can meet them by concentrating on the knowledge structures of people (such as what they know about a particular topic or their level of expertise in a particular process) and their cognitive processes (such as thinking, learning, and problem solving). It should be noted that this simplicity is also deceptive. There is, for example, active debate as to whether or not affective elements (feelings, emotions) are an appropriate part of this explanatory framework. In this chapter, the cognitive perspective omits affect, because thought processes and knowledge appear to be more directly relevant to a discussion of information needs.

The context for this discussion of the cognitive paradigm may be briefly outlined. The approach taken here is the perspective isolated by Cremmins (1992) in his analysis of lexical definitions, by Ellis (1992) in his comparison of paradigms, and by Frohmann (1992) in his discourse analysis. It is the approach that Hjorland and Albrechtsen (1995) contrast correctly with their data-centered approach to domain analysis. It is also the approach taken by Ingwersen (1992), derived originally from De Mey (1977). Admittedly, there are differences between the perspectives of each of these authors, but each of their analyses of the cognitive perspective emphasizes the importance of conceptual structures in understanding how people meet their information needs.

It may be appropriate at this point to identify and discuss the main philosophical weakness of the cognitive paradigm. Simply stated, the cognitive perspective uses mental entities, processes, and relationships to explain behavior. These mental entities (for example, thoughts and concepts), processes (such as thinking and remembering), and relationships (such as mental models) are not observable. The mind (as opposed to the brain) does not exist in space and time and so by definition cannot be observed by the mechanisms of science. The cognitive perspective is typical, in this weakness, of many perspectives of the social sciences, and Frohmann (1992) and Blair (1990), taking a Wittgensteinian perspective on the philosophy of language, have argued that there is no need to posit mental entities. The fact that other social sciences are equally guilty of developing explanatory constructs that are essentially unobservable does not make the situation any easier. In economics, for example, a marginal propensity to consume is essentially unobservable. It must be deduced from behavior, and then is given the task of explaining behavior: a rather vicious circle. Similarly, a social grouping, such as a bureaucracy, is not directly observable. Again, it is an explanation of behavior that is created from observing behavior.

This common trait of social science is characterized in the previous section as a weakness. This need not be the case. If high-level explanatory frameworks, such as those presented by the cognitive perspective, are seen as performing an explanatory function only, no difficulty emerges. It is when they are given additional characteristics and reified that they may serve to block understanding. Also, it is in the nature of an explanatory framework to be extremely difficult to negate. Science, proceeding by negation, may have to amass more evidence for the inappropriateness of an explanatory framework than for the nonexistence of an object or any other phenomenon. Accordingly, the scientist must remain particularly skeptical about any explanatory framework. The cognitive and, for that matter, the social explanations put forward in this book must be assessed by a twofold criterion. First, do they explain behavior? Second, do they serve as a basis for effective information-system design? At the same time, alternative philosophical perspectives, such as Wittgenstein's philosophy of language, should be subjected to the same tests.

Before the cognitive approach to information needs is discussed in detail, there is one additional element of context to be presented. The body of research that has contributed most to understanding information needs is composed of user studies that have investigated how user characteristics can affect the ways in which users interact with information systems. One subset of user studies focuses on the cognition of users: their knowledge structures, cognitive processes, cognitive abilities, and cognitive styles.

There is a subtle problem with this kind of user study. Information needs are expressed and described in terms that are determined at least in part by the information device, system, or service being used. It is quite possible that an individual will express the same information need to two different information sources in different terms. This effect is discussed in greater detail in Chapter 5. The effect of this problem is to make it difficult to develop a holistic understanding of information needs when investigators see needs only in the context of specific information systems or services.

User studies can obtain information on the use being made of the information system or service and limited information about the users as individuals or about the characteristics of users that influence their information behavior. However, because of the limitations cited previously, investigators can obtain little solid information on information needs in general from such studies. This shortcoming of user studies has led researchers to find alternative ways of understanding information needs.

Prominent in this change in emphasis has been the research and important theoretical framework of Brenda Dervin (1980). This work has established a pattern for investigations that try to understand information needs independent of the context of any particular information system or service. Dervin's model suggests that individuals who have information needs experience a gap that prevents them from making sense of their life situation. Information is sought to fill that gap. Perhaps not wanting to limit the general applicability of this model, Dervin and those who have adopted her understanding of information needs have provided little detail about the nature of a gap. In their research, they have discovered many different types of life situations in which gaps can occur and many different ways that people use to fill those gaps. The cognitive model given here supplements that of Dervin and provides a basis for understanding how information needs come to exist and how they can be met. This cognitive model suggests that what Dervin calls gaps are instances in which knowledge structures fail to indicate an appropriate course of behavior or action to an individual. As a result, the individual is placed in a situation in which making sense fails. Information can play a role in helping an individual learn about his or her situation, interpret it, and then select a course of action or behavior.

Belkin, Oddy, and their colleagues developed another influential way of understanding information needs. In the Anomalous State of Knowledge (ASK) approach to information needs, Belkin, Oddy, and Brooks (1982) suggest that information needs occur because individuals recognize something anomalous in their knowledge. These researchers and their colleagues then proceeded to investigate these anomalies by performing intensive linguistic analysis of presearch interviews. This analysis revealed something of the structure of the users' knowledge, but it was unable to lead to a profound understanding of information needs, because the presearch interviews occurred in a limited information context. What Belkin and his colleagues analyzed were not anomalous states of knowledge or needs, but rather statements of information need made in the context of a specific type of information system. These statements of need may reflect the information need, but only in an incomplete and filtered manner. The cognitive model of information needs presented here provides a means of understanding how a state of knowledge is recognized as anomalous and a way of differentiating between different kinds of anomalies in knowledge.

Cognition and Behavior

As mentioned previously, the cognitive perspective seeks to explain behavior by reference to how people think and what they know. In terms of the typology of approaches to information needs, this approach is the one that attempts to explain how individual variables influence individual behavior. The basis of the cognitive perspective is that two people will behave differently in identical situations because they have different understandings of that situation. Their understandings will be different because the knowledge structures of individuals are based on different past experiences. In other words, because no one has exactly the same set of past experiences, no one has exactly the same knowledge structures. This dissimilarity of knowledge structures means that any two people will not understand a situation in exactly the same way. Accordingly, people are likely to behave differently in any situation. The well-documented complexity and unpredictability of human behavior is explained (in this model) by differences in knowledge.

There are at least three ways that people's knowledge structures influence how they behave in any particular situation:

1. knowledge is employed in perception,
2. knowledge suggests alternative courses of action, and
3. knowledge is used to select a course of action.

The sections that follow consider each of these ways in which knowledge (or to use a more general term, cognition) affects the perception of a problem, the generation of alternative courses of action, and the selection of a course of action to resolve the problem.

Cognition and Perception

People perceive situations differently because they have different knowledge. A law enforcement officer may interpret the behavior of a group of young people gathering on a street corner as gang activity or as a drug deal in process, while an ordinary member of the public may see the behavior of the same group of people as a harmless social gathering. People who know each other well may be able to perceive behavior that is indicative of a good or a bad mood, while others will not be able to associate the same behavior with any particular state of mind. A mechanic listening to the sound of an automobile engine may be able to diagnose mechanical problems that will not be perceived by the average driver.

As an individual attempts to deal with a problem, the first step is to perceive the problem. Perceiving a problem is the same as perceiving any other aspect of reality. Knowledge structures, derived from the person's past experience, profoundly affect this process, and different knowledge structures result in different perceptions. An individual in a familiar situation will be less likely to perceive the situation as problematic than someone who has never experienced the situation before. Similarly, someone in a familiar situation is better able to identify what is happening and to deal with any problems presented by the situation. The person who is unfamiliar with the situation has no knowledge resources that provide coping strategies.

Cognition and Alternative Courses of Action

Even if people perceive a situation in the same way, they can behave differently, because different past experience (represented in knowledge structures) may suggest different alternative courses of action. One individual may act in a way that another individual literally would not consider. A law enforcement officer may behave differently from the average observer at the scene of a traffic accident. An intimate friend may know how to respond to an expression of anger from an individual, while someone without that inside knowledge may have no inkling of how to respond. In an information-seeking situation, someone who has a knowledge of information resources may know of productive approaches to satisfy an information need that will be a mystery to someone without such specialized knowledge.

Cognition and Alternative Selection

Even if two people perceive a situation identically and have enough common background that they think of the same possible courses of action, they may still behave differently because they can select different courses of action from the set of alternatives. For example, a motorist faced with two ways of getting to a certain city may avoid a certain highway because he or she knows that there is a lot of construction on that route. Without such specialized knowledge, the motorist may select the route with the construction delays. This trivial example can be generalized by noting that someone with a high level of knowledge of the outcomes associated with alternatives will be likely to choose a different alternative than someone without that knowledge.

Information Needs as Knowledge Gaps

Information needs occur whenever an individual's knowledge fails. Knowledge failures can be associated with perception, alternative identification, or alter-

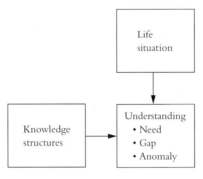

Figure 4
Knowledge gaps and information needs.

native selection. In this section, each of these knowledge failures or information needs is considered in detail. Figure 4 outlines in general terms how knowledge gaps are experienced as information needs. In Fig. 4, the user's life situation interacts with the user's knowledge or cognitive structures to create an understanding of the information need. This understanding may be expressed in terms of an information need, in terms of a gap in the user's ability to make sense of the world, or in terms of an anomaly in the user's state of knowledge. The following discussion considers in greater detail the kinds of situations in which this kind of knowledge gap can occur.

In some situations, knowledge appears to be unnecessary in determining how to behave: behavior can be automatic. There are certain kinds of action that are so frequently repeated that they require little or no conscious thought. Someone reading a book may turn the pages, understand the words, and create a mental summary of what is being read without having to refer any of these actions or processes to conscious interpretation. Automaticity produces a habitual kind of behavior. Habits of this sort are important, because they protect the individual from having to analyze every situation in detail, interpret what it contains, analyze alternative courses of action, and select appropriate behaviors. Rather, action comes automatically. The cognitive processes are reserved for analysis of more ambiguous situations. It is only when something unusual happens that conscious cognitive processes become involved in the behavior. For example, the reader may encounter an unfamiliar word and have to engage in some interpretation to figure out its meaning. This example demonstrates how conscious cognitive processes can activate information seeking. The reader may consult a dictionary to discover the meaning of the problematic word.

Thinking through this example suggests that there is a failure of some kind at the root of information-seeking behavior. In this example, the failure is one of automaticity. Highly programmed and automatic actions fail to produce the desired result, so conscious cognitive processes are employed. Interpretation of the problematic word requires not only conscious activity, but in this example, an effort to find information to assist in interpretation.

Highly determined behavior may also occur in situations that happen infrequently and where behavior is not automatic. In these situations, individuals consult their knowledge structures in order to interpret the situation and select a course of action. If these knowledge structures contain a single, highly authorized interpretation or course of action, the interpretation of the situation may be totally unambiguous to the individual, and the course of action can be so completely obvious that no question is raised. For example, behavior when standing on the edge of a high cliff is not automatic in the sense that reading behavior is automatic. This situation occurs relatively infrequently, and there has been no opportunity for the appropriate behavior to be overlearned to the point of automaticity. However, the course of action (keeping a safe distance from the edge) carries a strong sense of authorization or "rightness." Everything in an individual's experience dictates cautious behavior in that situation.

Other knowledge structures may become highly authorized even without repetition. The source of knowledge structures may convey particular authority to them. If a person learns from an authority figure, it is likely that the knowledge achieved will have a high degree of authorization. One example may occur in a work situation. If a course of action is recommended by a supervisor, it may be given greater strength than if it is suggested by a coworker. In other situations, courses of action suggested by authority figures may be unquestioned. There are obvious problems from an ethical point of view with just following orders, but most people are likely to stop when requested to do so by a police officer, simply because of the authorization attached to that course of action.

There are other sources of authorization. An action may be authorized because it corresponds closely to one's view of one's personal identity. In other words, a course of action may be highly authorized because it is the kind of action that a "person like me" will do. When asked to follow an alternative course of action, an individual may respond, "What kind of person do you think I am anyway?" Strong religious or moral beliefs are particular examples of this correspondence of action with personal identity. When asked why he or she did not follow an alternative course of action, the individual might respond, "I don't believe in doing something like that."

Some knowledge structures that lead to interpretations of situations or selection of courses of action may be highly authorized because of strong needs, fears, and drives. The action of staying well away from the edge of a cliff, which seems highly authorized in most people, may be even more highly authorized in acrophobics. The highly authorized action of enjoying a meal may be even more highly authorized for someone who has not eaten for many hours.

When a course of action is strongly indicated by existing knowledge structures, there is no need for interpretation and consequently no need for information seeking. It follows that an information need occurs when the knowledge structures of the user do not provide an unambiguous interpretation of the situation or do not provide a highly authorized course of action. These are situations in which stock understandings and standard courses of action are missing from knowledge structures. In such situations, individuals have to interpret the situation and assess alternative courses of action. They do so by using existing knowledge structures to interpret the novel situation. This process involves several related cognitive processes: interpretation, learning, and problem solving. In the course of these processes, information needs may be discerned, and information-seeking behavior may occur.

As a rule, these cognitive processes are engaged only when necessary. There is a rule of parsimony of effort that seems to lead people to accept stock interpretations and automatic behavior whenever possible. In fact, the stubbornness of people in maintaining a clearly inappropriate understanding or course of action testifies to the strength of this rule of parsimony of effort. For example, people may choose to ignore a reality that they do not wish to perceive. There are a variety of psychological attributes that are associated with this approach, such as the need to be certain (acknowledging an unpleasant reality can open a whole new area of uncertainty about how to behave) or the preference for taking or avoiding risks (if I ignore it, it will go away). Kellermann and Reynolds (1990) argue that ignorance is sometimes bliss: there are certain beliefs or approaches that are adopted without information-based testing. In experimental research using interpersonal communication, they found that the usual rational model, which assumes that people will want to reduce their uncertainty in social situations, failed to predict information seeking.

However, when people come up against a recalcitrant reality that forces them to engage in interpretation, their knowledge structures have failed them. They must decide how to behave in this novel situation. One way of adjusting to new situations is to rearrange one's knowledge structures into new assemblies that enable the novel situation to be understood. This creation of new knowledge structures may be a difficult task, because the parts to be assembled may be incomplete or may not fit together clearly. In these situations, information is essential to complete the missing components or to enable new structures to be fitted together.

Because information needs are most likely to occur during the cognitive processes involved in interpreting new situations by assembling new knowledge structures, the following section will examine these situations in greater detail.

Perception and Knowledge Structures

How can knowledge structures fail people? An extreme case is when people lack the knowledge that is necessary for them to perceive their situation. Failures of perception can occur because people use knowledge structures as an integral part of perception. They interpret sense data through knowledge structures that have been derived from their experience. If their experience does not provide appropriate knowledge structures, they will not see (or will not see correctly) what is presented in the situation.

One example of a lack of a knowledge structure allowing data to be interpreted meaningfully is found in the many accounts of native people exposed for the first time to European weapons. The native populations frequently had no basis upon which to perceive firearms and those who owned them as being dangerous. As a result, their behavior was painfully inappropriate. Christopher Columbus provided a brief account of this phenomenon:

> They do not bear arms or know them, for I showed them swords and they took them by the blade and cut themselves through ignorance. [Jane, Cecil (Ed.) (1980). *The journal of Christopher Columbus* (p. 24). New York: Bonanza.]

Cook's account of an encounter with the Maori in New Zealand also clearly illustrates this failure of perception:

> Monday 9th October [1769]. I went ashore with a party of men in the Pinnace and yawl accompanied by Mr Banks and Dr Solander, we land[ed] abreast of the Ship and on the east side of the river just mentioned, but seeing some of the natives on the other side of the river whome I was desirous of speaking with and finding that we could not ford the river, I order'd the yawl in to carry us over and the Pinnace to lay at the entrance. In the mean time the Indians made off; however we went as far as their hutts which lay about 2 or 3 hundred yards from the water side leaving four boys to take care of the yawl, which we had no sooner left than four men came out of the woods on the other side the river and would certainly have cut her off, had not the people in the pinnace discover'd them and called to her to drop down the stream which they did being closely pursued by the Indians; the Coxswain of the pinnace who had the charge of the Boats, seeing this fire'd two musquets over their heads, the first which made them stop and look round them, but the 2d they took no notice of upon which a third was fired and killed one of them upon the spot just as he was going to dart his spear at the boat; at this the other three stood motionless for a minute or two, seemingly quite surprised wondering no doubt what it was that had thus killed the commorade: but as soon as they recover'd themselves they made off draging the dead body a little way and then left it. [Price, A. G. (Ed.) (1971), *The Explorations of Captain James Cook in the Pacific as told by selections of his own journals 1768–1779*. New York: Dover.]

Many facets of modern life can produce equally disconcerting failures of perception. One of the areas most likely to produce this kind of culture shock is technological change. The first time someone encounters a new technological development, such as an automated teller machine (ATM) or an online library catalog, failures of perception may occur. People also have the opportunity to be more mobile than ever before. As a result, they are more likely to encounter situations in which perception can fail them. Sometimes the offensiveness associated with certain classes of tourists is caused by the inability of travelers to perceive (or to perceive appropriately) the people, artifacts, and situations of another culture.

Much more common than absolute failures of perception, in which no knowledge structure can be activated to make sense of a new situation, is the kind of failure of perception that occurs when people activate an inappropriate knowledge structure. Sometimes such failures of perception can be brought to people's attention through painful encounters with reality. If someone has come to expect doors at airports to open automatically, they may perceive all airport doors as being automatic doors. In a less modern airport, this failure of perception can result in the painful experience of walking into a door. Treating a sophisticated information-retrieval tool as if it were a card catalog is another example of misperception, which can result in inappropriate expectations of the tool and a failure to operate the tool successfully.

Other failures of perception are brought to people's attention as a result of failed intersubjectivity. People who perceive a situation in a certain way are likely to assume that others perceive it in the same way. Encountering courses of action that cannot be explained by that perception can be as revealing as encountering a recalcitrant reality. For example, someone may fail to perceive the difference between a formal restaurant and an informal one. Appearing at the former in informal attire and seeing all of the other diners wearing formal clothing reveals a failure of intersubjectivity. A library employee may fail to perceive the difference between two classes of users (for example, faculty and students) and use the same loan period or circulation regulations for both. This employee may naturally assume that all other employees are acting in the same manner. It will then come as a shock to see a fellow employee use a different loan period or circulation regulation for one class of users. Such failures of intersubjectivity will lead to an awareness of inadequacy, incompleteness, or anomaly in knowledge structures.[4]

Obtaining information to resolve failures of perception can be extremely difficult. The failure may be so complete that it is difficult or impossible to articulate the information need. The natives encountering firearms for the first time may have assumed they were seeing an elaborate version of the walking stick. But after their failure of perception was made clear in certain and painful terms, their questions may not have been explicit. If a person has been unable to activate any knowledge structure, then questions such as "What was that?" or "What happened?" are likely to occur. If a person has activated an inappropriate knowledge structure, then the awareness of the information need may be a bit more coherent: "I thought it was X, but it's not."

Resolving the type of failure of perception described in this section is the first step in problem solving: problem recognition. Cowan (1986) develops a theoretical model of problem recognition that reflects many of the considerations in the preceding paragraphs. His model consists of three stages: the gestation/latency stage, the categorization stage, and the diagnosis/definition stage. In the gestation/latency stage, the individual is engaged in situational scanning only. There is no failure of perception, and actions can proceed automatically. In the categorization stage, there is a recognition of a discrepancy between what is expected to happen

---

[4]This example is drawn from the dissertation research of my colleague Johanna Bradley (Bradley, 1991).

and what actually happens. During this stage, three processes occur. The first process is arousal. The individual starts paying attention to things that have occurred more or less automatically up until the discrepancy. The individual has a feeling of uncertainty and a motivation to explain what is going on. The second part of the categorization stage is clarification: an attempt to understand, to verify that something really has gone wrong. The third process in this stage is classification, in which the individual decides that the discrepancy is or is not really a problem. There is frequently considerable reluctance on the part of people experiencing discrepancies of this sort to classify them as problems, because this act of classification involves them in the subsequent labor of problem solving. The final stage of Cowan's model, diagnosis/definition, also consists of three processes. The first process is information search, in which additional evidence about the nature of the problem is gathered. Then inference occurs, during which conclusions are drawn about the evidence. Finally, problem description can occur: the problem is labeled as to its type and nature. Cowan's model uses different language and has some different emphases, but it matches fairly well the process of problem perception outlined in this chapter.

Models of information needs developed by other scholars also deal with failures of perception. Chew (1992) developed a typology of information needs in which the first stage is sensory awareness: a simple question of "What's going on?" This research found that, during the viewing of routine news broadcasts on television, people had more questions of this type. In other words, there was less of the more detailed processing that will be discussed in subsequent sections of this chapter. Similarly, information needs deriving from failures of perception correspond to the first two of the eight different types of information needs identified by Taylor (1991): enlightenment, in which the user is trying to understand a situation, and problem understanding, which allows the user to begin to plan to solve the problem. The approaches of Chew and Taylor are compared with the typology of information needs adopted in this chapter in the section titled "Selection of Alternative Courses of Action."

It is, however, important to recognize at this early stage of the discussion of information needs that information behavior is not always rational. In the preceding discussion, when an individual encountered a "reality check," it led to the recognition of an information need and subsequent information-seeking behavior. This rational problem-solving approach to information needs is, however, inadequate to explain all information behavior, because not all information-seeking behavior is rational. For example, people may refuse to recognize a problem, even when confronted with reality. This happens frequently in the area of health information. People will ignore all information about reality because they do not want to find out about a health problem or to engage in problem solving. Similarly, people making political decisions may act to limit the amount of information on which they are basing their decisions, or people deciding what consumer products to buy may act on feelings rather than information. Managers may engage in ritual uses of information or may disavow knowledge that is relevant to their decision making. In short, there are a variety of situations in which rational problem solving occurs, but in the context of a wide variety of less rational behaviors.

Even if irrational information behaviors could be predicted, it is not immediately clear if information systems should be designed around such behaviors. It is possible that systems that respond to rational information needs and behaviors will also be able to meet the needs that give rise to irrational information behavior. In any case, the remainder of this chapter will focus on rational, problem-solving behavior, although it is recognized that rational behavior is not necessarily the only type of information behavior that users will exhibit.

Identification of Alternative Actions

If the failure is not one of perception, but of alternative identification, then it may be easier to resolve the anomalous state of knowledge and its related information-seeking behavior. In such a situation, behavior is undetermined because there is no ready supply of alternative courses of action. In everyday life there are frequently situations in which perception is adequate but knowledge structures are inadequate to deal with them. Enough knowledge does not exist to suggest viable alternative courses of action. Knowledge can be seen as a series of knowledge structures (variously called schemata or frames) that contain a number of slots that can be filled. In cognitive psychology, schema theory is a popular approach to describing knowledge. A simple example may be the schema that contains a person's knowledge about swans. The swan schema will have a slot for type of animal, which will be filled with the value "bird," a slot for color, filled with the value "white" (at least until the individual encounters a black swan for the first time), a slot for habitat, filled with the value "aquatic," and so on. Filling the slots with values allows someone to perceive a swan. If an individual has a swan schema with enough slots filled, the process of perception is a simple matching process: a large, white, aquatic bird is observed, and because of the swan schema, the bird can be perceived as a swan. Perceiving the swan correctly is only the first step, however. As more knowledge is packed into that knowledge structure, individuals begin to identify alternative behaviors. For example, someone may know that swans are nervous and difficult to approach in the wild, but that in parks where they are fed by humans, swans can become aggressive and will chase people who may have food and sometimes bite them. This additional knowledge suggests possible courses of action. In the wild, swans should be approached cautiously, lest they fly away. In parks, they can be fed, but people should be aware of their aggressive tendencies.

To take the example of the natives encountering European weapons for the first time, it would be possible to tell them, "Yes, those are weapons. They are dangerous and they can harm from a great distance." At this point the failure of perception ends, and a failure to identify alternatives may begin. They know what is to be done: the weapons have to be avoided or rendered harmless. However, they have no idea how to proceed with this task. Specifically, how does one go about rendering this new kind of weapon harmless? That depends on many different characteristics, all of which are unknown (its mechanism, range, accuracy, etc.).

It should be emphasized that such a situation is still novel. Enough knowledge exists to provide a label for the entities or the situation, but not enough to decide on the appropriate action. Another way of looking at it is that the semantic problem has been resolved. Perception is possible. The episodic memory that will suggest possible courses of action is lacking.[5] Clearly, if a person has tried a variety of courses of action in the past and can remember what those were, there will be no failure at this stage.

Another example of a failure of alternative identification is if someone approaching an ATM or an online public access catalog (OPAC) terminal is told what it is. That person may respond "So that's what that is. I've heard of them. Now what do I do?" Failures of alternative identification resemble situations in which an individual has never played a particular game and needs to have the various procedures, steps, strategies, and tactics explained. Another way of thinking about failures of alternative identification is to ask how an individual goes about trying to discover alternative courses of behavior. One way is the familiar problem-solving process of trial-and-error. A novice computer user may know what the computer is, but still not have the faintest idea of how to turn it on. Such a person may very well push every button and turn every knob in sight until a reaction (appropriate or otherwise) is achieved. Other kinds of knowledge-acquisition activities may involve information seeking. Reading a manual is an obvious tactic in this situation. Manuals exist for a variety of situations, but there are many more situations for which there is no formal presentation of alternatives. In such situations, accounts of how others have coped in the past in similar situations would be of use.

Finally, there is the process of finding out everything about the novel situation or entity. Such knowledge may suggest courses of action, primarily by association or analogy. Learning more about a novel entity or situation involves identifying similarities with known entities or situations. Following these associative links can suggest courses of action. The thought process may be, "This situation seems to be similar to one in which a successful course of behavior was X. Therefore, let us try behavior X in this new situation."

It is clear that all of these ways of identifying alternatives require the assembly of new knowledge structures. Some of the components that are involved in this process may be fragments of existing knowledge assembled in new ways to understand the novel entity or situation. Some of the components may come from information-seeking behavior. The directions for assembly may consist of gen-

---

[5] This distinction between semantic and episodic knowledge, proposed by Endel Tulving (1983), distinguishes between general factual knowledge and knowledge (or memory) of specific events.

eral problem-solving strategies such as trial-and-error, or more specific problem-solving strategies such as reading a manual, finding out what others may have done in similar situations, or learning about the new situation and identifying alternative courses of action through analogy or association.

One example from the literature illustrates the kinds of processes that occur at this stage. Dukerich and Nichols (1991) investigated how managers, having diagnosed that a problem existed in their organization, went about filling in some of the details about that problem. As they tried to diagnose what was causing the problem, they sought information to confirm or disconfirm that a particular cause may be associated with the problem they faced. The amount of information they were able to find about potential causes affected the thoroughness of their approach to filling this crucial slot in their problem schema.

In the typology of information needs developed by Chew (1992), mentioned previously, pattern recognition leads to categorization of information, and then acceptance or rejection of that information. This stage seems to parallel the slot-filling approach previously outlined. In the research reported by Chew (1992), it was found that there was more of this type of in-depth understanding going on when people viewed serious news than when they viewed routine news on television. In other words, greater information seeking and depth of processing occurred when there was something special or urgent, while much of the processing during regular news watching was limited to basic awareness.

This kind of information seeking appears to correspond to three of the eight information needs in Taylor's (1991) typology. The first is instrumental needs, in which the user needs to obtain skills in order to proceed. This "how-to" need can be fulfilled by filling in slots in procedural schemata. The second is factual needs, in which the user requires precise data to be able to identify alternatives. The third is confirmational needs, in which users reinforce their knowledge of a specific topic or area. Although these needs have not been discussed in precisely this way, it seems clear that they fit the pattern of slot filling to identify alternatives.

Selection of Alternative Courses of Action

Once adequate knowledge has been achieved to ensure that a number of alternative courses of behavior have been identified, people may need help in selecting an alternative. In this case, there can be no clear and authoritative course of action dictated by the knowledge structures. In other words, the alternatives, whether identified from past experience or from an information search, present equally attractive courses of action. In evaluating courses of action, the source and strength of the authorization for each action are both important.

As previously described, sources of authorization may include the endorsement of authority figures, the experience of successful past use, and the association of actions with self-image or ethical positions. It is quite possible, however, that the alternative courses of action under consideration may have enough similarity in their authorization to lead to a state of confusion. This situation is clearly one in which the state of knowledge is anomalous: knowledge does not present a clearly authorized course of action.

Behavior in such situations may be selected on the basis of simple heuristics. For example, one may follow a trial-and-error problem-solving approach. Alternatively, one may have a rule that indicates, "When in doubt, do X." It is possible, however, that there may also be information-seeking aspects to selecting a course of action. One can assume that some of the general rules or heuristics take into account the consequences of actions. For example, behavior can be selected to maximize the probability of obtaining the best possible consequence or to minimize the probability of obtaining the worst possible consequence. Accordingly, selection of alternative behaviors requires some inquiry into the possible consequences of particular courses of action.

The action–consequence link can be obtained through information seeking that may provide accounts of individuals who have chosen a particular course of action in the past. Similar behaviors can be investigated to determine their consequences so that the action–consequence link can be determined via analogy or association. In these ways, the information that is available through information systems and services can be applied to this particular life situation.

There is a distinctive element in this kind of information need. What is required is a critical and evaluative approach to alternative courses of action. The leap from description of alternatives to evaluation of alternatives is big, but it is crucial. The task of the information system or service can be described as that of increasing the valence of one particular alternative so that it becomes the clear choice.

This situation is analogous to that experienced by graduate students. After learning the general to specific details of a topic, they are trying to evaluate alternatives, to select areas of research, and to decide whether one theorist provides a better explanation than another. An information system that provides evaluations of different ideas or concepts is invaluable in meeting this kind of information need. Evaluation consists of high-level analysis of courses of action.

To return to Chew's (1992) typology, the third type of information processing that can occur is in-depth processing (including reasoning, inference, elaboration, and retention). This final stage appears to correspond to the final stage of the model outlined in this section, because selection of an alternative requires precisely this kind of in-depth processing. Evaluation of alternatives will, inevitably, involve some level of reasoning about cause and effect, making inferences from what is known to what may happen in the future, and forming associative links between different ideas to create an elaborated understanding of the problem situation and how the problem may be successfully resolved. Chew (1992) found the kind of information processing that leads to decision making and opinion formulation occurred relatively rarely in regular news watching and more frequently when something particularly urgent was being reported. Three needs in Taylor's (1991) typology appear to fit into this alternative evaluation and selection area. The first is projective needs, which relate to estimation and assessment of probabilities. The

Table 1
Typologies of Information Needs

This book	Chew (1992)	Taylor (1991)
1. Perception (Schema activation)	1. Sensory awareness	1. Enlightenment
		2. Problem understanding
2. Identification of alternative actions (slot filling)	2. Pattern recognition	3. Instrumental needs
		4. Factual needs
		5. Confirmational needs
3. Selection of alternative courses of action (action–consequence links)	3. In-depth processing	6. Projective needs
		7. Motivational needs
		8. Personal/political needs

second need is motivational, in which users employ information to get started on the resolution of their problem. The third is personal/political information needs, in which people are able to feel that they can get control of their problem situation. Selection of an alternative course of action will involve estimation and assessment of probabilities of outcomes associated with certain actions; having made a selection, people will feel motivated to continue the resolution of their problem and will feel they are in control of the situation. The perspectives of Chew and Taylor augment the understanding of information needs associated with alternative selection presented here by concentrating on the kinds of thought processes and feelings that may occur when people experience and work through this kind of information need.

Table 1 compares the three types of information needs discussed in this chapter with the information needs identified by Chew (1992) and Taylor (1991).

Information Needs: A Social Model

This section discusses information needs from the social perspective, emphasizing the social embeddedness of the process of defining and meeting those needs and the social factors that influence how people approach information needs. Because people are always embedded in social situations, it is sometimes difficult to distinguish clearly between the individual and social influences on information-seeking behavior. The distinction may, in fact, be one of emphasis rather than of clear separation.

To avoid the problem of concentrating on the user in the narrow context of interacting with an information system, some user studies focus on groups of users and consider how membership in a group influences individual information seeking. Some of the earliest studies of this nature looked at groups of scientists, such as social scientists or chemists, and tried to ascertain their information needs and how they presented their needs to information services. More recently, studies of this nature have focused on particular social situations. Being a member of a group, such as abused spouses, cancer patients, senior citizens, or janitors, is seen as sufficient to influence individual information-seeking behaviors and patterns. For example, Chatman (1987) studied the information world of custodians and found that their information needs centered around health, career opportunities, and interpersonal relationships. An excellent overview of how social settings influence information needs is provided by Taylor (1991). Focusing on the professions, entrepreneurs, special interest groups, and special socioeconomic groups, he shows how information needs differ from group to group.

These user studies demonstrate the importance of social influences on how people see their information needs and ultimately on how they go about searching for information to meet those needs. Accordingly, it should be possible to design information systems tailored to the information-seeking behaviors of individuals who are members of groups. For example, these systems can work optimally in meeting the information needs of engineers, school children, or cancer patients.

Similarly, information institutions can be designed that are optimized for individuals from specific social settings. In fact, this occurs frequently in a variety of institutions. Special libraries established in academic communities may focus on the needs of individuals from that particular social setting, for example, an academic discipline. They may also focus on the needs of a specific group, for example, undergraduates. Thus, information services are often established to meet the needs of people in particular social settings: they may be patients in a hospital or customers in bookstore.

Social Influences and Individual Behavior

The social perspective seeks to explain information-related behavior by reference to the social settings in which people are found. The basic idea in the social perspective is that two people with different backgrounds will behave similarly in the same situation. This idea is the opposite of the assumption of the cognitive viewpoint discussed previously, in which people with different backgrounds are believed to behave differently in the same situation. Those who emphasize the cognitive perspective maintain that differences introduced by individual knowledge and background are sufficient to make the behavior different. Those who support the social perspective are likely to minimize individual differences, commenting on the underlying similarity of people's behavior in similar situations.

Individual knowledge structures are derived from experience, but that experience necessarily occurs in society. People who share experiences will therefore share knowledge structures. It is precisely this social reality that makes communication possible. If it were true that one person's knowledge structures are totally different from those of a second person, it would be difficult to see how communication would be possible (unless there were a translator present who embodied the knowledge of both of the individuals). It is at this point that the idea of a community of discourse is important. Communities share the background, experience, and ultimately language that enables communication. Even a characteristic as apparently individual as basic competence in arithmetic or reading is considered by some to derive from social influences. Elbers et al. (1991) presents a debate about the social context of competence, arguing that children develop competence amidst a storm of messages from adults that transmit perspectives on reality. These messages teach children what is worth knowing about a culture and so act to modify the children's abilities. The debate continues and serves to illustrate that social variables must be taken seriously in order to understand information seeking.

Social factors influence how people perceive the situations in which they are found. Most situations are, in fact, social situations. The individual is surrounded by other people, and how these other people behave will influence how the individual perceives the situation. Social influences also determine to some extent the different sets of alternative actions that are understood to be present, because they constrain the alternatives that may be considered. Social factors, particularly social values, also constrain the selection of a course of action.

Perception and Social Influence

The effects of social factors on perception can best be understood by examining situations where they are absent. The examples of failures of perception used in the cognitive model discussion worked not only because there were no appropriate knowledge structures in place, but also because there was no appropriate social resource which individuals could use in perceiving their problem situation. The indigenous people encountering European firearms for the first time could call on neither personal experience nor the example of their fellow tribespeople for an understanding of their situation. This failure of perception is noticed particularly when individuals are uprooted from their social context and placed in a situation in which they do not belong, in which they cannot understand their human surroundings.

Where problem situations occur less frequently and behavior is not automatic, but is still highly determined, the impact of social differences can be seen clearly. A single, highly authorized interpretation or course of action can derive from the social situation. Situations can be identified in which problems occur and solutions are not clear. However, if the situation is changed, solutions can become clear because they are highly authorized. An individual doing some work on his own house and encountering a problem may say, "If I were at work, I would know how to handle this." Similarly, in a religious situation, certain behaviors may be highly authorized that will not be considered appropriate in the work situation. One set of experiments that bears on this phenomenon is reported by Kruglanski, Peri, and Zakai (1991). They found that when people are already confident that they understand the situation and when they have a high need for cognitive closure (i.e., they want to decide quickly), they do little information seeking. When they have more alternatives and so are less certain that they understand the situation, they seek more information. An important point of this research is that the need for cognitive closure varies because of factors in the social situation; for example, by having the costs of inaccurate judgments stressed. Therefore, the amount of information search conducted depends on the (individual) feeling of confidence and the (socially induced) need for closure.

Much more common than absolute failures of perception, in which no social factor influences perception of the situation, is the kind of failure of perception that occurs when people are influenced by inappropriate social factors. Every individual is socialized into a large number of groups: occupation, work groups, national or community groups, or groups based on religion or avocation. An individual who behaves at church as if he or she were with bowling friends may find that the course of action dictated by one social influence is regarded as problematic in the recalcitrant reality of another social setting. Ways of dealing with members of the opposite sex that may be appropriate in one social setting (say, a night club) may be problematic or illegal in a work setting. Perhaps the best illustration of this phenomenon is sexual harassment. In a setting where one person has power over another, certain behaviors are inappropriate. Lord Acton's adage "Power tends to corrupt and absolute power corrupts absolutely" applies unmistakably to interpersonal relationships. However the power occurs, perhaps in an employer–employee or a teacher–student relationship, it serves to alter the perception (and the reality) of the interpersonal relationship in such a way that harassment occurs.

Awareness of an anomaly in social influences occurs as a result of a reality check. Examples have already been mentioned in which such an anomaly can result in a painful or unfortunate experience. It is in these anomalous situations that information seeking can be an important part of the problem's resolution, but obtaining information to resolve this sort of anomaly can be as difficult as obtaining information to resolve an inadequacy in knowledge structures. The failure of perception may be so complete that it is difficult or impossible to articulate the information need. Confusion leading to questions like "What happened?" or "What went wrong?" is likely. The individual in a religious context who behaves in a way that is appropriate while bowling (or vice versa) may be unaware of the anomaly. It is also possible, one suspects, for sexual harassment to occur because of a failure to perceive the poisoning effects of a power-structured social setting on interpersonal behavior. The question "What went wrong?" is, of course, a plea for information, but it can also be a call for help in the midst of a painful experience.

Identification of Alternative Actions

Situations in which the problem is clearly perceived must now be addressed. The social signals are unambiguous, but what is unclear is what alternatives may exist to resolve the problem. Again, this task of identifying alternatives is constrained by social factors.

In the previous discussion of the cognitive model, the example of someone needing to know the rules of a game is cited. It is sufficient to note at this point that the rules of most social encounters are socially determined. So, for example, the alternative courses of action available to an individual in a work situation may be considerably different from the courses of action available to someone at a party or in a restaurant. So the question "Now what do I do?" can only be asked in a constrained way. The appropriate question becomes "What do I do in this situation?"

The techniques and strategies for finding out what to do in any particular situation are largely interactional. Trial-and-error strategies are frequently attempted, but the success or failure of any particular trial can only be judged by the reaction of the group concerned. It is possible to observe others in similar situations and try to induce the possible courses of action. The social embeddedness of each situation makes information seeking more difficult. There are seldom instruction manuals that give directions for alternative acceptable courses of action in social situations. The nature of the information need is such that people experiencing that need may be looking for expert advice from someone who, through special training or previous experience, knows what the alternatives in this particular social situation may be.

Selection of Alternative Courses of Action

In situations where the possible courses of action that have been identified have approximately equal social endorsement, information needs associated with alternative selection may occur. If there are no courses of action that are strongly authorized by socially conditioned values, people need action–consequence links to decide what to do. However, in the social model, the action–consequence associations are not absolute, but relative to the specific social situation in which the individual is embedded. So it is not enough to be able to know that a particular action has been associated with a particular consequence in the past. Rather, one must know that the action–consequence association has been observed in a roughly analogous social setting.

Information seeking to meet this kind of information need must be constrained to the social situation described. The information system must have dual expertise, both topic-oriented and context-oriented. For example, a firm wishing to consider the available options for opening up a new market in Russia may wish to consult someone who is experienced with business practices and marketing and who has additional expertise and experience in Russia. To take another example, advice about what gift may be appropriate for a special occasion may vary considerably with socio-economic class, geographical setting, or ethnic influence. Again, the information provided must be expert in topic (what gifts are possible) and in social setting.

Social Cognition and the Collective Nature of Information Needs

No man is an *Iland*, intire of it selfe; every man is a peece of the *Continent*, a part of the *maine* . . . (John Donne, *Devotions on Emergent Occasions, Meditation XVII.*)

The discussion of the cognitive and social models of information needs employ examples that are intended to reflect common experience. Using a computer device for the first time or trying not to stand too close to the edge of a cliff are situations that emphasize individual behavior. But in reality, no action can be considered a totally individual action, which makes understanding information needs even more complex.

To consider how important this idea of collective behavior is for the recognition of information needs, it is necessary to reformulate the preceding discussion. To the extent to which behavior is not individual but is group or collective behavior, it is possible to consider the idea of group or collective information needs. It is argued here that there is a valid way of thinking of information needs that extends beyond the individual to the group. In this section, group information needs are discussed first, followed by a consideration of some of the individual factors that can influence group information behavior. The extent to which perception and knowledge are collective must be examined.

If perfect communication existed, the knowledge of a group would be the same as the knowledge of its members. However, communication is imperfect, and in any group, the perception of one individual can be shared only imperfectly with others. Groups perceive, know, and need information in different ways than their individual members. It follows that group and individual information needs and behaviors must be discussed separately.

If the important functions in which information plays a role are considered, numerous examples of group activity can be seen. Learning, for example, frequently occurs in groups. In a classroom situation, some individual learning occurs. Other learning activities will produce group learning: something that occurs to a group that cannot happen if the group were treated as individuals alone. Similarly, group problem solving will be familiar in most employment situations. Here, the group process is crucial to the solving of the problem, and the outcome may be entirely different if the individuals are not working together. By extension, situations in which information needs and information-seeking behavior are collective in nature can be identified.

If this is true, it follows that there can be both individual and social influences that determine the nature of the collective information-seeking behavior, just as these same influences determine (at least in part) the nature of individual information needs. However, individual factors that influence collective behavior differ from those that influence individual behavior. In the preceding discussion of the cognitive model, the focus is on the influence of individual knowledge and abilities on individual behavior. However, when groups are considered, the individual knowledge and abilities of the members of the group and the collective knowledge and abilities of the group must be discussed. In other words, the focus on groups leads to considering factors internal to the group as individual influences and factors outside the boundary of the group as social influences. The remainder of this section focuses on the individual (i.e., within-group) influences that influence group information needs and how these needs are satisfied.

Perception and Group Knowledge

Collective perception of any situation occurs when the group members not only perceive the situation individually but also note that other members of the collective see the situation in the same way. In other words, members of the collective must:

1. know that the situation is X (individual knowledge),
2. know that they know that the situation is X (metaknowledge[6]), and
3. know that other members of the collective know that the situation is X (intersubjectivity).

The group perception of a situation or problem is thus different from the sum of its parts. It is not enough to know how each member of the group perceives the situation. It is also important to know how the group, in an act of social cognition, perceives the situation. If the group is seen as a cognitive agent, then the perception of the group stems from the group's cognitive structures, which derive from its background and experience. Schaller (1991) gives examples of group knowledge structures: stereotypes that groups apply to other groups. In-group favoritism seems to occur automatically whenever groups are formed. There are, of course, many other examples of collective knowledge structures. If a group has been in a particular situation frequently, it may have developed a simple collective understanding of the situation that allows action to proceed automatically. It could be argued that military training, for example, is designed to make group reactions to a given situation automatic. If a squad comes under fire, they do not go through an elaborate process of developing a collective understanding of the situation. In-

---

[6] This use of the term "metaknowledge" is to be distinguished from that found in Connell (1995). In her work, metaknowledge is high-level, integrated knowledge that can be expressed in rules. As used here, however, metaknowledge is knowing (or feeling) that one knows something.

stead, all members of the group react promptly and virtually automatically to counter the threat. The same phenomenon can be seen in team sports. Someone fumbles the ball, and the defensive team reacts immediately to the situation. In these examples, groups can have the equivalent of the knowledge structures previously discussed for individuals. Through those knowledge structures, the group can perceive the situation. If the knowledge structures are sufficiently developed, they may provide a basis for automatic action.

If the group has not encountered the situation before or has no training that will enable it to respond automatically, a process of building a collective perception must occur. One example of this phenomenon is chronicled in Kuhn's book on scientific revolutions (Kuhn, 1970), which has been repeatedly supported in works on the social psychology of science, in particular in the work of Latour (see, for example, Latour & Woolgar, 1979). Although an individual scientist may work in isolation to some extent, scientific facts are group constructs. The scientists gradually evolve a collective understanding of the situation (Kuhn calls this a paradigm), which remains intact until supplanted, more or less violently, in a scientific revolution.

The point of this example is that science proceeds by persuasion. An individual scientist is not just recounting the truth as observed, but rather is doing his or her best to persuade fellow scientists of a particular perception of reality. This social construction of truth also occurs in work groups, groups such as gangs, and other tightly knit groups that have a collective cognition. One member of the group may perceive the situation in a certain way. That member then is responsible to not only to communicate his or her perception of the situation, but to persuade the other members of the group that the perception is a good one (i.e., truthful, veridical, explanatory, workable). Some members of the group may not be easily persuaded to that particular perception, having viewed the situation somewhat differently. In a political process, groups of adherents holding different individual perceptions will come together. It is in this process that the group perception emerges. Without the political process, a misperception previously described as a failure of intersubjectivity may occur. One may assume that one's perception is shared by other members of the group, but find that this assumption is incorrect. This assumption is an example of a particularly recalcitrant reality, but within the political process, it is possible to see that all members of the group come to assent to the perception of one member. This consensus is an indispensable element of a social cognition.

Collective perception can be as subject to failure as individual perception. Indeed, collective perception, based on a necessarily imperfect communication of individual perception, seems more likely to have gaps that will cause it to fail. In a previous example, the case of aboriginal people failing to perceive the true nature of firearms when encountered for the first time is considered. When these aboriginal people are considered not as individuals but as a group, the social basis for information inadequacies can be seen. One individual, upon seeing the deadly consequences of mistaking a firearm for a walking stick, could quickly adjust his or her knowledge structures, but communicating that new knowledge structure to the community would be a different matter. The individual could tell his compatriots, "This is a weapon, it's deadly, and it strikes from a great distance," but there is always a conservative tendency in any community that would lead it to disregard the warning. To many in the society, this idea of a deadly fire-stick would be incredible. They would resist the idea, against increasing evidence, until finally the collective knowledge structures were changed. In scientific society, this process is known as a paradigm shift. The collectivity of scientists is likely to ignore initial evidence that challenges their collective understanding of the world and how it works. It is only after increasing evidence and more challenges that their worldview is called into question.

Technological change can produce substantial culture shocks for groups such as occupations. This change is, however, slow to be recognized and accepted in professional groups and similar occupations. Occupational groups tend to be conservative, protecting their previous way of doing things by legal and contractual provisions, yet surrounded by the change that will make their occupation obsolete. Transition, when it occurs, can be revolutionary: an entire occupational group will give up its existence and another will be formed.

Much more common than absolute failures of perception, in which no collective understanding can be found to make sense of a new situation, is the kind of failure of perception that occurs when groups misinterpret phenomena. Such misperceptions occur in national groups that continue to maintain a national mythos in the face of evidence to the contrary. This tendency is amply illustrated in the history of hominid anthropology, for example, in the instances of the Moulin Quignon jaw, discovered in 1863 in France, and of Piltdown Man, a more recent English discovery.

> The English felt the point was settled (the finds were fakes or planted); so did the French (the finds were real) . . . What became clear in the debate over the Moulin Quignon materials was the power of national pride to blind the eyes of learned men to the suspicious nature of their finds.
> The real lesson in this [Piltdown] episode lies in its revelation of the dangerous power of theory over fact. Good scientists in paleontology—competent anatomists, incisive thinkers—were taken in by a forgery that neatly matched their preconceived ideas, that embodied their pet theories. [Trinkhuas, E., & Shipton, P. (1993). *The Neandertals: Of skeletons, scientists and scandal* (pp. 95–96, 298). New York: Knopf.]

The discussion of individuals notes that there can be failures of intersubjectivity that can result in misperceptions of reality. This phenomenon also happens in groups. There are many examples of intergroup and international agreements that have foundered because the nations or groups involved assumed intersubjectivity when none existed. The failure of the League of Nations or of ecumenical movements can be seen in this light. These examples highlight an issue in collective information processing. It is not enough for the group to collectively perceive the external reality. There must be a continual process of perception within the group: group members perceiving the group processes. Feedback between members is crucial to the collective operation of the group. Accordingly, if feedback fails, intersubjectivity may fail seriously. The group can no longer successfully maintain its collective consciousness. Robinson and Weldon (1993) point out how internal group perception through feedback can provide self-assessment and self-validation and therefore improve both group performance and group morale.

Just as individual misperceptions can be difficult to resolve and may lead to information needs that are difficult to address, collective misperceptions can be difficult to clear up and may lead to information needs that are as hard to express as they are complex and difficult to resolve. When entire groups, including occupations, nations, and religious groups, ask the collective question "What went wrong," it may take more than a brief visit to the local library to resolve the question. One is reminded of the prevalence of the stab-in-the-back perception in Weimar and National Socialist Germany. This explanation was apparently more acceptable than one that emphasized the inherent weakness of any one nation-state or bloc in conflict with massive external coalitions.

> "The war is not yet won. We will win it if the homeland no longer stabs the army in the back and if the army, by receiving that to which it is entitled, can maintain trust and confidence" (Ludendorff).
>
> If the stab-in-the-back idea itself was a legend, the series of accusations of which it was constituted were not always completely false. It was precisely this fact that made it so potent and effective. The German wartime governments were woefully inadequate, and their machinery was slow moving, ponderous, and bureaucratic. But most important was the absence of adequate leadership. . . .
>
> It was the home front that had destroyed the morale of the army and it was the home front that let the army down at the end of the war. [Feldman, G. D. (1966). *Army industry and labor in Germany 1914–1918*. (pp. 502–505). Princeton: Princeton University Press.]

Groups, including nations, can experience failures of perception that are as dangerous to their continued well-being as are the failures of perception that individuals experience.

Identification of Alternative Actions

If the collective failure is not one of perception, but of alternative identification, then resolving the collective information need may be no easier to deal with. In such a situation, behavior is undetermined because there is no ready supply of alternative courses of action. To take the example of the natives encountering European weapons for the first time, eventually they would overcome the built-in conservatism of any group and recognize that they were dealing with lethal, long-range weapons. Collectively, this group would now have to come to grips with the ways in which they should react to opponents who have technological superiority in weaponry. Their alternatives in this situation are circumscribed, and yet it is amazingly hard to predict what any group may decide to do. The obvious choices are to fight to extinction or to give up and trust to the mercy of the newcomers (with approximately the same results). However, other possible responses exist. One alternative response may be characterized as the religious response, and certain aspects of the Ghost Dance religion can serve as an example.

> The Lakota added several new traits that were in line with their visionary and militant ethos: they became entranced while dancing; they pondered military action against the whites; and they covered their upper bodies with white "ghost shirts," decorated with spiritual emblems. The ghost shirt was supposed to protect the wearer magically against enemy bullets. [From "Ghost Dance" by Ake Hultkrantz. Reprinted with permission of Macmillan Library Reference USA, a Division of Simon & Schuster, Inc., from THE ENCYCLOPEDIA OF RELIGION, Mircea Eliade, Editor in Chief. Vol. 5, pp. 544–547. Copyright © 1987 by Macmillan Publishing Company.]

In this development, the collective adaptation to a new reality was religious in nature, with predictable and unfortunate results for those who accepted the invulnerability myth. When a group seeks to identify alternatives, it has no procedures manual to which it can turn and so is thrown back on collective memory for ways of dealing with problem situations. Collective memory includes history, mythology, and religion, none of which is necessarily an appropriate guide for action. But these are the raw materials from which new collective knowledge can be formed. A kind of collective information seeking can be associated with this use of collective memory.

More frequently, however, the group delegates one of its members to collect information. There is a great deal of power in this role of information agent and much responsibility. The information-seeking process must create an understanding of the possible alternatives that will fit with the existing group perception of the problem situation. If the information collected fails to respond to that existing perception, the alternatives will not be accepted. This group influence places the individual information seeker in a highly constrained situation. Alternatives that are germane to some unacceptable interpretation of the situation will be ignored, unless the individual concerned is willing to begin again the involved political process of renegotiating the collective perception of reality. This phenomenon may give the individual the perception of being highly inflexible in his or her information search, but in fact the inflexibility comes from the collective nature of the information search.

Selection of Alternative Courses of Action

Once adequate knowledge has been achieved to ensure that a number of alternative courses of behavior are identified, groups must select one course of action. Again, it is presumed that the various courses of action suggested by collective memory or by current information seeking are equal competitors.

The identification of action–consequence links requires information about similar groups who have made similar selections. It seems at least possible that this task will be easier for groups than for individuals. There is a high level of similarity between groups that may enhance the predictive power of an example from history. Because groups tend to submerge individual differences between their members, it is possible to typify groups rather simply. Religious groups, for example, are categorized by ideology, nation-states by economic systems, and organizations by governance structures. Given relatively simplistic classification schemes like these, it should be possible to identify organizations that have faced similar alternatives and to suggest from the consequences of previous decision what the consequences will be in a new situation.

This discussion allows consideration of the kinds of situations in which groups experience information needs, where the collective knowledge of the group does not provide for an unambiguous perception of what is going on, nor for automatic or highly authorized solutions. The parallel with the discussion of the cognitive model is exact. The group has a collective perception that augments individual perceptions, a collective set of stock alternatives that constrain individual perceptions of alternatives, and a collective set of values that lead to the selection of one of the alternatives. When this collective problem solving fails, the group must engage in information seeking to perceive the problem, to identify alternatives, or to select an alternative. When groups come up against a recalcitrant reality that forces them to engage in interpretation, their collective knowledge structures have failed them. They must decide how to behave in this novel situation. One way of adjusting to new situations is to rearrange the group's knowledge structures into new assemblies that enable the novel situations to be understood. This may be a difficult task, because the parts to be assembled may be incomplete or may not fit together clearly. In these situations, information is essential to complete the missing components or to enable new structures to be fitted together.

The preceding discussion uses examples of the various kinds of groups that may collectively experience information needs. It may, however, be helpful to consider in more detail the kinds of information needs that can occur in specific groups. Groups must deal with their component parts. In the case of an individual, this kind of problem is taken care of by the organic homeostasis of an organism, but as was noted previously, groups are not organisms, because of their inadequacies of communication. A group, for example, can choose to banish or excommunicate some of its members. It can (and must) enforce some kind of collective ideology among its members, and it must consciously adapt to external forces.

In the discussion of individual information needs, it is clear that much information is devoted to understanding the relationship between individuals and their surroundings. Individuals discover that some airport doors are not automatic, that some walking sticks are really firearms, or that some computers have a power switch hidden in a remote location on the back of the box. Groups must also cope with their external environment. That environment provides input to, absorbs output from, and regulates and controls the group. How the social environment influences group behavior is the subject of the next section in this chapter.

Information Needs: The Organizational Perspective

Just as individual influences in terms of the knowledge structures developed and maintained by a group can influence how that group perceives problems and deals with them in a variety of ways, including information seeking, so also can groups be influenced by their larger social context. Individuals find their options in perceiving or in acting to be constrained by social values and norms. Groups find their options similarly constrained. There are many examples of groups whose collective activities are embedded in social contexts that constrain their behaviors. However, the best example may be the complex business organization, where a network of work groups exists. Some of these groups are based on function (for example, the accounting department) and others on ties of personal friendship (the workers on the line who go out for a beer at the end of each shift). There may be a group of people working on an assembly line who have a collective way of thinking about their work that separates them from other groups who work on the same assembly line with them, but all of these groups find their understanding of their situation constrained by the larger social situation of the organization as a whole.

The objective in considering these factors is to suggest ways in which information systems and institutions can be designed for specific settings. Clearly, in an organization such as a business, there are many different information systems in place, ranging from the corporate library to the accounting system. The functioning of all of these systems can be assessed most fully from an organizational perspective (i.e., by considering how the information needs of groups within the organization are constrained by the organization itself and by providing mechanisms for meeting those information needs).

Social Influences and Collective Behavior

The social perspective seeks to explain information-related behavior by reference to the social settings in which groups are found. The basic idea in the social perspective is that two groups with different internal structures and histories will behave similarly in the same situation. This is completely opposite to the assumption of the social cognition perspective discussed previously, in which it was argued that what makes groups behave in a certain way is the internal structure of those groups and the way the members work together to achieve consensus. Those who emphasize the social cognition perspective maintain that differences introduced by internal makeup and history are sufficient to make group behavior different. Those who support the organizational perspective are likely to minimize internal differences, commenting on the underlying similarity of the behavior of work groups. The basis for emphasizing the similarity of group behaviors within an organization is that, for the most part, the groups exist within the social structures and value structures of the organization. Groups who share the corporate frame-work and values will, therefore, necessarily share collective knowledge structures.

There are at least three ways that organizational influences determine how groups behave in any particular situation. First of all, organizational factors influence how groups perceive the situations in which they are found. The work group is surrounded by other groups, and the behavior of these other groups influences how the group perceives their situation. Second, social influences determine to some extent the different sets of alternative actions that are understood to be present. Again, the influence of those other groups who surround the work group may constrain the alternatives that may be considered. Finally, the organizational situation can operate to constrain the selection of a course of action. The values expressed by the organization can constrain the ability of the work group to behave in a particular way.

Collective Perception and Social Influence

The examples of perception failures used in the discussion of the social cognition model worked because there were no appropriate collective knowledge structures in place and because there was no appropriate organizational resource upon which the group could call to help them perceive their problem situation. However, work groups become socialized to particular ways of perceiving reality. As noted previously, there are situations that occur frequently in which behavior occurs automatically. The example given was the activity of a military squad responding to an attack. Yet even in this kind of automatic activity, there is a level of organizational influence. There are rules of engagement that establish for any particular context the amount of force that may be applied in response to specific threats.

When situations occur less frequently and behavior is not automatic, but is still highly determined, the impact of organizational differences can be seen clearly. The evolution of a single, highly authorized interpretation or course of action depends on the organizational situation. There are situations in which problems occur and the solution is not clear. However, if the situation changes, the solution becomes clear because it is highly authorized. Sometimes an assembly line goes down temporarily, and work groups are reassigned from that line to some alternative activity (say, quality control). If, in that unfamiliar setting, a problem occurs (for example, one of the workers injures himself), the group may be at a loss for an appropriate course of action, because they are away from their familiar organizational context.

Every group is socialized into a large number of alternate organizations: the organization as the bosses perceive it, the organization as occupational groups or trade unions perceive it, and the organization as other work groups perceive it. A work group that behaves as the trade union's perception of the organization would dictate may find itself in a certain amount of disagreement with the way the organization's administrative group expects it to behave. Awareness of an anomaly in organizational influences occurs as a result of a reality check. It is in these anomalous situations that information seeking can be an important part of the resolution of the problem, but obtaining information to resolve this sort of anomaly can be as difficult as obtaining information to resolve an inadequacy in internal group processes. The failure of perception may be so complete that it is difficult or impossible to articulate the information need. Confusion leading to questions like "What happened?" or "What went wrong?" is likely.

Identification of Alternative Actions

There are situations in which the problem is clearly perceived. The organizational signals are unambiguous. But what is unclear is what alternatives may exist to resolve the problem. Again, this task of identifying alternatives is constrained by organizational factors. The preceding discussion of the social cognition model, which uses the Ghost Dance religion as an example, emphasizes how difficult it can be for groups to identify appropriate alternative courses of action. In an organization, the identification of alternatives may be organizationally constrained. So, for example, the alternative courses of action available to a work group on the assembly line may be considerably different from the courses of action available to the same work group temporarily assigned to a quality control task. So the question "Now what do we do?" can only be asked in a constrained way. The appropriate question now becomes "What do we do in this situation in this organization?"

The techniques and strategies for finding out what to do in any particular organization are largely interactional. It is possible to observe other work groups in similar situations and try to induce the possible courses of action. Analogy or association with other related situations may be another strategy for suggesting actions, but the organizational embeddedness of each situation may make information seeking somewhat easier. There may be instruction manuals or authority figures that can give directions for alternative acceptable courses of group action in organizational situations. Where these are absent or ambiguous, there may still be an organizational ethos or culture that may suggest alternatives.

Selection of Alternative Courses of Action

A group's choice of action can also be determined, at least in part, by organizational factors. Here, as in the social cognition model, the group needs action–consequence links to decide what to do. However, in this situation, the action–consequence associations are not absolute, but are relative to the specific organization in which the group is embedded. So it is not enough to be able to know that a particular action has been associated with a particular consequence in the past. Rather, one must know that the action–consequence association has been observed in a roughly analogous organizational setting. Evaluation of alternatives, as discussed previously, is a function that may be accomplished in part by recourse to an information system, but such information seeking must be constrained to the organizational situation described. This can make the search for action–consequence associations somewhat easier. On the other hand, the expertise required to respond to information needs of this sort is complex. The informant needs to know about the particular problem situation and also about the organization in which the group is working. Failure to include this second kind of expertise will lead to advice that may be inappropriate for the group.

The Person-in-Situation Model

Information needs happen to individuals who are embedded in a range of social situations. This section outlines how individual and social influences can lead to different ways of understanding and resolving information needs; one can then conclude that only a complex, person-in-situation model can provide a complete understanding of information needs. The first element in this model must be recognition that any individual may be influenced by several groups simultaneously. People are influenced by the families, nations, and occupations to which they belong. Sometimes they choose to be members of other groups, such as voluntary associations, religious groups, or businesses, and so they pick up additional social influences. At the same time, individuals have information needs that cannot be tied to any particular social grouping. For example, they need to know how to prepare a particular recipe or what is the least expensive vacation package to Mexico. So as individuals, people are engaging in individual perception, alternative identification, and alternative selection on an ongoing basis; at the same time, they are being influenced in all of these activities by the social situations in which they are embedded.

The preceding paragraph looks at things from the individual's perspective. From the perspective of the group, the situation is equally complex. Each collection of individuals has its own information-seeking activities. At the same time, each group encompasses all of the individual information activities of its members. The fact that someone in the group knows about inexpensive vacations in Mexico may have nothing to do with the group's collective activities, but this knowledge may form part of the collective knowledge base and may be used if necessary by the group. The information-seeking activities of groups have an impact on individuals because they share in the collective consciousness and memory of the group. Similarly, the activities of each of the group's members in other social settings contribute to a group's knowledge about itself and its external environment.

In addition, each group may be embedded to some extent in an organizational setting that constrains its ways of perceiving reality and solving problems. So it is not just the internal makeup of the group and its internal political process that determine how the group engages in information seeking. The larger organizational context acts as an important part of this entire process.

There is a highly complex interaction between personal and collective information needs. At any point in time, an individual must express an information need for it to be relevant to an information system or institution; Chapter 5 focuses in detail on this expression. However, in expressing that information need, the individual is governed by a complex set of cognitive structures: those of the individual and those of all groups that include the individual. It is therefore crucial for the functioning of the information process that the individual be placed in the context of the situation that encompasses all relevant social groupings.

To make this more clear, consider an example. When an individual presents himself or herself to an information system with an expression of information need, it will be necessary to understand the following individual and collective facts to fully understand the need.

The individual is a member of the following groups:

- the physics department,
- graduate students,
- feminists,
- Dr. Lu's lab, and
- the team investigating high energy particles.

The individual is:

- highly knowledgeable about physics,
- trying to decide on a dissertation topic (presumably something related to high-energy particles), and
- thoroughly frustrated.

To meet this individual's information needs in a way that is sensitive to the various characteristics of the individual and his or her social settings requires information systems that can adjust, or be adjusted, to the individuality of the information need. The chapters that follow will consider some aspects of information systems, services, and institutions that may arise from a focus on the individuality of users and their needs.

The discussion presented thus far in this chapter is presented at a fairly general, even theoretical level. Many different factors influence information needs. In any concrete situation, these different factors will combine to provide information needs that are unique to that situation or to that user group. To illustrate how some specific needs can be influenced by individual, social, and group factors, the remainder of this chapter presents a few detailed analyses of types of information needs and some approaches to meeting those needs that have received research attention. These examples and the research on which they are based provide support for the model of information needs presented in this chapter and concrete instances of how people approach their needs for information.

Example 1: Health Information Needs

One area of information-seeking behavior that has received a great deal of attention is health information needs. What goals, purposes, and objectives lie behind these information needs? What cognitive and social factors constrain them? An excellent review of these issues is provided by Kreps (1988). The following discussion is intended to provide a few representative examples of research into health information needs as one way of illuminating information needs in general.

One of the approaches to health information can be tied directly to information needs based on failure of perception. These are areas of health education. For example, an individual may not perceive the risk of unprotected sex, so the objective of AIDS education is making people aware of that particular reality. Advertising campaigns that present the seven warning signs of cancer or the symptoms of diabetes or substance abuse are all designed to lead to perception, to counter the failure of perception that is associated with incomplete knowledge structures. It is true, however, that some people prefer not to perceive their health situation. Such individuals engage in a strategy labeled "blunting": they ignore information that may allow them to perceive dangerous situations or health problems. Blunting is a kind of activity that escapes the rational, problem-solving approach presented in this chapter.

Ferguson and Valenti (1991) considered different types of risk takers in their analysis of individual differences in health information seeking. Some people chose to ignore messages that would have led to the perception of a potential health problem. Interestingly, this choice to ignore health education messages depended in part on the source of the message and how it was presented. Risk preferences influenced the willingness of individuals to ignore aspects of reality and thus maintain the status quo. The implication of this finding, of course, is that different risk-taking preferences will generate different kinds of information seeking to resolve failures of perception.

The blunting strategy is contrasted with an information-seeking or "monitoring" approach to health problem solving. Davey, Tallis, and Hodgson (1993) found that blunting was associated with lower levels of psychological health, and that blunters' tendency to ignore initial illness cues made them more likely to report problems with opportunistic infections such as cold or flu. On the other hand, blunting or information avoidance can be a positive coping strategy in health situations. Thompson (1994), reporting on the information-seeking strategies of school-age children about to undergo elective surgery, found that both information seeking and information avoidance controlled the stress of the anticipating hospitalization. Interestingly, those children who sought information about some aspects but not others reported the highest levels of pre-surgery anxiety. In a similar study, Bar Tal (1994) found that people who are high monitors (i.e., people who engage in active information seeking about their health) can experience high levels of stress, particularly when they are unable to structure and categorize the information they receive. By contrast, people who avoid information may have considerably less stress.

Brouwers and Sorrentino (1993) found that people's orientations toward uncertainty led to differences in how they approached information seeking. Uncertainty-oriented people were more likely to recognize the failure of perception, accept the uncertainty, and seek information to help them perceive their problems. Certainty-oriented people, on the other hand, did not want to know anything new about themselves. They did not want to perceive the problem and so were unlikely to engage in information seeking.

Borgers, Mullen, Meertens, and Rijken (1993), surveying information behavior of cancer outpatients, found that 58% of patients did not intend to discuss their illness and treatments with medical specialists who were treating them. This tendency was influenced by their own needs for information, their values and beliefs, and the behavior of the medical specialist. Another quantitative estimate of the distribution of information-seeking patterns is provided by Pierce (1993), who found that only 15% of female patients diagnosed with breast cancer engaged in active information seeking. These patients were labeled "deliberators." Far more frequent were individuals who left the decision to others ("deferrers," 41%) and individuals who delayed making a decision about treatment ("delayers," 44%). This finding is confirmed by the investigation of Hack, Degner, and Dyck (1994), who found that 23% of breast cancer patients were classed as "active." These patients sought more information than others.

What leads people to adopt a monitoring or blunting approach to medical information? Van Zuuren and Wolfs (1991) found that some personal characteristics had an effect, such as locus of control. Monitoring strategies were associated with an internal local of control and with problem-focused coping. Blunting was associated primarily with a "wishful-thinking" coping mechanism. As noted above, risk preferences and need for certainty seem to generate different approaches to medical information.

Once people are in the problem-solving mode, they need to know their alternatives and the consequences attached to each so they can make choices. Treatment selection is an obvious example. The diagnosis of a disease is very much a case of perception of a problem. The question now becomes how to deal with that problem. Identification and evaluation of alternatives obviously lead to information needs.

Prince-Embury (1992) found that when people received information they perceived to be reliable about health situations, they experienced a feeling of loss of control. It is easy to see how this can happen. The entire problem-solving model has the result of bringing people to the point of selecting a course of action. The more information is obtained, the more constrained the choices become. The information-seeking process can say to the individual, in effect, "This is your best, really your only option." In that situation, individuals may feel that they now have less control of the situation. Individuals who wish to maintain control over their lives (at least in the short run) may prefer not to engage in information-seeking behavior.

Other research (Johnson & Meischke, 1993) suggests that health information seeking has little to do with individual health situations, but rather relates to more general information-seeking behaviors or to a general attitude about self care. If people are information seekers in other areas, they will also seek information about health. If they usually do not seek general information, they will be unlikely to search for health information. This idea of a general predisposition to be an information seeker relates to some of the psychological factors identified previously (for example, locus of control or monitoring strategies), but it also may relate to the social situations in which people are embedded. Rakowski, Rice, and McHorney (1992) found that, in the case of older adults, this general information-seeking predisposition can be more narrowly defined as a fundamental tendency toward self care, and that this predisposition is largely independent of demographic variables such as age, education, and income.

At the same time, health information behavior is embedded in social situations, and so social factors influence whether and how people will search for health information. Rakowski et al. (1990) found that health information seeking is associated with other health-related tasks. In other words, people who are dealing with physicians and other health-care professionals are more likely to seek health information. This seems an obvious finding, but it raises the question of causality. Are people seeking health information because they are engaged in related health tasks, or are they engaged in the related health tasks because they are seeking information? One suspects that neither is true. Rather, the social situation in which people are found leads them to be concurrently engaged in both health information seeking and other health activities. As a side note, it is interesting to see that this research found that females are more likely to be involved in such social situations than males. It seems likely that there are gender differences that affect the willingness of people to deal with health issues.

Hsia (1987) found that social influences such as education and income also influenced the likelihood of information seeking about health issues. Again, this seems straightforward. Individuals who cannot afford health care are unlikely to want to find out about their health problems or the alternative treatments that may be suggested. This research also found that most information seeking about health issues included family and friends as information sources. This result is an example of a more general trend, in which information is sought from close-by and familiar sources, even if those sources are less than expert. It also relates to the socioeconomic variables just discussed. Family and friends tend to provide information free, while other sources may be much more expensive.

Langer and Warheit (1992) studied adolescent health information seeking and found that what adolescents were interested in finding out about and how they searched for information depended on their "directedness." In what is probably an oversimplification, Langer and Warheit identified three kinds of orientation among adolescents: parent orientation, in which parental values and attitudes direct the behavior of the adolescents; peer orientation, in which values and attitudes of peers direct their behaviors; and self orientation, in which social embeddedness was less important than individual values and attitudes. Despite this oversimplification, it seems clear that combinations of these motivations and orientations would indeed influence how adolescents reacted to health education or whether they sought further information about their alternatives.

One of the most socially embedded health information needs are those of the caregiver or family member. Fortinsky and Hathaway (1990) assessed these information needs in Alzheimer's caregivers and found that self-education about the disease (a matter of individual cognitive structures) and addressing their emotional well-being through counseling and support (a social function) were the primary information needs of caregivers at the time of diagnosis. The sorts of information sought fit clearly into the alternative-identification area of the problem-solving model. Caregivers were most interested in topics such as how the disease progressed, medication, and other treatments. This information would allow them to assess alternatives to assure the continued health and treatment of their ill relatives or friends. This pattern of findings also occurred in the investigation of Meissner, Anderson, and Odenkirchen (1990) into the information needs of significant others of cancer patients. The interest in disease and treatment details paralleled those of the patients themselves, but there was an additional need for information on support services such as counseling. Gowen, Christy, and Sparling (1993) found the same dual pattern of needs in parents of children with special needs. An interesting variant on this pattern was reported by Main, Gerace, and Camilleri (1993), who found that family members of individuals with schizophrenia sometimes engaged in information avoidance or denial and sometimes found that information was important, but were still reluctant to share it. In other words, there are differing levels of openness to information among family members, just as there are among many patients. It seems clear that the patient–caregiver group is an example of a collective that can have information needs. It is particularly notable that these groups seek information, not just about the task with which they are engaged, but also about how to maintain the cohesiveness and ongoing functioning of the group.

Two studies of parents of children with emotional or behavioral problems suggested that the usual pattern of information seeking (finding information from family and friends) tends to break down in this area. Sontag and Schacht (1994) and Sonuga-Barke, Thompson, and Balding (1993) found that parents preferred to meet information needs about their children from medical specialists (physicians and therapists), then from written sources, and least of all from (the usually popular) friends and family. This finding may indicate that there is a level of social embarrassment that refers parents to more formal sources for information in this area. Once again, the strong influence of social variables on health information behavior is visible.

Although it may be premature to discuss information systems, a few studies may be cited here that illustrate some of the ways people with complex information needs approach information systems and how their information needs may be resolved through interaction with these systems. For example, Cameron et al. (1994) found that, for hospital patients, verbal information was more important than written information and there was a substantial mismatch between the patients' interests and the information presented. For example, there was ample information about the hospital's administrative routines, something that had only a low level of interest for patients. At the same time, there was little information about drug effects, a topic of considerable interest to patients.

Johnson and Meischke (1994) found that there was little difference in the media that women preferred as information sources relating to cancer, but that human informants were much preferred to media informants. This result is related to McIntosh and Parkes' (1974) conclusion that a mutually supportive therapeutic community is needed in which the information needs and emotional needs of patients, relatives, and staff can be recognized and met.

In summary, the full range of individual, social, and group factors influence health information needs. This example demonstrates that an analysis of these factors is needed as a basis for information-system design. Of additional importance in this research is the blunting approach taken by some users. It must be recognized that there are information behaviors that may lead people to avoid any information system that is created to meet health information needs.

Example 2: Consumer Information Needs

Another group of individuals whose information needs and information-related behaviors have been studied in some detail is consumers. The principal motive for this research is economic: if marketers can understand how people decide what products to purchase, they can design advertising campaigns to influence those decisions. As represented in standard works in this area, however, the information that contributes to consumer decision making is treated as actively present in the marketplace. All the consumer has to do is to attend to the messages that are presented, remember them, and process them into a decision. In fact, there is considerable skepticism about treating the consumer as an active decision maker. Research indicates that many purchase decisions occur without conscious decision making (see, for example, Mowen, 1993; Horton, 1984). Indeed, there is a justifiable emphasis on the limited cognitive capabilities that individuals have to devote to consumer information seeking, the clearly bounded rationality of consumer decisions, and the roles of affect and group behavior in such decisions. Similarly, there is debate about the role of cognition in purchase decisions. The model once proposed, of cognition leading to affect leading to behavior, is certainly too simplistic (Holbrook, 1986). Cognition and affect must interact in complex ways when purchase decisions are made.

Much of this research deals with the individual variables that influence information-related behavior in this kind of decision making. For example, Cole and Balasubramanian (1993) investigated age differences in information-seeking behavior. They found few age differences in information seeking during normal shopping, but when consumers were put in laboratory situations that were designed to emphasize the information-seeking aspects of consumer decisions, they found that older consumers were less likely to search intensively for information to help them make appropriate purchase decisions. The authors attributed this difference to age-related changes in information-processing ability.

The other end of the age spectrum was investigated by Moschis and Moore (1979). Their research showed that adolescents had reasonably sophisticated decision-making processes, backed up by information seeking about consumer products. Although social approval was important in purchase decisions, price and brand names were the most important criteria in making purchase decisions. Age was correlated with evaluation of products according to brand name, and even younger adolescents had well-defined sex roles when it came to defining the responsibility for the decision to purchase certain products.

Schmitt, Leclerc, and Dube-Rioux (1988) examined gender differences in information processing, and found that there were strong differences between genders in how they processed information from advertising and packaging. There was another aspect of their research, however, that did not work out as well. The authors hypothesized that strongly sex-typed individuals would behave differently from non-sex-typed individuals in their processing of consumer information. This hypothesis turned out not to be true, which calls into question the idea that gender-based self-perception influences information processing. This result is of particular interest, because (as already mentioned) metacognitive variables such as feeling-of-knowing do influence information performance. It appears that certain aspects of self-concept are stronger predictors of information behavior than others.

Another aspect of individual variables influencing the information-search process was investigated by Verplanken, Hazenberg, and Palenewen (1992). They found that a variable called "need for cognition," which measures how strongly individuals are intrinsically motivated to learn, strongly influenced consumer information searches. Individuals with high levels of this particular need sought more information and expended more effort on information behavior than others.

Other research in this area focuses on the actual process of searching for consumer information. Ozanne, Brucks, and Grewal (1992) conducted an experimental investigation of consumers trying to categorize a new product while faced with different levels of contradictory information. This research found that information seeking will continue as long as the contradictions in the information are moderate, but that high levels of discrepancy will tend to cut off information seeking. In terms of the model presented in this chapter, these findings make sense. If an individual is unable to engage in slot filling because the information seeking uncovers a massively contradictory set of information, the individual is likely to give up on the problem and perhaps try to reformulate the problem in new way.

Murray (1991) studied the sources of information that consumers use in making their purchase decisions and found that personal sources are preferred. This outcome is not terribly surprising and is in line with studies of preferred information sources in other areas. The more interesting result of this research was that people who were in the market for services rather than goods were likely to regard this purchase decision as carrying a higher level of risk. Accordingly, shopping for services involves distinctive consumer information needs.

There is an additional element in consumer information seeking that seems important to a consideration of information needs. This is the phenomenon, observed by Davidsson and Wahlund (1992) and to a lesser extent by Hauser, Urban, and Weinberg (1993), that consumers avoid negative information in making their purchase decisions. This confirmation bias suggests that people want to have a particular alternative supported, but are less interested in having alternatives attacked.

The research into consumer information needs once again shows the limitation of the problem-solving model in understanding behavior. Some people will make purchase decisions without engaging in the problem-solving process of alternative identification and alternative evaluation. Again, the bounded rationality of consumer decision making must be emphasized. The other element that must be emphasized in this research is the apparent lack of consideration of group or collective decision making in consumer behavior. It seems likely that some of these decisions are actually group decisions, perhaps made by families or by groups such as service associations or religious groups. In business, major purchase decisions are almost always group decisions, although these may more properly be considered managerial decision making (see the following) than consumer information needs. The research is clear about individual and social effects on consumer information needs, but it appears that more research is required into the phenomenon of collective consumer information needs.

Example 3: Political Information Needs

One of the commonly held opinions or myths of democratic society is that voters make informed decisions. If this is true (and there is much cause for skepticism), it follows that information seeking and information needs are central to the political process. There is a body of scholarship that outlines the role of information seeking in voter decision making. Popkin (1993) outlines the value of information shortcuts that people use in considering voting decisions. This idea is based on the understanding that information seeking is a labor-intensive activity and the expected returns from the investment of effort may be quite small. As a result, people acquire the information upon which they base their decisions through a number of shortcuts. They rely on the opinions of others, use the party affiliation of candidates as a surrogate for detailed information about the candidates and where they stand on issues, use the demographics of candidates and their supporters to estimate policy positions, and so on. Particularly interesting is the reliance upon a small number of specialists and "news junkies" for information about candidates. These sources of information appear to hold gatekeeper roles and to have the potential for significant influence in political decision making. Grofman and Withers (1993) reinforce the importance of information shortcuts and stress the importance of information about societal choices (for example, reports of public opinion polls) in opinion formulation. Similarly, Bowler, Donovan, and Happ (1992) showed how the effort required to obtain information can be measured in voter behavior. They found that as the number of ballot propositions and initiatives increased, voters engaged increasingly in avoidance behaviors. For example, they may omit items, vote "No" on all propositions, or vote only on the top half of the ballot.

Ottati and Wyer (1990) summarized the ways in which information shortcuts influence how people receive, process, and think about political information. General background knowledge and expertise, party identification, and affect and image can influence the attention paid to political information, how that information is stored, and the inferences that are drawn from the information. Another influence is simple geographical location. Bowler, Donovan, and Snipp (1993) found that local patterns in voting were tied to availability of information about candidates in the local media market. Uncertainty about candidates increased with distance from the home base of the candidate.

On the other hand, Cutler and Danowski (1980) studied an individual characteristic (age) and found that information seeking without any real interest in the topic increased with age. This is a phenomenon called "process gratification," in which people engage in information behavior without any real need, simply because the process pleases or amuses them. One can perhaps understand the attitudes of those older citizens who regard the political process as a matter of amusement rather than as an information need to be taken seriously. Bennett (1981), in a thorough review of the individual processes of perception and learning in political information processing, mentions other individual characteristics that may influence how people search for this kind of information. In particular, cognitive styles, such as dogmatism and rigidity, or field dependence, may influence the kinds of information seeking that occur in political decision making.

It is not necessary, however, for all individuals to be equally informed. In their research, Sniderman, Glaser, and Griffin (1990) posit two different kinds of voter decision making. Well-informed voters were able to locate candidates against the background of political parties, points of view, and policy preferences. Less-informed voters were still able to make political choices, but they did so by treating the choice as a referendum on the incumbent. Clearly, different types of information are appropriate for different approaches to decision making, and it is difficult to be judgmental about either type of political involvement.

Chaffee and McLeod (1973) assessed the relative contribution of individual and social predictors of information seeking and found that social predictors were particularly important in explaining political information seeking. For example, individuals who had recently discussed the election with friends were most likely to request campaign pamphlets. Other social predictors of political information seeking were investigated by Surlin and Gordon (1977). They found that respondents with lower socioeconomic status and African-American respondents showed the attributes of low-energy information seekers: they were more favorably oriented toward negative advertising during political campaigns. Strong social orientation (i.e., strong feelings of membership in their groups) enhanced this information-seeking tendency for some respondents. This result illustrates that the impact of political information depends on a number of social factors, including social value systems.

There has been a great deal of attention on the influence of both social and organizational factors on political information seeking. Huckfeldt and Sprague (1990) emphasize that political behavior is anchored in social contexts and political environments in complex ways. The process of political opinion formulation begins with an individual within a context. That context structures the social interaction patterns through which political information is conveyed. The political opinion derived from that information is thus influenced twice: once by the context, and once by the social interaction factors.

To close this discussion of information in politics, it can be noted that there appear to be two underlying views of the individual that drive much of the research into information seeking and information processing in political contexts. Donohew and Springer (1980) contrast the information-seeking and information-diffusion paradigms. In the first approach, individuals are seen as active agents, engaging in information seeking in order to produce change in their communities and in their individual lives. In the second approach, individuals are viewed as recipients of information aimed at them by groups and individuals who wish to persuade them of a particular viewpoint or to motivate them to a particular kind of action. The two approaches are not mutually exclusive, but the literature appears to indicate that the diffusion paradigm is much more important to political studies. In addition, the decision process here is always considered within the individual and never within a group. Certainly, political decisions tend to be made on an individual basis, but one wonders if collective decisions may not occasionally be in evidence.

Example 4: Newcomer Information Needs

Newly hired employees in any organization provide a convenient example for how individuals use information to cope with novel situations. Morrison (1993a) showed that employees who seek information facilitate their socialization into the organization. This socialization has a long-term effect on their mastery of their jobs, their understanding of their role in the firm, and their integration into the social life of the organization. It should be emphasized that these positive effects are found for individuals new to a firm who take the initiative in seeking out information about their jobs, rather than for those who passively wait to be informed by their supervisors. In a further report of this research, Morrison (1993b) considers the types of information sought from different information sources. Written information, such as employee manuals, are consulted infrequently and mostly for technical information. For information about the social system of the organization or for understanding the values of the firm, people tend to obtain information by observation or by asking others, particularly their supervisors.

Ostroff and Kozlowski (1992) found results that anticipated those of Morrison. They found that the most important information for newcomers to acquire was task information (what they were supposed to do) and role information (how they were supposed to fit in with other workers). The most effective information-seeking techniques were observation of others, asking supervisors, and asking coworkers (in that order).

On the other hand, there are some indications that this type of newcomer information seeking may not produce results that managers may expect. Gundry (1993) and Gundry and Rousseau (1994) studied how newcomers to an engineering firm succeeded in interpreting the organization's values and norms. This investigation found that the newcomers perceived the norms as calling for competition between workers and defensive interpersonal relations. However, the managers of these newcomers perceived their organization norms as calling for achievement and collaboration. In addition, the newcomers found less consistency and clarity in what they learned about the organization than their managers perceived.

The research reported by Bauer and Green (1994) extends these investigations of newcomer information seeking. They examined newcomers to academic Ph.D. programs, rather than newcomers to a firm, looking at information seeking that occurred before entry into the program, instead of at information seeking that occurred on the job. The results, however, were exactly parallel to those reported in the preceding literature. Individuals who had collected information they perceived as realistic or who had relevant knowledge about the university or research from previous experience experienced less role conflict, were more engaged, and were more productive in their academic work.

This small but interesting body of research demonstrates both the individual and social factors that influence information needs and presents the importance of information seeking for sense making. The fact that individuals who engaged in appropriate information behavior were more successful in adapting to their jobs than those who failed to seek information appropriately represents in microcosm the essential role information has in making sense of what goes on in life experiences.

Example 5: Managerial Decision Making

There has probably been more written about managerial decision making than about any other information-need situation. The sheer volume of this literature prevents more than a representative sampling, and any such sample cannot represent the richness of the scholarship that underlies the understanding of information search in management contexts. It should also be recognized that there is an equally interesting body of research that relates to decision making in other contexts, such as politics and policy making. One source that can be recommended as an overview of research in this collateral area of decision making is Weiss and Bucuvalas (1980).

Research into decision making in the management context makes it clear that information seeking is central to decision making. For example, Thomas, Clark, and Gioia (1993) found that there were significant positive relationships between high levels of information use during the scanning phase of decision making and the quality of interpretation of strategic issues displayed by managers. On the other hand, experimental research by Gilliland, Schmitt, and Wood (1993), Gilliland and Schmitt (1993), and Hulland and Kleinmuntz (1994) has demonstrated that a number of factors can constrain the amount of information that managers will seek while assessing situations in which decisions must be made. Two of these factors are the cost of the information and the redundancy of the information. Higher cost and higher redundancy reduced the amount of information seeking that occurred.

Consistent with this concern for the use of information in decision making is the research of Timmermans (1993), who found that increased decision complexity reduced the amount of information seeking that accompanied decisions. This result makes sense, particularly because complex decisions with many alternatives provide a high level of cognitive load. Accordingly, decision makers balance this high level of cognitive load by reducing the amount of information seeking they accomplish. Macrae, Hewston, and Griffiths (1993) found that when information processing is difficult or demanding, people tend to fall back on stereotypes to understand situations and make decisions. This type of situation is quite different from situations in which there are low processing demands, in which case, information inconsistent with stereotypes is more likely to be sought and used. Brown and Prentice (1987) show that, if the decision has higher levels of risk, there will be an increased level of information seeking. Even here, however, the decision-making use of information is constrained: only certain types of information are sought, even where the risks associated with the decision are high. Boynton, Gales, and Blackburn (1993) show that the amount of information that managers seek in decision-making situations depends on an interaction between their perceptions of the risks associated with the decision and the availability of information to support the decision. They found curvilinear relationships between information-search activities and both the perceived risk and the perceived availability of information.

This result means that, at low levels of risk and availability, managers use limited information in coming to their decisions. But at high levels of risk and availability, they also reduce the information they gather to support their decision. Limitations on information use in decision making appear to run counter to the rules for optimal decision making proposed in rational, step-wise models. Kleinmuntz (1993) suggests that this apparently ineffective decision making may arise because decision makers fail to perceive the dynamic nature of the situations in which they are working. Another likely explanation, however, is that decision-making shortcuts, like the shortcuts observed previously in the discussion of political information seeking, are really a way of reducing cognitive effort and load.

There are different types of managerial decisions to be made. Lindquist (1988) contrasts routine, incremental, and fundamental decisions. In the first, situation-monitoring information is most appropriate; this information is analyzed for indications that higher levels of decisions may become necessary. In incremental decision making, analysis of alternatives predominates, and information useful for that function is sought. In fundamental decision making, in-depth information derived from research may be necessary to study a problem intensively. Related to this typology of decisions, Carpinello, Newman, and Jatulis (1992) looked at information seeking in different types of evaluation. They found that traditional evaluation used a variety of information types, including descriptive, financial, and opinion-based evaluative information. Other types of evaluation, particularly accreditation, make no comparable use of information. Clearly, the type of decision being made has a bearing on the information that will be sought.

At the same time, it is clear that there are important social and individual factors that influence how information is used in managerial decision making. Slocum (1982) provides a brief review of some of the research that delineates these factors. The place of the decision makers within the organization can influence how they use information. Particularly, where the decision makers are placed with regard to boundary spanners and information gatekeepers will influence how much information they can obtain. At the same time, differences in cognitive styles, including preferences for perceiving or judging, can influence information use in decision making. Pincus and Acharya (1988) investigated the differences between individuals who cope with decisions (particularly in crisis situations) by seeking information and those who try to avoid the decision. Avoiders resist information about the crisis, deny that the crisis exists, and may be in information paralysis due to an inability to engage in complex, integrated thought. The research makes it clear that this type of reaction to decision making may be common in crisis situations and that it constitutes an example of information dysfunction within an organization.

Social factors are, of course, crucial in organizational decision making. Rediker, Mitchell, Beach, and Beard (1993) looked at the strength of the organization's belief structures and values and how these social factors influence decision making. They found that a strong, agreed-upon, and tightly constructed set of beliefs reduces the amount of information sought in decision making and also (in a simulated hiring situation) produces more negative decisions. Because many management decisions are group decisions, the impact of group behavior on information seeking is also important. Robertson (1980) found that groups can be easily overloaded with information and increased information can increase, rather than decrease, the uncertainty attached to decision making. It is therefore essential that information be managed appropriately in group decision making: a task that has recently been attempted by the developers of Group Decision Support Systems (GDSS).

In a systematic review of how information is used in organizations, Feldman and March (1988) point out that the actual collection and use of information extends beyond a rational decision-making approach. They state that much of the information that is gathered and communicated has little decision relevance, and information collected to support a decision tends to be sought after the decision is already substantially made. Also, information collected to support a decision is frequently not used at all, and more information is requested regardless of the amount of information available to support the decision. Part of the reason for these discrepancies is that information is seen as intrinsically good; it provides a "ritualistic assurance that appropriate attitudes about decision making exist" (Feldman & March, 1988, p. 418). Another part of the reason for this apparently illogical emphasis on information is that information is collected for all sorts of purposes other than decision making (e.g., surveillance). This latter approach to collecting and using information seems to distinguish entrepreneurs from managers, according to Gilad, Kaish, and Ronen (1989). They found that entrepreneurs are more open to information because they are trying to keep alert to new opportunities, while managers appear to engage in a more classical and rationally focused search for information.

Another apparent information dysfunction is called "knowledge disavowal" (Deshpande & Kohli, 1989). Reliable information deemed relevant to the decision is gathered within the organization, but is not shared among decision makers. Centralization of decision making, for example, will make it more likely that knowledge will not be shared. Similarly, disagreements among decision makers can lead to disavowal. This research suggests that different aspects of information are in conflict in some decision making. Insofar as information represents power and control, it will not be shared, even though sharing information will contribute to more effective decision making.

It is fascinating to speculate about developing Management Information Systems that may correspond to some of the management information behaviors mentioned in this discussion that fall outside the rational problem-solving model. On the other hand, it has been amply demonstrated in this chapter that rational problem solving is affected by a wide variety of individual, social, and group factors that make it complex. The approach in this book is to focus on the design implications of the information needs associated with problem solving.

Summary

The discussion in this chapter proposes a way of understanding information needs that combines individual and social variables into a person–in–situation model. This approach can be seen as both a guide for research in information science and as a basis for developing principles that will guide the development and design of information systems.

It seems clear that a unified and coherent understanding of information needs can only be obtained as researchers consider the problem situations that give rise to needs and the information-seeking behaviors that resolve those needs in terms of interactions between personal and situational variables. Achieving this understanding will clearly require more complex research designs and more sophisticated data analyses than studies that simply focus on situational or individual variables.

The second implication of the person–in–situation model developed in this chapter is that it carries with it the seeds of a principled approach to user-centered information-system design. Understanding information needs has direct implications for the design of information systems and services. From the general model of information needs presented here, system designers can develop plans for investigating the needs of the user populations they serve. They can, for example, assess whether their users experience failures of perception or collective needs involving within-group communication. At the same time, system designers can use this general model to focus on the social and organizational constraints that act on their user population. Plotting these constraints can help to delineate the nature of information systems that can meet their users' needs, because information needs occur in social and organizational contexts. Finally, system designers can use the general model developed here to identify the kinds of individual and social resources that their users bring to their information seeking. System designers will, of course, investigate these resources as they consider the actual tasks that their users accomplish and will apply their understanding of these resources in creating usable information systems.

References

Allen, B. L. (1991). Cognitive research in information science: Implications for design. *Annual Review of Information Science and Technology, 26*, 3–37.

Bar Tal, Y. (1994). Monitoring, blunting, and the ability to achieve cognitive structure. *Anxiety, Stress and Coping: An International Journal, 6*(4), 265–274.

Bauer, T. N., & Green, S. G. (1994). Effect of newcomer involvement in work-related activities: A longitudinal study of socialization. *Journal of Applied Psychology, 79*(2), 211–223.

Belkin, N. J., Oddy, R. N., & Brooks, H. M. (1982). ASK for information retrieval. Part I: Background and theory. *Journal of Documentation, 38*(2), 61–71.

Bennett, W. L. (1981). Perception and cognition: An information-processing framework for politics. In S. L. Long (Ed.), *The handbook of political behavior* (Vol. 1, pp. 69–193). New York: Plenum.

Blair, D. C. (1990). *Language and representation in information retrieval*. New York: Elsevier.

Borgers, R., Mullen, P. D., Meertens, R., & Rijken, M. (1993). The information seeking behavior of cancer outpatients: A description of the situation. *Patient Education and Counseling, 22*(1), 35–46.

Bowler, S., Donovan, T., & Happ, T. (1992). Ballot propositions and information costs: direct democracy and the fatigued voter. *Western Political Quarterly, 45*(2), 559–568.

Bowler, S., Donovan, T., & Snipp, J. (1993). Local sources of information and voter choice in state elections: Microlevel foundations of the "friends and neighbors" effect. *American Politics Quarterly, 21*(4), 473–489.

Boynton, A. C., Gales, L. M., & Blackburn, R. d. S. (1993). Managerial search activity: The impact of perceived role uncertainty and role threat. *Journal of Management, 19*(4), 725–747.

Bradley, J. R. (1991). *Bureaucratic and individual knowledge and action in the public services units of an academic library*. Unpublished Ph.D. dissertation, University of Illinois at Urbana-Champaign.

Brouwers, M. C., & Sorrentino, R. M. (1993). Uncertainty orientation and protection motivation theory: The role of individual differences in health compliance. *Journal of Personality and Social Psychology, 65*(1), 102–112.

Brown, R. D., & Prentice, D. G. (1987). Assessing decision making risk and information needs in evaluation. *Evaluation Review, 11*(3), 371–381.

Cameron, P., Corbett, K., Duncan, C., Hegyl, K., Maxwell, H., & Burton, P. F. (1994). Information needs of hospital patients: A survey of satisfaction levels in a large city hospital. *Journal of Documentation, 50*(1), 10–23.

Carpinello, S. E., Newman, D. L., & Jatulis, L. L. (1992). Health decision makers' perceptions of program evaluation: Relationship to purpose and information needs. *Evaluation and the Health Professions, 15*(4), 405–419.

Chaffee, S. H., & McLeod, J. M. (1973). Individual vs social predictors of information seeking. *Journalism Quarterly, 50*(2), 237–245.

Chatman, E. A. (1987). The information world of low skilled workers. *Library and Information Science Research, 9*(4), 265–283.

Chew, F. (1992). Information needs during viewing of serious and routine news. *Journal of Broadcasting and Electronic Media, 36*(4), 453–466.

Cole, C. A., & Balasubramanian, S. K. (1993). Age differences in consumers' search for information: Public policy implications. *Journal of Consumer Research, 20*(1), 157–169.

Connell, T. H. (1995). Subject searching in online catalogs: Metaknowledge used by experienced searchers. *Journal of the American Society of Information Science, 46*(7), 506–518.

Cowan, D. A. (1986). Developing a process model of problem recognition. *Academy of Management Review, 11*(4), 763–776.

Cremmins, E. T. (1992). Value-added processing of representational and speculative information using cognitive skills. *Journal of Information Science, 18*(1), 27–37.

Cutler, N. E., & Danowski, J. A. (1980). Process gratification in aging cohorts. *Journalism Quarterly, 57*(2), 269–276.

Davey, G. C., Tallis, F., & Hodgson, S. (1993). The relationship between information-seeking and information-avoiding coping styles and the reporting of psychological and physical symptoms. *Journal of Psychosomatic Research, 37*(3–4), 333–344.

Davidsson, P., & Wahlund, R. (1992). A note on the failure to use negative information. *Journal of Economic Psychology, 13*(2), 343–353.

De Mey, M. (1977). The cognitive viewpoint: Its development and scope. In: *CC77: International workshop on the cognitive viewpoint* (pp. xvi-xxxii). Ghent: Ghent University.

Dervin, B. (1980). Communication gaps and inequities: Moving toward a reconceptualization. In B. Dervin & M. Voigt (Eds.), *Progress in communication sciences* (Vol. 2, pp. 73–112). Norwood, NJ: Ablex.

Deshpande, R., & Kohli, A. K. (1989). Knowledge disavowal: Structural determinants of information processing breakdown in organizations. *Knowledge, 11*(2), 155–169.

Donohew, L., & Springer, E. R. (1980). Information seeking versus information diffusion: Implications for the change agent of an alternative paradigm. *Community Development Journal, 15*(3), 208–213.

Dukerich, J. M., & Nichols, M. L. (1991). Causal information search in managerial decision making. *Organizational Behavior and Human Decision Processes, 50*(1), 106–122.

Elbers, E., Grossen, M., Kanner, B. G., Wertsch, J. V., Moshman, D., Saljo, R., & Siegler, R. S. (1991). The development of competence and its social context. *Educational Psychology Review, 3*(2), 73–94.

Ellis, D. (1992). The physical and cognitive paradigms in information retrieval research. *Journal of Documentation, 48*(1), 45–64.

Feldman, M. S., & March, J. G. (1988). Information in organizations as signal and symbol. In J. G. March (Ed.), *Decisions and organizations* (pp. 409–428). Oxford: Blackwell.

Ferguson, M. A., & Valenti, J. M. (1991).Communicating with environmental health risk takers: An individual differences perspective. *Health Education Quarterly, 18*(3), 303–318.

Fortinsky, R. H., & Hathaway, T. J. (1990). Information and service needs among active and former family caregivers of persons with Alzheimer's disease. *Gerontologist, 30*(5), 604–609.

Frohmann, B. (1992). The power of images: A discourse analysis of the cognitive viewpoint. *Journal of Documentation, 48*(4), 365–386.

Gilad, B., Kaish, S., & Ronen, J. (1989). Information, search, and entrepreneurship: A pilot study. *Journal of Behavioral Economics, 18*(3), 217–235.

Gilliland, S. W., & Schmitt, N. (1993). Information redundancy and decision behavior: A process tracing investigation. *Organizational Behavior and Human Decision Processes, 54*(2), 157–180.

Gilliland, S. W., Schmitt, N., & Wood, L. (1993). Cost benefit determinants of decision process and accuracy. *Organizational Behavior and Human Decision Processes, 56*(2), 308–330.

Gowen, J. W., Christy, D. S., & Sparling, J. (1993). Informational needs of parents of young children with special needs. *Journal of Early Intervention, 17*(2), 194–210.

Grofman, B., & Withers, J. (1993). Information-pooling models of electoral politics. In B. Grofman (Ed.), *Information, participation and choice: An Economic Theory of Democracy in perspective* (pp. 55–64). Ann Arbor, MI: University of Michigan Press.

Gundry, L. K. (1993). Fitting into technical organizations: The socialization of newcomer engineers. *IEEE Transactions on Engineering Management, 40*(4), 335–345.

Gundry, L. K., & Rousseau, D. M. (1994). Critical incidents in communicating culture to newcomers. *Human Relations, 47*(9), 1063–1087.

Hack, T. F., Degner, L. F., & Dyck, D. G. (1994). Relationship between preferences for decisional control and illness information among women with breast cancer: A quantitative and qualitative analysis. *Social Science and Medicine, 39*(2), 279–289.

Hauser, J. R., Urban, G. L., & Weinberg, B. D. (1993). How consumers allocate their time when searching for information. *Journal of Marketing Research, 30*(4), 452–466.

Hjorland, B., & Albrechtsen, H. (1995). Toward a new horizon in information science: Domain analysis. *Journal of the American Society for Information Science, 46*(6), 400–425.

Holbrook, M. B. (1986). Emotion in the consumption experience: Toward a new model of the human consumer. In R. A. Peterson, W. D. Hoyer, & W. R. Wilson (Eds.), *The role of affect in consumer behavior: Emerging theories and applications* (pp. 17–52). Lexington, MA: Heath.

Horton, R. L. (1984). *Buyer behavior: A decision-making approach.* Columbus, OH: Merrill.

Hsia, H. J. (1987). The health information seeking behavior of the Mexican Americans in west Texas. *Health Marketing Quarterly, 4*(3–4), 107–117.

Huckfeldt, R., & Sprague, J. (1990). Social order and political chaos: The structural setting of political information. In J. A. Ferejohn, & J. H. Kuklinski (Eds.), *Information and democratic processes* (pp. 23–58). Urbana, IL: University of Illinois Press.

Hulland, J. S., & Kleinmuntz, D. N. (1994). Factors influencing the use of internal summary evaluations versus external information in choice. *Journal of Behavioral Decision Making, 7*(2), 79–102.

Ingwersen, P. (1992). *Information retrieval interaction.* London: Taylor Graham.

Johnson, J. D., & Meischke, H. (1993). A comprehensive model of cancer related information seeking applied to magazines. *Human Communication Research, 19*(3), 343–367.

Johnson, J. D., & Meischke, H. (1994). Women's preferences for cancer related information from specific types of mass media. *Health Care for Women International, 15*(1), 23–30.

Kellermann, K., & Reynolds, R. (1990). When ignorance is bliss: The role of motivation to reduce uncertainty in uncertainty reduction theory. *Human Communication Research, 17*(1), 5–75.

Kleinmuntz, D. N. (1993). Information processing and misperceptions of the implications of feedback in dynamic decision making. *System Dynamics Review, 9*(3), 223–237.

Kreps, G. L. (1988). The pervasive role of information in health and health care: Implications for communication policy. *Communication Yearbook, 11,* 238–276.

Kruglanski, A. W., Peri, N., & Zakai, D. (1991). Interactive effects of need for closure and initial confidence on social information seeking. *Social Cognition, 9*(2), 127–148.

Kuhn, T. S. (1970). *The structure of scientific revolutions.* Chicago: University of Chicago Press.

Langer, L. M., & Warheit, G. J. (1992). The pre-adult health decision making model: Linking decision making directedness/orientation to adolescent health related attitudes and behaviors. *Adolescence, 27*(108), 919–948.

Latour, B., & Woolgar, S. (1979). *Laboratory life: The social construction of scientific facts.* Beverly Hills: Sage Publications.

Lindquist, E. A. (1988). What do decision models tell us about information use? *Knowledge in Society, 1*(2), 86–111.

Macrae, C. N., Hewstone, M., & Griffiths, R. J. (1993). Processing load and memory for stereotype based information. *European Journal of Social Psychology, 23*(1), 77–87.

Main, M. C., Gerace, L. M., & Camilleri, D. (1993). Information sharing concerning schizophrenia in a family member: Adult siblings' perspectives. *Archives of Psychiatric Nursing, 7*(3), 147–153.

McIntosh, J., & Parkes, C. M. (1974). Processes of communication, information seeking and control associated with cancer: A selective review of the literature. *Social Science and Medicine, 8*(4), 167–187.

Meissner, H. I., Anderson, D. M., & Odenkirchen, J. C. (1990). Meeting information needs of significant others: Use of the Cancer Information Service. *Patient Education and Counseling, 15*(2), 171–179.

Moschis, G. P., & Moore, R. L. (1979). Decision making among the young: A socialization perspective. *Journal of Consumer Research, 6*(2), 101–112.

Morrison, E. W. (1993a). Longitudinal study of the effects of information seeking on newcomer socialization. *Journal of Applied Psychology, 78*(2), 173–183.

Morrison, E. W. (1993b). Newcomer information seeking: Exploring types, modes, sources, and outcomes. *Academy of Management Journal, 36*(3), 557–589.

Mowen, J. C. (1993). *Consumer behavior.* New York: Macmillan.

Murray, K. B. (1991). A test of services marketing theory: Consumer information acquisition activities. *Journal of Marketing, 55*(1), 10–25.

Ostroff, C., & Kozlowski, S. W. (1992). Organizational socialization as a learning process: The role of information acquisition. *Personnel Psychology, 45*(4), 849–874.

Ottati, V. C., & Wyer, R. S., Jr. (1990). The cognitive mediators of political choice: Toward a comprehensive model of political information processing. In J. A. Ferejohn & J. H. Kuklinski (Eds.), *Information and democratic processes* (pp. 186–216). Urbana, IL: University of Illinois Press.

Ozanne, J. L., Brucks, M., & Grewal, D. (1992). A study of information search behavior during the categorization of new products. *Journal of Consumer Research, 18*(4), 452–463.

Pierce, P. F. (1993). Deciding on breast cancer treatment: A description of decision behavior. *Nursing Research, 42*(1), 22–28.

Pincus, J. D., & Acharya, L. (1988). Employee communication strategies for organizational crises. *Employee Responsibilities and Rights Journal, 1*(3), 181–199.

Popkin, S. L. (1993). Information shortcuts and the reasoning voter. In B. Grofman (Ed.), *Information, participation and choice: An Economic Theory of Democracy in perspective* (pp. 17–35). Ann Arbor, MI: University of Michigan Press.

Prince-Embury, S. (1992). Information attributes as related to psychological symptoms and perceived control among information seekers in the aftermath of technological disaster. *Journal of Applied Social Psychology, 22*(14), 1148–1159.

Rakowski, W., Assaf, A. R., Lefebvre, R. C., Lasater, T. M., Niknian, M., & Carleton, R. A. (1990). Information seeking about health in a community sample of adults: Correlates and associations with other health related practices. *Health Education Quarterly, 17*(4), 379–393.

Rakowski, W., Rice, C., & McHorney, C. A. (1992). Information seeking about health among older adults: An examination of measurement and structural properties. *Behavior, Health, and Aging, 2*(3), 181–198.

Rediker, K. J., Mitchell, T. R., Beach, L. R., & Beard, D. W. (1993). The effects of strong belief structures on information-processing evaluations and choice. *Journal of Behavioral Decision Making, 6*(2), 113–132.

Robertson, R. D. (1980). Small group decision making: The uncertain role of information in reducing uncertainty. *Political Behavior, 2*(2), 163–188.

Robinson, S., & Weldon, E. (1993). Feedback seeking in groups: A theoretical perspective. *British Journal of Social Psychology, 32*(1), 71–86.

Schaller, M. (1991). Social categorization and the formation of group stereotypes: Further evidence for biased information processing in the perception of group behavior correlations. *European Journal of Social Psychology, 21*(1), 25–35.

Schmitt, B. H., Leclerc, F., & Dube-Rioux, L. (1988). Sex typing and consumer behavior: A test of gender schema theory. *Journal of Consumer Research, 15*(1), 122–128.

Slocum, J. W., Jr. (1982). Decision making: An interdisciplinary focus. In G. R. Ungson & D. N. Braunstein (Eds.), *Decision making: An interdisciplinary inquiry* (pp. 288–292). Boston: Kent Publishing.

Sniderman, P. M., Glaser, J. M., & Griffin, R. (1990). Information and electoral choice. In J. A. Ferejohn & J. H. Kuklinski (Eds.), *Information and democratic processes* (pp. 117–135). Urbana, IL: University of Illinois Press.

Sontag, J. C., & Schacht, R. (1994). An ethnic comparison of parent participation and information needs in early intervention. *Exceptional Children, 60*(5), 422–433.

Sonuga-Barke, E. J., Thompson, M., & Balding, J. (1993). Everyday beliefs about sources of advice for the parents of difficult children. *Child Care, Health and Development, 19*(4), 251–260.

Surlin, S. H., & Gordon, T. F. (1977). How values affect attitudes toward direct reference political advertising. *Journalism Quarterly, 54*(1), 89–98.

Taylor, R. S. (1991). Information use environments. *Progress in Communication Sciences, 10*, 217–255.

Thomas, J. B., Clark, S. M., & Gioia, D. A. (1993). Strategic sensemaking and organizational performance: Linkages among scanning, interpretation, action, and outcomes. *Academy of Management Journal, 36*(2), 239–270.

Thompson, M. L. (1994). Information seeking coping and anxiety in school age children anticipating surgery. *Children's Health Care, 23*(2), 87–97.

Timmermans, D. (1993). The impact of task complexity on information use in multi attribute decision making. *Journal of Behavioral Decision Making, 6*(2), 95–111.

Tulving, E. (1983). *Elements of episodic memory.* Oxford: Clarendon.

Van Zuuren, F. J., & Wolfs, H. M. (1991). Styles of information seeking under threat: Personal and situational aspects of monitoring and blunting. *Personality and Individual Differences, 12*(2), 141–149.

Verplanken, B., Hazenberg, P. T., & Palenewen, G. R. (1992). Need for cognition and external information search effort. *Journal of Research in Personality, 26*(2), 128–136.

Weiss, C. H., & Bucuvalas, M. J. (1980). *Social science research and decision-making.* New York: Columbia University Press.

4

Information Needs and Information Design

Introduction

Chapter 2 outlines the basis for user-centered information-system design: to investigate the nature of users' needs (their goals, purposes, and objectives), the tasks they accomplish in meeting those needs, and the resources they use to complete the tasks. Then the different levels of these resources that are available to users can be assessed, and systems can be designed that take advantage of existing resources or augment those resources by system features. The result will be usable information systems or systems that will bring users to the point that they can meet their overall goals and satisfy their needs. Of this agenda, only the first step has thus far been completed, the investigation of users' needs. Chapter 3 outlines a number of general approaches to information needs that can serve as a basis for understanding the specific needs of users.

It should be emphasized that this analysis of information needs, although important, does no more than provide a context for the discussions of more specific information tasks that are found in Chapters 5 and 7 and the detailed analyses of information-system design in Chapters 6 and 8. It is what users do, rather than their internal state of need, that has the most impact on the design of information systems and services. On the other hand, an attempt to tie the discussion of information needs to the practical business of meeting those needs is appropriate. This chapter draws out some of the implications of the nature of information needs for the design of information systems, services, and institutions.

Design Directions: Some Initial Hints

At this point in the analysis, the nature of information needs has been considered from a variety of perspectives. This analysis does not permit any conclusions about the design of specific information systems to be drawn, because it has not considered the real world of the information interaction. In fact, the discussion of information needs was conducted on a fairly theoretical plane, despite the inclusion of

Some information needs arise from failure of perception.

> A. Failure of perception can be either individual or collective.
>
> B. If individual, failure of perception can arise from inadequate knowledge structures, inappropriate or ambiguous social influences, or a combination of both.
>
> C. If collective, failure of perception can arise from inadequate knowledge structures, inadequate group communication processes, inappropriate or ambiguous social and organizational influences, of some combination of these factors.

Some information needs are associated with a process of exploring a topic area so as to identify alternative courses of action.

> D. Failure of perception needs can be either individual or collective.
>
> E. If individual, they can result from inadequate knowledge structures, inappropriate or ambiguous social signals, or a combination of the two.
>
> F. If collective, they can result from inadequate knowledge structures, inadequate group processes, inappropriate or ambiguous organizational signals, or some combination of these factors.

Some information needs arise from the need to associate alternatives with outcomes.

> G. Such needs can be individual or collective in nature.
>
> H. If individual, needs associated with alternative selection and evaluation are driven by inadequate knowledge structures, inadequate or conflicting social signals, or both.
>
> I. If collective, needs associated with alternative selection and evaluation are driven by inadequate knowledge structures, inappropriate or inadequate group processes, conflicting organizational values, or some combination of these factors.

People can, and frequently do, engage in information avoidance. They interact with their environment by limiting their intake of information, ignoring information if it is associated with negative outcomes, and taking information shortcuts. Organizations are frequently equally irrational in their collection, processing, and use of information.

Figure 5
Characteristics of information needs.

real-life examples. It is possible, however, to begin to identify some areas of challenge that face system designers. This chapter suggests four general design principles derived from these areas of challenge and discusses each of them along with specific design implications for information systems and services. These four general design principles give rise to nine specific implications for information-system design; these principles and implications are provided in Fig. 5 for the purpose of comparison and synthesis.

Failures of Perception

In Chapter 3, the discussion follows the problem–solving model, in which the first step is perception and recognition of the problem. Knowledge structures, both individual and collective, determine not only how people perceive and recognize problems, but also whether they perceive problems. This consideration of the importance of knowledge structures leads to the conclusion that the absence of knowledge structures can result in a failure of perception and individuals and groups may recognize this absence of knowledge structures, thus experiencing a need for information to fill in the gap. From this discussion, the following general design principle and implications can be derived.

General Design Principle
Some information needs arise from failures of perception.

Specific Design Implications
A. Failures of perception can be either individual or collective.

There are many factors that influence how people will behave in any situation. Some of these relate to the individual: an individual may be tall or short, male or female, or (more relevant to a discussion of information seeking) may have higher or lower levels of individual knowledge or cognitive ability. Other factors that influence behavior are social in nature. An individual may be a member of an occupational group, a socioeconomic class, a minority ethnic group, or a street gang. All of these types of membership in social groups determine how individuals react in situations.

The same types of factors influence group behavior. The individual and social variables influence not only how individual members behave, but how the group behaves. For example, these variables influence how the group works to achieve consensus about its purpose and focus. From these considerations, two additional implications that may guide the development of information systems and services can be drawn.

B. If individual, failures of perception can arise from inadequate knowledge structures, inappropriate or ambiguous social influences, or a combination of both.

C. If collective, failures of perception can arise from inadequate knowledge structures, inadequate group communication processes, inappropriate or ambiguous social and organizational influences, or some combination of these factors.

Approaches to the development of information services that follow from the principle and implications can now be considered.

Some information needs arise from failures of perception.

This general design principle implies that, in any information setting, there are going to be people who are (at least metaphorically) wandering around and wondering what went wrong. They may be confused, inarticulate, or frustrated. Information-system designers and information professionals who create information services and manage information institutions must accomplish several tasks that relate to these individuals. The first is to decide whether or not to attempt to serve people who are experiencing this type of information need. This is not a trivial decision. Any objective observation of information systems and services found in most communities leads to the conclusion that the decision has usually been to ignore people with this type of need. For example, library systems usually require users to be able to produce a concise and clearly formatted statement of their information need, something that is beyond the capability of people experiencing failures of perception. The current wisdom in reference librarianship, derived from many years of research and practical experience, is that users who do not initially produce such a concise and clearly formatted statement of need should be interviewed by librarians to discover what their real information need may be. However, no amount of interviewing of users experiencing failures of perception will be likely to produce more elaborated statements of need. Data-centered approaches require the user to have an articulated information need that approximates the format of the data. Because the data of a library online catalog contains subject headings, users must generate subject headings. Because the data of an airline reservation system contains airport designations, users must produce airport names. There is no place in these highly data-centered information systems for the previously described users: those who are confused because they have experienced an unpleasant or even painful failure of perception.

Other services are more able to deal with poorly articulated needs. For example, a hospital may be able to diagnose and treat someone who remains unconscious throughout the procedure. In the information domain, experts may be able to work with people to diagnose their information needs and to define for them the reality they are facing so they can perceive it clearly. However, an information system or service that will provide this kind of information may be rather different from current information systems and services.

This discussion leads to a consideration of the next task facing information systems and services. If the systems must attempt to meet the needs of people experiencing failures of perception, they must develop some means for identifying and making contact with such people. The hospital, with its ability to treat people who cannot articulate their need for treatment, serves as an example. Hospitals have developed a number of mechanisms, such as referral networks and ambulance contracts, to sweep the community for this type of customer. Again, libraries provide an example of information agencies that have failed to address adequately the needs of people experiencing failures of perception. Libraries expect users to be aware enough of their need for information to be able to present themselves to the library and identify their need. Given the nature of the mental state of people experiencing failures of perception, this seems an unlikely occurrence. Information agencies that choose to deal with this type of information need will need a mechanism with which to sweep their communities for users, thus bringing users into contact with experts.

The final step necessary in meeting information needs of this type is to develop information systems and services that are adapted to the task. This development problem requires a more detailed analysis of the information tasks accomplished by people who experience failures of perception. A general framework for this analysis is presented in Chapters 5 and 7, and sketches of an information system that may respond to this type of need can be found in Chapters 6 and 8. For the present, it can be noted that typical, data-centered information systems seem poorly designed to meet the information needs associated with failures of perception. Because these systems are built on the data that is produced by people who not only perceive the problem clearly, but are to some extent experts in the problem area, there is a considerable cognitive gap between such systems and people who are unable even to perceive their problem. Data-centered systems may attempt to bridge this gap with an interface, but this seems an impossible task even for the most artfully developed interface. Developing information systems and services to meet this type of information need seems to demand user-centered design for the entire system development process.

Failure of perception can be either individual or collective.

The preceding discussion considers individuals facing failures of perception. In groups, the information need deriving from failures of perception is extended beyond what individuals experience. In a group, it is not enough for individual members to come to perceive the problem (through expert intervention). Individual members must persuade the group that their perception of the problem is correct. This understanding of group processes leads to the conclusion that information systems and services that attempt to meet collective information needs have a responsibility to facilitate the group processes involved in building consensus about the problem, as well as to provide the kind of expert assistance that will diagnose and identify the problematic reality. Once again, information agencies have to make the decision as to whether or not they should attempt to deal with collective failures of perception. The evidence is fairly clear that many information agencies have abandoned group information needs altogether. For example, the design of online bibliographic retrieval systems emphasizes the interaction between one user and the retrieval device. Most of the work on interface design for information systems has failed to consider the possibility that a group may be interacting collectively with the system. In the area of management information systems, it is only recently that support for group decision making has become a priority.

Having decided to meet these needs, the information agency must develop mechanisms for finding and making contact with groups experiencing failures of perception. Contacting groups appears to have been ignored by traditional, data-centered information systems and services. As indicated previously, most current information systems seem to assume that individuals working alone will be the principal users. This assumption has made it difficult for designers of such systems to consider the ways that groups work together to resolve information needs and to arrange avenues through which groups could come into contact with the information they need in a collective manner.

Having decided to try to help and having developed contact mechanisms, information-system developers must establish system designs that will assist the group consensus processes. In data-centered system design, the designers have typically had so little idea of who may be using the data and for what purpose the data would be used that it probably made no difference to them that users may be groups rather than individuals. In the user-centered paradigm, designers must take into account the fact that some groups make use of information systems. Some systems, such as Group Decision Support Systems (GDSS) (Rao & Jarvenpaa, 1991) and systems for Computer Supported Cooperative Work (CSCW) (Nunamaker, Dennis, Valacich, Vogel, & George, 1991), have features that seem to meet this kind of need. It may be possible for the information system to facilitate the group processes involved in building a common understanding of what is to be done or what information may bear on the collective purpose. Information obtained by one member of a group can be posted to some central information space where all group members will see it. A collective understanding of the topic being investigated can be kept in a central information space and revised from time to time as group members evolve their expression of the topic or as aspects of the problem are resolved.

> If individual, failures of perception can arise from inadequate knowledge structures, inappropriate or ambiguous social influences, or a combination of both.

Information needs can be derived from these inadequacies. Consideration of how to design information systems and services that will address these information needs must be based on the individual and social factors that influence these needs. Clearly, an information system can meet an information need by providing information that will fill gaps in individual knowledge structures. Experts in a topic area are ideally placed to diagnose where those inadequacies lie and to assist the user in a learning process that will result in new knowledge structures where none existed previously. With these new knowledge structures, individuals will be able to perceive the problem clearly and move to the next steps in problem solving. However, the social constraints on the processes of perception and learning are equally important, and it seems clear that creating information systems without considering these factors will result in lower levels of usability. It is essential for the experts to know not only the topic that contains the gap, but also the social situation in which the user is found. So, for example, it will be necessary for experts giving information on dinosaurs to students to be familiar with the classroom situation and curriculum. Without this sensitivity to the social context of the information need, appropriate information may not be provided in an appropriate manner.

> If collective, failures of perception can arise from inadequate knowledge structures, inadequate group communication processes, inappropriate or ambiguous organizational influences, or some combination of these factors.

The knowledge structures of individuals in the group and the group communication processes that turn them into group knowledge structures have been discussed. However, the organizational influences have not yet been addressed. It seems clear that the expertise making the provision of individual information sensitive to social setting must also be present in information systems responding to collective information needs. Information agencies must provide expertise that is sensitive to the organizational settings in which groups are working, so they are able to provide appropriate and usable information.

Alternative Identification

Chapter 3 next considers the information needs associated with filling in detailed information so as to explore alternative problem-solving approaches. This type of information need assumes that the problem was perceived, but an individual now needs to find out about possible solutions. At the same time, it is recognized that groups who have achieved a collective understanding of the problem they face may also need to explore a topic area in more depth to identify ways of addressing the problem. This type of information need, both in groups and in individuals, is associated with failures of knowledge structures to identify alternatives. The general principle that may guide the design of information systems and services is articulated in the following section.

General Design Principle
Some information needs are associated with the process of exploring a topic area so as to identify alternative courses of action.

Specific Design Implications
D. Such information needs can be individual or collective.

Chapter 3 notes that both individual and social factors can influence the need for information. An individual's own knowledge of alternatives may be constrained by an understanding of acceptable alternatives that derives from social groups in which he or she is a member. Similarly, a group's knowledge and understanding of alternative ways of addressing its collective problem may be constrained by organizational culture and values. The implications that guide the design of information systems and services may be articulated as follows:

E. If individual, they can result from inadequate knowledge structures, inappropriate or ambiguous social signals, or a combination of the two.

F. If collective, they can result from inadequate knowledge structures, inadequate group processes, inappropriate or ambiguous social or organizational signals, or some combination of these factors.

Some information needs are associated with the process of exploring a topic area so as to identify alternative courses of action.

The first decision facing information agencies is whether or not they will try to address these information needs in individuals. It may be argued that this type of information need is easier to address than those associated with failures of perception. Here, the problem has been diagnosed and defined, and all that remains is to add details. In fact, most traditional information services seem to make this kind of information need the focus of their activities. There are areas of difficulty, however, that may make some information agencies less interested in developing the resources to deal with this type of information need. There are, for example, real differences that arise from the nature of the problem being resolved. An individual facing one kind of problem may need to explore a topic area in a different way than an individual facing a different kind of problem. This kind of problem-based flexibility in the presentation of information is not frequently found in current information systems. In part, this inflexibility may be attributed to the data-centered approach, which focuses on the data rather than on the uses to which the data can be applied. It is also true that implementing information systems that can tailor their functioning to the different problems faced by users is far more difficult than implementing systems with less flexibility.

Having decided to address information needs of this nature, the information agency must identify and attract to its services and systems the people who are experiencing these needs. This task seems to be primarily a matter of marketing. If individuals are in possession of enough information to be able to articulate their information need, it seems fairly straightforward to attract them to an agency that can fill in the details they need. Finally, the information agency must put in place systems and services that will permit flexible yet easy exploration of topic areas. To anticipate some of the design characteristics that will be considered in detail in subsequent chapters, there must be mechanisms that will enhance exploration both hierarchically through information structures and laterally across information structures. The term "information structures" should be amplified. Dealing with information-as-knowledge, which has as its foundation a body of publicly accepted knowledge, requires an understanding of the structure of that public body of knowledge. So, for example, an encyclopedia can be arranged to allow readers to move from more general to more specific topics. On the other hand, in information-as-process, the information structures are much more individualized. Different individuals may have different ways of structuring their own knowledge, and these differences in individual knowledge structures will influence how people will perceive information that they receive. Individual as well as public information structures exist, and this fact complicates the matter of exploration and navigation. While it may be fairly simple to allow individuals to explore both hierarchically and laterally across public information structures, it seems considerably more difficult to design information systems that will allow users to navigate in similar ways through individual information structures.

Such information needs can be individual or collective.

This implication draws attention to the needs of groups for this kind of information. Again, it is important to point out that a group's exploration of a topic area in order to identify alternative courses of action differs considerably from the same kind of exploration undertaken by an individual. Different members of the group may explore the area differently because of their individual knowledge structures. Accordingly, members of the group may propose rather different sets of possible solutions. The group must act collectively to direct the exploration so that all aspects are explored and then must act collectively to agree on the set of possible solutions to its problem. The information agency that addresses this kind of information need will be faced with facilitating group processes that are more complex than those associated with problem perception. It will have to address consensus building about search strategy and interpretation of results. Information systems and services that will accomplish this kind of group facilitation will also have to deal with the special roles of boundary spanning and gatekeeping adopted by some group members.

If individual, they can result from inadequate knowledge structures, inappropriate or ambiguous social signals, or a combination of the two.

This implication emphasizes that the identification of alternatives cannot occur in a social vacuum. Rather, the viable alternatives that a user can consider relate to the social setting in which that user is found. As noted previously, this means that the information system or service must contain expertise not only on the topic, but on the social situations that influence the information need. Such considerations are, of course, foreign to the data-centered perspective, where data, decontextualized and value-free, is the basis for design. In the user-centered approach, the social and organizational context of alternative identification is much more important to the design task.

If collective, they can result from inadequate knowledge structures, inadequate group processes, inappropriate or ambiguous social or organizational signals, or some combination of these factors.

As discussed previously, this means that information agencies that propose to meet collective information needs associated with alternative identification must contain enough expertise about the organizational situation to be sensitive to the constraints that the organizational setting places on alternatives.

Alternative Selection

The most detailed information need is that associated with evaluating alternative solutions and selecting a course of action. The gap in knowledge may be seen as relatively narrow. An individual or group knows almost everything there is to know about the problem situation. But at the same time, the gap is profound.

Knowledge associated with alternative evaluation can come from a wide variety of areas. There may be many people who have experienced the outcomes of a particular solution and their experiences may be quite diverse. Pulling together all of this knowledge and focusing it on the task of evaluation can be demanding. The general design principle and associated implications derived from the discussion in Chapter 3 of this type of information need are provided in the following sections.

General Design Principle

Some information needs arise from the need to associate alternatives with outcomes.

Specific Design Implications

G. Such needs can be individual or collective in nature.

In accordance with the approach taken throughout this book, the individual and social factors that can influence this type of information need and how it is satisfied must be distinguished. While an individual or group may be able to entertain a wide variety of solutions as being best for their problem, the social or organizational context may prevent some of these solutions from being considered seriously. Accordingly, there are two additional implications:

H. If individual, needs associated with alternative selection and evaluation are driven by inadequate knowledge structures, inadequate or conflicting social signals, or both.

I. If collective, needs associated with alternative selection and evaluation are driven by inadequate knowledge structures, inappropriate or inadequate group processes, conflicting social or organizational values, or some combination of these factors.

Some information needs arise from the need to associate alternatives with outcomes.

Information agencies may consider carefully whether they wish to address this type of need. The task of assembling information from widely scattered informants in a uniform format that will allow appropriate evaluation is not an easy one. Evaluative tasks, such as those envisioned in meeting this set of information needs, require information systems of considerable complexity, and it seems that most data-centered systems have chosen to neglect this area because of its complexity. Secondly, an information agency will have the task of identifying and attracting people who have this type of information need. It seems that this is the easiest task likely to be faced by information professionals. If an information agency can do a good job of advising people how best to solve their problems, the world will beat a sizable path to its door. Finally, an information agency will have to put systems and services in place that will do the good job mentioned in the previous sentence. This may well be the most difficult task that information professionals have to face.

It seems clear even at this early stage of analysis that information systems that can address this type of need will provide an analyzed or processed information package to the user. Evaluation requires that alternatives be compared, linked with different outcomes, and (ultimately) selected. Raw data will not satisfy this information need, at least not without considerable additional work by the user. It seems clear that some synthesis of the available literature or the results of different experiments must be provided to meet information needs of this type.

> Such needs can be individual or collective in nature.

The individual's evaluative information need has already been discussed. Clearly, enabling a group to decide on the best solution to its collective problem is rather more complex. One member of the group may decide on the basis of available information that one particular solution is best. Another member acting on identical information may select another solution. The political process of persuading all members to a particular point of view is one of the most critical in group processes such as problem solving and decision making. It follows that information systems and services put in place to assist groups in evaluating and selecting solutions will have to address the group dynamics associated with reaching a consensus on the best solution.

> If individual, needs associated with alternative selection and evaluation are driven by inadequate knowledge structures, inadequate or conflicting social signals, or both.

Although individuals may be in a position to select one alternative on the basis of their individual assessments of the outcomes from that alternative, social values and norms may dictate other alternatives. Accordingly, the information system or service put in place to advise people on which alternative is best will have to apply expert knowledge of the social settings in which users find themselves.

> If collective, needs associated with alternative selection and evaluation are driven by inadequate knowledge structures, inappropriate or inadequate group processes, conflicting social or organizational values, or some combination of these factors.

The conflicting organizational values can make it even more difficult for groups to select a course of action. Accordingly, any information system that proposes to assist groups in resolving this type of information need will have to sensitively apply an expert knowledge of organizational constraints on alternative selection.

Bounded Rationality

Chapter 3 notes that the problem-solving model, so instrumental in the consideration of information needs in the first parts of this chapter, does not really do a good job of representing some information activities. These information activities may be typified by noting that the rationality of the actors is bounded to some greater or lesser extent. It is always possible to label activities irrational and so have good reason for ignoring them. But it seems doubtful whether adequate information systems can be developed if the ways in which real people behave in real information situations are ignored. Accordingly, an additional general design principle that can guide the development of information systems and services can be derived from the discussion in Chapter 3.

General Design Principle

People can, and frequently do, engage in information avoidance. They interact with their environment by limiting their intake of information, ignoring information if it is associated with negative outcomes, and taking information shortcuts. Organizations are frequently equally irrational in their collection, processing, and use of information.

Data-driven information-system design can, perhaps, be forgiven for assuming a purposive, rational, information-seeking process. Because user characteristics are not the driving factor in this kind of design, it is understandable that information systems developed under this paradigm will be blind to the kinds of uses made of the information. If people choose to ignore information generally or to make irrational uses of it, there will be no impact on design. However, in the user-centered paradigm, there is no excuse for ignoring the bounded rationality of information behavior. In fact, a case can be made that many information needs are information-avoidance needs. And information systems that pay attention to user needs will have to have information–avoidance design features. This is something that is increasingly understood by those who are designing information filters to handle e-mail messages or other networked information. Such systems are built on the recognition that a kernel of vital information can be buried in an avalanche of useless or trivial messages and that an information system should not just deliver data, but rather should process, analyze, and filter it to meet information needs. This is, however, a concept that has not been well developed in more traditional information systems, where the underlying and driving assumption seems to be that more information is always better.

Part of the blame for ignoring the limited rationality of information behavior must be shared by user studies. Chapter 3 notes the wide variety of user studies that have been conducted and have provided a great deal of insight into information needs. But, as Wilson (1981) points out, the problem with user studies is that investigators concentrate on users of a particular information system or service and therefore see only those individuals who have elected to use that system or service. They fail to see all of the people who have elected not to use the system or service, perhaps because they wish to avoid information at all costs, they are already overloaded with information, or there are organizational constraints that prevent them from seeking information from that particular system or service. In other words, user studies give an inadequate picture of information needs and information behavior. In particular, they seem unlikely to capture the less rational aspects of information behavior.

Other aspects of information-processing irrationality at the organizational level can have implications for the design of group information systems. It is not enough to provide a central space in which information can be shared. It can be important that this central information repository be processed, analyzed, and filtered for each member of the group. In fact, group processes may demand that each group member receive a different version of the information. This kind of group information support system is light-years away from typical data-centered information devices.

Each of these points can be considered in more detail. Information agencies must first decide whether they wish to deal with individuals who limit their intake of information, ignore information when it may be inconvenient, or take information shortcuts. There exists in libraries, for example, a kind of Puritan ethic that decries information shortcuts. Some public libraries, for example, refuse to stock Cliffs Notes, one convenient form of information shortcut for students. Managers of information institutions may well feel that, if people choose not to seek information, the needs of those individuals should not be considered in the design of information systems and services. The managers may well note that their resources are sufficiently strained by meeting the needs of people who are seriously and purposively pursuing information. As justification for their positions, the managers may ask why should they divert resources toward the task of informing people who really do not want to be informed.

It would therefore be understandable if information agencies ignored those who avoid information, but it is at least conceivable that a less critical approach is to be recommended. A community is not neatly divided into blunters and monitors. Rather, some people may seek some kinds of information and ignore others. Their orientation to information may also change as their individual situations change. When serving people who are actively and purposively seeking information, agencies may simultaneously be serving people whose approach is less rational. The appropriate approach, some may argue, will be to provide people with the amount of information on topics of interest that they may need at any moment. In some cases, users may need detailed information; in other cases summary information; and in others, no information at all. However, if information systems and services are optimized to provide only one or two sets of information, they will not be sensitive to the needs of people who avoid information.

If information agencies agree to attempt to provide information flexibly to users depending on their needs (rational or otherwise), they will face the task of attracting people to their services. Marketing of information services to people whose main wish is to avoid information is, to put it mildly, difficult. One is reminded here of a typical shopper in a department store. The author may serve as an ideal example here. When I am just browsing and really do not want help from a salesperson, it seems that they accost me at every corner. But when I really need help with a purchase, it seems that I cannot find a salesperson anywhere. The ideal, of course, is to attract people to the information service by promising them that they will not be forced to learn anything they do not want to learn, at the same time assuring them that they will be given the help they need with their information problems.

This discussion applies to the design of information systems and services to meet a wide range of user needs. It is clear from the beginning that the one-size-fits-all approach found in most data-centered information systems simply will not work. In those systems, the attention is firmly on the data. People are free to use as much or as little as they wish, but users are not given the access devices they need in order to select as much or as little as they wish. Accordingly, users are left with a large task. The system figuratively dumps a great pile of documents on them and lets them winnow and process the pile so as to select the amount of information that they need or desire. Without anticipating all of the design details considered in the next several chapters, the need for information-filtering devices of many kinds to allow individuals to adjust the amount of information they will receive can be emphasized.

The first decision that information agencies must face is whether they will ignore the bounded rationality of organizational information seeking and processing. For example, in an organization, some members of the group may engage in information collection for symbolic reasons. Perhaps they are demonstrating their dedication to the task of decision making. In an information system focusing on individual needs, the symbolic nature of information seeking may be ignored, but in a group information system, the superfluous information will be evaluated by the group and some of it will be entered into the group knowledge base. Processing group information to reach a consensus about problem solving and decision making is difficult enough without imposing additional and unnecessary loads on the group process, so the group information system cannot be justified in ignoring the bounded rationality of this type of information behavior.

If group information systems are to take into account activities such as symbolic uses of information or information withholding behaviors, they must incorporate system features that will allow them to filter and apportion information appropriately to group members. This can be done by developing a kind of member profile that directs information to specific individuals, while keeping the group communication channels reasonably clear for consensus building.

Conclusion

All of the individual and social variables that influence the information needs outlined in Chapter 3 lead inevitably to the conclusion that user-centered design will produce complex information systems. In data-centered design, it is customary to take a one-size-fits-all approach. The data dictates the nature of the system, and users (if considered at all) are accommodated through user-friendly interfaces.

If information systems are to meet individual needs and take into account the many variables that influence those needs, it seems inevitable that the systems must be customized for or adapted to the needs of individual users. Similarly, when discussing groups with collective information needs, it seems inevitable that each group will be able to establish an information system that will facilitate their group processes and allow them to achieve their collective objective. This task of adapting a system to a group seems likely to be more complex than customizing systems to individual users.

In summary, the discussion of information needs has illuminated the complexity of these needs and has provided a great deal of insight for information-system design. A variety of anomalous states of knowledge have been identified. Failures of perception, of alternative identification, and of selection can lead to these anomalies, which in turn may produce information-seeking behavior. There are challenges that face the designers of information systems and services if they try to meet all information needs. The distinction between individual and collective information needs appears to be equally important to system design, as are the individual and social variables that affect information seeking and information processing. The next chapter presents a more detailed analysis of statements of information need as the first step in an in-depth study of information tasks.

User-Centered Design: A Practical Guide II

Note: At the end of each even-numbered chapter of this book, a brief guide to the practical aspects of design is provided. This guide summarizes discussions in preceding chapters as they relate to the practical aspects of conducting user-centered design. Contents that have been added to this version of the guide are shown in boxes.

1. Identify a user population. The first and obvious step in user-centered design is to find a user, or more appropriately, a user population. Sometimes user identification is dictated by the mission of the organization where the designer works. In other cases, users may be selected by the designer. The identification of the user population is such an obvious step that it is sometimes omitted. This omission results in systems that are not particularly usable for any set of users.

> The user population may be composed of either individuals or groups or perhaps a combination of both. Because different design decisions will be necessary for groups, they should be identified separately when they occur within the user population.

2. Investigate the information needs of your user group. The users identified in step 1 have a number of information needs. These can be investigated using a wide range of research methods, which are easily accessible in manuals on social science research or market research. The key element of this step is to talk to users and find out what kinds of information they need to resolve problems they encounter. No information system can meet all of the information needs of a user group. Once the full range of information needs has been identified, system designers must select those that their information system will be designed to meet.

User needs can be identified by reference to a problem-solving model. According to this model, information needs can be associated with problem perception, alternative identification, or alternative selection. Each of these classes of information needs will require different approaches to system design. User needs can also be typified by their setting. Information needs can occur in individuals or in groups. Group needs are sufficiently different from individual needs to require different design approaches.

Both individual and social factors influence the information needs that may occur within a user population. Designers should investigate the social and organizational settings in which information needs occur, because these settings may give rise to or constrain the information needs experienced by users. Figure 5 summarizes the design principles that emerge from a consideration of user information needs.

---

3. Discover the tasks that users accomplish as they meet these information needs. Again, research methods from social science and market research are useful in this step. The key element is to talk to users and observe them as they work on meeting their information needs. Identify the tasks that users employ as they meet their information needs and how they accomplish these tasks. Note the sequential ordering of the tasks. Try to distinguish between the tasks that are essential and those that are optional. The result will be one or more task models for each information need.

Tasks may be accomplished individually or collectively. Where users are observed to be completing tasks as a group, it is important to consider these group tasks separately from individual tasks in the design of information systems.

Tasks accomplished may be dictated by the social setting in which information seeking occurs. Social and organizational factors must be analyzed carefully, because they may constrain the number of tasks that individuals and groups choose to accomplish. When social factors constrain tasks in this way, information-system design can be considerably simpler than when users can select from a broader range of tasks.

4. Investigate the resources that users require to complete these tasks. Each task completed by a user who is meeting an information need requires a variety of resources: background knowledge, procedural knowledge, and abilities. List the resources required for each task and identify the level of the resources required. For example, expert knowledge or high levels of verbal ability may be required to complete a task involving vocabulary selection. At the same time, it is important to note the levels of these resources that users possess. Some users, for example, may have less expert topic knowledge or lower levels of verbal abilities, and gaps between resources required and resources possessed are obvious areas of concern. Research methods to investigate the resources possessed by users can be found in any text on psychometrics.

Resources may be individual or collective in nature. Where individual knowledge and ability are concerned, psychometric methods are adequate to identify levels of resources possessed by users. In the case of collective knowledge and ability, however, it is essential to investigate the group processes by which consensus is reached. Collective resources may differ considerably from the sum of the individual resources of group members.

Resources may derive from and be constrained by social factors. Accordingly, it is important to investigate the social and organizational setting in which resources are being applied to the completion of information tasks. These settings may provide additional resources or may constrain how resources are applied to tasks.

5. Summarize the preceding steps in user models. For each distinct user group to be served by the information system, there will be a number of information needs that the system is designed to meet. For each of these information needs, there will be a number of tasks that must be accomplished. For each of the tasks, there will be a list of resources that are necessary. Integrating these elements together results in a user model that can be used to guide design decisions or that can be implemented as part of the information system to direct how the system will respond to users. For example, user models can form the basis for the preset options for how the information system will work, but users will be able to change the options to make the system conform to their own preferences.

      6. Consider each design decision in the light of resource augmentation and enabling. The goal of system design is to allow users to complete the tasks that will meet their information needs. With this in mind, system features that will augment the resources of users when necessary will enable them to complete the tasks. Some of these features will be required by all users, while others will be required by only a portion of the user group. In the latter case, system features are best implemented as user-selectable options. Experimental research to identify interactions between user resources and design options can be used to select system features that should be implemented as user-selectable options.

References

Nunamaker, J. F., Dennis, A. R., Valacich, J. S., Vogel, D. R., & George, J. F. (1991). Electronic meeting systems to support group work. *Communications of the ACM, 34*(7), 40–61.

Rao, V. S., & Jarvenpaa, S. L. (1991). Computer support of groups: Theory based models for GDSS research. *Management Science, 37*(10), 1347–1362.

Wilson, T. D. (1981). On user studies and information needs. *Journal of Documentation, 37*(1), 3–15.

5

Expressing Information Needs

Introduction

Chapter 2 notes that the second step in user-centered information-system design is task analysis. This step occurs after needs analysis has been completed and before analyzing the resources used in information task completion, user modeling, and information system design. Task analysis involves investigating what people actually do as they resolve their information needs. This chapter turns to the first of the information tasks that users of information systems must perform, which is to express the information need in such a way as to produce the desired result: an informative response from an information system. The information needs discussed in the two preceding chapters (failures of perception, of alternative identification, and of evaluation of alternatives) exist in the minds of those who experience them. The first external, observable behavior associated with any need is its expression. The statement of need is a translated, filtered, public manifestation of the internal need state.

In keeping with the model for user-centered design, this chapter will examine in detail the task accomplished by users as they express their information needs and the resources they use in completing this task. Resources may be available to some users, but not to all. Alternatively, the resources may be available to users of information systems in different degrees. To enable users to accomplish their tasks, information systems must ensure that all users have access to the resources they need. In other words, the objective of this discussion is to build information systems that take advantage of the resources that users have and to augment these resources where necessary and appropriate. In this way, users will be able to complete their information tasks and satisfy their needs. The next chapter will consider the design implications of the analysis of the resources used in the task of expressing information needs.

The focus here is on how statements of information need that may be presented to an information system come into existence and how the filtering effects of language are felt in both individual and collective statements of need. Before beginning this discussion, however, it is appropriate to examine the traditional, data-driven approach to information-system design, if only to identify the problems with that approach that may be addressed by user-centered design. Data-centered information systems have access points that are derived from the data itself or from interpretations of that data given by information professionals as they accomplish value-added tasks such as indexing or abstracting. As a direct result of the data-centered approach, the language that subject experts and information professionals use to talk about their area of expertise is the language demanded by the information system. A user approaching this type of system must generate a query using expert language. In other words, the expression of information need must be created using a linguistic structure that is (at least potentially) foreign to the user.

User interfaces can be created to bridge this gap. Some of them allow users to select terms from a list or from a hierarchically organized display. Such interfaces assume, however, that the user has enough familiarity with the expert language to enable the user to select appropriate terms. Although it is premature to consider design implications in detail, one of the issues for user-centered design may be "How can users express their information needs in their own terms and still obtain information that will meet their information needs?"

The information task discussed in this chapter can also be related to the approach to cognitive engineering presented by Norman (1986). In this general understanding of user-centered system design, Norman identifies two gulfs that must be bridged to bring about successful interaction between a user and an information system. The first is the gulf of execution and the second the gulf of evaluation. The gulf of execution represents the difficulty that users experience in making contact with information systems and expressing their needs. Norman suggests that this gap can be bridged by the user who formulates an intention, specifies an action sequence, executes the action, and finally makes contact with the interface. These steps represent in general terms the task of expressing an information need. This chapter considers the individual, social, and organizational influences that determine how information needs are expressed. In other words, it considers how the gulf of execution is bridged when users make contact with an information system. The gulf of evaluation is the focus of Chapter 7.

Individual Expressions of Information Need

The statements of information need generated by individuals form the initial focus of this discussion. Just as there are individual and collective information needs, there are also individual and collective statements of need. Collective statements of need, originating from a group that has a joint task and a common understanding of that task, are quite complex and deserve separate treatment. In order to build an understanding of statements of information need progressively, the less complex question of individual needs will be discussed before proceeding to more complex collective needs. Figure 6 presents a graphical illustration of the

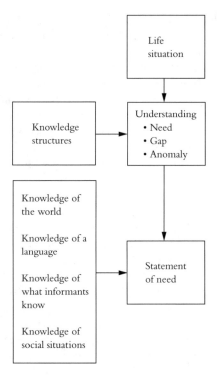

Figure 6
Individual expressions of information need.

process by which individual information needs come to be expressed. It will be noted that the top part of this figure is identical to Fig. 4 from Chapter 3.

Figure 6 shows how the information need, derived from a comparison of a real-life situation and existing knowledge structures, is processed into a statement of need using additional knowledge structures. Four types of knowledge structures are central to the ways in which individuals express their information needs. These are:

- knowledge of the world in which the information need occurs,
- knowledge of a language,
- knowledge of what informants may know, and
- knowledge of what is appropriate in different social situations.

In the terms used previously to describe the user-centered approach, these four types of knowledge are the resources used by individuals as they complete the tasks of information-need expression. Accordingly, these knowledge resources provide the framework for the following discussion of how different types of information needs are expressed.

Questions and Question Answering

World Knowledge

Much of the relevant research into the expression of information needs can be found in work in linguistics and psychology on questions and question answering. In linguistics, for example, attention has been paid to the presumptions and presuppositions that lie behind questions (Kaplan, 1983). What this means is that questioners (or searchers for information) build into their questions (or statements of information need) a certain amount of their own knowledge structures. For example, the question "Is the King of France bald?" presupposes that a King of France exists in some world, even if that world is one of imagination. Otherwise the question would be nonsense. So it is true that for every statement of information need there must be knowledge structures that describe the world in which the information need occurs. More specifically, the user's knowledge of the situation that gives rise to the information need is crucial. However, as is discussed in the following sections, the amount of knowledge that users have about the situation that gives rise to their information need will vary significantly from one type of information need to another. In other words, people have different levels of this particular type of knowledge resource that is so central to completing the task of expressing an information need.

Knowledge of a Language

Knowledge of a language seems so obvious a resource for expressing information needs that it can be easily overlooked, but the significance of this knowledge for generating statements of need is easily understood when the question-and-answer process is considered. People who have traveled in foreign countries will be familiar with the process of asking for something when there is no shared language between the questioner and respondent. Ordering a meal, shopping for basic necessities, or finding directions from one place to another can be rather frustrating experiences. The habit, for example, of repeating a question in a louder tone of voice in the hope of generating a response is not limited to American tourists. Extravagant gestures represent another communication strategy that may have limited success. This example is an extreme case of a language gap between questioner and answerer. But such experiences also occur between native English-speakers who do not share a specific sublanguage. Sublanguages include, for example, the technical jargon of a scientific discipline or profession. In the case of the generation of a statement of information need, sublanguage knowledge may be central. If technical language is not shared between questioner and informant, situations may occur in which the statement of need is unintelligible or (alternatively) in which the response is not informative.

Shared Knowledge

The third knowledge resource that drives the successful creation of statements of information need is the knowledge of what informants may know. Galambos and Black (1985) give an illustration of the question "Why did Sam eat dinner at the Copper Beach restaurant?", which could be answered in several different ways: because he was hungry, because he had heard that it was a good restaurant and wanted to try it out, or because his wife was out of town and he can't cook. They go on to say:

> Questions typically occur in a situation with two people exchanging information. Given the potential for ambiguity in any question and wide range of potentially appropriate answers, it is almost miraculous that question answering works at all. However, it does work because the participants share much pragmatic knowledge. (p. 158)

It follows that statements of information need represent the state of knowledge of the searcher for information and that they are restricted by the requirement that the informant share pragmatic knowledge (i.e., knowledge of the situation that provides the context for the information need).

In expressing an information need, the questioner needs to know that the informant has some understanding of the kind of situation in which the questioner is found. One is reminded here of the annoying verbal mannerism frequently associated with adolescent Americans of interpolating the question "you know?" several times in every sentence. To the extent to which this habit has a meaningful purpose, it may be considered a means of checking that the respondent understands what is being said. Shared understanding of the situation is crucial to the success of the question-and-answer process, and knowledge of the pragmatic knowledge shared by questioner and respondent is a resource that is used to generate the statement of information need.

Social Constraints

The fourth knowledge resource that is important to expressions of information need is the understanding of the social constraints upon question asking. There are social conventions that limit how people address questions to certain informants, and these conventions are quite specific to social situations. For example, there are limits on how patients will question physicians in the hospital or consultation room. There are different limits on how patients will question physicians if they meet in social situations or on the golf course. Understanding these social constraints is a central factor in generating appropriate statements of information need.

Expressing Failure of Perception

Probably the most difficult information need to express is the need attendant upon a failure of perception. This situation occurs if there is no existing knowledge structure that will account for the recalcitrant reality an individual has encountered. The discussion of information needs in Chapter 3 notes that this kind of failure of perception gives rise to questions like "What went wrong?" or "What was that?" These situations are relatively common. It seems as if people have developed a number of successful strategies for dealing with them. Chapter 1 notes that stopping to ask for directions when one is driving in an unfamiliar part of the world is a good example of information-seeking behavior. This is one example of a failure of perception. The question may be as vague as "Where am I?" or may represent the information need in the plaintive query "Help, I'm lost!"

This kind of information-seeking strategy is actually quite general in application. In the case of failure of perception, expression of the information need may be approached through the following steps:

- finding an expert,
- approaching the expert,
- identifying the problem (usually in a few words), and
- asking for help.

There is a direct correspondence between each of these four steps and the four knowledge resources discussed previously. In finding an expert, knowledge of what informants may know is crucial. In approaching the expert, knowledge of what is appropriate in different social situations plays an important role. In identifying the problem, knowledge of the world in which the information need occurs is the central resource. Finally, in asking for help, knowledge of a language is the most important of the four knowledge resources.

Finding an Expert

Examples of this strategy for expressing an information need abound. The lost tourist must first find an informant, a stage at which many searches for information may be aborted. I sometimes find myself visiting an unfamiliar city and being accosted by another tourist who asks for information. In such situations, the choice of informant is not a good one. In other cases of failure of perception, the selection of informant may be relatively straightforward. Medical problems are a case in point. An individual experiencing physical pain may not perceive the nature of the problem, but can usually select a medical expert who can (hopefully) diagnose and treat the problem. Alternatively, people take their ailing vehicles to an expert mechanic, who may be able to find out what the problem is and fix it. Similarly, if one is trying to identify a physical object or something from the natural world, informants are usually easy to identify. The gardener who has a particular beetle destroying his or her crops may approach an entomologist from the nearest university, clutching an example of the offending beastie, and ask for help. If someone finds an unidentified object in an attic, they may take it to a museum curator to learn about its identity, history, and use.

On occasion, the unidentified reality may be human in form. Here the question is "Who was that person, anyway?" A teacher, failing to recognize the amount of knowledge already possessed by a student, may begin to explain some subject at an inappropriately simple (or advanced) level. A junior officer may give orders to a senior officer whose real seniority is not perceived. Selection of an informant is less straightforward here: the ideal informant would be someone who knows the unidentified person and can clarify their identity and role, but such informants may not be conveniently labeled, as are medical or scientific experts.

Another type of failure-of-perception information need is the "What went wrong?" type of experience. An individual may encounter a situation in which expected events do not occur. One example is an automobile or boating accident. The people involved in the accident do not expect or intend to engage in a damaging episode, but something goes wrong. People who have experienced this may be unable to identify precisely what it was that went wrong. Reconstruction of the episode may require a special kind of expertise that can work from external evidence, eyewitness accounts, and so on. The informant may be an accident investigator who can piece together the events that occurred and deduce what went wrong during the automobile accident. Such an expert informant has knowledge of the kinds of things that may go wrong in any set of circumstances and the ability to collect and assess evidence that will identify the probable cause of the accident.

Similarly, personal situations can lead to the "What went wrong?" information need. An individual can do things that are intended to have a positive outcome for a personal relationship, only to find that something has gone wrong and the outcome is a negative one. Perhaps a particular gift is not appreciated, a way of expressing oneself is offensive, or an insult is felt where none is intended. Personal relationships are built on such uncertain foundations that the "What went wrong?" expression of failure of perception and resulting information need can be expected with a certain frequency. Identifying an informant in cases of this sort can be straightforward: one may approach a counselor or therapist whose professional expertise enables them to assess what went wrong in a friendship or marriage. Alternatively, one may approach someone who has had experience with similar personal problems.

Approaching the Expert

Having identified the informant, the next step is to approach him or her. There may well be social constraints that govern this process. One does not normally approach a physician at a cocktail party and ask for help with a physical pain. An appointment normally has to be made to approach the expert. Alternatively, the social conventions may dictate that one must use a certain tone of voice or polite manner when approaching the informant. More crucially for the expression of information needs, the language that one uses may be constrained by social convention.

Identifying the Problem and Asking for Help

The next steps are to identify the problem and to ask for help. In a case involving a failure of perception, there will be little or no semantic knowledge with which to create an elaborate statement of need. Rather, this kind of information need will be expressed in minimal semantic form. The point should be emphasized that this is information seeking in the absence of perception or in the presence of minimal perception ("I see it, but I have no idea what it is"). Frequently, the information need is expressed by pointing out the offending body part to the physician, holding out the bug to the entomologist or the artifact to the curator, and saying "It hurts" or "What is this thing that's eating my potato plants?" or "What is this?" Little or no definition of the information need in semantic terms is possible or, in fact, necessary. In some cases of failure of perception, enlisting the aid of an expert informant may require a slightly more detailed expression of information need. The person who is asking "What went wrong?" may have to verbalize the general set of things that were happening when that something went wrong. The informant will be able to examine the known details of the circumstance in which the unexpected event occurred, but may have to elicit from the information seeker other relevant details that will help to establish what may have happened.

Understanding Informative Responses

As indicated previously, this kind of expression of information need is relatively common and so is quite standardized by social convention. The process of answering this kind of question is equally standardized. It consists of two steps: using expert knowledge to identify the unknown entity or process and using linguistic knowledge to transform the expert knowledge into terms that will be understood by the inquirer. The first step is one of diagnosis and identification, and the second is one of definition.

The expert who is approached for information will frequently be able to diagnose or identify the reality from personal knowledge. In other cases, collection of relevant data by doing tests or examining the accident site may be a necessary precursor to answering the question. In all cases, however, there must be a body of knowledge that an informant uses to identify the recalcitrant reality. The importance of this consideration can be fully appreciated by reflecting on those cases in which the knowledge base does not exist. Asking a local resident for directions is a trivial example, but it can be exceedingly frustrating if that local resident has no idea how to get to the destination. More significant are situations in which a physician cannot diagnose an illness. New diseases, associated with new viruses, can be deadly reminders of the inadequacies of the body of medical knowledge.

The body of knowledge can be inadequate in another way. Instead of failing to diagnose or identify the reality, it can wrongly identify the reality. Misdiagnosis of a disease may lead to the application of a treatment that will be useless or worse. Misdiagnosis can occur in many social situations as well. The important point here is that there must be an epistemological match between the body of knowledge and the information need. If this does not occur, misdiagnosis or incorrect interpretation may occur.

In diagnosis and identification, the expert informant places a label on the unidentified object. If the individual has encountered the label in the past and has the label in his or her semantic store, the act of labeling the unidentified object activates the existing semantic knowledge and completes the process of answering the question. One can imagine, for example, someone who has heard of a particular species of bird, but has never seen an example of that species. Seeing one for the first time, in the presence of an expert informant, such a person may ask "What kind of bird is that?" This question is typical of the kinds of questions associated with failures of perception. The expert responds with a label: "That's a pileated woodpecker." The individual may respond "Oh, that's what they look like. I've never seen one before." This example introduces the idea of a label: a word that serves as a short form of identification for a knowledge structure. Being able to attach a label to a previously unidentified reality is the first step in gaining knowledge of that reality. A knowledge structure exists and it is associated with the reality. The next step, of course, is to fill in the details of that knowledge structure; this is dealt with in the next section, where the task of expressing an information need for slot filling is considered.

Another instance in which a label may activate existing elements in one's semantic store is the case of a descriptive label. My parents had an odd piece of ironmongery, consisting of a handle, several gears, and projections, that held (for most people) no identifiable purpose. It was something of a family game to present this apparatus to guests and have them guess what it might be. The answer was that it was an apple peeler. Once that label was given, the purpose of the various parts could be discerned, and the apparatus' function was clear. This understanding occurred even though people had never heard of the existence of such a piece of equipment. The fact that they knew what apples were and what a peeler might do was enough to construct a new element in their semantic store and to associate it with a particular object. The process of building a new semantic element from pre-existing knowledge is not, however, without difficulties. There are labels that appear to be of the descriptive sort just described, but are in fact quite different. In certain parts of the country, for example, a euphemistic label for a beer bottle opener is a "church key." Someone who hears such a label can, arguably, be misled.

Usually labels are not a great deal of help, so the second step in meeting this type of information need is to define the object: to translate the label into language that the person asking the question will understand. In response to a "What was that?" question, an expert may respond with a label that is not in the semantic store of the questioner, either as a single element or as several component elements. In the example of indigenous people encountering European weaponry for the first time, it is conceivable that it would not be very helpful to learn that the weapon in question was a matchlock. In fact, people from more contemporary cultures may find that their semantic store lacked the element matchlock. Upon being given this notably unenlightening piece of verbiage by the expert informant, the questioner may well respond (irritably), "That's very nice. But what the devil is a matchlock?"

The task of definition must link the existing semantic store with the new element. It is a weapon, it is lethal, and it kills from a great distance. All of these elements can be associated with other elements in the semantic store: other weapons, other lethal things, and other things that act at a distance. This task of creating an elaborated network of links between knowledge elements is part of the learning process. In this sense, the expert informant becomes a teacher who facilitates the learning process. The process of definition is continued until there is a satisfactory understanding. In other words, it continues until a network of associative links ties the new experience into the knowledge gained from previous experiences.

The preceding analysis allows the characterization of this information task in terms of the resources that it uses. To express an information need in a failure-of-perception situation, questioners employ first of all their knowledge of the world. This knowledge, however, is quite limited. It may contain only a description that something went wrong or that something is eating the potato plants. In the case of an automobile accident, this knowledge may consist of a confused account of what was happening before and during the event. As the examples given in this section make clear, limited knowledge of the situation that gives rise to the information need is a hallmark of this type of information-need expression.

Three other types of knowledge are important to the selection of an informant: knowledge of a language, knowledge of what informants know about the situation in which the questioner is found, and knowledge of social constraints. Because of the minimally verbal nature of information-need expression, there is usually no concern that an expert informant will not understand the question. In such cases, knowledge of a specific sublanguage is important to the understanding of the response from the expert. As indicated previously, there may be a need for the technical labels attached to the unidentified reality to be translated into the language of the questioner. This act of translation involves linking to the questioner's existing linguistic knowledge.

Knowledge of what informants know about the pragmatic situation in which the questioner is found can also be crucial in selecting an informant. It may mean, for example, that the gardener will address an expert in the Agriculture Department rather than one in the Biology Department. The expert knowledge may be as great (or greater) in the Biology Department, but it may not address the practical situation of growing potatoes as clearly. Finally, as indicated previously, knowledge of social constraints can be crucial to the expression of this kind of information need.

The kinds of questions and answers that are associated with failures of perception can now be summarized. The questions involve placing the person who has the information need in proximity with an expert and having that person describe to the best of his or her limited abilities what the problem is and what was going on when the problem occurred. The expert informant then draws on a body of knowledge to identify the reality that was not fully perceived, label that reality, and associate that label with existing knowledge in the cognitive structures of the inquirer. Chapter 6 will use the implications of this analysis for the design of information systems, services, and institutions. For the moment, the reader may wish to reflect on how little this type of question-and-answer situation resembles those normally found in data-driven information systems.

Expressing Needs for Slot Filling and Alternative Identification

The more an individual knows, that is to say, the more complete his or her knowledge structures are, the more semantic content can be included in the statement of information need. In instances of the second type of information need, in which individuals experience a failure, not of perception, but of slot filling, the first knowledge resource that is important to the task of information-need expression (knowledge of the world in which the information need occurs) is more in evidence than it was in the case of a failure of perception. People with this kind of information need have more knowledge of the situation that gives rise to their need. This knowledge is, however, incomplete and may not contain enough detail to allow the user to ascertain the alternative ways of behaving that are possible in the situation.

The expression of information need may well consist of a label. The user knows enough to label the situation that gives rise to the information need, but that may be all the user knows. Alternatively, the user may have an understanding of the situation that is partial and can include in the statement of information need not only a label, but an account of what is already known. Therefore, the basic format of questions used to express needs for information that will fill in the empty slots in the user's knowledge structures is "What can you tell me about X?" Sometimes the question may be phrased "What can you tell me about X that I don't already know? What I know is . . . ."

Answers to this type of question seem relatively straightforward. The informant begins to relate details that are associated with the label in question. There is, however, a potential problem. As the informant recounts the details, there will be ideas that are not understood by the questioner. In an interactive conversational setting, these will give rise to interruptions from the questioner, usually phrased in terms like "What's that?" or "Stop, I didn't understand what you just said." These situations, embedded in a slot-filling or alternative-identification process, are easily recognized as examples of failures of perception. In each case, the question-and-answer process outlined previously will be invoked to inform the user sufficiently so that understanding is achieved. There is, accordingly, a probability that there will be an oscillation back and forth between slot filling and failures of perception during the answer.

Another aspect of answers to these kinds of questions is that they may provide new associative links between existing knowledge structures. An individual may present a label and ask for more information about the reality represented by that label. During the course of the answer, the user may recognize that the situation he or she is trying to understand resembles situations previously encountered. However, that resemblance has not been understood, because there was no association between the two situations. During the course of understanding the answer, the user may come to realize that the situation was already well understood, if only the associative links had been in place. This crucial building of associative links can influence the way the informant proceeds. It is possible, for example, to encounter information question-and-answer dialogues with the following form:

> Q: What can you tell me about eating in a Japanese restaurant?
> A: Well, have you ever eaten in a Chinese restaurant?
> Q: Sure.
> A: Well, it's like that, only . . .

The informant is basing the response on an existing knowledge structure, linking the needed information to that previous experience and then elaborating the nature of the associative links. The question explicitly or implicitly presents a need for information that is in sufficient depth, but not too great depth. The function of slot filling and alternative identification provides a framework for problem solving without actually solving the problem. The framework identifies the nature of the problem, suggests some of its ramifications and extent, and provides basic semantic and procedural knowledge that can be used and reused in similar problem situations. At this stage, however, the detailed evaluation of all of the alternatives need not be accomplished. Rather, some of the alternatives identified will be ignored, some of the semantic knowledge will be stored but not used or explored in greater detail and some of the procedures will be considered inappropriate. Having enough information to consider the problem intelligently without necessarily getting into the detailed solution of the problem is the objective here. In an information-seeking dialog, the user may turn off or may interrupt the informant if the answer is in too great detail.

The rest of the resources that allow users to accomplish the task of expressing an information need of this type are equally important. The linguistic knowledge implied by the preceding description of slot-filling questions is reasonably limited. The fact that an individual can ask a question with a label or some similar piece of technical language may lead the informant to respond with more details than the user's language abilities can handle. Hence, the respondent may provoke failures of perception as described previously. Again, an illustration may help to clarify this point. Sometimes a traveler in a foreign country will memorize a question in the language of that country. Expressing this question with a reasonable accent may lead a native of the country to respond with a raft of verbiage that the tourist has no hope of understanding. It may be better to stick to gestures and broken language than to give the respondent the idea that one really understands the foreign language. This phenomenon is also true in the case of slot-filling information needs. Having one or two bits of knowledge that can be expressed in the sublanguage of the special topic area may indicate to the informant that detailed information in that special topic area will be understood easily. Of course, this may lead to a failure of communication. It seems reasonably important not only to provide the label or the one or two bits of technical knowledge one possesses, but also to draft the statement of information need in such a way as to indicate one's limitations in the use of the sublanguage of the field.

As in the case of failures of perception, the shared pragmatic knowledge of the situation that gives rise to the information need is important in slot filling and alternative identification. The previous discussion typifies questions that express these information needs by the question "What can you tell me about X?" Of course, this kind of question must be contextualized in a particular life situation that the informant understands. Otherwise, the informant's response may be of limited relevance to the situation that engenders the information need. Health information needs provide good illustrations. The information that will be relevant to a questioner who asks "What can you tell me about breast cancer?" will differ depending on the state of the illness. Information needed at the stage of prevention will be different from information needed during selection of treatment. Similarly, the information that is relevant to the question depends on the status of the questioner: patient, family member, or caregiver. The point of this discussion is that users may select their information source and express their information needs differently, depending on their knowledge of what the informant knows about the questioner's life situation.

Once again, a knowledge of social constraints will affect how the question is asked. The situation here is not very different from the case of statements of need attendant upon failures of perception, but certain informants will be more highly authorized than others in answering information questions. In particular, their level of topic knowledge and understanding of the pragmatic situation that gives rise to the information need may lead people to address their information needs to one informant rather than another. This phenomenon is discussed in more detail in the following section.

Expressing Needs for Evaluation of Alternatives

Finally, if the existing knowledge of the user is sufficient to identify alternatives, the search for consequences of these alternatives can proceed. In such a situation, there will be a great deal of existing knowledge that can be used to elaborate the statement of information need. Each alternative may have its own set of vocabulary, which can be added into the description of the information need by the searcher. At this stage, the problem may not be the lack of semantic content, but rather the selection of appropriate contents for the statement of information need from an abundant store of semantic memory.

It is also true that there will be a highly elaborated and interlinked set of knowledge structures that lies behind the statement of information need at this point and that may get built into the statement of need. Some of these associations may be part of the general knowledge base. For example, causal linkages between events or taxonomic relationships between different species of animal are likely to be shared by all members of a linguistic group. However, there are other forms of links that are individual. I tend to associate the statistical techniques involved in handling large and sparse matrices with studies of demographic mobility, because I first encountered these techniques in those studies. For other researchers, this association would be less obvious. What this means is that questions associated with this type of information need are complex and problematic, not because the questioner has too little information to pose an appropriate question, but because the questioner may have a great deal of information, some of it rather idiosyncratic in nature.

Accordingly, the knowledge of the world that a questioner brings to the task of formulating a statement of need at the point of alternative selection may be quite thorough. Similarly, the knowledge of language may be at a high level. Consideration of the knowledge of what the informant knows leads to conclusions similar to those discussed previously. In the specific pragmatic situation in which people find themselves when they are trying to evaluate and select an alternative, they may need a different kind of information than the survey of details required for slot filling and alternative identification. Chapter 3 discusses the association of actions and consequences that gives the basis for the evaluation of alternatives. This kind of association requires reasonably detailed accounts of individuals who have been in similar problem situations, selected particular alternatives, and recorded the consequences of that selection.

The question that is likely to be posed here is quite a complex one. It may take the form, "This is my problem situation. I know quite a bit about it already [followed by a summary or enumeration of what is known]. What's the best thing for me to do? What might happen if I did X?" In response to this question, an informant may well respond by saying that people tend to find X a suitable alternative or that, in several instances, X proved a disastrous choice. One can imagine a rather detailed conversation in which the various alternatives are discussed in detail. However, it should be noted that the informant needs a broad understanding of the pragmatic situation, as well as a highly developed expertise in the topic area, to be able to engage in this kind of conversation. Accordingly, knowledge of what the informant knows can be crucial in formulating this kind of information-need expression. The selection of an informant may be quite constrained, because of the high level of expertise required, and accordingly, the expression of the information need may be highly constrained.

The social constraints on informant selection and form of expression are as real in this kind of information need as in the ones discussed previously, and no further elaboration is necessary at this point. The reader may wish to think about how an information system may respond cooperatively and helpfully to this kind of question. It is also possible to reflect on how poorly data-centered information systems can respond to statements of need of this type.

Informant Selection and Statements of Need

The third resource that is used to complete the task of expressing an information need is a knowledge of what the informant knows. Although the previous discussion of the expression of different information needs provides an opportunity to consider some of the details of this resource, a more detailed analysis of how informant selection can influence the nature of the information-need statement follows.

Galambos and Black (1985) emphasize that the information source can only understand and respond to the information need if there is a substantial basis of commonality between the information searcher and the information system. It follows that the same information need will be expressed differently to different informants. If the informant is seen as having a great deal of understanding of a particular body of knowledge, then the information seeker will be justified in presenting the information need in terms likely to be understood by the source. On the other hand, if the information seeker does not have a particularly good grasp of the topic, he or she may approach a truly expert informant with a certain amount of trepidation. This caution may be carried into the information interaction, with the user expressing the information need carefully and frequently interrupting the informant for clarification and explanation.

It is also true that the perception of the information seeker about the informant may be inaccurate, thus leading to a failure of communication. Someone addressing a source perceived as being particularly knowledgeable may use language that will be incomprehensible to a less knowledgeable informant. Accordingly, perceptions of the nature of informants have a filtering effect on the expression of information needs.

To frame a statement of information need, a user must select the information system or service, extract as much of his or her semantic knowledge as possible (or as much as is indicated by the social situation), edit that semantic knowledge in such a way as to conform with the expectations or perceived expectations of the information system, and then make contact. Selection of the source is the first step. If an information service has been particularly good in the past at responding to certain types of questions, a searcher for information will likely draw on memory and return to the source. However, the effect of past experience may go even further in dictating the perception and selection of an information source. If a source has been particularly helpful, seekers for information may consciously or unconsciously change their perception of the nature of their information need or problem situation to conform to the purpose or expectations of that information source. Suppose, for example, that an individual has two colleagues: a chemist and a biologist. The individual finds that the chemist is always ready to chat and has a wealth of information about research in areas of mutual interest. On the other hand, the biologist seems a taciturn individual, with a limited range of expertise in areas of mutual interest. Now a question comes up in the area of biochemistry. The individual can, theoretically, consult either colleague. However, because of past experience, the problem may be expressed, and may even be seen by the individual who needs the information, as a chemistry problem rather than a biology problem. Past experience and expectations have filtered the understanding and expression of the information need.

Sometimes past experience may be encapsulated and generalized into procedures or scripts. Procedure development happens with frequently occurring functions that entail a number of steps. A knowledge structure develops that essentially gives the steps in the order in which they are to be accomplished. Such procedures may also have a heuristic function, suggesting that if A fails, B should be tried. Again, there are both positive and (potentially) negative aspects that arise from procedures and scripts. Of course they make life much simpler. There is an established mechanism for dealing with different situations. On the other hand, they are so convenient that it may be unlikely that they will be abandoned in favor of newer, more efficient, or more effective procedures. In the domain of information seeking, this may mean that a searcher for information will address himself or herself to a particular information source as a matter of procedure, rather than because that source matches the information need particularly well.

The possibility exists that an individual may ignore a variety of potentially useful information sources to seek out the one recommended by a rule generalized from memory of past success. One can imagine a situation in which someone always looks in a particular handbook for facts of a particular nature, such as the *Handbook of Chemistry and Physics* for physical and chemical constants. A question regarding a mathematical formula comes up, and the searcher immediately turns to the *Handbook* for the answer. Now the searcher may in fact find the appropriate formula in that source, but it may be a great deal easier to find that information in another more appropriate tool.

It is by no means clear that users will have the necessary knowledge structures to identify the best (the nearest, the most useful, the cheapest) information source. A kind of secondary information need can develop: that of obtaining appropriate knowledge structures to identify potential information sources. This example shows how one statement of information need can spawn other statements of information need. In this case, the "Who can I ask?" question is important, because its answer will open up not only a series of possible information sources, but also a series of possible formulations of the information-need expression.

Having identified a potential source of information, the user now is in a position to express the information need. However, the user's perception or model of the information source is likely to affect the expression of that need. For example, asking a human source for information may involve a discursive expression of the need. Using a reference tool or bibliographic service may involve a terse, subject-heading-like expression. It is clear that users who approach a reference librarian are more likely to express themselves in terms that they believe the librarian will understand, asking for books on a specific topic.

In essence, what is involved at this stage is a reperception of the information need. As soon as a source is considered, the linguistic structures embodied in the source (i.e., its social status or its stated linguistic preferences) present an alternative knowledge structure for the expression of the information need. As one considers a variety of alternative information sources, one is in effect considering a variety of alternative expressions of the information need.

It seems that the decision to make contact with a particular source involves a set of high-level knowledge structures. A situation can be conceptualized in which a user is comparing an initial understanding of a problematic life situation with a set of alternative expressions of that understanding. Is the expression that is closest to the original most likely to be chosen? Or is the expression that is closest to some previously resolved situation likely to be chosen? At this point, a user can choose from a variety of possible universes the one in which he or she wants to live. Once the decision is made, the information need will be expressed to the selected source in the language associated with that source.

There is also a social dimension. Social constraints may dictate ways in which information needs are expressed. A formal information system or service may require, either as a matter of policy or etiquette, that the information need be expressed in a particular formal manner. On the other hand, an informal informant, such as a friend, colleague, or family member, may be likely to be addressed in a much more colloquial manner.

It is in this context that the model of Sitter and Stein (1992) may be of some interest. They note that questions can be asked in a number of ways: directives, questions, and assertions, for example. Questions can also be answered in a variety of ways: questions, answers, offers, or statements of evaluation, for example. The objective of this research, which models the illocutionary aspects of information seeking, was to compile a grammar of all possible dialogs between an information seeker and an information provider. A related point is made by Pomerantz (1988), in an analysis of the manner in which people sometimes ask questions that present a candidate answer, so as to reveal the questioner's attitudes or expectations. The many ways of asking questions have also been incorporated into an automated system (Golding, Graesser, & Millis, 1990; Graesser & Franklin, 1990; Graesser & Hemphill, 1991) that can analyze questions and specify information sources that should furnish answers. Weijts, Widdershoven, Kok, and Tomlow (1993), in a study of how patients ask their physicians for information during gynecological consultations, found that most of the questions concerning the nature or procedure of treatment are formulated in a straightforward manner. However, questions about what may have caused the medical problem are approached through indirect questions. This example indicates that there may be social or personal constraints that influence how patients ask for information.

The social influences that govern the nature and extent of question answering seem particularly strong. Tabak (1988) reports that some patients waiting to see a physician were given a booklet that encouraged them to ask questions, while others were given a booklet that was neutral on question answering. The booklet had no effect on the number of questions patients asked. Simple treatments of this nature seem ineffective in altering strongly conditioned behaviors. Other research has demonstrated how individual variables interact with social variables in question asking. Wallen, Waitzkin, and Stoeckle (1979) analyzed taped recordings of patient–physician interviews and conclude that although women ask more questions than men, they receive the same amount of explanation as men. Allwinn (1991) explored the interrelationship between social factors and knowledge factors in question formulation, and found that knowledge variables led to the selection of form of question (open or closed), but that social variables influenced both the form of the question and the politeness with which it was posed.

The Social Nature of Statements of Information Need

The fourth resource identified previously that is used in generating statements of information need is knowledge of what is appropriate in different social situations; i.e., the social constraints and authorizations that lead people to select certain informants and phrase their questions in certain ways. This resource deserves some additional attention.

Asking a certain question in a specific situation may be considered bad form. It is generally considered gauche to ask professionals for their advice and opinions during social occasions. Similarly, going to a public library information desk and asking about what went wrong in your marriage relationship may be inappropriate, not to mention unfulfilling. Not only is there a time and place for each of the various statements of information need, there is also a need to edit or revise the statement depending on the informant. Social knowledge can authorize certain forms of expression in certain social situations and so is important in how statements of need are expressed. This social knowledge may arise from a number of social contexts. There may, for example, be different forms of expression that are associated with work situations or with social situations. This social knowledge leads to a selection from the many different ways that people may have of asking a question. Some organizations, for example, have their own specialized language. Most professions and occupations have their own jargon. If individuals are working within the social context established by an organization or occupation, they are constrained in the vocabulary they can use in expressing their information needs.

Another area of social influence on information-need expression is that of cultural constraint. It is well understood in psychological research, for example, that individual traits of personality or belief system are filtered and mediated by cultural differences. This filtering makes cross-cultural communication particularly problematic (Adler & Gielen, 1994). Being embedded in a particular culture may place constraints on the language forms people can use to express their information needs. If the informant is from a different culture, there may be an incompatibility in forms of expression that will make the information interaction strained or perhaps unproductive. Cultural differences need not be limited to ethnic differences. Giles, Coupland, Coupland, Williams, and Nussbaum (1992) show how cross-cultural communication models help explain the communication barriers between older and younger individuals. Here, as in communication across ethnic boundaries, stereotypes and prejudices can be activated in communication, resulting in reduced openness to messages. This reduced openness may constrain the information-need expression to the point that the information interaction is no longer cooperative.

This examination of the factors that influence the expression of individual information needs has demonstrated how complex this task really is. The task of user-centered information-system design is to facilitate the completion of the task by making use of the resources that users bring to the task and by supplementing these resources when necessary. There is, however, an additional factor that complicates how a user's knowledge resources are employed in expressing an information need: the presence of a human intermediary as part of the information system and the role that such an intermediary plays in expressing information needs.

Intermediaries and Need Expressions

The role of the information intermediary in facilitating the resolution of information needs is a complex one. In the first case, the interaction with the user must lead to some shared understanding of the information need. This shared knowledge involves an understanding on the part of the intermediary of the user's life situation, the understanding of that situation that has been reached by the user, and the knowledge structures that have been instrumental in generating the statement of need. In coming to this understanding of the user, the intermediary employs knowledge structures.

One of the functions of this shared understanding is a translation of the information need into other terms. This translation serves a variety of purposes. Sometimes, translation or reexpression of the information need can have a direct role in resolving the information need. In other cases, the translation is a necessary step in the use of a variety of information sources. In the most general case, the intermediary's own linguistic structures are by definition different from those of the user, and the translation or redefinition simply enables the intermediary to participate meaningfully in the information search.

It may be useful to examine the contribution of the intermediary in terms of perception, identification of alternatives, and selection of alternatives. Intermediaries may bring to the information interaction knowledge that will influence how users perceive their information need and the problem situation from which that need arises. It is also possible that the specialized knowledge possessed by intermediaries may suggest different alternatives for resolving the problem situation. Finally, the experience of a human intermediary in dealing with information problems may bring about a reevaluation of alternatives on the part of the user.

It is possible through interaction between the user and the intermediary to elicit information that was not selected by the user for input to the statement of information need. This additional detail can be important in elucidating and clarifying the knowledge that the user has of the problem situation. It is sufficient to note that, as an individual interacts with an intermediary, the linguistic structures that lead to the expression of a statement of information need may change yet again.

Group Expressions of Information Need

The discussion thus far has focused on expressions of individual information needs. It now turns to a consideration of groups with information needs and how these are likely to be expressed. The crucial question to be resolved here is whether the expression of group information needs can be accounted for and explained by taking into account the statements of information need of the individual members of the group. In other words, it must be ascertained whether the group statement of information need can be adequately understood by summing all individual expressions of need of the group members.

The analysis begins with an examination of these individual expressions of need. In a group situation, two types of questions and answers can be distinguished. The first occurs when one member of the group asks another member of the group for information, and the second occurs when one member of the group asks an outside source for information.

There has been a substantial body of research that examines within-group exchanges of information. In studies of group learning in education and investigations of group problem solving and decision making in business, a great deal of emphasis has been placed on internal statements of information need. For example, Moreland and Levine (1992) identify the internal communication that occurs as groups build a consensus about a problem. Stasser (1992) analyzed the extent to which group members share information and found that there is a great deal of individual knowledge that does not get shared in a group problem-solving situation. Webb (1992) surveys a large body of research into the group learning process, with special attention to how students who are learning together seek help from each other. Similarly, Berlin and Jeffries (1992) focus on how consultants can share information with apprentices within the same group using specific communication technology. Olson, Olson, Carter, and Storrosten (1992) analyze small group meetings and find that about 40% of the time was spent on the actual task in hand. The remainder of the time is split between taking stock of progress and coordinating group activities. They also find that groups clearly follow the standard problem-solving approach in stating issues, identifying alternatives, and evolving criteria for judging alternatives.

The development of within-group statements of information need is aided by the development of specialized versions of the four resources discussed previously. These are:

- knowledge of the world in which the information need occurs,
- knowledge of a language,
- knowledge of what informants may know, and
- knowledge of what is appropriate in different social situations.

Groups working together on a problem, making a decision, or learning about a topic area are likely to have a reasonably detailed knowledge of the world situation that gives rise to the information need. In fact, as noted in Chapter 3, there can be a shared cognition developed within the group that defines the problem situation or the objective of the group's activities. In such situations, within-group communication may not need to rely on the question-and-answer process. Because there is a collective understanding of the problem situation, the group communication process can be seen as one of continually updating and revising that collective understanding. Krauss and Fussell (1990) describe how this mutual knowledge is developed and how it influences within-group communication. Wellens (1993) emphasizes that developing a group situation awareness requires concerted effort. Information is important in developing this awareness, but quality of information is more important than quantity of information. In other words, the creation of a collective understanding is something that requires a great deal of human effort and is one in which the information technology itself is of limited assistance.

Cannon-Bowers, Salas, and Converse (1993) describe the shared mental models used in group decision making and assess both their positive and negative aspects. Of course, a collective understanding of the task is crucial to within-group communication, but at the same time, the shared mental model can act to prevent group members from coming to grips with other perspectives on the problem they are facing. Superimposed on the collective understanding of the group's task is an understanding that group members have of each other. As Chen, Lynch, Himler, and Goodman (1992) found, a common knowledge of hot topics being considered by the group is augmented by knowledge of the special expertise of group members. Therefore, the knowledge of the task held in common can be augmented by knowledge of the individual expertise and contributions of group members.

This collective knowledge of the world situation can give rise to a common specialized language. In fact, Winograd (1988) suggests that cooperative or collective work must always have a linguistic side and that a common language is the basis for a common understanding and collective work. As Tushman and Katz (1980) point out, within-group communication in some groups depends on locally shared semantic knowledge that defines, labels, and organizes the complex reality that is the focus of the group's activities. The nature of the work that the group is doing is crucial in determining whether a specialized group language will develop. In the results reported by Tushman and Katz (1980), it is clear that groups that are working on locally defined projects (e.g., development projects) are likely to develop these specialized languages, and groups that are working on universally defined projects (e.g., research projects) are less likely to develop specialized languages. This result means that researchers, using a more general scientific language, do not have access to a sublanguage that is specific to the group. Specialized internal sublanguages are a valuable resource for aiding within-group communication, such as expressing information needs between group members.

The third resource that is employed in expressing information needs is knowledge of what informants know about the problem situation. Because informants are also members of the group, a common understanding of the situation is assumed. In other words, informant selection is less likely to relate to what the informant knows and more likely to relate to social constraints that are local in nature. These social constraints come out of the internal dynamics of the group and may include the development of subgroups, leader–follower relationships, and so on. The internal politics of groups is no less complex than the patterns of interaction that are authorized and conventionalized in social settings. However, because the group is relatively smaller than society as a whole, the social constraints that govern expressions of information needs in the group may be more easily understood and are less likely to provide barriers to need expressions.

When the resources required to complete the task of within-group expression of information needs are compared with those required by individuals to express their needs in more general information settings, it appears that the resources required for within-group expression of needs are more specialized. The group may have a collective world knowledge, a specially developed internal language, and enhanced knowledge of what each member knows about the problem situation. In addition, the social constraints, while every bit as real as those involved in individual question-and-answer situations, depend on the internal dynamics of the group. It seems likely that this combination of specialized resources will tend to allow enhanced communication of information within the group. In other words, the task of expressing information needs will be somewhat easier than in more general information-need situations.

There are also situations in which group members express information needs to outside informants. One way this process occurs is through boundary-spanning individuals who have the ability to obtain external information and translate it into terms that will fit into the group's specialized understanding of the problem situation and into the group's specialized sublanguage. This ability usually arises from a gatekeeper role, in which an individual has strong connections both internally (within the group) and externally (to some other group or external information resource). Tushman and Katz (1980) distinguish this gatekeeper role from boundary spanning more generally; this role can include individuals who serve representational roles and who are not effective or highly used information resources. Similarly, Friedman and Podolny (1992) differentiate gatekeeping from three other types of boundary-spanning activities in the context of labor negotiations. This research also indicates that the role of gatekeeper may be more complex than simply going outside the group, finding the information, and translating it into the group's special terms. In some instances, gatekeepers may introduce group members to outside resources or broker contacts between outsiders and group members and so help group members engage in information seeking outside the group. In this sense, the gatekeeper role has some of the attributes of the intermediary role discussed previously. Newell and Clark (1990) examine one particular source of external information that may be used by gatekeepers: professional associations. There seems to be a relationship between the involvement of group members in these associations and the innovativeness of the group, implying that information about new technological developments obtained from the professional associations is incorporated into the group's understanding of its task and focus. Similarly, Galaskiewicz and Wasserman (1989) show how contacts outside the organization not only facilitate information transfer, but also help managers make decisions on how to deal with uncertainty. Their evidence suggests that managers will mimic other managers or other influential individuals whom they have encountered through boundary-spanning activities.

The gatekeeper role, within the larger context of research into boundary-spanning activities, has been researched in some detail. Friedkin (1982) found that boundary-spanning individuals tend to have weaker ties to members of their own group than the group members without boundary-spanning roles. This research suggests that a group composed of people with both strong and weak within-group ties will produce the best information flow. Strong ties will make for good internal communication, while weak ties will be associated with boundary spanning. In addition, it is clear that the nature of the work being done makes gatekeeping more or less important (Tushman & Katz, 1980). If the group does not develop a specialized language (as in the case of researchers who employ the language of their science), then gatekeepers can actually impede the performance of the group. It will be more effective for all members of the group to communicate with external informants in such cases. Second, the relationship of the group to its environment seems crucial in determining whether gatekeepers will be needed or be effective. High levels of interdependence between the group and its environment, coupled with high levels of uncertainty in the environment, tend to lead to an increase in boundary spanning (At Twaijri & Montanari, 1987). In a related discussion, Clark, Varadarajan, and Pride (1994) note that organizations that seek not only to obtain information from, but to have an effect on their external environment are more likely to engage in boundary-spanning activities. This effect of the organization on the environment can be reciprocated, sometimes to the detriment of the organization. While it is clear that boundary spanning allows organizations to influence their political environment, it is also true that boundary spanning can open the organization or group to outside control. Finet (1993) provides a case study of one organization in which the political power obtained by a boundary-spanning subordinate through interaction with outside agencies was sufficient to counteract the direction taken by the management of the organization. Finally, this analysis of the social influences on gatekeeping can note the study reported by Shrum (1990). This work suggests that boundary-spanning activities are influenced by social status. If the boundary-spanning individual has less status than his or her outside contacts or if the social signals are mixed, the information exchange may be less effective.

The personal characteristics of group members can also have an impact on the use and effectiveness of gatekeepers. Dailey (1979) investigated personality characteristics as well as group and task characteristics and found that all three are important in determining the effectiveness of boundary-spanning activities. Of the individual characteristics studied, locus of control is found to be significantly associated with boundary-spanning activities.

The four resources examined in this chapter remain important for the communication task in which group members ask outside informants for help. These resources are used by gatekeepers or by other group members, although the majority of the research has focused on gatekeepers. First, those who are expressing information needs must have an understanding of the problem situation facing the group. This understanding is developed collectively, so the task of formulating the statement of need implies participation in the collective cognition of the problem or topic being addressed by the group. Second, those who are expressing information needs must have an understanding of a language. If the group has developed its own specialized sublanguage, then the questioner must actually know two languages: the language of the group and the language of the external source. In other situations, the two languages will be identical and there will be no barrier to be overcome by the use of a gatekeeper. There remains one important function for the gatekeeper, however, even if the group does not use a specialized language. This is the social function of intermediary, which relates directly to the two final resources: knowledge of what informants know and knowledge of the social constraints on asking for information. The gatekeeper, as an active member of the outside group that contains informants, can serve to direct the information-seeking group through his or her knowledge of the informing group.

It is now possible to summarize the understanding of group expressions of information needs. The resources used to complete this task are identical to those used to express individual information needs. There are, however, two versions of this information task: the internal and the external statements of information need. In the case of internal expressions, the dynamics of the group, its collective understanding of the task being accomplished, and its specialized language may make it easier to express information needs than it would be in the case of individual needs. In external statements of need, the resources in question may be concentrated in individuals who act as gatekeepers. Because the role and function of gatekeepers differ depending on group task, group environment, and individual characteristics, these variables can affect the external information-need expression task, thus adding complexity to the way the task is accomplished.

The emphasis in this chapter has been on the resources that individuals and groups employ as they complete the task of expressing an information need. These knowledge resources are, of course, available in varying degrees to the people who make up the user population of any information system. It remains to be seen how this understanding of both individual and group information-need expression can inform the process of user-based information-system design. That is the topic of the next chapter.

References

Adler, L. L., & Gielen, U. P. (Eds.) (1994). *Cross-cultural topics in psychology*. Westport, CT: Praeger.

Allwinn, S. (1991). Seeking information: Contextual influences on question formation. *Journal of Language and Social Psychology, 10*(3), 169–183.

At Twaijri, M. I., & Montanari, J. R. (1987). The impact of context and choice on the boundary spanning process: An empirical extension. *Human Relations, 40*(12), 783–797.

Berlin, L. M., & Jeffries, R. (1992). Consultants and apprentices: Observations about learning and collaborative problem solving. In J. Turner & R. Kraut (Eds.), *CSCW '92: Sharing perspectives: Proceedings of the conference on computer-supported cooperative work* (pp. 130–137). New York: ACM.

Cannon-Bowers, J. A., Salas, E., & Converse, S. (1993). Shared mental models in expert team decision making. In N. J. J. Castellan (Ed.), *Individual and group decision making: Current issues* (pp. 221–246). Hillsdale, NJ: Lawrence Erlbaum.

Chen, H., Lynch, K. J., Himler, A. K., & Goodman, S. E. (1992). Information management in research collaboration. *International Journal of Man Machine Studies, 36*(3), 419–445.

Clark, T., Varadarajan, P. R., & Pride, W. M. (1994). Environmental management: The construct and research propositions. *Journal of Business Research, 29*(1), 23–38.

Dailey, R. C. (1979). Group, task, and personality correlates of boundary spanning activities. *Human Relations, 32*(4), 273–285.

Finet, D. (1993). Effects of boundary spanning communication on the sociopolitical delegitimation of an organization. *Management Communication Quarterly, 7*(1), 36–66.

Friedkin, N. E. (1982). Information flow through strong and weak ties in intraorganizational social networks. *Social Networks, 3*(4), 273–285.

Friedman, R. A., & Podolny, J. (1992). Differentiation of boundary spanning roles: Labor negotiations and implications for role conflict. *Administrative Science Quarterly, 37*(1), 28–47.

Galambos, J. A., & Black, J. B. (1985). Using knowledge of activities to understand and answer questions. In A. C. Graesser & J. B. Black (Eds.), *The psychology of questions* (pp. 157–189). Hillsdale, NJ: Lawrence Erlbaum.

Galaskiewicz, J., & Wasserman, S. (1989). Mimetic processes within an interorganizational field: An empirical test. *Administrative Science Quarterly, 34*(3), 454–479.

Giles, H., Coupland, N., Coupland, J., Williams, A., & Nussbaum, J. (1992). Intergenerational talk and communication with older people. *International Journal of Aging and Human Development, 34*(4), 271–297.

Golding, J. M., Graesser, A. C., & Millis, K. K. (1990). What makes a good answer to a question? Testing a psychological model of question answering in the context of narrative text. *Discourse Processes*, *13*(3), 305–325.

Graesser, A. C., & Franklin, S. P. (1990). QUEST: A cognitive model of question answering and question asking. *Discourse Processes*, *13*(3), 279–303.

Graesser, A. C., & Hemphill, D. (1991). Question answering in the context of scientific mechanisms. *Journal of Memory and Language*, *30*(2), 186–209.

Kaplan, J. (1983). Cooperative responses from a portable natural language data base query system. In M. Brady & R. C. Berwick (Eds.), *Computational models of discourse*. Cambridge, MA: MIT Press.

Krauss, R. M., & Fussell, S. R. (1990). Mutual knowledge and communicative effectiveness. In J. Galegher, R. E. Kraut, & C. Egido (Eds.), *Intellectual teamwork: Social and technological foundations of cooperative work* (pp. 111–145). Hillsdale, NJ: Lawrence Erlbaum.

Moreland, R. L., & Levine, J. M. (1992). Problem identification by groups. In S. Worchel, W. Wood, & J. A. Simpson (Eds.), *Group processes and productivity* (pp. 17–47). Newbury Park, CA: Sage Publications.

Newell, S., & Clark, P. (1990). The importance of extra organizational networks in the diffusion and appropriation of new technologies: The role of professional associations in the United States and Britain. *Knowledge*, *12*(2), 199–212.

Norman, D. A. (1986). Cognitive engineering. In D. A. Norman & S. W. Draper (Eds.), *User centered system design: New perspectives on human–computer interaction* (pp. 31–61). Hillsdale, NJ: Lawrence Erlbaum.

Olson, G. M., Olson, J. S., Carter, M. R., & Storrosten, M. (1992). Small group design meetings: An analysis of collaboration. *Human–Computer Interaction*, *7*(4), 347–374.

Pomerantz, A. (1988). Offering a candidate answer: An information seeking strategy. *Communication Monographs*, *55*(4), 360–373.

Shrum, W. (1990). Status incongruence among boundary spanners: Structure, exchange, and conflict. *American Sociological Review*, *55*(4), 496–511.

Sitter, S., & Stein, A. (1992). Modeling the illocutionary aspects of information seeking dialogues. *Information Processing & Management*, *28*(2), 165–180.

Stasser, G. (1992). Pooling of unshared information during group discussion. In S. Worchel, W. Wood, & J. A. Simpson (Eds.), *Group processes and productivity* (pp. 48–67). Newbury Park, CA: Sage Publications.

Tabak, E. R. (1988). Encouraging patient question asking: A clinical trial. *Patient Education and Counseling*, *12*(1), 37–49.

Tushman, M. L., & Katz, R. (1980). External communication and project performance: An investigation into the role of gatekeepers. *Management Science*, *26*(11), 1071–1085.

Wallen, J., Waitzkin, H., & Stoeckle, J. D. (1979). Physician stereotypes about female health and illness: A study of patient's sex and the informative process during medical interviews. *Women and Health*, *4*(2), 135–146.

Webb, N. M. (1992). Testing a theoretical model of student interaction and learning in small groups. In R. Hertz-Lazarowitz & N. Miller (Eds.), *Interaction in cooperative groups: The theoretical anatomy of group learning* (pp. 102–119). Cambridge, UK: Cambridge University Press.

Weijts, W., Widdershoven, G., Kok, G., & Tomlow, P. (1993). Patients' information seeking actions and physicians' responses in gynecological consultations. *Qualitative Health Research*, *3*(4), 398–429.

Wellens, A. R. (1993). Group situation awareness and distributed decision making: From military to civilian applications. In N. J. J. Castellan (Ed.), *Individual and group decision making: Current issues* (pp. 267–291). Hillsdale, NJ: Lawrence Erlbaum.

Winograd, T. (1988). A language/action perspective on the design of cooperative work. *Human–Computer Interaction*, *3*(1), 3–30.

6

Designing Systems to Meet Expressed Information Needs

Introduction

The task of expressing an information need in a statement of need is examined in Chapter 5. From that analysis, a design principle and a number of implications for information-system design can be drawn, and it may be helpful to enumerate these implications at the beginning of this chapter. Each will be examined in detail, and information-system design decisions will be associated with each implication.

The general design principle derives from the resources used in expressing these needs. These resources are particularly important, because they form the basis of designing for usability. If the extent to which users possess the resources required to complete an information task such as expressing an information need can be determined, designers can create information-system features that will ensure that users have access to appropriate resources to complete their information task. The system provides users with an enabling state, bringing them to the point where they can accomplish information tasks and so meet their information need.

General Design Principle

Information systems must take advantage of the knowledge resources that users possess and augment those resources when necessary.

Specific Design Implications

From the four knowledge resources discussed in the previous chapter, four specific design implications can be drawn.

A. Information systems must take advantage of the knowledge that users possess of the world in which their problem situation arises and where necessary must supplement that knowledge with expertise contained in the system.

B. Information systems must take advantage of the linguistic knowledge that users possess (as it relates to their information needs) and augment that linguistic knowledge when appropriate with knowledge contained in the system.

C. To respond cooperatively and intelligibly to statements of information need, information-systems must share with the users an understanding of the pragmatic situation in which they are found.

D. To respond to statements of information need, information systems must be aware of the social constraints that lead to the selection of informants and formulations of need expressions and be able to assist in resource selection and need expression.

The next set of implications relate to how the four resources are applied in creating statements of the different kinds of information need.

E. An information system that will respond cooperatively and helpfully to a statement of failure of perception will:

- accept minimal semantic expressions of need,
- contain or refer to expert knowledge, and
- be able to define new ideas in such a way as to lead to user understanding.

F. An information system that will respond cooperatively and helpfully to a statement of need relating to alternative identification and slot filling will:

- accept labels or labels with statements of existing knowledge,
- allow systematic exploration of an area of interest, and
- facilitate semantic links en route to full understanding of the area of interest.

G. An information system that will respond cooperatively and helpfully to a statement of need relating to alternative evaluation and selection will:

- accept detailed statements of existing knowledge,
- assemble and summarize information that may help in evaluation, and
- advise users about the alternatives they face.

The final implication derives from the discussion of group or collective information needs.

H. An information system that will respond cooperatively and helpfully to group information needs will:

- facilitate the internal sharing of essential information between group members,
- allow the evolutionary development of the focus of group activities and of the special language that may evolve around that focus,
- facilitate the activities of gatekeepers in importing information to the group, and

- facilitate the activities of gatekeepers in performing an intermediary function to outside information sources.

Designing for World Knowledge

The remainder of this chapter will consider in turn each of these implications for design and begin to sketch some of the details of generic information systems that correspond to these design implications. The first step is a consideration of the knowledge resources that users employ in the task of expressing information needs.

> Information systems must take advantage of the knowledge that users possess of the world in which their problem situation arises and where necessary must supplement that knowledge with expertise contained in the system.

It seems clear from the discussion in Chapter 5 that users create statements of need from a wide range of levels of world knowledge. At one extreme are statements of need that derive from failures of perception, in which knowledge of the situation may be limited to a simple understanding that something (unspecified) has gone wrong. At the other extreme are statements of need that reflect an in-depth knowledge of the situation, fully developed except for a few gaps in information elements that will enable evaluation of alternatives to proceed. Information systems will have to respond differently to users whose statements of information need are based on these different levels of world knowledge. One approach is to design several different types of information system and switch back and forth between them on the basis of user preferences. In the discussion of information-system design that is presented in this chapter, three different information systems are considered, each designed to address the information needs attendant upon failures of perception, identification of alternatives, and evaluation and selection of alternatives.

The design principle being proposed here is that there should be a mechanism for matching statements of information need with informants, based not just on topic, but also on depth of understanding of the situation displayed by the user. If the informants are represented by stored documents, designers may seek to expand traditional indexing of such stored representations by including annotations about the amount of user knowledge presumed by the informant. A serious attempt to deal with this kind of issue, with an appropriate vein of levity, is the series of manuals including *Internet for Dummies* and *Access for Dummies*.

This approach, however, is inadequate. It fails to address the fact that each user's interpretation of the appropriateness of any informant to their state of knowledge may differ. What seems to be required is a multiplicity of assessments of each informant's suitability. These different assessments can be captured by asking each individual who uses a particular informant to state the following: how much does the individual know about his or her problem situation and how does the informant match that level of situation knowledge. This approach, obtaining user input about information resources, is called cumulative user-supplied indexing in this book. It plays an important role in the system-design recommendations provided here, so a brief elaboration of the idea is appropriate. Koenig (1990) introduces this approach in a library context, referring to user-supplied data in library online catalogs.

The first element of this approach is that the descriptions of informants are provided by users. This element is a distinct change from most value-added processes, in which information professionals of various kinds provide the descriptions of informants (or the documents that informants have created). It is also a major change from the approach that generates descriptions of informants or documents as metadata by computer processing of the data itself. The idea is simply that users are best able to comment on the topic covered by an informant, the depth of knowledge displayed by that informant, or the appropriateness of the informant's approach for use in different problem-solving activities. It is recognized that users will not be unanimous about any informant. This is a good thing. Diversity of opinion adds to the richness of the representations that are part of the information system. Of course, such a lack of unity implies that there will be some process to summarize and represent the diversity of opinion about an informant. If opinions are collected using standard techniques of questionnaire design, such as Likert scales with ordinal anchors, there are a variety of statistical techniques (e.g., calculation of median opinions and the use of confidence intervals) that can be used to present diversity of opinion in a coherent manner, so this seems a minor problem.

It is also important to consider the function of the intermediary in bringing users and informants together. Intermediaries, to the extent that they know about the situation in which the user is found, are ideally placed to assess the suitability of informants for users' existing knowledge levels. Intermediaries can use their knowledge of information needs to diagnose the situation that gave rise to the user's information need, and their knowledge of information sources to recommend informants to users.

Designing for Knowledge of a Language

> Information systems must take advantage of the linguistic knowledge that users possess (as it relates to their information needs) and augment that knowledge when appropriate with knowledge contained in the system.

Most information systems produced by data-driven design make use of linguistic structures derived from expert informants to organize information for access. These expert language structures may be opaque to users who generate their statements of information need from less-than-expert perspectives. Further, most information systems do not have the capability to analyze the linguistic structures of users or to attach language elements from users' linguistic structures to the language used by experts. This shortcoming means that the onus is entirely on the user to adapt his or her language to the expert language of the information system.

There is a variety of ways that information systems can extract user language structures during the information interaction. The first is to ask users who have been in contact with an informant to describe in their own terms the area of expertise of that informant. Another approach is to have users describe their information needs in their own terms and then assess how useful informants are to that information need. Either mechanism builds up a set of user linguistic structures and links between these structures and the expert knowledge structures already in place. This linking provides the basis for translation between statements of information need and expert language and thus for enhanced information retrieval. Intermediaries may be able to serve as translators between the language of users and the language of informants by applying their knowledge of both the technical language of expert informants and the ordinary language of information users to the translation function.

The design of usable information systems does not require a complete representation of a user's linguistic knowledge. The complexity of language will in any case prevent a complete representation from being developed. The techniques sketched in this section can provide a limited but adequate understanding of how a user may express an information need or interact with an expert informant. Using this understanding of linguistic structures in information systems has the potential to improve usability.

Designing for Source Selection

> To respond cooperatively and intelligibly to statements of information need, information systems must share with the users an understanding of the pragmatic situation in which they are found.

A bird-watcher, walking along a trail in the Rockies, needs a particular type of informant in his or her backpack: a field guide to birds. This guide is an information resource that is designed specifically to meet the information needs that arise in that particular pragmatic situation. There are, of course, many such information resources that are keyed to specific pragmatic situations: the car repair manual for someone stripping down the engine of a '57 Chevy, the baby-name book for prospective parents, or Cliffs Notes for high school students of English literature.

There is also an indefinitely large number of informants or information resources that are not dedicated to any particular pragmatic situation. It is impossible to predict in advance the extent to which there will be a shared pragmatic knowledge of the information situation between any particular user and any particular informant. The task facing information-system designers is to match the user with an informant whose knowledge of the user's situation is profound and congruent with the user's understanding of the situation. For example, an engineering professor may be preparing for class and may need an example of a certain physical principle. The best possible informant is someone who knows a great deal about that physical principle, but from the perspective of an educator rather than (for example) a researcher. Someone who has prepared lectures on the topic and who has used a variety of examples of the physical principle will be a good informant. Someone who has researched the physical principle extensively, but has never tried to communicate it to a class of undergraduates, will be a less satisfactory informant.

One approach to accomplishing this matching of informant with information seeker, is to describe informants not just by the topic they cover, but also by the perspective or approach they take to the topic. This is, for example, what has been done with some degree of success by the *MLA Bibliography*. In that database, role indicators can be included in descriptor searches. Someone wanting to find informants addressing a particular audience can use the "for (audience)" role indicator. Someone wanting informants who give study examples of a particular approach can use the role indicator "study example." Someone wanting an informant who discusses a particular idea applied to a specific problem area can use the "applied to" role indicator.

As innovative and potentially useful as this approach is, it fails to address the fact that each user's interpretation of the appropriateness of the informant's perspective may differ. Multiple assessments of each informant's suitability can be obtained through cumulative user-supplied indexing. Users can express their understanding of their situation in terms of variables, such as depth of knowledge required or desired approach to the knowledge, and how the informant matches that understanding of the situation. Is the informant knowledgeable enough about the situation? Too knowledgeable? Does the informant address the topic from a useful perspective? Building an evaluative set and matching the evaluations with details from the user model will enable a far more complete matching of user knowledge with informant knowledge.

Intermediaries can provide a supplement to cumulative user-supplied indexing. With their knowledge of the need situation of users and their understanding of the approaches taken by informants, they can act to bring together users and informants in such a way as to facilitate the meeting of information needs. Users can share their experiences with each other, and intermediaries can facilitate the process.

Designing for Social Understanding

To respond to statements of information need, information systems must know about the social constraints that lead to the selection of informants and formulations of need expressions, and be able to assist in resource selection and need expression.

Chapter 5 notes that statements of information need are necessarily selective in the terms they use. One major set of factors that leads users to generate statements using particular terms are the social constraints on selection of informants and formulations of need statements. The discussion of health information needs reveals that some patients will not ask their physicians about certain aspects of their health situation. Rather, they are more likely to ask their friends about those aspects of their health problem. Even when questions are asked of physicians, they are likely to be asked in particular ways. There is a real constraint on the way patients ask questions in the authority-laden nature of the patient–physician relationship. In response to this phenomenon, physicians and other medical practitioners have tried various methods to increase the question asking that occurs in health settings. This recognition of the importance of questioning is exactly analogous to reference librarians conducting a reference interview to elicit more detail about the information needs of their patrons.

Information-system characteristics can reinforce social constraints on asking certain types of questions or asking them in a certain manner. The physical setting of the information encounter (for example, a busy library reference desk) may reinforce social constraints against asking personal or sensitive questions. Alternatively, the nature of the interface to an information device may require questions to be posed in specific ways (for example, with certain punctuation or using a specific controlled vocabulary).

At the same time, information-system characteristics can counteract social constraints when necessary. For example, advance directives have been shown to increase patients' willingness to ask questions of physicians (Tabak, 1988). Similarly, Allen (1989) shows that different forms of questions have more power to elicit details of an information need. The role of intermediaries in encouraging alternative or more verbose expressions of need is also important.

Because information needs are embedded in social situations, users must be reassured that their questions are being expressed in socially acceptable ways. This reassurance can be provided by another version of user-supplied cumulative indexing. If past users are asked to characterize their information need and to comment on the appropriateness of posing their question to the informant, records of these assessments, summarized to aid in decision making, will greatly facilitate the selection of informants. Similarly, intermediaries who are sensitive to the social constraints on information-need expression can assist users in selecting appropriate informants and expressing their needs appropriately.

Examination of the resources that users employ to generate statements of information need suggests some of the features that may be incorporated into user-centered information systems. The idea of collecting user reactions to and opinions of informants and incorporating this data into the information system is one such design element. At the same time, information systems can augment the knowledge resources that users possess by making extensive use of human intermediaries. The discussion that follows will explore how these emergent design features can be incorporated into a more detailed design sketch for information systems.

Designing for Failure of Perception

An information system that will respond cooperatively and helpfully to a statement of failure of perception will

- accept minimal semantic expressions of need,
- contain or refer to expert knowledge, and
- be able to define new ideas in such a way as to lead to user understanding.

The kind of information systems that will be able to help users who have expressed an information need associated with a failure of perception can now be discussed. The first feature is that such information systems must accept minimal semantic expressions of need. Chapter 5 considers such questions as "What happened?" or "What went wrong?" or "What's this thing?" or "Doctor, why does my arm hurt?" There are examples of information devices in print form that will accept these kinds of statement of information need. Field guides are good examples. If an individual has something in his or her hand or has seen something in the backyard and knows enough to identify it as an animal, bird, plant, or mineral, the individual can turn to a field guide and try to match its pictures and illustrations with the object in question. The matching process may be aided, to a certain extent, by classificatory structures of various kinds. Objects may be grouped by size, color, geographical location, and so on. Such structures may be helpful, but frequently identification of the object in question requires a large-scale sequential scan of many object representations to isolate the one that most closely matches an object in hand. Similar functions are served by guides to collectibles, which are frequently well illustrated. Here again, the information need is of a most general nature, expressed in questions like "What is this, and is it worth anything?" Browsable information resources like these can be helpful in meeting information needs of this sort. It is important, therefore, to discuss the nature of browsable systems and how they can be designed to effectively meet the information needs related to failure of perception.

Browsing: Classification

Answering questions like "What was that?" or "What's going on?" is hardly what normal information devices are set up to do. These devices tend to require semantic material to work. What seems to be needed instead is an information device that can be entered at some point (perhaps chosen to represent the best estimate of the problem area), which will then navigate toward the information that will resolve the information need. One feature of information devices that has not always been used to its best advantage in meeting this kind of information need is the classified arrangement of knowledge.

This feature of information systems employs an associative network. To perceive and understand something new, the novel experience must be linked to something already known and understood. For example, a novel situation can be understood if its similarities with other, well-understood situations are made clear. Someone who has never seen a hovercraft may experience a failure of perception upon being exposed to one. However, once the similarities with other, more familiar entities like ships and aircraft have been identified, the perception will no longer fail, and the state of knowledge will no longer be anomalous. The associative network inherent in classification systems may enable individuals to fill in the gaps in their knowledge structures without having to express a detailed information need.

Many information sources have either explicit or implicit classifications that enable their use in meeting this kind of information need. Explicit classifications include classification schemes such as those used in organizing documents in libraries or taxonomies such as those used to organize chemicals, animals, or plants. Implicit classifications include the syndetic structures that are incorporated in thesauri. Here the association between broader, narrower, and related terms reflects an understanding of the underlying classification of the entities that correspond to those terms. Even information sources that appear to be organized purely by alphabet may have an underlying classification in the way terms are chosen for inclusion. For example, a geographic source may include data on places above a certain size. This size limit has a classificatory basis. Similarly, selective information sources (those that cover only a particular topic) establish the basis for inclusion in the source in a classificatory manner.

Classification is, then, an essential component of most information sources. To be useful in meeting information needs, however, the classification must be both understood by the user (i.e., presented in some intelligible manner) and navigable by the user. The ideal, as described previously, is that a user who is unable to express in clear language the topic of the information need should be able to enter the information source at some (perhaps random) point and move toward the information that will meet the information need by explaining what the unknown entity is (i.e., provide links to known entities). The field guides mentioned previously are examples of classificatory principles being used to aid browsing to find, identify, define, and learn about an unknown and unexpressed object of information need.

Browsing behavior has been researched by Marchionini & Liebscher (1991), who show that navigation through the associative and classificatory networks of an electronic encyclopedia can be an effective means of access to information. This finding is in accord with research from educational psychology (for example, O'Donnell, 1993), which shows that browsing through knowledge maps is a viable means of finding information in a learning environment. Savoy (1993) reports about a hypertext device in which the user does not need to express an information need verbally, but rather starts selecting (possibly) relevant materials during browsing. As this process continues, the system monitors user choices and uses spreading activation along multiple indexing paths to retrieve additional relevant nodes for browsing. Similar use of associative networks can be found in the work of Cakmakov and Davcev (Cakmakov & Davcev, 1991; Davcev & Cakmakov, 1993). Their information-retrieval device, implemented in the area of mineralogy, employs a network of concepts, which may be either chunks of text or images linked together with hierarchical and relevance relationships. In other words, this associative network combines classificatory elements with semantic relationships. Users can, presumably, browse from a particular text to a related image, then to other related texts, exploring the information contained in the system. A similar ability to browse from text to alternative representations can be found in the Worm Community System developed by Bruce Schatz and his colleagues (Pool, 1993).

It is interesting to note that many standard methods from bibliometrics can be used to develop knowledge maps; these maps, based on bibliographic coupling or citation analysis, can be considered comparable to the knowledge representations that experts in a topic area may have (Tijssen, 1993). These approaches, however, are open to the criticisms already voiced about using expert knowledge representations if the users are nonexperts. At the very least, user mental maps should be linked to the expert mental maps. User mental maps can only be developed with detailed investigations of how users think about what they already know and how they visualize the gaps in that existing knowledge. Investigations of this sort have discovered not only what users know, but how they organize their knowledge and perceive or feel about their knowledge. Research into user knowledge maps is an important component of designing usable information systems.

Browsing: Interfaces

Browsing can also be aided by interface design. There has been a great deal of attention to interface design in information-science literature [see Shaw (1991) for a review of this literature]. In many cases, however, designers have turned to interfaces to carry the whole burden of user-centered design. They take a data-centered approach to the selection, indexing, and organization of the information-retrieval device. This approach is most likely to produce a system that is unusable. Then, in order to try to salvage a bad job of information-system design, the designers add on a user interface that they hope will reflect a user model or user preferences. Examples of this hybrid approach include many graphical user interfaces to library online catalogs. As Donna Harman has correctly observed, designers' attention should be directed toward making user-friendly information systems, rather than designing user-friendly interfaces (Harman, 1992).

One text that takes a solidly user-centered approach to interface design is that of Lansdale and Ormerod (1994). They recognize that interfaces exist not only to provide procedural information (for example, through help screens), but also to help users understand what they find and explore the information. To help users understand what they find, interfaces can provide mental models. These models (for example, using their mental models of print encyclopedias to understand the information presented in an electronic encyclopedia) act as advance organizers. An advance organizer is a technique frequently used in classroom teaching. When an organizational framework is presented before the new material to be learned, students tend to learn more quickly because they already have a way of organizing the new knowledge they are receiving. Similarly, in information-system interfaces, the interface that uses a metaphor or mental model can provide users with a way of organizing their understanding of the new knowledge. Marchionini and Liebscher (1991) examine the effect of such organizational frameworks on users of electronic encyclopedias. They show how undergraduates used their mental model of print encyclopedias to develop proficiency in using electronic encyclopedias. Of course, there is a problem with this. Using an approximate metaphor as a mental model to understand information provides only a minimal level of understanding. It seems clear that, to advance beyond this minimal level, users will have to adopt more sophisticated models of the system. Accordingly, the interface will have to be an adaptive one, incorporating a series of conceptual models that will support more comprehensive user understanding.

Probably more important than facilitating understanding, interfaces can enhance exploration. It can be important for users to be able to express their information needs and to move toward information that will meet those needs in a nonverbal and exploratory manner. Lansdale and Ormerod (1994) suggest that interfaces can use such features as "display-based problem solving" or "learning by doing" to enhance exploration. Again, these approaches are familiar from educational psychology. Display-based problem solving includes features that will allow a user to diagram the various components of the problem they are facing. Learning by doing is a trial-and-error approach that works well in developing an understanding of procedures or a mastery of skills. These examples show that interface design, if taken as part of a user-centered design program, is an essential component of the design process, and several systems show great potential in helping users who are unable to express their information needs in detailed semantic form.

Various icon-based systems have been developed to allow people to express their information needs in a minimally verbal manner. Perhaps the best example is the Book House, developed by Mark Pejtersen and used as an example in Rasmussen, Pejtersen, and Goodstein (1994). This system, designed to allow people (particularly young people) to find fiction materials, allows users to specify aspects of their information need by selecting an icon. It also provides classified lists of aspects such as geographical settings and expected emotional responses. The result is a good example of a system that may meet information needs attendant upon failures of perception.

Similarly, Schur, Feller, Devaney, Thomas, and Yim (1991) designed an icon-based office that organizes information into books, notebooks, and so on, as a browsable approach to scientific data to be used by researchers. Card, Robertson, and Mackinlay (1991) designed an interface to allow users to visualize the information workspace, using a series of three-dimensional rooms as a metaphor. A simple example of using interface metaphors to enhance browsability was reported by Mander, Salomon, and Wong (1992). Here, they decided to organize documents in piles, not unlike the piles that many people create in their own offices. The advantage of these particular piles is that they could be clicked on with a mouse to show their contents. This feature would make the process of browsing through informally organized collections of documents considerably easier. Another simple example is reported by Brown (1991), who created a bibliographic database that makes use of the outline metaphor. The outline allows users to move hierarchically through different levels of the outline until they are able to find the detailed information they need.

The efficacy of these icon-based interfaces is explained by the concept of "affordances" (Strong & Strong, 1991; Gaver, 1991). Certain objects and information layouts determine certain kinds of information processing. For example, if an interface uses the room metaphor as its information layout, there is a built-in, three-dimensional browse capability that is absent if one uses a file metaphor, which is two-dimensional. However, if the room is presented visually as a library (as in the Book House), then the browsing dimensionality is reduced to a single dimension (the linear arrangement of books on shelves). Because certain information layouts afford certain kinds of behaviors, the selection of a layout to facilitate browsing is crucial.

The first aspect of designing information systems to answer statements of information need that arise from failures of perception is the ability to accept statements of need in minimal semantic form. Browsing allows people to enter an information space with little in the way of semantic labels for their need and to navigate to information that may be helpful. The second aspect of such systems derived from the discussion of statements of need is the ability to present or refer to expert knowledge.

Experts and Failures of Perception

In many cases of failures of perception, what the user needs is access to an expert. This is someone who, at a glance, can diagnose the problem, identify the recalcitrant reality, and then interpret that reality to the questioner. The preceding discussion uses the example of a naturalist's field guide as an example of an information device that presents precisely this kind of expertise to the user. Such devices present an ordered set of representations of objects (or possibly of people) to help questioners identify what they have seen and provide enough basic information linked to the representations to enable questioners to define the unknown entity in their own semantic terms.

Beyond the identification, labeling, and explanation of objects, such as those covered by field guides, other types of expertise are also important. The ability to diagnose legal or medical problems or to generate cause–effect explanations for events that are poorly understood goes beyond expert knowledge of objects. This is the domain of expert systems, whose knowledge bases and inference rules provide exactly this sort of expertise. In restricted domains, some expert systems seem to work. Plantamura, Soucek, and Visaggio (1994) present a detailed discussion of a variety of knowledge-based systems. One that is of particular interest to the current discussion is the "Help Desk": a system that allows users to input a problem description, which is matched against "cases" (descriptions of problems previously encountered and resolved). This type of approach resembles closely the expert advice described in this chapter, although it is clearly limited by the number of stereotypical problem cases that can be made part of the system and by the ability of the rule-based matching system to distinguish between the cases.

It is, however, a bit impractical to recommend that medical diagnosis (for example) be incorporated into information-system design, even if the expert systems are sufficiently reliable and capable (which they are not). Rather, this discussion leads to a definition of the boundary between information-retrieval systems and other information systems in their environment. What this means is that at some point the information system must be able to refer users to experts (presumably human) who will be able to provide the expertise needed to respond to statements of information need. One such approach is through a bulletin-board service, in which users pose their questions and experts monitoring these queries engage in further interaction (electronically or in person) to diagnose the information need.

A significant potential for the referral of users to experts exists in the information-system intermediaries. The idea is that users expressing their information needs to an intermediary, even in the most inarticulate and unstructured form, will provide enough information to enable the intermediary to recommend an outside expert to whom the question should be addressed. In this sense, the intermediary is a connector to the larger world of expert information, opening up a wide range of possible advice and help to the user.

There is a third implication for user-centered information-system design derived from the discussion of statements of information need deriving from failures of perception. Users should be able to have the situation defined and explained to them. Rather than simply providing a label, it may be necessary to define what that label means by linking it to what is already known. It is that function of definition and explanation that will now be explored.

Definition of and Explanation for Failures of Perception

The task of definition is usually associated with dictionaries. It is hard to think of a more basic element to be introduced into the design of information-retrieval systems. One model for the incorporation of dictionary definitions into information systems is given by statistical packages such as SPSS. This system allows the user to select any technical term used in statistical analysis output, and by clicking on an icon on the toolbar, obtain a definition of that term. As users struggle with the task of understanding what an information system has given them, a simple dictionary lookup will be of great help to them. This approach and some elaborations of it will be considered in more detail in Chapter 8.

In addition to definition, the process of informing someone who has expressed a failure of perception may require some explanation. Moore (1995) outlines a process by which an information device with a sufficiently large knowledge base can explain things to users. In addition to having the knowledge that underlies the explanation, the system also needs an elaborate linguistic structure that allows it to monitor the dialogue, plan how the explanation will be given, and react to feedback from the user. This system, however, is experimental and works only in limited domains. It seems clear that information systems that have the ability to explain completely the information they are giving to users are unlikely to be available in the near future.

On the other hand, analogies have great power to explain new ideas to people. The trick is to identify another area that is similar to the area of information need with which the user is familiar and to explain the novel information by associating it with the already familiar set of ideas. Saying that a hovercraft is like an aircraft employs an analogy that may be useful in remedying failures of perception. Recounting the similarities and differences between a Japanese restaurant (the novel experience) and a Chinese restaurant (the familiar experience) may help the user to understand what has been a failure of perception. For an information system to perform this kind of explanation by analogy, it has to possess a knowledge base of linked examples, so that when one example is the subject of a query, the linked examples can be used in the explanation. Such a knowledge base will resemble knowledge structures that are already in use in information systems. For example, in thesauri, terms that are related to each other in specific ways are identified. In classificatory structures, there are links between similar ideas, experiences, and events. So it may not be too much of a stretch of the imagination to suggest that information systems can make use of this kind of associative structure to explain through analogy.

This kind of explanation should be distinguished from those systems, proposed or developed, that include explanations of their own behavior. Explanation of system function is, presumably, of only moderate interest to most users. Users have a problem to solve and tasks to complete. All they want is a system that helps them, not one that can explain its own function. So the explanation functions suggested by Belkin (1988) and Ingwersen (1992) or the system described by Fischer, Henninger, and Redmiles (1991) is of little interest or help here.

At this point, the role of experts not only as informants but as teachers must be considered. The real task of explanation (given current technology) is in the hands of expert informants. Once the information system, including its intermediaries, puts the user in contact with a human expert, the task of responding to the expression of information needs associated with failures of perception can be regarded as accomplished.

The design implications developed in the previous section can be summarized as follows. Information systems, at least those that propose to respond to questions of failure of perception, can employ:

Browsing and navigational systems to allow users to access information in a minimally semantic fashion. These systems include classificatory and associative networks and interfaces that facilitate browsing.

Expert knowledge encoded as associative networks of images of objects, as diagnostic expert systems, or as human experts linked to the information system by electronic messaging or referral.

Definitions of words, perhaps implemented through a dictionary lookup, and explanations of the information provided accomplished through explanation systems, analogy, or human experts.

Because this is the first information system to be addressed in specific design terms, it will be called System 1. An implementation of the preceding design principles may look something like the following scenario. A person who has experienced a failure of perception approaches the information system. The first element of the system that the user encounters is a human intermediary, to whom the user expresses the equivalent of the minimally semantic questions discussed previously. The human intermediary may be present in the flesh or may be communicating with the user through a telecommunication link. By interacting with the user, the intermediary establishes a general domain that will suggest an expert informant, as well as an understanding of the level of topic and language knowledge the user possesses. The intermediary may also be able to discern the pragmatic situation and social context of the information need. On the basis of this interaction, the intermediary may recommend an expert informant. Alternatively, the intermediary may recommend that the user browse through a series of high-level representations of informants. These representations may consist of bibliographic information (for example, a bibliographic description of a field guide to birds) or personal information (for example, an expert on marital relationships). User-supplied cumulative indexing may be attached to these representations, which may allow the user to assess the nature of the informant, particularly the topic expertise, familiarity with the user's pragmatic situation, and expert knowledge of the social constraints facing the user.

As the result of the recommendation by the intermediary or selection from the browsable list of informants, the user comes into contact with an informant. This contact can occur through a browsable interface that permits navigation through recorded information, through a connection to a diagnostic expert system, or through a telecommunication (or personal) link to a human expert. If the information is recorded, the user will be able to click on a word or picture at any time to receive a definition of the item identified. Similarly, most expert systems allow definitions and explanations as part of their capabilities. In the case of human experts, one can imagine an electronic messaging system that has a dictionary lookup system available to the person reading a message. Alternatively, the user can ask the expert for definitions or explanations.

Finally, there must be a mechanism for the intermediary to check on the progress and success of the encounter with the expert and to collect the kind of evaluative user-supplied indexing that will cumulatively provide a thorough description of the capabilities of any informant. This mechanism will increase the ability of the information system to match individual user needs (and the social situations that constrain them) with appropriate experts. As the quantity of user-supplied indexing increases because more people are using the system, the usability of the system will be enhanced.

The discussion thus far has been based on the assumption that people who have experienced failures of perception wish to perceive clearly and in a balanced manner, and that they seek information that will help them to perceive what has previously been unknown to them. This assumption is severely limiting. Some people may wish not to perceive their situation. Perhaps more likely is a situation where the user wants to perceive the situation selectively. In other words, the user may be delighted with explanations of a certain type, but may avoid explanations of other types. Selective perception is, of course, something that people use to cope with the variety and sheer bulk of the information with which they may be inundated.

In other words, the design sketch for System 1 does not recognize the bounded rationality of information behavior and, as a result, does not take into account the need for people to avoid information. It is possible, for example, to implement a system feature that resembles a volume control. In specifying the nature of the need, the user can use this control to specify the amount of information wanted: a low setting produces a brief sketch while a higher setting produces a more detailed explanation. This feature seems to be a fairly straightforward addition to the design sketch.

Selective volume controls are rather more difficult to implement in an automated way. For example, people and communities are frequently faced with decisions about developments such as new industrial plants, toxic waste dumps, or military installations in their neighborhoods. Some individuals may wish to focus their perception on the economic benefits (or drawbacks) associated with a decision, while others may prefer to focus on concerns relating to personal health. As people seek information in order to perceive this unknown reality, they may have distinct preferences as to the type of expert information they wish to receive. This seems to be the domain of the human intermediary. The information specialists who work with users must be sensitive to the amounts and kinds of information that people may seek and those that they prefer to avoid.

Designing for Alternative Identification

An information system that will respond cooperatively and helpfully to a statement of need relating to alternative identification and slot filling will:

- accept labels or labels with statement of existing knowledge,
- allow systematic exploration of an area of interest, and
- facilitate semantic links en route to full understanding of the area of interest.

The discussion now turns to alternative identification. What is needed here are information systems that will work from a label, either alone or in combination with a moderate amount of semantic content, to fill in the slots in the knowledge structure and to make connections between the new knowledge and existing knowledge. The first two points suggest an encyclopedia. Here, more than in any other type of information resource, the user can begin with a single word or simple concept and move systematically through an exploration of an area of interest. In addition, the encyclopedia is likely to provide an appropriate level of detail in its information: sufficient detail to understand the options that exist, but (probably) not enough to complete a detailed evaluation of the alternatives. In fact, encyclopedias have existed for millennia, and it is possible to speculate that the reason for their ongoing success and successful adaptation to new information media is that they are so able to meet exactly this type of information need. Another similar information resource may be a selective, structured bibliography. If the bibliography is well indexed, the information system will accept a single word as an input point, then allow the user to move through a discussion of the literature of the area of interest.

The third point listed previously is the ability to link what is learned from the information system with what is already known, so as to understand thoroughly the new area of interest. In an encyclopedia, it may be possible to follow associative links to related topics. In fact, most encyclopedias have "see" references, and electronic encyclopedias have hypertext links that enable browsing along associative links.

Another information resource that seems ideally suited to alternative identification is the how-to manual. If the problem is identified (i.e., perceived), then the question remains "How do I deal with this problem?" or "How do I fix it?" The information resource should allow the user to move quickly to the appropriate instructions, usually by an index of problems or tasks. The user should then be able to explore the alternatives systematically (in this case, in a step-by-step fashion). Finally, there should be links to related problems or tasks to help the user attain full understanding of what is being recommended. It will be clear that this kind of information source is similar to many of the characteristics of the encyclopedia mentioned previously.

It is important to note how different the encyclopedic type of information system is from the field-guide type of information system described as being appropriate for dealing with failures of perception. In this system, the browsing that is done is *within* the topic of interest, rather than *to* the topic of interest. However, both types of browsing can make use of classificatory and associative networks. In the case of navigating to a topic, the process is one of eliminating possibilities or, as in the childhood game, getting "warmer" or "colder," depending on how close one is to the desired information. In the case of navigating within a topic, it is more like a child seeing the family's new house for the first time. The child runs from room to room, exploring every part of the house. In information systems, one kind of associative network that can facilitate this kind of exploration is the general-to-specific topical organization. This movement from general to specific may proceed in several directions, either sequentially or in parallel, but it can be fruitful. Another useful classificatory approach is whole–part organization, which allows the exploration of a topic beginning with the whole, then moving to details about each of the components or parts of the topic. This kind of organization is particularly useful in exploring (for example) how a corporation functions, how the circulatory system functions, or how to fix the steering system of a vehicle. However, it is not clear that current information systems, with their emphasis on lexical and logical relationships, implement the part–whole classification in a useful manner.

Chapter 1 notes parenthetically that some information activities are not problem-solving in nature, but rather treat information as a collectible, either in its own terms or because of its association with some other interest (e.g., professional sports). It seems clear that the kind of information system that responds to alternative identification may also meet the needs of collectors. Someone who wishes to know what happened yesterday on *General Hospital* may be in possession of a great deal of knowledge already and just needs to fill some specified empty slots in that knowledge framework. A general-to-specific information approach, providing it moves quickly enough to the specifics, seems to be ideal. In fact, some telephone services that charge a fee for providing this kind of information are organized precisely in a series of general-to-specific hierarchical menus.

In current generations of information systems, a simple, one-word query is likely to produce a large stack of documents. This stack may include documents of various types and will usually not be organized to facilitate general-to-specific exploration. Nor are there convenient "see" references to related documents. In other types of information systems, alternative identification can be impeded by the way the information is presented. Airline reservation systems, for example, may present first the flights of the particular airline that created the system. Alternatively, because the data is organized by city pairs, it may be impossible to explore systematically the many options involving multiple city pairs involved in a particular trip. What is needed, again, is something like an encyclopedia that allows users to explore each topic (in this case, each trip) in some detail. The ideal information system may resemble a how-to manual, with step-by-step instructions for exploring the possible connections between cities and their different fares.

To give some substance to these information-system design implications, a particular information system can be considered (called System 2 for convenience). In this information system, users may browse through an alphabetical or classified list of topic labels or may input a topic label. The first response from the system will be a discussion of the topic equivalent to what is found in an encyclopedia or a general textbook on the topic. Each of the headings of this text serves as a hypertext link to more detailed discussions of the various components or aspects of the topic. Each of the chunks of text in this encyclopedia-like or textbook-like presentation will be linked to search formulations that can be run in real time against document collections to provide either lists of document representations or access to full text. At the top (general or whole) level, the searches will identify only general discussions. As the user proceeds to more specific levels or examines the detailed aspects of the topic, the searches will start to retrieve more specific or detailed results. Of course, it will be desirable for these bibliographies to be selective and annotated. One can anticipate using the cumulative user-supplied indexing described to select those documents most illustrative of a given point or considered to be the most interesting or readable. The objective here is to avoid dumping (metaphorically) a huge stack of documents on the user. Rather, the searches should be carefully restricted using qualitative criteria. This, of course, implies that qualitative judgments are incorporated into the bibliographic representations.

One problem of such a structured retrieval system is that not all topics may be included in the encyclopedia, or rather that a user may fail to discover the label that corresponds to his or her information need in the list of topics covered by the encyclopedia. Any list of topics must be considered a manifestation of public knowledge (information-as-knowledge). However, individual information needs may be understood in ways that are individual (i.e., that differ from the commonly accepted classification of topics). To accept statements of information need that diverge from the common classification, this information system will require full-text searching of the encyclopedia-type materials, as well as the document representations or full text. This capability should allow the system to assemble paragraphs that are relevant to any individual topic and to link the resulting topic description to relevant documents on demand. Transaction logging enables information professionals to identify novel topics as they arise and to rewrite the assembled paragraphs into a coherent document if sufficient demand is revealed.

One other aspect of this redesigned text-retrieval system must be emphasized. The encyclopedia-like or textbook-like documents that are retrieved as the first or second step of document retrieval must have lateral links to related topic areas. These "see" or "see also" references will allow users to build an elaborated comprehension of the topic they want to understand by associating that topic with other related topics.

Systems of this sort may be designed to deal with a variety of different problems. The information that is included in the encyclopedia-type article and the organization of that material into presented text must take into account the practical, pragmatic situation in which the user is found, the social context that may constrain the types of alternatives that can be considered, and of course the knowledge the user has of the topic and the language used to discuss it. The text and other informative elements that may be part of an encyclopedia-type article must be individually indexed and described, so they can be composed into alternative forms of informative articles with a flexibility not achieved by current electronic encyclopedias.

To achieve the ability to format an article that will match a user's state of knowledge about the topic, problem situation, and social context, each chunk of text, probably no bigger than a paragraph, can be rewritten in a variety of ways. Each alternative chunk can be described by readability measures, assessed to see how much knowledge of the topic it presupposes, and evaluated for its appropriateness to different problem situations or social contexts. Only users can evaluate its appropriateness to problems of social settings, through an ongoing form of cumulative user-supplied indexing. The creation of alternative forms of the informative text by assembling text chunks will be under the direct control of the user. There is, however, a possibility that human intermediaries can assist users in generating statements about their situation that move beyond a simple label and that will provide the basis for selecting and compiling a suitable article.

One information system that seems promising in providing some elements of this kind of redesigned information system is reported by Erickson and Salomon (1991). The system uses a system metaphor of reporters, which are retrieval mechanisms programmed individually to select information on a topic with (for example) a certain depth of search. These mechanisms can be automated after being programmed so that they can be run repeatedly to gather more information. Along with the reporters, information is modeled using the metaphor of newspapers and notebooks, each containing information of different types and with different uses. It seems clear that some such mechanism will facilitate retrieval by users trying to identify alternatives and also will be useful later in the evaluation and selection of alternatives.

Once again, however, the bounded rationality of individual users and their need to avoid information as well as obtain it must be taken into account. Clearly, the volume-control approach described previously will work both for the amount of information provided in the primary, encyclopedia-type article, as well in the links to more detailed information. Because of the availability of lateral associations implemented through hypertext links, it will be possible for users to navigate from one aspect of information on a topic to another. But at the same time, users will be able to ignore some of these routes if they wish to keep their understanding of the alternatives selective, rather than trying for a balanced and complete understanding. Allowing a large degree of user control over the nature and amount of the information that is displayed seems the best approach to dealing with knowledge-avoidance needs.

It is possible to summarize the design implications for meeting this type of information need. An information system modeled on an encyclopedia, a textbook, or a how-to guide will allow the kind of easy access through labels, systematic topic exploration, and elaboration of understanding that is necessary to respond satisfactorily to statements of need for alternative identification. If the information is suitably indexed, it will be possible for the system to generate a large number of alternative versions of this information, so that users with different levels of knowledge and language abilities and with different problem situations and social constraints will be able to be served in a customized way. The encyclopedia-type article, acting as an initial or primary information source, will be linked to a number of search statements that can be continuously updated as users' interests evolve. These search statements will provide direct links to more detailed information on any of the topics covered by the primary source. Human intermediaries will be available to assist users in selecting appropriate ways of expressing the nature of their information need, but in general, users will have a large degree of direct control over the nature, amount, and organization of the information presented by the system.

Designing for Evaluation

An information system that will respond cooperatively and helpfully to a statement of need relating to alternative evaluation and selection will:

- accept a detailed statement of existing knowledge,
- assemble and summarize information that may help in evaluation, and
- advise users about the alternatives they face.

The discussion now turns to evaluation of alternatives. Neither of the approaches to information systems discussed previously is appropriate for responding to statements of need associated with alternative evaluation. In discussing expert advice systems modeled on naturalists' field guides, statements with little semantic content were expected. Similarly, the information systems for alternative identification modeled on encyclopedias expected labels or relatively simple topic descriptions. Here, the systems are dealing with users who know a lot about the topic and are able to express their information needs quite discursively.

Similarly, the type of information provided by a system responding to information needs related to alternative evaluation will be different from the types already discussed. Rather than the beginning stages of investigation or problem solving, for which diagnosis and exploration are the appropriate tasks, this system deals with people who need evaluative information and advice about the alternatives they face. Existing information sources may provide some of the answers. The texts that are found in full-text databases contain accounts of individuals or groups who have been in specific problem situations and selected particular alternatives. These texts may also indicate the consequences of those actions. For example, a scientific article will present the benefits and drawbacks of a methodology chosen to investigate a particular topic. If a user is interested in choosing a methodology in a related area, this kind of discussion can serve as a valuable link between choices and consequences. Similarly, if one is considering alternative ways of traveling from Paris to Avignon, travel books with accounts of bicycle trips, barge trips, etc. will be of great help.

The problem with using full-text information to respond to this kind of statement of information need is that documents, such as scientific reports or travel books, contain far more than justification of methodological choices or comments on modes of travel. It seems clear that the information required for alternative evaluation will be buried in a mass of additional verbiage that is of little interest to the user with a specific query. In addition, the required evaluative information may be found scattered through many documents. It is probably not enough to find a single justification of a methodological choice in order to select an analytical technique. Rather, one needs the appropriate sections from a reasonably representative selection of scientific report articles. Similarly, the perspective of one author of a travel book may be appropriately balanced by that of another author writing on the same type of travel. Perhaps an appropriate model for the kind of document that will best respond to this kind of statement of need is a review article or a meta-analysis.

The next point to make about the documents found in typical document-retrieval systems is that they are not organized appropriately to provide information that will enable the evaluation of alternatives. As described previously, these systems typically dump a stack of documents on the user and leave to him or her the task of winnowing out the useful evaluative comments. What is required to meet this kind of information need is to step away from the detail about an entity or situation and provide a high-level overview of it. The kind of output that will be useful is, "Most people think that X is the right interpretation, but a minority thinks Y and one person suggests Z." Alternatively, "Most people do X, but some do Y, and one person tried Z." Once again, the idea of a review or summary of the relevant literature or a meta-analysis combining the results from a number of studies seems to provide a fruitful model.

Here is one way that an information system may be designed to meet this need. It can be called System 3, to distinguish it from the first two systems sketched in this chapter. First, the system must obtain the semantically rich and extensive statements of information need from users and do something with them. The vector-space model, as developed by Salton (1988, pp. 313ff), treats statements of need exactly as if they were documents. This assumption of a high level of similarity between user queries and documents has been challenged, but in the case of this type of information need, it seems to be defensible. These users are those who are closest in terms of their semantic knowledge to the experts who are creating documents, so treating the semantically rich statements of need as if they were documents seems quite justifiable.

It will, however, be necessary to redefine what constitutes a document for the purposes of this type of document retrieval. It seems clear that entire documents may be an inappropriate basis for matching with statements of need. Rather, it is only the sections or parts of documents that discuss the particular alternatives being considered that should serve as the basis for retrieval. It is, of course, computationally demanding to calculate similarity measures between statements of need and individual paragraphs or sections of documents. However, given the observation that relevant evaluative comment may be buried in a mass of less interesting verbiage, there seems to be no alternative. It may be possible to use features of text structure to limit the searching that is done. If, as in the preceding example, the alternatives being evaluated are methods of addressing a particular scientific problem, the system can limit the searching to those sections of scientific report articles that discuss methods used. Similarly, if meta-analysis is desired, one can limit searching to the findings reported.

Using vector-space retrieval on paragraphs or sections of documents will produce a group of selections from documents, ranked by their similarity to the statement of need. While this is not a review article or a meta-analysis in any real sense, it is at least the raw materials from which such a document can be produced. It enables the user to undertake the task of alternative evaluation. To this basic capability, two elements mentioned in earlier sections of this chapter can be added. If transaction logs show a high level of demand for evaluative material in a specific area, it is possible for information specialists to incorporate into the information system actual review articles covering the high-demand area. These articles are then associated, through hypertext links, with the source documents. The result resembles the encyclopedia-like information system described as being appropriate for alternative identification, but rather than a series of encyclopedia articles, there can be a series of review articles that constitute the first document retrieved by users. It is equally possible that information specialists can create review articles from the raw materials described previously, where such articles are not available from the literature.

The discussion of System 2 notes that the system has to deal effectively with the needs of users who have different levels of topic knowledge and language abilities and who are dealing with different problem situations and sets of social constraints. For this to happen, the system has to be highly flexible and must have the ability to present one of many alternative versions of information based on the user's description of the information need and extensive indexing of the chunks of text that constitute the primary retrieval document. It seems clear that, in System 3 as well, there will be a need to adapt the information presented to meet a wide variety of different information needs. Simply presenting a user with a large stack of raw materials from a literature review will not be a sufficiently flexible alternative, given the variety of needs that an information system may have to address.

It seems possible that cumulative user-supplied indexing will be the key to resolving this problem. If the document chunks considered as the basis for retrieval are enhanced by descriptions and evaluations obtained from previous users, the vector-space model may be able to retrieve a selection of raw materials closely tailored to the individual circumstances of the user. Chapter 8 considers more details of how this may work.

Finally, there is no substitute for expert advice when trying to decide on a course of action. The importance of expert help in perceiving and diagnosing the problem was previously noted, and it was suggested that the information system be linked to human experts who could interact either electronically or face-to-face with users. The same feature seems to be useful here. An information system is unlikely to be able to provide advice except through its human elements. Intermediaries may have some expertise they can apply to advising users on alternative selection, but a network of human experts will expand the ability of information systems to help users in this task.

As in the sketches for Systems 1 and 2, some allowance must be made here for the somewhat bounded rationality of users of information systems. Fortunately, the nature of the information system sketched here makes this easy. If people wish to avoid information or to limit their intake of information, they can limit their information tasks to a consideration of the first items retrieved. Because documents are presented in descending order of calculated similarity to the statement of need, the highly relevant information is likely to be presented first. In addition, a relatively minor change to the typical vector-space model will allow users to specify terms that should receive a high negative weight. This negative weight will allow users to eliminate areas of discussion from the retrieved set.

The design features appropriate for information systems that can respond to statements of information need associated with alternative evaluation and selection can now be summarized. A vector-space model will accept verbose and reasonably expert statements of need. Matching the resulting representation of the statement of need against document paragraphs or sections seems most appropriate, and this may be facilitated by using the text-linguistic structures of documents to limit retrieval. The resulting documents will resemble the raw materials from which review articles or meta-analyses can be created. When demand is sufficient, actual review articles can be obtained or created to serve as the initial retrieval element, just as encyclopedia-like articles are the initial retrieval element in System 2. Linking to human experts who can provide advice is also to be recommended.

At this point, a comparison can be made among the information systems that will respond to statements of information need that are likely to occur during the various tasks of problem solving: perception and diagnosis, alternative identification, and alternative evaluation and selection. For those who are trying to perceive the problem, a browse-based system with associative links (perhaps classificatory or perhaps based on more general associations) seems ideal. What is needed is a system that will allow people to enter this system with minimal verbal expression and navigate toward their information need. Linked experts that can provide the identification and diagnosis that people need can supplement such a system. This expertise can be provided on a purely human basis, although it seems clear that some of the needed expertise can be incorporated into information systems through devices like field guides.

For those trying to identify alternatives by completing their understanding of a topic, a general-to-specific information system that allows selective exploration of topics in depth, while at the same time providing lateral links to related topics, is needed. The electronic encyclopedia, textbook, or selective annotated bibliography may represent the kind of information service that can be useful in this process.

For those trying to select alternatives, in-depth information, arranged in such a way as to permit specific-to-general consideration and evaluation of alternatives, is needed. At this point, the information system can provide advice about the consequences of various alternatives. A vector-space retrieval engine adapted to create the raw materials of review articles or meta-analyses may be most appropriate here.

All of these systems are within the realm of possibility. None of them require radical innovation in information-system design. It must also be emphasized that none of these systems is recommended for implementation. This discussion has been at as specific a level as possible, given the highly general and generic analysis of information needs and their expression provided in Chapters 3 and 5. System designers addressing the needs of specific populations will be able to conduct a far more detailed analysis of the kinds of statements of information need that their users present. Based on this detail, they will be able to create systems far more closely matched to their users' needs than anything presented in this chapter. The ideas presented here are representative and illustrative of the kind of outcome that can be achieved when designers pay serious attention to users and make users the center of their design initiatives.

If designers follow this pattern, they will end up with many different information systems. A highly general analysis identifies three quite different designs, each of which uses different data, has different organizational features, and uses different retrieval techniques. Clearly, this is a different approach than creating multiple interfaces to a single underlying system. The systems are different because they are supporting different user tasks. This point seems obvious, but it raises the specter of a user approaching an information service and being confronted with a confusing multiplicity of information systems. It seems clear that user models will be a necessary feature of information systems in this kind of environment, and the first task of the interaction between the user and the rest of the information system (the device and the intermediary) will be to diagnose the kind of information task that is being attempted and to match that task with the appropriate information system.

Designing for Group Information

Chapter 5 notes that group information needs are more complex than a simple summation of the information needs of individual group members. Information systems that can cope with and facilitate the ways that groups function require design features that go beyond designs that respond to individual expressions of need. Some of these additional design features can now be considered.

An information system that will respond cooperatively and helpfully to group information needs will:

• facilitate the internal sharing of essential information between group members,

- allow the evolutionary development of the focus of group activities and of the special language that may evolve around that focus,
- facilitate the activities of gatekeepers in importing information to the group, and
- facilitate the activities of gatekeepers in performing an intermediary function to outside information sources.

A family of information systems exists that is designed specifically to deal with groups as they deal with information needs. These systems do not usually call themselves information systems, nor do their designers and users think of them as such, but they are highly relevant to group information tasks. These systems are those designed to facilitate computer-supported cooperative work (CSCW) and to support group decisions [Group Decision Support Systems (GDSS)]. A quick overview of the state of the art in these systems may help to focus the discussion.

The first point that derives from the discussion of group statements of information need is that information systems should facilitate within-group (internal) communication between group members. Communication is one of the main functions accomplished by systems for CSCW. The literature abounds with descriptions of such systems. For example, Nakauchi, Itoh, Sato, and Anzai (1992) present a description of a model and prototype for within-group communication. Nunamaker, Dennis, Valacich, Vogel, and George (1991) describe a system that captures the activities of group meetings for later replay and analysis, thus creating a kind of collective memory. Luff, Heath, and Greatbatch (1992) compare electronic and paper communication devices for within-group communication. Wolf, Rhyne, and Briggs (1992) describe a pen-based system to enhance group communication and capture group processes for later use. Ackerman (1994) reports on a study of a system called the Answer Garden that was designed to make recorded knowledge retrievable and to make knowledgeable individuals (specifically, group members) accessible to other group members. Fowler et al. (1994) develops and investigates a hypertext-based notebook system that serves as the basis for within-group communication.

However, more interesting to this author than the tedious details of the electronic plumbing that goes into these communication systems are the analyses of the effectiveness of information systems to support group learning, decision making, and problem solving. Aiken and Riggs (1993) suggest that a system that supports electronic brainstorming can enhance creativity and productivity in group decision making. McLeod (1992) conducted a meta-analysis of experimental studies regarding electronic support of group work and found that such support improves decision quality, time to reach decisions, equality of participation, and task focus. Interestingly, electronic support of group work decreases feelings of consensus and satisfaction with the decisions made. Supporting this meta-analysis is the work of Lea and Spears (1991), who reexamine the phenomenon of higher decision-making polarization among computer-supported groups than among other groups. They suggest that computer-mediated communication between group members has its own social and normative context, which influences the behavior of group members. Poole, Holmes, Watson, and DeSanctis (1993) also compared groups who communicate electronically during decision making with those who use more traditional means of communication and found that the work process in the computer-supported groups is more organized and group members have more insight into the decision-making process that occurs.

It is also interesting to note that there is little in the CSCW or GDSS literature that refers to the gatekeeper or boundary-spanning role. One system described by Musliner, Dolter, and Shin (1992) is tangentially relevant. This system allows group members to enter the bibliographic references that they find in their information-gathering activities outside the group, thereby communicating these results to other group members. However, this system is really an internal communication device rather than something that will actively facilitate gatekeeping.

This review indicates that there exists a wide range of information technologies performing the first function required of information systems that will respond to group statements of information need: they facilitate the internal sharing of information between group members. Citera et al. (1995) detail the barriers that such systems must overcome in bridging between the task being accomplished by the group and the organizational processes through which the tasks are accomplished.

The second requirement for such systems, identified previously, is to allow the evolutionary development of the focus of group activities and of the special language that may evolve around that focus. One or two words of explanation may be in order here. This requirement recognizes that how the group collectively perceives its problem and states it to each other and to outside agencies will change over time. Further, the focus of the group on what it is doing at the moment must change reasonably quickly as the group proceeds with the tasks of decision making, learning, or problem solving. The group's statement of how it perceives its problem, coupled with a statement of its current focus, is a kind of Selective Dissemination of Information (SDI) profile. In other words, if the group is going to monitor outside information resources for material related to their task, their statement (as it evolves over time) is the basis for monitoring those outside resources. Similarly, if the group is going to request information from outside resources that will help it complete the tasks and activities on which it is currently focused, the statement of current focus will be the basis for that request for information.

What this system requirement envisages is a separate workspace in which the group collectively maintains a statement of its collective interest, which can be compiled and run against a variety of external information resources from time to time. Appended to that statement is a statement of focus, changing rather more rapidly than the statement of interest, which again can be compiled and run frequently against external resources. The results of these information-retrieval activities will be reviewed by the group and incorporated into the group's collective information store when appropriate. In this discussion, the nature of the outside information resources has been left deliberately vague. It is possible that any of the three types of information systems developed for responding to individual statements of information need can be selected by the group. They may need basic diagnosis and definition, topic exploration for alternative identification, or help in evaluating alternatives.

This discussion leads to the third requirement of information systems for collaborative group work: to facilitate the activities of gatekeepers in importing information to the group. The collective statement of information need maintained and used as input to external information resources should provide the group with a basic foundation of information that can be used in its collective function. However, particularly if the group has developed a specialized language to discuss what it is doing, the process of searching outside resources using the language of the group may be less than successful. One of the features of gatekeepers is that they are active in two groups and (presumably) reasonably fluent in the languages of both. This cross-group function gives them the ability to translate the group information need into the terminology of an external informant. Accordingly, it is possible to imagine a workspace adjacent to the one containing the statements of interest and focus, in which a gatekeeper expresses the interest and focus in the language of some external group that can act as an information resource. The maintenance of this workspace will be the responsibility of the gatekeeper, although the activities of maintaining and using these statements will be visible to the entire group. A sketch of how this gatekeeper information workspace may look is presented in Fig. 7.

As information is provided, either through the activities of the group as a whole in editing its statements of interest and focus or by individual gatekeepers as

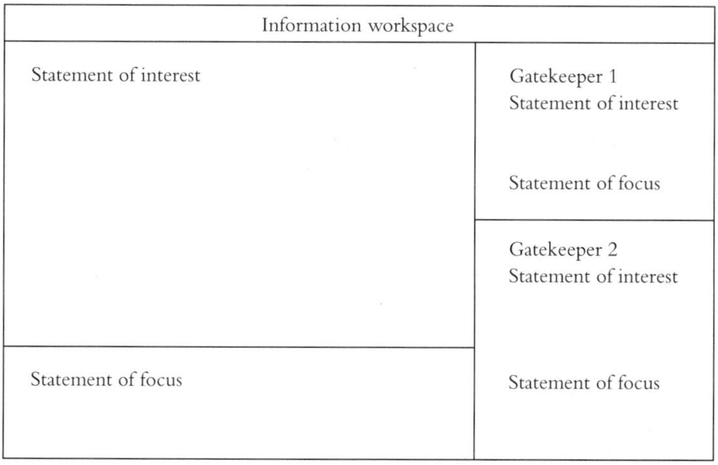

Information workspace	
Statement of interest	Gatekeeper 1 Statement of interest Statement of focus
	Gatekeeper 2 Statement of interest
Statement of focus	Statement of focus

Figure 7
Gatekeeper information workspace.

they use their linguistic expertise to collect additional information from outside systems, the results will appear in the information workspace to be reviewed by group members and transferred, where appropriate, to the collective information store. Again, depending on the nature of the external system being tapped, the material that appears here can be expert advice, review articles, documents, or images of various kinds.

The final function for group information systems suggested previously is that they should facilitate the activities of gatekeepers in performing an intermediary function to outside information sources. This requirement presupposes that group members will individually be contacting external information sources, and that they have a kind of cheat sheet or external memory to remind them what those resources are and what sorts of language are appropriate for approaching them. In effect, group members need to augment their own resources in those areas already described as central to the creation of statements of information need: source selection (including the knowledge that informants have of the problem situation and social constraints on contacting the informants) and linguistic skills.

The group information system sketched previously can be adapted to perform this function. The gatekeeper sections of the information workspace will now contain a brief statement of the information systems that exist in one or more areas outside the group, in addition to the statements of need and focus already noted. Group members can copy search language from the gatekeeper workspaces into the collective statements of interest and focus areas and then use these statements to generate queries to be run against the external information resources. The output from these searches, serving as input to the group's collective knowledge, seems to correspond to what Star and Griesemer (1989) describe as "boundary objects." In their description of a particular institution, they identify repositories and piles of documents as examples of boundary objects. These objects can be interpreted differently by different members of the group and can in fact facilitate the process of translating between viewpoints, thus helping to develop a common understanding. As the information obtained by gatekeepers is introduced to the group, then assimilated by a process of reinterpretation and consensus to form part of the collective knowledge store, it acts to redefine the nature of the group and its task.

The discussion of group information behavior notes that organizational factors influence the kinds of information that may be sought or used by groups. The use of an information workspace of the kind sketched previously should be able to incorporate these organizational factors. For example, the collective understanding of the task and focus will, necessarily, be expressed in terms that are dictated by the organization. The group members may not be particularly aware of these influences, but organizational culture and values can be so pervasively present in work situations that they can lead to ways of thinking about a task or focus that inevitably condition the kind of information search that occurs. Similarly, the nature of gatekeepers' activities in importing information into the group may be constrained by organizational factors. Again, there seems to be little need to adapt the design of the information workspace to allow organizational factors to play a role.

These factors are operational in any communication or information system used in the workplace.

It is possible, however, to consider that the group information system may need design features to deal with the less rational approaches to information that can be found in groups. The over-enthusiastic collection of information to display (in a symbolic manner) one's commitment to the decision-making process or the failure to share information with other group members can be accommodated by having individual information spaces that are separate from, but linked to, the group information space. In the information spaces maintained by individual members, the task may be expressed and the focus understood in different terms. The information retrieved may be shared with the group through the information space, but it may also remain only in the individual information store. It seems clear that no group can totally submerge the individuality of its members. The collective understanding will be continually negotiated, but will always lag somewhere behind the individual understandings. The group information system is not in a position to enforce conformity, but rather to facilitate consensus. So it seems inevitable that individual information spaces will remain on the periphery of the group information space, frequently (but not always) contributing to the collective understanding of task and focus and to the collective information store.

Summary

The design implications discussed in this chapter can now be summarized. First, users have knowledge of their problem situations that varies considerably in detail. Information systems can be adapted to these different levels of knowledge through browse searching, general-to-specific classifications, vector-space searching, or the creation of interest and focus workspaces for groups.

Second, users have different levels and types of linguistic structures. Information systems can be adapted to these different levels by incorporating dictionary lookup into the system, by using encyclopedia-type or review-type texts as a first stage in retrieval, or by providing opportunities for gatekeepers to act as intermediaries using specialized language from their outside group contacts.

Third, informants have different levels of knowledge of the problem situations that give rise to user statements of information need. Information systems can account for these different levels by using intermediaries and gatekeepers as guides to source selection and by using a network of experts to whom users can turn for advice and help.

Finally, there are social constraints that lead users to select informants and express their needs in particular ways. The same combination of intermediaries, gatekeepers, and expert informants can enable information systems to respond flexibly to users. In addition, it is possible for these components of the information system, interacting with users, to counteract or reinforce (where appropriate) the social norms that constrain information seeking. This chapter has sketched representative information-system designs that incorporate these ideas and suggest ways in which working information systems can be designed to respond cooperatively, helpfully, and appropriately to the wide variety of information-need expressions that are generated by users.

User-Centered Design: A Practical Guide III

Note: At the end of each even-numbered chapter of this book, a brief guide to the practical aspects of design is provided. This guide summarizes discussions in preceding chapters as they relate to the practical aspects of conducting user-centered design. Contents that have been added to this version of the guide are shown in boxes.

1. Identify a user population. The first and obvious step in user-centered design is to find a user, or more appropriately, a user population. Sometimes user identification is dictated by the mission of the organization where the designer works. In other cases, users may be selected by the designer. The identification of the user population is such an obvious step that it is sometimes omitted. This omission results in systems that are not particularly usable for any set of users.

The user population may be composed of either individuals or groups or perhaps a combination of both. Because different design decisions will be necessary for groups, they should be identified separately when they occur within the user population.

2. Investigate the information needs of your user group. The users identified in step 1 have a number of information needs. These can be investigated using a wide range of research methods, which are easily accessible in manuals on social science research or market research. The key element of this step is to talk to users and find out what kinds of information they need to resolve the problems they encounter. No information system can meet all of the information needs of a user group. Once the full range of information needs has been identified, system designers must select those that their information system will be designed to meet.

User needs can be identified by reference to a problem-solving model. According to this model, information needs can be associated with problem perception, alternative identification, or alternative selection. Each of these classes of information needs will require different approaches to system design. User needs can also be typified by their setting. Information needs can occur in individuals or in groups. Group needs are sufficiently different from individual needs to require different design approaches.

Both individual and social factors influence the information needs that may occur within a user population. Designers should investigate the social and organizational settings in which information needs occur, because these settings may give rise to or constrain the information needs experienced by users. Figure 5 summarizes the design principles that emerge from a consideration of user information needs.

Some information needs arise from failure of perception. Some information needs are associated with a process of exploring a topic area so as to identify alternative courses of action. Some information needs arise from the need to associate alternatives with outcomes.

People can, and frequently do, engage in information avoidance. They interact with their environment by limiting their intake of information, ignoring information if it is associated with negative outcomes, and taking information shortcuts. Organizations are frequently equally irrational in their collection, processing, and use of information.

3. Discover the tasks that users accomplish as they meet these information needs. Again, research methods from social science and market research are useful in this step. The key element is to talk to users and observe them as they work on meeting their information needs. Identify the tasks that users employ as they meet their information needs and how they accomplish these tasks. Note the sequential ordering of the tasks. Try to distinguish between the tasks that are essential and those that are optional. The result will be one or more task models for each information need.

Tasks may be accomplished individually or collectively. Where users are observed to be completing tasks as a group, it is important to consider these group tasks separately from individual tasks in the design of information systems.

Tasks accomplished may be dictated by the social setting in which information seeking occurs. Social and organizational factors must be analyzed carefully, because they may constrain the number of tasks that individuals and groups choose to accomplish. When social factors constrain tasks in this way, information system design can be considerably simpler than when users can select from a broader range of tasks.

Expressing an information need is one key task that users will typically accomplish while meeting information needs. Different types of needs produce different types of need expressions and accordingly place different requirements on information-system design.

---

4. Investigate the resources that users require to complete these tasks. Each task completed by a user who is meeting an information need requires a variety of resources: background knowledge, procedural knowledge, and abilities. List the resources required for each task and identify the level of the resources required. For example, expert knowledge or high levels of verbal ability may be required to complete a task involving vocabulary selection. At the same time, it is important to note the levels of these resources that users possess. Some users, for example, may have less expert topic knowledge or lower levels of verbal abilities, and gaps between resources required and resources possessed are obvious areas of concern. Research methods to investigate the resources possessed by users can be found in any text on psychometrics.

Resources may be individual or collective in nature. Where individual knowledge and ability are concerned, psychometric methods are adequate to identify levels of resources possessed by users. In the case of collective knowledge and ability, however, it is essential to investigate the group processes by which consensus is reached. Collective resources may differ considerably from the sum of the individual resources of group members.

Resources may derive from and be constrained by social factors. Accordingly, it is important to investigate the social and organizational setting in which resources are being applied to the completion of information tasks. These settings may provide additional resources or may constrain how resources are applied to tasks.

Resources particularly important to the expression of information needs are knowledge of the problem situation, linguistic knowledge, knowledge of informants and what information they have, and knowledge of the social constraints that govern the expression of information needs.

---

5. Summarize the preceding steps in user models. For each distinct user group to be served by the information system, there will be a number of information needs that the system is designed to meet. For each of these information needs, there will be a number of tasks that must be accomplished. For each of the tasks, there will be a list of resources that are necessary. Integrating these elements together results in a user model that can be used to guide design decisions or that can be implemented as part of the information system to direct how the system will respond to users. For example, user models can form the basis for the preset options for how the information system will work, but users will be able to change the options to make the system conform to their own preferences.

6. Consider each design decision in the light of resource augmentation and enabling. The goal of system design is to allow users to complete the tasks that will meet their information needs. With this in mind, system features that will augment the resources of users when necessary will enable them to complete the tasks. Some of these features will be required by all users, while others will be required by only a portion of the user group. In the latter case, system features are best implemented as user-selectable options. Experimental research to identify interactions between user resources and design options can be used to select system features that should be implemented as user-selectable options.

For those who are trying to perceive a problem, a browse-based system with associative links seems ideal. What is needed is a system that will allow people to enter the system with minimal verbal expression and navigate toward their information need. Linked experts that can provide the identification and diagnosis that people need can supplement such a system.

For those trying to identify alternatives by completing their understanding of a topic, a general-to-specific information system that allows selective exploration of topics in depth, while at the same time providing lateral links to related topics is needed. The electronic encyclopedia, textbook, or selective annotated bibliography may represent the kind of information service that can be useful in this process.

For those trying to select alternatives, in-depth information, arranged in such a way as to permit specific-to-general consideration and evaluation of alternatives, is needed. Advice can be provided by the information system about the consequences of various alternatives. A vector-space retrieval engine adapted to create the raw materials of review articles or meta-analyses may also be appropriate.

References

Ackerman, M. S. (1994). Augmenting the organizational memory: A field study of Answer Garden. In R. Furuta & C. Neuwirth (Eds.), *Proceedings of the conference on computer supported cooperative work* (pp. 243–252). New York: ACM.

Aiken, M., & Riggs, M. (1993). Using a group decision support system for creativity. *Journal of Creative Behavior, 27*(1), 28–35.

Allen, B. L. (1989). Questions on search request forms. *Online Review, 13*(4), 283–288.

Belkin, N. J. (1988). On the nature and function of explanation in intelligent information retrieval. In Y. Chiaramella (Ed.), *Proceedings of the 11th international conference on research and development in information retrieval* (pp. 135–195). Grenoble: Presses Universitaires de Grenoble.

Brown, M. E. (1991). Design for a bibliographic database for non-professional users. In J. Griffiths (Ed), *ASIS '91. Systems understanding people. Proceedings of the 54th Annual Meeting of the American Society for Information Science* (Vol. 28, pp. 276–282). Medford, NJ: Learned Information.

Cakmakov, D., & Davcev, D. (1991). A multimedia cognitive-based system model. In *Proceedings of the 5th European Computer Conference on Advanced Computer Technology, Reliable Systems and Applications—CompEuro '91* (pp. 282–286). Piscataway, NJ: IEEE.

Card, S. K., Robertson, G. G., & Mackinlay, J. D. (1991). The information visualizer, an information workspace. In S. P. Robertson, G. M. Olson, & J. S. Olson (Eds.), *Human factors in computing systems.*

Reaching through technology. CHI '91 Conference Proceedings (pp. 181–188). New York: Association for Computing Machinery.

Citera, M., McNeese, M. D., Brown, C. E., Selvaraj, J. A., Zaff, B. A., & Whitaker, R. D. (1995). Fitting information systems to collaborating design teams. *Journal of the American Society for Information Science, 46*(7), 551–559.

Davcev, D., & Cakmakov, D. (1993). An application of a multimedia cognitive-based information retrieval system (AMCIRS) in mineralogy. In *Proceedings, 1993 ACM Computer Science Conference* (pp. 284–290). New York: ACM Press.

Erickson, T., & Salomon, G. (1991). Designing a desktop information system: Observations and issues. In S. P. Robertson, G. M. Olson, & J. S. Olson (Eds.), *Human factors in computing systems. Reaching through technology. CHI '91 Conference Proceedings* (pp. 49–54). New York: Association for Computing Machinery.

Fischer, G., Henninger, S., & Redmiles, D. (1991). Intertwining query construction and relevance evaluation. In S. P. Robertson, G. M. Olson, & J. S. Olson (Eds.), *Human factors in computing systems. Reaching through technology. CHI '91 Conference Proceedings* (pp. 55–62). New York: Association for Computing Machinery.

Fowler, J., Baker, D. G., Dargahi, R., Kouramajian, V., Gilson, H., Long, K. B., Petermann, C., & Gorry, G. A. (1994). Experience with the virtual notebook system: Abstraction in hypertext. In R. Furuta & C. Neuwirth (Eds.), *Proceedings of the conference on computer supported cooperative work* (pp. 133–143). New York: ACM.

Gaver, W. M. (1991). Technology affordances. In S. P. Robertson, G. M. Olson, & J. S. Olson (Eds.), *Human factors in computing systems. Reaching through technology. CHI '91 Conference Proceedings* (pp. 79–84). New York: Association for Computing Machinery.

Harman, D. (1992). User-friendly systems instead of user-friendly front ends. *Journal of the American Society for Information Science, 43*(2), 164–174.

Ingwersen, P. (1992). *Information retrieval interaction.* London: Taylor Graham.

Koenig, M. E. D. (1990). Linking library users: A culture change in librarianship. *American Libraries, 21*(9), 844–849.

Lansdale, M. W., & Ormerod, T. C. (1994). *Understanding interfaces: A handbook of human-computer dialogue.* London: Academic Press.

Lea, M., & Spears, R. (1991). Computer-mediated communication, de-individuation and group decision-making. *International Journal of Man-Machine Studies, 34*(2), 283–301.

Luff, P., Heath, C., & Greatbatch, D. (1992). Tasks-in-interaction: Paper and screen based documentation in collaborative activity. In J. Turner, & R. Kraut (Eds.), *CSCW '92: Sharing perspectives: Proceedings of the conference on computer-supported cooperative work* (pp. 163–170). New York: ACM.

Mander, R., Salomon, G., & Wong, Y. Y. (1992). A 'pile' metaphor for supporting casual organization of information. In P. Bauersfeld, J. Bennett, & G. Lynch (Eds.), *CHI '92 conference proceedings: ACM conference on human factors in computing systems: Striking a balance* (pp. 627–634). New York: Association for Computing Machinery.

Marchionini, G., & Liebscher, P. (1991). Performance in electronic encyclopedias: Implications for adoptive systems. In J. Griffiths (Ed.), *ASIS '91, Systems understanding people, Proceedings of the 54th Annual Meeting of the American Society for Information Science* (Vol. 28, pp. 39–48). Medford, NJ: Learned Information.

McLeod, P. L. (1992). An assessment of the experimental literature on electronic support of group work: Results of a meta-analysis. *Human–Computer Interaction, 7*(3), 257–280.

Moore, J. D. (1995). *Participating in explanatory dialogues: Interpreting and responding to questions in context.* Cambridge, MA: MIT Press.

Musliner, D. J., Dolter, J. W., & Shin, K. G. (1992). BibDb: A bibliographic database for collaboration. In J. Turner & R. Kraut (Eds.), *CSCW '92: Sharing perspectives: Proceedings of the conference on computer-supported cooperative work* (pp. 386–393). New York: ACM.

Nakauchi, Y., Itoh, Y., Sato, M., & Anzai, Y. (1992). Modeling and implementation of multi-agent interface system for computer-supported cooperative work. *Ergonomics, 35*(5–6), 565–576.

Nunamaker, J. F., Dennis, A. R., Valacich, J. S., Vogel, D. R., & George, J. F. (1991). Electronic meeting systems to support group work. *Communications of the ACM, 34*(7), 40–61.

O'Donnell, A. (1993). Searching for information in knowledge maps and texts. *Contemporary Educational Psychology, 18*(2), 222–239.

Plantamura, V. L., Soucek, B., & Visaggio, G. (Eds.) (1994). *Frontier decision support concepts.* New York: Wiley.

Pool, R. (1993). Networking the worm. *Science, 261*(5123), 842.

Poole, M. S., Holmes, M., Watson, R., & DeSanctis, G. (1993). Group decision support systems and group communication: A comparison of decision making in computer-supported and nonsupported groups. *Communication Research, 20*(2), 176–213.

Rasmussen, J., Pejtersen, A. M., & Goodstein, L. P. (1994). *Cognitive systems engineering.* New York: Wiley.

Salton, G. (1988). *Automatic text processing: The transformation, analysis and retrieval of information by computer.* Reading, MA: Addison-Wesley.

Savoy, J. (1993). Searching information in hypertext systems using multiple sources of evidence. *International Journal of Man Machine Studies, 38*(6), 1017–1030.

Schur, A., Feller, D., Devaney, M., Thomas, J., & Yim, M. (1991). EASI. An electronic assistant for scientific investigation. In *Proceedings of the Human Factors Society 35th Annual Meeting* (pp. 393–397). Santa Monica, CA: Human Factors Society.

Shaw, D. (1991). The human–computer interface for information retrieval. *Annual Review of Information Science and Technology, 26*, 155–195.

Star, S. L., & Griesemer, J. R. (1989). Institutional ecology, "translations" and boundary objects: Amateurs and professionals in Berkeley's Museum of Vertebrate Zoology, 1907–39. *Social Studies of Science, 19*(3), 387–420.

Strong, G. W., & Strong, K. E. O. (1991). Visual guidance for information navigation: A computer–human interface design principle derived from cognitive neuroscience. *Interacting with Computers, 3*(2), 217–231.

Tabak, E. R. (1988). Encouraging patient question asking: A clinical trial. *Patient Education and Counseling, 12*(1), 37–49.

Tijssen, R. J. W. (1993). A scientometric cognitive study of neural network research: Expert mental maps versus bibliometric maps. *Scientometrics, 28*(1), 111–136.

Wolf, C. G., Rhyne, J. R., & Briggs, L. K. (1992). Communication and information retrieval with a pen-based meeting support tool. In J. Turner & R. Kraut (Eds.), *CSCW '92: Sharing perspectives: Proceedings of the conference on computer-supported cooperative work* (pp. 322–329). New York: ACM.

7

Information Tasks

Interacting with Information Systems

This chapter discusses the tasks that are accomplished by users of information systems as they interact with those systems. The previous chapters trace the development of an awareness of an information need and its expression to an informant. Clearly, this is just the beginning of the information interaction. As that interaction develops over time and the process of becoming informed proceeds, a number of additional tasks become apparent.

The delineation of these tasks and the resources that are used to complete them begins with a discussion of what happens when an individual (defined generically) interacts with an information system (defined in an equally general manner). The statement of information need, presumably formatted in some acceptable manner, leads to the display of some response from the system. The user must deal with this response. Scanning the response from the system seems likely to be the first task in dealing with it. The information presented must then be evaluated (as being useful, useless, or somewhere in between). Concurrent with evaluating the potential usefulness of the information system's response to the statement of need, the user may learn from the response. This task of learning may contribute to the resolution of the information need, but in some cases, it may also transform the information need, because the user may find elements in what the system presents that lead him or her to reformulate or reconsider the expression of the information need or to develop a new understanding of the information need itself. Finally, dealing with an informative response from an information system may lead a user to adjust his or her approach to the information need. This change in the user's understanding of the information need requires the user to plan the development of a course of additional action required to meet the information need. Accordingly, there are four information tasks that are considered in this chapter: scanning, evaluating, learning and planning.

The generality of the preceding description is not limited by any device specifics. The display of output from the device can come in response to a well-formulated command, a menu choice, a browse move along a classificatory network, or even a simple appearance before the system. In some information systems with human intermediaries, all the user has to do is show up in order to generate some response from the system. Similarly, the nature of the response given by the system may be highly varied, ranging from text to images, documents to human experts, or research to gossip. Any interaction with an information system will require that the user scan (for want of a more neutral term) the response from the system, evaluate the response, learn from the response, and plan a course of additional action.

Russell, Stefik, Pirolli, and Card (1993) suggest that the greatest costs (in terms of both effort and actual dollar costs) in information retrieval are likely to occur in these additional tasks. They describe these tasks as central to sense making, although there are also a number of sense-making steps involved in recognizing and expressing an information need. They refer to these additional tasks as data extraction: finding the documents, selecting them, and transforming them into canonical (i.e., useful) form. It seems clear that the tasks discussed in this chapter represent a general approach to data extraction.

In terms of the focus on user-centered system design presented by Norman (1986), this discussion deals with the gulf of evaluation. In Norman's model, this gulf can be bridged by considering first the output display of the information system, then how that display is processed by the perception of users, and finally the interpretation and evaluation of the material presented by the system. This chapter focuses on each of the steps that are necessary to bridge this gulf between the user and the information system by considering the tasks of scanning, evaluating, learning, and planning.

Chapter 2 surveys a number of approaches to information-seeking tasks that are found in the literature. A brief review will provide a context for the discussion of this chapter. Kuhlthau's (1993) six-step information search process contains the following steps:

1. Task initiation: to recognize the information need
2. Topic selection: to identify the general topic
3. Prefocus exploration: to investigate information on a general topic
4. Focus formulation: to decide on a narrower topic
5. Information collection: to gather information on the narrower topic
6. Search closure: to complete the information search

Task initiation, topic selection, and focus formulation are tasks relevant to the chapters on information needs and information-need expressions. Three tasks remain to be considered in this chapter: prefocus exploration, information collection, and search closure. These tasks are special examples of scanning materials presented by an information system, evaluating the information, and learning from the information. In other words, these three tasks all require a more or less detailed interaction with an information system.

Similarly, only two of Marchionini's (1992) five information tasks (listed again here) remain to be discussed:

1. defining the problem,
2. selecting the source,
3. articulating the problem,
4. examining the results, and
5. extracting the information.

Clearly, examining the results and extracting the information require scanning, evaluating, and learning.

As noted in Chapter 2, each of these tasks must incorporate a variety of sub-tasks. The model of information needs in Chapter 3 and the model of statements of information need in Chapter 5 do not attempt to cover all possible specific information needs or means of expression. Rather, they attempt to provide a general framework so that information-system designers can apply that general outline to the specific user populations they serve. In the same way, this chapter will not attempt to cover all possible tasks nor all possible levels of detail in analysis of the tasks. Rather, it will present a general model that can be adapted to the specific user populations for which systems are being designed. In addition, it presents the resources that users bring to their completion of these tasks. By taking into account the different degrees to which these resources are available to users, a foundation can be established for designing usable information systems: systems that will enable users to complete the essential information tasks as they interact with information systems to resolve their information needs.

Scanning

It is possible to deal with these four tasks in sequence, without assuming that there is necessarily a linear sequence involved in their completion. Individual users may move backward through the sequence, they may loop repeatedly through parts of the sequence before moving on, and so on. However, to be systematic, this discussion begins with scanning. The task of scanning material presented by an information system seems a straightforward one. However, there exists a body of scientific evidence that shows that people complete this task differently. To develop an understanding of how people complete the scanning task, it is first necessary to ascertain what kinds of variables affect the performance of this task. Making this understanding more complicated is the fact that scanning what information systems present is not a simple task. The material presented may consist of lists of words, texts, text representations, hypermedia links to other texts, or pictures. The purpose of the scanning task may be to select vocabulary, to identify likely texts or text representations, or to find an appropriate direction in which to navigate. Scanning requires attention to and perception of the system and what it is doing. There are a variety of cognitive resources that are important factors in paying attention to and perceiving these media, and these can be found enumerated in any textbook on cognitive psychology. Some people are more able than others to attend to multiple stimuli at once. Some are less likely to be distracted than others. Some have the ability to attend selectively (which is different from perceiving selectively). In addition, Chapter 2 notes that there are specific tasks that are required to decipher maps or graphs or to browse hypertext, so specific resources must be brought to these tasks. In this more detailed discussion, it is important to consider both the general resources that must be brought to bear in scanning any response from an information system and the specific resources that are demanded by distinct forms of response.

Before beginning this examination, however, there is one caveat that should be expressed. Most of the research in this area has been into tasks that are somewhat different from scanning. For example, in considering how students interact with text materials, psychologists and educators have tended to study tasks such as finding specific items. It seems likely that the resources employed in searching for specific items are similar to those employed in scanning, and accordingly that research is reviewed here. The task being considered here is that of scanning, preparatory to evaluation and use of information, but it should be emphasized that scanning may not use the resources in exactly the same balance as the more detailed search task.

Scanning Text

Anyone who has observed people using information devices will be familiar with the process: someone sits, flipping quickly through the pages of a book. More recently, an observer will have seen the process of someone sitting, paging repeatedly through lists of references in an electronic document-retrieval system. Wiberley and Daugherty (1988) reviewed this phenomenon and subsequently did some interesting research (Wiberley, Daugherty, & Danowski, 1990) that shows how much scanning actually occurs in this kind of setting.

There appears to be a relatively superficial level of comprehension that occurs during these tasks. However, from time to time, a reader will slow down and carefully peruse a passage, or someone sitting at a screen will stop to make a note or to press the print key. In such instances, the deeper processing associated with review, evaluation, and learning may be occurring. To begin analyzing the task of scanning, however, the resources required for the act of scanning for simple (and perhaps superficial) comprehension will be explored.

The first set of factors that enter into the scanning process are found in the individual. The ability to perceive a stimulus is critically related to the amount of knowledge one already has. That is to say, much perception is "top-down," or driven by one's concepts and expectations, as opposed to "bottom-up," or driven by the stimuli. Guthrie (1988) formulates a model of the subtasks involved in searching text and later (Guthrie, Weber, & Kimmerly, 1993) expands it to include a variety of document types. The tasks that this model identifies are:

1. goal formation,
2. category selection,
3. information extraction, and
4. integration.

The first two of these tasks are top-down in nature: they depend on the goals and knowledge of the user. The goals formulated by the user determine the aspects of the document that will receive attention, and the user's knowledge of the topic and the structure of the documents determine the categories of information that will be perceived during the scan. These points may be clarified by an example. Suppose that a user is scanning some material presented by an information system to locate previously unfamiliar documents on earthquakes. This goal predisposes the user to pay particular attention to documents that contain words that relate to seismology and in particular to anything containing the word "earthquake" or its variants. Now, suppose that the user knows that documents are structured in a particular way by the information system. Perhaps there are topic summaries or titles that are indicative of content. This knowledge will lead the user to focus particularly on those topic-oriented categories of the information. There may be one additional level of influence of user knowledge here. If the user knows that a particular indexing expression or classification code applies to the topic of interest, the user may scan for that exact phrase or code. This discussion emphasizes the importance of user goals and knowledge in driving the scanning task.

Research into text searching, if modified to account for the differences between searching and scanning, emphasizes this influence of individual characteristics on scanning. The importance of different goals that individuals may have in searching for information from text is emphasized in some studies. In some cases, these goals are individual in nature [see, for example, the achievement goals investigated by Butler (1993)]. On the other hand, many goals are derived from social situations. For example, Glynn (1994) reports experimental research with information processing where two different social situations are involved: work and play. These situations influence how information is perceived and used to form judgments. Those who see themselves in a work situation attend to information about the quantity of their performance, while those who see themselves as playing attend to information about the quality of their performance. Similarly, Small and Grabowski (1992) found that motivation was a crucial factor in determining performance of people searching through a hypermedia information system.

Individual knowledge is clearly one of the most important variables influencing how scanning is done. Armbruster and Armstrong (1993) study children's abilities to locate information in text, using a model similar to that of Guthrie (1988). They found that older readers are better able to find information in text and knowledge of both text structure and the topic searched are also important. Symons and Pressley (1993) confirm that prior knowledge is a key element of success in finding information in texts, but Byrnes and Guthrie (1992) found that topic knowledge, organized in a certain way, only helps if the texts are organized in a congruent manner. Dillon (1991) found that readers possess and use a knowledge of the organizational structure of text (in this case, scientific report articles) in scanning text.

The point made previously about the importance of users knowing specific indexing terms or phrases or particular classification codes to assist in the scanning task is supported by some of the research into text search. Yussen, Stright, and Payne (1993) found that text searches succeed if the book index contains the ideas being sought. Dreher and Brown (1993) found that equipping searchers with terms that may be found in the textbook's index and giving them planning prompts (advice about how to plan their search for information) produces higher levels of success in finding and extracting information from texts. Similarly, Dreher and Guthrie (1990), after analyzing the tasks involved in text search, found that successful searchers spend more time on the category selection subtask, where terms are selected for the search using a locator system such as a table of contents or an index. This result is confirmed by the work of Guthrie, Britten, and Barker (1991). As a result of making better choices of terms to find, more efficient searchers can spend less time actually finding and extracting the information. Again, it is necessary to adapt these findings from the search task to the scanning task, but it seems clear that if individuals have particular, rather small chunks of text for which they are scanning and particularly if those chunks of text are found predictably in the same place in the input from the information system, scanning will be enhanced.

Perceptual abilities are also important individual resources used in the scanning task. Allen (1992, 1994) shows that perceptual speed and spatial orientation have an effect on the scanning task as well as on the learning task discussed in the following section. It appears that in scanning input from an information-retrieval system, users may adopt a number of strategies. Some, particularly those gifted with high levels of perceptual speed, adopt a sequential scanning approach. Others, particularly those with lower levels of perceptual speed but higher levels of spatial orientation, do not try to scan everything, but rather watch for the data elements that appear in specific places. Lee-Sammons and Whitney (1991) completed research that focuses on memory for text rather than text scanning, but which can perhaps be extended to explain scanning. They found that working memory capacity has an impact on what people remember of texts they read. In particular, people who are lower in working memory span seem to compensate for their deficit by making greater use of a perspective to guide their comprehension. If this research is generalized to the scanning task, it may be argued that users with less working memory capacity are likely to scan rather inflexibly, sticking to their previously set goals, while users with more working memory capacity are able to shift their attention to other potentially interesting materials during the course of scanning.

Of course, individual variables are not all that influence the scanning task. The nature of the text must have some influence on how scanning occurs. Verbal imagery, for example, has the ability to draw attention and enhance perception. Sadoski, Goetz, and Fritz (1993) tested the comprehensibility and interest of text that contained concrete language (words and ideas that encourage readers to create mental images of the topic covered) as opposed to texts that were more abstract (and consequently less apt to be encoded as images). They found that concreteness was highly related to the comprehensibility of text. Again, it is necessary to generalize from this finding to the scanning task, but it seems reasonable to assume that the memorability of concrete text begins with the perception of the text; some texts will attract attention during the scanning process more than others.

In summary, scanning is a task that draws on a number of individual and social resources. The goals and knowledge of users, both of which may be influenced by social as well as individual variables, help to determine the extent to which users will pay attention to different parts of the information presented. Individual abilities also influence scanning strategies, and text characteristics play a role.

Scanning Documents

Many documents consist of text in combination with a variety of figural elements. These include images (pictures or illustrations), graphs, charts, drawings, and maps. Lohse, Walker, Biolsi, and Rueter (1991) examined a large number of these figural contents of documents and found that they can be grouped into five categories: graphs/tables, maps, diagrams, networks, and icons. Two principal dimensions seem to characterize these groups: the amount of spatial information they contain and the amount of cognitive processing effort they require. Scanning documents that contain graphic elements may use resources that are not required for scanning simple text. For example, Winn (1993) studied people searching for information in diagrams and found that there is a crucial knowledge element needed to make sense of diagrams: a knowledge of symbol systems and conventions. This is knowledge that is not typically used in finding text information.

At the same time, some ways of conveying information in a document seem better for certain purposes than others. It may be easier to scan some kinds of figural elements than it is to scan text, depending on the content. Kelly (1993) found that statistical information from tables and graphs is more efficiently processed than similar information in text. This finding should be qualified by the results of Boehm-Davis, Holt, Koll, Yastrop, and Peters (1989), who examined spatial, tabular, and verbal displays of information and concluded that it was important to match the display format to the type of information needed to answer a question. For example, if a table presents information in the best way to answer a question, it is much more difficult for people to process a verbal or spatial display to obtain the required information. It seems unlikely that any one form of data presentation is always easier to scan and process than another. This conclusion is supported by the research of Sparrow (1989), who found that different types of graphic representations (spreadsheets, pie charts, line graphs, bar charts, etc.) are effective for meeting different types of information needs. For example, trends are more easily assessed from line charts, proportions from pie charts, and so on. These results lead to the conclusion that the user's goal is crucial in determining the appropriateness of any display format.

Guthrie *et al.* (1993) found that there were really two kinds of processing going on when people learn from graphs, tables, and illustrations. One is the search for specific facts, similar to the processes described previously for text searching. If it is possible to generalize from searching to scanning, it seems to follow that scanning figural information formats has a basic similarity to scanning text. The user's goals, the user's knowledge of both the topic and the presentation medium, and the user's abilities influence how well the task of scanning will be completed. The second type of processing, that goes on when people learn from documents is more global processing, which requires summarizing information into gist representations, understanding trends, and developing generalizations and abstractions from the specific information presented. This type of processing is really a matter of learning from the text, so discussion of it is best postponed to the section on learning that appears later in this chapter.

Scanning Electronic Documents

Electronic documents include those that mimic paper documents and new formats such as hypertext that appear only in the electronic environment. There have been a number of comparative studies that have examined the difference that electronic presentation can make in scanning effectiveness. For example, McGoldrick, Martin, Bergering, and Symons (1992) found that scanning a computer presentation of text was more time-consuming than reading a print presentation of the same text, although students were eventually able to find the same amount of information from both media. They also found that computer presentation of text was associated with higher levels of use of an outline presented at the beginning of the text. This result seems to indicate that a directed search is more likely to be used in finding information from computerized text and a scanning approach is more likely in print. Nygren, Lind, Johnson, and Sandblad (1992) compared reading from paper and reading from the screen. They found that many cues present in printed materials that help scanning and comprehension were absent from the screen or were different and unfamiliar in electronic text. They suggest that information systems should be designed to create the same kind of automatic processing that occurs in reading printed materials. On the other side of the ledger, Riding and Chambers (1992) found that electronic presentation of information produces higher levels of success in scanning for answers to a variety of questions than paper presentation of the same information. Gray, Barber, and Shasha (1991) developed a system they call "dynamic text," in which text is linked to a series of questions asked of readers. Depending on how readers respond to the questions, different pieces of the text are displayed. They found that once readers had learned how to use the electronic version, they were able to scan more effectively to find the answers to difficult questions. None of these approaches to electronic text compares with the thorough and elegant approach of Dillon (1994), whose genuinely user-centered approach to designing electronic documents is discussed in Chapter 2.

Hypertext documents are (typically) electronic documents, so they present some of the scanning problems associated with other electronic documents, but they are also organized in ways that may influence the way that scanning occurs. Mynatt, Levanthall, Farhat, and Rohlman (1992) found that hypertext allows users to scan for facts embedded in text and printed books are superior to hypertext only in finding facts on maps. They conclude that hypertext can be a good information-seeking medium, even for users with minimal training. Considering the use of visual aids in knowledge representation in a hypermedia or hypertext environment raises additional questions, however. For example, hypertext can create virtual spaces or information spaces in which individuals can browse from one point to another. On the other hand, graphs and charts create Euclidean spaces in which the dimensions have a different representational purpose. As Shum (1990) suggests, the coexistence of these two spatial principles may lead to confusion or excessive cognitive load.

In scanning hypertext, users sometimes have problems understanding the nature of the hyperlinks they are following. In other words, hypertext requires an additional knowledge resource that people reading standard paper or electronic texts do not require: a knowledge of links and how they affect the scanning process. Mohageg (1992) found that hierarchical links lead to more effective scanning than linear or network links. Given the importance of hierarchical exploration to meeting information needs, particularly those needs associated with alternative identification, this finding will come as no surprise. Welsh, Murphy, Duffy, and Goodrum (1993) studied how knowledge about link types could be communicated to users to facilitate scanning. They found that none of the methods they tried were completely successful. It must be concluded that scanning in hypertext presents problems that remain to be solved. Hypertext scanning requires knowledge resources not required for other texts, and information systems using hyperlinks must successfully address the question of how to augment the user's knowledge resources in this area before such systems will be truly usable.

This discussion of scanning can be summarized by noting the resources that users employ in completing this task. They use their existing knowledge of a topic and of the index terms describing the topic to guide the scanning process. In addition, they use their understanding of data formats, including text structures, to direct their attention to specific parts of the material presented. Finally, they make use of perceptual abilities, such as perceptual speed, in scanning. Because users possess perceptual abilities to different degrees, they develop scanning strategies that optimize use of their abilities. Chapter 8 will explore how the resources used in scanning can have an impact on information-system design.

Reviewing and Evaluating

Of course, scanning by itself is not a satisfactory process. Unless one receives gratification from interacting with an information system, as some people appear to receive from watching television, the simple act of scanning is just the first step. For more complete processing, one expects some kind of review or evaluation of what is perceived. Concurrent with scanning what the information system presents, the user must make some decisions about what he or she sees. Sometimes a system may present vocabulary that can be used to redefine the information need or redirect the information search. This relationship of the vocabulary to the way the information need is currently being expressed must be evaluated. Sometimes a system may present documents of various types. These documents must be assessed for their relevance to the information need. The questions to be resolved are straightforward: Is this information good or bad, useful or useless?

The many approaches to relevance that have been adopted in information science are reviewed by Schamber, Eisenberg, and Nilan (1990). More recently, there has been a move toward user-centered relevance (Froehlich, 1994; Park, 1993, 1994; Smithson, 1994). Barry (1994) identifies a number of criteria that users may consider in judging information presented by an information system. Some of these criteria are presented (inappropriately) as characteristics of the information itself, for example, the depth, accuracy, clarity, and recency of the information. Such criteria, however, are not inherent in the information itself. Assessment of clarity, for example, depends on the reading ability of the user. Judgment of recency depends on the user's knowledge of the domain. Other criteria, such as novelty, are specifically associated with users. Assessments of the novelty of the information presented depend on what else the user has seen, but the subjectivity of this judgment is no more pronounced than the subjectivity of any of the perceptions that Barry associates with the information itself. Bruce (1994) places this kind of perception of relevance within the context of cognitive structures, thus emphasizing the individual nature of information judgment. This individuality of the process of evaluating information is repeated frequently in the contemporary literature on relevance. Howard (1994) associates judgments of pertinence with personal constructs, and Wyatt, Pressley, El Dinary, and Stein (1993) examine some of the questions that are articulated by readers in associating judgments of relevance with personal constructs. Typical of these questions are "Is the text relevant to my purpose?", "Is the content already known to me?", and "Is the text consistent with my biases, beliefs, and expectations?" All of these investigations have established the importance of individual knowledge resources in assessing the relevance of information.

Other individual resources are used to successfully complete the evaluation tasks. For example, Allen (1993) shows that a cognitive ability called "logical reasoning" is important in determining how selective people are when they judge the potential usefulness of information. Individuals with higher levels of this ability tend to be more selective than others. In addition, there are a variety of abilities associated with reading that affect the judgments people make of what they read. In particular, the way people interact with text (or other media of communication) affects their assessment of what is presented to them. One example of this phenomenon is given by Baker and Wagner (1987), who show that people do not always review incoming information for truthfulness or for consistency with what they already know. Particularly if information is presented in a grammatically or logically subordinate part of the text, people may simply ignore the incongruent information.

Despite the intense focus on individual variables as influencing how people evaluate what is seen, there are indications in the literature that there are also social influences involved in evaluation. For example, Janes (1994) compared the evaluative judgments of individuals with those of others (in this case, information intermediaries) and found that there was a reasonably good but imperfect match between the judgments of users and intermediaries. This finding suggests that there is a certain level of commonality in evaluations that may be associated with a community of discourse. People who are members of a community share many knowledge structures and personal constructs and so are likely to agree in their evaluations of materials. Sutton (1994) found that attorneys tend to adopt a particular approach to evaluation of materials. As members of a specific occupation, they seem to have been socialized or trained to adopt an approach in which they construct dynamic mental models and judge the usefulness of cases they are reading by a complex, multidimensional process of fitting the cases into their mental models of the law. Wilson, DePaulo, Mook, and Klaaren (1993) showed that the socially negotiated importance of an article's topic influenced how individual scientists assessed the article. They found that a higher level of importance linked with a topic (e.g., heart disease versus heartburn) was associated with more lenience in judging methodological rigor and publishability.

Evaluating Text

People seem to read text by focusing only on parts of the document. Blanchard and Carey (1992) studied college students learning from text. These students considered information important if it began or ended the text they were reading, began a paragraph, or preceded or surrounded examples of the main points being discussed in the text. Also of interest is that the students appeared to process chunks of text that were not considered important for any of the preceding reasons by picking out words that appeared at somewhat equal intervals in this otherwise unimportant text and focusing on them. Clearly, the ideas presented in the text, the physical structure of the text, and the scanning strategy employed all had an effect on the judgments of importance that students made. This observation is in agreement with that of Janes (1991), who found that relevance judgments change as different parts of documents are made available to users. In particular, when dealing with document representations, people appear to focus primarily on abstracts and titles in making assessments of the potential relevance of the documents.

Evaluating Documents

Judging other forms of information presentation is subject to different individual factors. It has already been noted that scanning different types of documents requires different kinds of knowledge. The same considerations relate to judging the quality of other types of representations. It seems clear from the work of Tufte (1983, 1990) that judging the quality of information presented in visual or figural displays is inextricably bound up with judging the quality of the display itself. The appropriateness of the medium to the information being expressed is crucial to both scanning and judging the information. Different forms of display can have the effect of concealing information, misleading readers, or focusing attention on irrelevant or collateral details. It appears that judging information presented using graphs, charts, and images requires a two-step assessment: first, that the form of presentation is appropriate, and second, that the information itself is useful or relevant.

Evaluating Electronic Documents

It is also true that medium of presentation can have an effect on user judgments. A body of research going back to the initial introduction of computers into education, information retrieval, and related domains has demonstrated that users regard computer-presented information as more trustworthy, accurate, and believable than information presented in more traditional formats [for example, printed information sources or human information sources; see, for example, Hess & Tenezakis (1973)]. This phenomenon is represented in the naive but pervasive statement, "The computer says it, so it must be true." This kind of suspension of critical judgment has led many users of electronic information-retrieval systems to inappropriate assessments of the quality, completeness, or accuracy of information received.

Once again, the discussion of the task of evaluating materials can be summarized by noting the variety of resources that people employ to complete this task. Knowledge of the context of the information need is obviously important to evaluating the potential usefulness of any material. Other knowledge resources employed in this task include knowledge of data display formats, such as text structures, and knowledge of the topic being investigated. Personal characteristics such as reading abilities and logical reasoning abilities also influence how people evaluate information. Chapter 8 will explore how these resources and the degree to which different users have access to them can be instrumental in designing usable information systems.

Learning

From a cognitive perspective, the task of review or evaluation is the first step of the learning process. In a sense, the entire discussion up to this point has been prefatory to a consideration of learning. Learning is central to the problem-solving process. People learn how to perceive and define the problems they are facing. They learn the alternative solutions they can adopt. They learn about the consequences and outcomes of those alternatives as they move toward selecting a course of action. Clearly, learning is one of the most crucial information tasks that must be completed in order to meet information needs. There are a number of good textbooks that consider learning from a cognitive perspective [see, for example, Anderson (1995)]. From this perspective, the learning task consists of several distinct steps. The first step is comprehension. A new stimulus must be understood (i.e., placed in the context of existing knowledge structures). The second step is elaboration. New connections among existing knowledge structures are generated, resulting in a richer understanding of phenomena. The third step is the creation of new knowledge structures. The memory structures that individuals have are enriched by new memories that they can subsequently recall. They know more than they did before. This rough outline of the learning process can be used to consider some of the individual resources that users bring to the task of learning from an information system.

In a simple example, an information system presents vocabulary to a user. This vocabulary may be contained in a list of possible terms for searching, a label for a point on a semantic network, or part of a document (text or a graphic). The first step in learning, which is comprehension, requires placing the new vocabulary in the context of existing knowledge structures. For example, the user who sees vocabulary presented by an information system may respond with the thought, "Yes, that's another word that may be used to describe what I'm looking for." In that case, subsequent processing of information or interaction with the information system benefits from incorporating this additional vocabulary.

The second step in learning, which is elaboration, requires new associations to be made. For example, the user who sees vocabulary presented by an information system may respond with the thought, "That's interesting. I would never have thought of using that word in this context." However, seeing the word in the context of the information interaction may well be enough to forge a new link between the word presented by the system and the vocabulary of the statement of need. A simple example can illustrate this phenomenon. If a user is searching for information on techniques of high-powered microscopy, encountering the word "tunneling" in that context may provoke surprise. However, after reconsideration, the user will understand that the term is being used in an appropriate but very specialized sense in this field. This realization can lead to the reexpression of the statement of need.

The third step in learning, which involves additions to memory, requires the user to know a word that he or she did not know before. For example, the user who sees vocabulary presented by an information system may respond with the thought, "That word is totally unfamiliar to me. What does it mean?" This question is the first step in a process in which the user looks up the new word in a dictionary or finds out its meaning from a friend, thus adding it not only to the vocabulary that is associated with the particular information need, but also to the user's understanding of the language.

This vocabulary presentation example serves well as a simple illustration of learning from an information system. However, the kinds of information systems considered in Chapter 6, and in fact most operational information systems, present users with more than just vocabulary. They contain documents of various types from which users may learn vocabulary, but from which they also may learn a great deal more. Presentation of ideas in text or image form can lead to the activation of existing knowledge (of all kinds) in thinking about and resolving the information need. Users first comprehend the information presented by the information system and place it in the context of their information need. Ideas presented in documents can be linked with the topic of the information need in ways previously not considered. This kind of elaboration of ideas by creating associations is the second step in learning, as noted previously. For example, in learning about the historical events that preceded the French revolution, one may encounter descriptions of food riots associated with high prices for bread and shortages of grain. Elaborated understanding may suggest that these food riots can be compared and associated with those in the reign of the Emperor Claudius, the experience of price inflation in Weimar Germany, or the endemic food shortages in East Africa. Learning about mountain formation may be enhanced by an association with knowledge about how plastic warps when heated. The richer the elaboration, the more complete the learning experience is. For example, Cardinale (1993) shows how embedding analogical explication in a science textbook can enhance learning.

Finally, learning results in the addition of new knowledge to memory. One suspects that, in the school environment, where much activity is ostensibly addressed to new knowledge acquisition, there is actually little new knowledge being added to memory. Classroom learning frequently emphasizes elaboration and reinforcement of existing knowledge rather than learning of new knowledge. However, the information presented by an information system can be so novel to a user that a process of knowledge acquisition is initiated. The student researching the antecedents of the French Revolution may well encounter the physiocrats[7] for the first time and learn something new. The role of physiocratic ideals in the food shortages of the eighteenth century may be explored, and in the end the student will have a knowledge of people like the elder Mirabeau that he or she did not previously possess. Similarly, someone exploring mountain building will certainly come into contact with plate tectonics. It can be assumed that, of those who encounter plate tectonics in this context, many are hearing the term for the first time. As a result of their exposure to the material presented by an information system, they are able to add a new set of knowledge to their memory stores.

Learning from Text

A variety of individual resources influence how people learn from text. Learning disabilities can impede learning; good learning heuristics and procedures can enhance it. General intelligence or any of its component cognitive abilities can also be crucial to learning. Chan, Burtis, Scardamalia, and Bereiter (1992) examine how children interact with textual materials. Five kinds of interaction are identified: word-level reactions, in which students focus only on the words they read and not on the text as a coherent unit; text-level reactions, in which students engage in verbatim learning or respond to things they find in the text; paraphrasing, in which students assimilate the text and are able to reformulate it in their own words; problem-solving, in which students are able to relate the text to their personal knowledge; and extrapolation, in which students can construct inferences that go well beyond the text itself. The authors found that the kind of response students had to the text was determined in part by their age and their prior knowledge of the topic and that the kind of response they made to the text determined the amount of learning that occurred. Clearly, students who are able to deal with the text at the level of paraphrasing, problem-solving, or extrapolation are engaging in deeper processing and more learning than students who respond only to individual words or to verbatim chunks of text. This result is confirmed by the large-scale investigation reported by Kardash and Amlund (1991). They found that higher levels of processing, such as elaboration and the internal reorganization of textbook materials, are found primarily in students who earn higher grade point averages in college. Another individual trait, that of creativity, was found by Popov (1992) to be associated with a variety of measures of learning from text. In particular, measures of the kind of higher-order processes outlined previously, such as constructing an abstract or criticizing a text, were correlated with measures of creativity.

It is not only individual characteristics such as age, creativity, and previous knowledge that influence learning from text. Yochum (1991), who also examined

---

[7]Physiocrats were eighteenth-century philosophers who believed that land and its products were the only true wealth and that freedom of property and trade were the hallmarks of a desirable political system.

children's learning in a classroom situation, found that both prior topic knowledge and the way the text was organized influenced learning from text. It will be recalled from the analysis of scanning text that a match between the organization of the text and the goal of the user seems to be required for easy scanning. It now appears that this match is also important in learning, which can be seen in the research of Schraw, Wade, and Kardash (1993). They found that the reader's goals (the tasks they were trying to accomplish) and the organization of the text (for example, the way main ideas were presented) lead them to focus on and learn from certain parts of the text. These two factors, which they call text-based and task-based importance, interact to influence learning from text.

Other text variables are also important factors in determining the way learning occurs. For example, differences in the way text is presented have an impact on learning. This observation leads to a consideration of the literature on text design to facilitate learning. For example, Moreno and Di Vesta (1994) found that using analogies as advance organizers helped students to engage in the kinds of higher-order processes that are associated with enhanced learning from text. Similarly, text that is interesting to readers is processed and remembered more easily than uninteresting (but important) text elements (Wade, Schraw, Buxton, & Hayes, 1993).

The discussion of scanning notes that it is influenced by social factors, particularly those that are associated with motivation. It seems clear that motivation is equally crucial to the learning task and that social factors that may have a bearing on motivation can be important in the learning task. For example, studies have linked socioeconomic status and linguistic abilities associated with language production (Walker, Greenwood, Hart, & Carta, 1994), and the impact of family settings on educational achievement is also well documented (Blake, 1989; Marjoribanks, 1979). The effects of social variables on specific tasks, such as learning from text, have not been extensively investigated. However, it is possible to generalize to this task the findings from more general studies of educational achievement. In addition, the preferences of people from different social settings for different media of information can be considered as evidence for social influences on how people learn from those media. This phenomenon is noted in the discussion of health information needs in Chapter 3. In a more general study, Goodman (1992) focuses on the types of information sources likely to be used by elderly people. The use of print media and interpersonal channels is influenced by individual variables such as age and education and by social variables such as income. Accordingly, social factors must be considered relevant to the task of learning from information-retrieval systems.

Learning from Documents

The next focus of this discussion is learning from documents that contain both text and other forms of knowledge representation: the figural elements described previously that include graphs, images, and drawings. The first point that becomes clear immediately from a perusal of the literature on learning is that such documents have a real advantage over materials that contain only text. The source of this advantage is what Paivio (1990) calls the "dual-coding" approach. This understanding of the learning process states that people learn and remember information two ways: as propositions and as images. Propositions are linguistic representations of what they know; images are figural representations of what they know. It is true that dual coding can operate on plain text. For example, if a text describes a location, people will remember not only the words that describe the place, but will also create a spatial representation of the location in their mind that they will remember as well. Similarly, as previously noted, language that is highly concrete or that uses verbal imagery is more apt to lead to the creation of a mental image to accompany the learning that is derived from the language of the text.

On the other hand, documents that contain both textual and figural forms of representation seem to have a real advantage in stimulating learning. Waddill and McDaniel (1992) found that pictures in text enhanced understanding of and learning from the text, although they note that this enhancement is limited by the skills of the readers in processing images. It appears clear that learning from pictures is different than learning from text and that to obtain the maximum advantage of dual coding, readers must have the ability to do both kinds of processing. There has also been a substantial body of research that shows how maps enhance learning from texts (Kulhavy, Stock, Woodard, & Haygood, 1993; Kulhavy, Stock, & Kealy, 1993; Rittschof, Stock, Kulhavy, & Verdi, 1994). This dual-coding phenomenon also requires that readers have additional resources to comprehend and learn from maps: the ability to process both the individual features on the map and the structural relationships between those features. It also appears that there is a distinct advantage in terms of learning to examining the map first, then processing the text related to the map. The map provides an organizational structure, or a mental model, that helps the reader understand and remember the text information and provides a separate figural encoding of the information (Schnotz, Picard, & Hron, 1993).

Guthrie *et al.* (1993) found that there are two kinds of processing going on when people learn from graphs, tables, and illustrations: the search for specific facts and a more global processing that requires summarizing information into gist representations, understanding trends, and developing generalizations and abstractions from the specific information presented. It appears that the second kind of processing, focusing on complex abstraction, is particularly important in learning from this kind of information representation. Other research has shown how this kind of complex abstraction can be assisted. For example, Mayer (1994) found that referential connections between verbal and visual representations of information help individuals comprehend graphics. Keying the graphic to the text is sometimes awkward in standard print information media, but is accomplished more easily in multimedia or hypermedia approaches. Such direct links between the two representations is a way of ensuring that they can refer to each other in the process of recall. Similarly, Peeck (1993) suggests that drawing attention to the illustrative pictures and assisting readers' visual literacy are ways of increasing the impact of images presented in text.

The importance to learning of having figural and textual representations together in a document must be qualified. First, not all representations of the same data have the same informing value. Kaplan, Hammel, and Schimmel (1986) investigated the presentation of the risks of medical treatment as probabilities or through a graphic visual aid (presenting the probabilities as dots). They found that patients had difficulty processing the probabilities and they tended to make different decisions based on how the information was presented. Learning from documents is more likely to occur when the information is presented in a simplified manner. This point is reinforced by Sweller, Chandler, Tierney, and Cooper (1990). They found that some representations accompanying text can distract the reader from the task of understanding the text and these representations can impose a high cognitive load. Simpler representations are preferred over multiple, competing representations of information in learning from documents. There is a second reservation that must be voiced: not all readers learn equally well from all representations of information. Riding and Douglas (1993) found that cognitive styles of learners (for example, whether they were verbalizers or imagers) help to determine how well they learn from different combinations of text and images. Kirby (1993) investigated the ways that text and graphics can be combined so that the verbal and spatial processes of learners can collaborate with each other to enhance learning, rather than compete with each other to lessen learning. The conclusion of this research was that the kind of information to be learned is of central importance in determining the appropriate balance between the textual and graphical information presented and that students may need help in dealing with some combinations of these elements.

Learning from Electronic Documents

In the discussion of scanning presented previously, it is noted that electronic documents present special problems and opportunities for scanning information. The same is true of learning from the information presented by electronic information devices. Learning some kinds of information seems to be helped considerably by the presentation of information in the form of hypermedia. Cognitive flexibility theory, advanced by Rand Spiro and his students [see, for example, Jacobson & Spiro (1993)], suggests that if a problem is badly defined, different problem-solving or learning processes are appropriate than if a problem is well defined. In an ill-defined area, learners benefit from the ability to explore a variety of ways in which the topic can be elaborated, and of course hypertext or hypermedia excels in facilitating precisely this kind of learning. A number of hypermedia information systems in ill-defined domains have been developed to facilitate learning of the type suggested by cognitive flexibility theory. One example, focusing on the topic of transfusion medicine, was reported by Jonassen, Ambruso, and Olesen (1992).

One form of electronic document increasingly being used in business and related organizations is the electronic message. Walther (1992) examines in some detail the individual factors that influence communication in this medium and suggests that computer-mediated communication can be as good an information source as other interpersonal information sources, once users develop sufficient familiarity with the medium. In other words, one can learn from this kind of electronic document once one has an understanding of the conventions that govern its use. Here again, as in the various figural sources of information discussed previously, there is an additional knowledge resource that users must employ if they are going to obtain optimal learning from the medium. Rice, Grant, Schmitz, and Torobin (1990) conducted an early study of the appropriateness of adopting this source of information. They found that, in addition to the conventions governing the use of the medium, individual variables (e.g., attitudes and expectations) and social information-processing variables (e.g., communication patterns) influence the success of electronic messaging in providing information in an office setting.

Electronic communication systems that incorporate electronic messaging may take over the roles formerly served by a variety of text forms, such as reports, memos, and forms. When these functions are taken over by computer-media communication, some of the characteristics of the paper media may be lost, resulting in barriers to learning and communication. Croft, Krovetz, and Turtle (1990) comment on the cognitive differences between different information sources such as reports, memos, and forms. Although the content of the sources is likely to be more important than the different layout attributes in determining whether a source is relevant to a particular information need, the layout attributes help in comprehension of and learning from the sources. Clearly, any information system that incorporates a variety of text forms must allow users to deal in a flexible and informed manner with them. The OFFICER prototype described by Croft *et al.* (1990) seems a logical first step, although it seems to focus too much on the data and not enough on the user's knowledge and understanding of the data in its different forms. Another approach to office information systems that makes use of the way users think about information resources is described by Lansdale and Edmonds (1992). The MEMOIRS information system organizes documents around events rather than around topics. This approach seems to represent an interesting design for a personal filing system, but it will require a strong collective understanding of the history of the work group or organization if it is to be employed in facilitating group recall and learning.

Learning from People and Media

The discussion of information needs in Chapter 3 notes that, for many kinds of information, people prefer to learn from personal communication with family and friends, from direct communication with professionals such as physicians or social workers, and from media such as television and newspapers. The discussion of system design presented in Chapter 6 incorporates links to human experts as something that may be valued in information systems that respond to statements of failure of perception or to statements of need for advice in evaluating alternatives. Given this recognition of the importance of people and media in information seeking, it may seem strange that this discussion of learning has focused entirely on documents of various kinds.

The focus on documents can be justified by noting that documents are nothing more than recorded messages from people. The same processes are involved in comprehension, evaluation, and learning when information is presented directly by a person and when that communication is mediated by a recorded message. The user must know something about the topic and must understand the structure of the message. The processing of the message can occur at several levels and involve different ways of coding or representing the message in memory. There are real differences between processing spoken and written information, but there are also great similarities in the way learning occurs. For example, hearing a lecture or reading a lecture will produce essentially the same learning experience, and both experiences will be subject to the same individual and social influences.

When it comes to mass media, however, there are important differences that must be recognized. The main difference between television and documents can be highlighted by the uses-and-gratifications approach mentioned in Chapter 3 (Gantz, 1978). Television appears to be particularly prone to multiple uses. For example, a television news broadcast may be seen as a learning experience or it may be treated as entertainment. Robinson and Davis (1990) question whether the great increase in the number of television news programs actually produces a better informed public. The answer seems to be a negative one. People who report that they get most of their information from television have lower news comprehension scores than those who use other media. In such cases, a task that one may consider an information task is actually serving another goal. There is a sense in which all information sources may be considered as having multiple uses, and one use can interfere with another. In making information and communication systems more interesting and lively, designers may reduce their informativeness. Abelman (1987) adds complexity to this with regard to a specific television information medium: religious programming. This investigation found that in addition to the usual uses-and-gratifications motivation for using the information medium, there is a reactionary motivation: people reacting against the usual television programming. This research points out the importance of assessing people's motivations to use different media when building information systems.

The resources individuals employ in learning from materials presented by an information system are diverse. Knowledge resources similar to those already discussed in the context of scanning and evaluating come into play: existing knowledge of the topic being investigated, knowledge of text structures and related display formats, and knowledge of the context of the information need. In addition, personal characteristics, including learning abilities and creativity, drive the learning process. The challenge of incorporating an understanding of these resources into information-system design will be considered in Chapter 8.

Planning

The focus now shifts to the task of planning. Many information searches must be regarded longitudinally as a series of goal-directed activities. As users move closer to their goal, they evolve plans that may take them the next few steps. These plans are subject to continuous revision. This revision process is driven by a feedback loop that is well documented in the literature. The first part of that loop is that people seek information in order to make plans. The second part of the loop is that people make plans to seek information.

Researchers in different domains have investigated the information seeking that goes into the planning of any activity. Berger and DiBattista (1992) show that, as people plan for certain social outcomes, they seek information. The more complex the plan, the more information they require. Hartman, Lundberg, and White (1993) show that information-processing strategies normally outlined as being appropriate in planning are not actually used in business planning. They suggest that other implicit strategies are operating. In these two studies, the fact that information is sought and processed during planning is clear. In fact, Abernethy (1993) found that some level of information is necessary for any plan, even those involving motor skills.

The evidence that people construct plans to search for information is more anecdotal. Basch (1993) interviewed experts in searching bibliographic data files and found that planning search strategies was a key element in their success. In addition, the work of Bates (1979) points out the importance of plans in conducting specialized searches of this kind. A plan frequently is derived from a knowledge structure such as a script. Derived from repeated experience in similar situations, a script includes a step-by-step approach to completing the task in question. Even when there is no script from which to derive a plan for what to do next in information seeking, there may be more general heuristics that users may bring to the task. These may be as simple as trial-and-error approaches to problem solving, or they may be more elaborate coping mechanisms. These knowledge structures are important resources that users bring to the task of planning for information retrieval. In general, they allow users to decide on an appropriate sequence of actions, given an understanding of the current situation in which they are found.

In addition to scripts or heuristics, people employ a knowledge of the task they are accomplishing, their current state in accomplishing their plan, and their environment in developing plans. In the case of planning for information retrieval, users combine their goal, purpose, or objective with an understanding of the current state of their knowledge and the nature of the informant or information source in activating and using a particular script or heuristic that will generate a plan of action. It seems likely that cognitive abilities also affect the planning that people do. For example, higher levels of creativity in problem solving may lead to more elaborate or unique plans of action.

In addition, social factors can influence how people plan for information seeking. The nature of scripts and heuristics is that they are derived from experiences in society. There are, therefore, social constraints on the kinds of behavior that are included in these knowledge structures. The classic example is the restaurant script: a step-by-step summary of how one behaves while obtaining and consuming a restaurant meal. The social nature of this task is self-evident and so also is the fact that different social situations may lead to quite different versions of the script. It follows that an individual's plans for information seeking are likely to be constrained by social factors. These may authorize (or prevent) certain sequences of steps particularly related to specific information systems or resources. For example, there may be social constraints placed on how one learns from a particular informant, or how one may repeatedly approach that informant.

The resources employed in planning are somewhat different from those discussed in the context of scanning, evaluating, and learning. Here, the knowledge resources employed include knowledge of scripts and heuristics in addition to knowledge of the topic and the context of the information need. Although not emphasized in the preceding discussion, it seems clear that there are individual differences that affect the kinds of planning people will complete. Again, an understanding of this combination of knowledge and abilities must be incorporated into user-centered information-system design.

Cognitive Load

The concept of cognitive load provides a basis for synthesizing the discussion of individual information seeking presented in this chapter. All of the tasks discussed, scanning, judging, learning, and planning, place a demand on the cognitive processes of the individual. To meet that demand, a number of resources are employed. One research approach to cognitive load (Carey, Nonnecke, Lungu, & Mitterer, 1993) suggests that aversion to risk and cognitive load drives the selection of research approaches by users. For example, users may employ a method they perceive as safe, perhaps because it is familiar, even if that method is less efficient than other search techniques. The cognitive load of learning a new, more efficient approach to searching is avoided at the cost of less-efficient (or possibly less-effective) search results.

Users in this perspective seek to maximize the return they achieve for a given amount of effort or minimize the amount of effort required to achieve a certain amount of information. This maximization of return can be achieved if the information system is optimized to correspond to the resources that users have, either because they bring them to the tasks or because the information system is structured in such a way as to augment naturally occurring resources.

Collective Interaction with Information Systems

The preceding discussion concentrates on how individuals interact with information systems. The question that must be considered now is whether groups can interact collectively with information systems in ways that are not fully explained by the interactions of individual group members with those systems. In other words, do groups perform differently in the tasks of scanning, judging, and learning from information? Do they plan their information activities differently from individuals?

The answers to all of these questions are almost certainly in the affirmative. Collective scanning of information requires that individuals scan the information and then communicate with each other about what they are seeing. It was noted previously that individuals may scan materials differently depending on the state of their knowledge of the topic, their knowledge of the structure of the materials being scanned, their task, and their cognitive abilities. If the individuals in a group possess these resources in different ways, it can be predicted that the individuals will see different things in the materials presented by an information system. If the group is engaging in collective scanning, then the question of what the group saw will have to be negotiated by the group members.

This point becomes clearer when the question of evaluating and judging the materials presented by an information system is considered. If the system presents vocabulary, group members may have different perceptions of the appropriateness of any given vocabulary element to the description of their collective information need. If the system presents documents, group members may have different perceptions of the usefulness of a given document to the task at hand. The amount of negotiation about the relevance of required materials will depend on the extent to which there is a clear and shared understanding of the group's collective knowledge and on its collective understanding of the task it is accomplishing. Even if there is absolute consensus on these points, individual group members are still likely to present different material evaluations because they have different understandings of the information structure presented or different levels of cognitive abilities used in making such judgments. So, again, the task of collective evaluation of materials is one that will necessarily involve some level of negotiation among group members.

Collective judgments of the usefulness or appropriateness of information to a collective information task combine all of the individual and social variables cited previously with the dynamics of group assessment. To arrive at a group assessment of information, the group must first agree on the criteria against which materials are to be evaluated, then come to a consensus about the extent to which any particular information matches those criteria. The first level of agreement, associated with defining criteria, requires ongoing discussion among group members. It seems likely that, as the group process continues, the criteria by which information is judged will evolve. It follows that there must be an ongoing discussion about exactly what constitutes good (or appropriate) information for meeting the group's needs. Again, the role of persuasion seems crucial here. If a particular group member has a strong feeling that only information that matches a particular set of biases or perspectives is useful, he or she will have to convince the other group members about the value of that criterion.

The second level of agreement, that attached to the application of criteria to any particular piece of information, requires ongoing negotiation. For example, there may be a process through which group members present candidates for good information to be assessed by the group. There are a variety of approaches that this assessment may adopt. First, information deemed relevant by any group member can be considered by the group. Alternatively, any group member may have the power to veto any information presented for use by the group. There can be approaches of consensus, majority vote, or inclusion of information with a weighting system based on the proportion of the group that regards the information as useful. Clearly, group interactions with information systems are highly complex, and this complexity adds to the difficulty of designing information systems for group use.

Collective learning is also different from individual learning. As observed in Chapter 3, it is not enough for one member of a group to learn something. This learning must be communicated to other group members. This communication may involve more than simple conversation and may require persuasion. Learning a new way of thinking about the problem that the group is solving, the decision it is making, or the ideas it is studying requires a renegotiation of the group's focus, in which personal and political factors play an important role. The preceding discussion of individual learning notes the importance of elaborating knowledge structures, creating new links by analogy or other kinds of associative learning. Elaboration in the group setting requires that the elements to be linked or associated are present in the collective knowledge base and that all members of the group come to understand the elaboration. An example may clarify this point. One member of a research team may tell his or her colleagues of an analogy that seems to illuminate the problem they are investigating particularly well: "You know, in 1928 Schultz faced exactly the same problem we're facing in trying to get the cyclotron to cycle." One colleague may ask, "Who was Schultz?", while another may respond, "No, his problem was completely different from ours." To create an elaborated collective understanding of the problem, there will have to be a great deal of interaction between group members to ensure that the collective knowledge of the problem has the elements to be linked and that the link is a productive one. Finally, the addition of new knowledge to the collective understanding will require reaching consensus that the new knowledge element is appropriate. Again, this involves that the members of the group come to know something new, they recognize that they know something new, and they recognize that all of the other members of the group share that knowledge. These exercises in individual cognition, meta-cognition, and social cognition are achieved at the expense not only of cognitive load, but also of an investment of group time and effort.

The ongoing task of planning how information seeking will proceed is also rather more complex in the group environment. As the group comes to understand its own nature and the nature of its task, there will necessarily be a new understanding of the next steps to be accomplished in seeking information. This understanding may occur differently in the minds of group members as they call upon different heuristics that they have learned in the course of individual information seeking. As a result, the group must focus its activities at least for a time on deciding a plan to which all members agree.

The counterpart of cognitive load in group information seeking is group-process load. In collective activities of the kind discussed in this book, each task that is accomplished by an individual at the expense of some cognitive load must be accomplished by the cognitive load absorbed by each of the group members, plus a group process load. This will usually be computed as the amount of time and effort expended in reaching a collective understanding. The tasks of group information seeking can present a substantial bill to pay in the area of group-process load.

Conclusions

Interactions between people and information systems involve a number of tasks, only a few of which have been discussed here. This chapter has focused on the more general interaction tasks, and it is clear that, with specialized information systems, the tasks to be considered will differ. System designers who adopt the user-centered approach will necessarily be in the position of investigating the tasks that must be accomplished by their own users as they interact with the information systems being designed. Throughout this discussion, it has been clear that the tasks of interaction draw upon many different resources: individual knowledge, cognitive abilities, socially approved procedures, and the processes of group dynamics. The task of user-centered design requires that these resources be taken into account in deciding which design features will be included in the system. Understanding what resources are available to users and in what degree and combination will allow designers to build systems that take optimal advantage of existing resources and augment those resources with design decisions where possible.

The next chapter considers the general design features that may be considered to enhance information-system usability by paying attention to the tasks of interaction and the resources required to accomplish those information interaction tasks.

References

Abelman, R. (1987). Why do people watch religious TV?: A uses and gratifications approach. *Review of Religious Research, 29*(2), 199–210.

Abernethy, B. (1993). Searching for the minimal essential information for skilled perception and action. *Psychological Research/Psychologische Forschung, 55*(2), 131–138.

Allen, B. L (1992). Cognitive differences in end-user searching of a CD-ROM index. In *15th International Conference on Research and Development in Information Retrieval Proceedings* (pp. 298–309). Baltimore, MD: ACM.

Allen, B. L. (1993). Logical reasoning and retrieval performance. *Library and Information Science Research, 15*, 93–105.

Allen, B. L. (1994). Perceptual speed, learning and information retrieval performance. In W. B. Croft and C. J. van Rijsbergen (Eds.), *SIGIR '94: Proceedings of the Seventeenth International Conference on Research and Development in Information Retrieval* (pp. 71–80). London: Springer-Verlag.

Anderson, J. R. (1995). *Learning and memory: An integrated approach.* New York: Wiley.

Armbruster, B. B., & Armstrong, J. O. (1993). Locating information in text: A focus on children in the elementary grades. *Contemporary Educational Psychology, 18*(2), 139–161.

Baker, L., & Wagner, J. L. (1987). Evaluating information for truthfulness: The effects of logical subordination. *Memory and Cognition, 15*(3), 247–255.

Barry, C. L. (1994). User defined relevance criteria: An exploratory study. *Journal of the American Society for Information Science, 45*(3), 149–159.

Basch, R. (1993). Secrets of the super searchers: Planning search strategies. *Online, 17*(5), 52–54.

Bates, M. J. (1979). Information search tactics. *Journal of the American Society of Information Science, 30*(4), 205–214.

Berger, C. R., & DiBattista, P. (1992). Information seeking and plan elaboration: What do you need to know to know what to do? *Communication Monographs, 59*(4), 368–387.

Blake, J. (1989). *Family size and achievement.* Berkeley: University of California Press.

Blanchard, J., & Carey, J. (1992). What makes information important and its influence on learning in self directed study. *Perceptual and Motor Skills, 75*(1), 323–333.

Boehm-Davis, D. A., Holt, R. W., Koll, M., Yastrop, G., & Peters, R. (1989). Effects of different data base formats on information retrieval. *Human Factors, 31*(5), 579–592.

Bruce, H. W. (1994). A cognitive view of the situational dynamism of user centered relevance estimation. *Journal of the American Society for Information Science, 45*(3), 142–148.

Butler, R. (1993). Effects of task and ego achievement goals on information seeking during task engagement. *Journal of Personality and Social Psychology, 65*(1), 18–31.

Byrnes, J. P., & Guthrie, J. T. (1992). Prior conceptual knowledge and textbook search. *Contemporary Educational Psychology, 17*(1), 8–29.

Cardinale, L. A. (1993). Facilitating science learning by embedded explication. *Instructional Science, 21*(6), 501–512.

Carey, T., Nonnecke, B., Lungu, D., & Mitterer, J. (1993). Access methods for online information: A cost/benefit approach to users' choices. In *Proceedings of the 1993 IEEE International Professional Communication Conference* (pp. 268–272). Piscataway, NJ: IEEE.

Chan, C. K., Burtis, P. J., Scardamalia, M., & Bereiter, C. (1992). Constructive activity in learning from text. *American Educational Research Journal, 29*(1), 97–118.

Croft, W. B., Krovetz, R., & Turtle, H. (1990). Interactive retrieval of complex documents. *Information Processing & Management, 26*(5), 593–613.

Dillon, A. (1991). Readers' models of text structures: The case of academic articles. *International Journal of Man Machine Studies, 35*(6), 913–925.

Dillon, A. (1994). *Designing usable electronic text: Ergonomic aspects of human information usage.* London: Taylor and Francis.

Dreher, M. J., & Brown, R. F. (1993). Planning prompts and indexed terms in textbook search tasks. *Journal of Educational Psychology, 85*(4), 662–669.

Dreher, M. J., & Guthrie, J. T. (1990). Cognitive processes in textbook chapter search tasks. *Reading Research Quarterly*, *25*(4), 323–339.

Froehlich, T. J. (1994). Relevance reconsidered: Towards an agenda for the 21st century. *Journal of the American Society for Information Science*, *45*(3), 124–134.

Gantz, W. (1978). How uses and gratifications affect recall of television news. *Journalism Quarterly*, *55*(4), 664–672.

Glynn, M. A. (1994). Effects of work task cues and play task cues on information processing, judgment, and motivation. *Journal of Applied Psychology*, *79*(1), 34–45.

Goodman, R. I. (1992). The selection of communication channels by the elderly to obtain information. *Educational Gerontology*, *18*(7), 701–714.

Gray, S. H., Barber, C. B., & Shasha, D. (1991). Information search with dynamic text vs. paper text: An empirical comparison. *International Journal of Man Machine Studies*, *35*(4), 575–586.

Guthrie, J. T. (1988). Locating information in text: Examination of a cognitive model. *Reading Research Quarterly*, *23*(2), 178–199.

Guthrie, J. T., Britten, T., & Barker, K. G. (1991). Roles of document structure, cognitive strategy, and awareness in searching for information. *Reading Research Quarterly*, *26*(3), 300–324.

Guthrie, J. T., Weber, S., & Kimmerly, N. (1993). Searching documents: Cognitive processes and deficits in understanding graphs, tables, and illustrations. *Contemporary Educational Psychology*, *18*(2), 186–221.

Hartman, S. J., Lundberg, O., & White, M. (1993). The processing of information by students and business planners. *Journal of General Psychology*, *120*(4), 421–435.

Hess, R. D., & Tenezakis, M. D. (1973). Selected findings from "The computer as a socializing agent: Some socioaffective outcomes of CAI." *AV Communication Review*, *21*(3), 311–325.

Howard, D. L. (1994). Pertinence as reflected in personal constructs. *Journal of the American Society for Information Science*, *45*(3), 172–185.

Jacobson, M. J., & Spiro, R. J. (1993). *Hypertext learning environments, cognitive flexibility, and the transfer of complex knowledge: An empirical investigation* (Technical Report # 573). Champaign, IL: Center for the Study of Reading.

Janes, J. W. (1991). Relevance judgment and the incremental presentation of document representations. *Information Processing & Management*, *27*(6), 629–646.

Janes, J. W. (1994). Other people's judgments: A comparison of users' and others' judgments of document relevance, topicality, and utility. *Journal of the American Society for Information Science*, *45*(3), 160–171.

Jonassen, D. H., Ambruso, D. R., & Olesen, J. (1992). Designing a hypertext on transfusion medicine using cognitive flexibility theory. *Journal of Educational Multimedia and Hypermedia*, *1*, 309–322.

Kaplan, R. M., Hammel, B., & Schimmel, L. E. (1986). Patient information processing and the decision to accept treatment. *Journal of Social Behavior and Personality*, *1*(1), 113–120.

Kardash, C. M., & Amlund, J. T. (1991). Self reported learning strategies and learning from expository text. *Contemporary Educational Psychology*, *16*(2), 117–138.

Kelly, J. D. (1993). The effects of display format and data density on time spent reading statistics in text, tables, and graphs. *Journalism Quarterly*, *70*(1), 140–149.

Kirby, J. R. (1993). Collaborative and competitive effects of verbal and spatial processes. *Learning and Instruction*, *3*(3), 201–214.

Kuhlthau, C. C. (1993). Seeking meaning: *A process approach to library and information services*. Norwood, NJ: Ablex.

Kulhavy, R. W., Stock, W. A., & Kealy, W. A. (1993). How geographic maps increase recall of instructional text. *Educational Technology Research and Development*, *41*(4), 47–62.

Kulhavy, R. W., Stock, W. A., Woodard, K. A., & Haygood, R. C. (1993). Comparing elaboration and dual coding theories: The case of maps and text. *American Journal of Psychology*, *106*(4), 483–498.

Lansdale, M., & Edmonds, E. (1992). Using memory for events in the design of personal filing systems. *International Journal of Man Machine Studies*, *36*(1), 97–126.

Lee-Sammons, W. H., & Whitney, P. (1991). Reading perspectives and memory for text: An individual differences analysis. *Journal of Experimental Psychology: Learning, Memory, and Cognition, 17*(6), 1074–1081.

Lohse, G., Walker, N., Biolsi, K., & Rueter, H. (1991). Classifying graphical information. *Behaviour and Information Technology, 10*(5), 419–436.

Marchionini, G. (1992). Interfaces for end-user information seeking. *Journal of the American Society for Information Science, 43*(2), 156–163.

Marjoribanks, K. (1979). *Families and their learning environments: An empirical analysis.* London: Routledge & Kegan Paul.

Mayer, R. E. (1994). Visual aids to knowledge construction: Building mental representations from pictures and words. In W. Schnotz & R. Kulhavy (Eds.), *Comprehension of graphics* (pp. 125–138). Amsterdam: North-Holland.

McGoldrick, J. A., Martin, J., Bergering, A. J., & Symons, S. (1992). Locating discrete information in text: Effects of computer presentation and menu formatting. *Journal of Reading Behavior, 24*(1), 1–20.

Mohageg, M. F. (1992). The influence of hypertext linking structures on the efficacy of information retrieval. *Human Factors, 34*(3), 351–367.

Moreno, V., & Di Vesta, F. J. (1994). Analogies (adages) as aids for comprehending structural relations in text. *Contemporary Educational Psychology, 19*(2), 179–198.

Mynatt, B. T., Levanthall, L. M., Farhat, J., & Rohlman, D. S. (1992). Hypertext or book? Which is better for answering questions? In P. Bauersfeld, J. Bennett, & G. Lynch (Eds.), *CHI '92 conference proceedings: ACM conference on human factors in computing systems: Striking a balance* (pp. 19–25). New York: Association for Computing Machinery.

Norman, D. A. (1986). Cognitive engineering. In D. A. Norman & S. W. Draper (Eds.), *User centered system design: New perspectives on human-computer interaction* (pp. 31–61). Hillsdale, NJ: Lawrence Erlbaum.

Nygren, E., Lind, M., Johnson, M., & Sandblad, B. (1992). The art of the obvious. In P. Bauersfeld, J. Bennett, & G. Lynch (Eds.), *CHI '92 conference proceedings: ACM conference on human factors in computing systems: Striking a balance* (pp. 235–239). New York: Association for Computing Machinery.

Paivio, A. (1990). *Mental representations: A dual coding approach.* New York: Oxford.

Park, T. K. (1993). The nature of relevance in information retrieval: An empirical study. *Library Quarterly, 63*(3), 318–351.

Park, T. K. (1994). Toward a theory of user based relevance: A call for a new paradigm of inquiry. *Journal of the American Society for Information Science, 45*(3), 135–141.

Peeck, J. (1993). Increasing picture effects in learning from illustrated text. *Learning and Instruction, 3*(3), 227–238.

Popov, A. (1992). Creativity and reading comprehension. *Journal of Creative Behavior, 26*(3), 206–212.

Rice, R. E., Grant, A. E., Schmitz, J., & Torobin, J. (1990). Individual and network influences on the adoption and perceived outcomes of electronic messaging. *Social Networks, 12*(1), 27–55.

Riding, R., & Chambers, P. (1992). CD-ROM versus textbook: A comparison of the use of two learning media by higher education students. *Educational and Training Technology International, 29*(4), 342–349.

Riding, R. J., & Douglas, G. (1993). The effect of cognitive style and mode of presentation on learning performance. *British Journal of Educational Psychology, 63*(2), 297–307.

Rittschof, K. A., Stock, W. A., Kulhavy, R. W., & Verdi, M. P. (1994). Thematic maps improve memory for facts and inferences: A test of the stimulus order hypothesis. *Contemporary Educational Psychology, 19*(2), 129–142.

Robinson, J. P., & Davis, D. K. (1990). Television news and the informed public: An information processing approach. *Journal of Communication, 40*(3), 106–119.

Russell, D. M., Stefik, M. J., Pirolli, P., & Card, S. K. (1993). The cost structure of sensemaking. In

S. Ashlund, K. Mullet, A. Henderson, E. Hollnagel, & T. White (Eds.), *INTERCHI '93 conference proceedings: Conference on human factors in computing systems INTERACT '93 and CHI '93: Bridges between the worlds* (pp. 269–276). New York: Association for Computing Machinery.

Sadoski, M., Goetz, E. T., & Fritz, J. B. (1993). Impact of concreteness on comprehensibility, interest, and memory for text: Implications for dual coding theory and text design. *Journal of Educational Psychology, 85*(2), 291–304.

Schamber, L., Eisenberg, M. B., & Nilan, M. S. (1990). A re-examination of relevance: Toward a dynamic, situational definition. *Information Processing & Management, 26*(6), 755–776.

Schnotz, W., Picard, E., & Hron, A. (1993). How do successful and unsuccessful learners use texts and graphics? *Learning and Instruction, 3*(3), 181–199.

Schraw, G., Wade, S. E., & Kardash, C. A. (1993). Interactive effects of text based and task based importance on learning from text. *Journal of Educational Psychology, 85*(4), 652–661.

Shum, S. (1990). Real and virtual spaces: Mapping from spatial cognition to hypertext. *Hypermedia, 2*(2), 133–158.

Small, R. V., & Grabowski, B. L. (1992). An exploratory study of information-seeking behaviors and learning with hypermedia information systems. *Journal of Educational Multimedia and Hypermedia, 1*(4), 445–464.

Smithson, S. (1994). Information retrieval evaluation in practice: A case study approach. *Information Processing and Management, 30*(2), 205–221.

Sparrow, J. A. (1989). Graphical displays in information systems: Some data properties influencing the effectiveness of alternative forms. *Behaviour and Information Technology, 8*(1), 43–56.

Sutton, S. A. (1994). The role of attorney mental models of law in case relevance determinations: An exploratory analysis. *Journal of the American Society for Information Science, 45*(3), 186–200.

Sweller, J., Chandler, P., Tierney, P., & Cooper, M. (1990). Cognitive load as a factor in the structuring of technical material. *Journal of Experimental Psychology: General, 119*(2), 176–192.

Symons, S., & Pressley, M. (1993). Prior knowledge affects text search success and extraction of information. *Reading Research Quarterly, 28*(3), 250–261.

Tufte, E. R. (1983). *Visual display of quantitative information*. Cheshire, CT: Graphics Press.

Tufte, E. R. (1990). *Envisioning information*. Cheshire, CT: Graphics Press.

Waddill, P. J., & McDaniel, M. A. (1992). Pictorial enhancements of text memory: Limitations imposed by picture type and comprehension skill. *Memory and Cognition, 20*(5), 472–482.

Wade, S. E., Schraw, G., Buxton, W. M., & Hayes, M. T. (1993). Seduction of the strategic reader: Effects of interest on strategies and recall. *Reading Research Quarterly, 28*(2), 93–114.

Walker, D., Greenwood, C., Hart, B., & Carta, J. (1994). Prediction of school outcomes based on early language production and socioeconomic factors. *Child Development, 65*(2), 606–621.

Walther, J. B. (1992). Interpersonal effects in computer mediated interaction: A relational perspective. *Communication Research, 19*(1), 52–90.

Welsh, T. M., Murphy, K. P., Duffy, T. M., & Goodrum, D. A. (1993). Accessing elaborations on core information in a hypermedia environment. *Educational Technology Research and Development, 41*(2), 19–34.

Wiberley, S. E., & Daugherty, R. A. (1988). Users' persistence in scanning lists of references. *College and Research Libraries, 49*(2), 149–156.

Wiberley, S. E., Daugherty, R. A., & Danowski, J. A. (1990). User persistence in scanning postings of a computer driven information system: LCS. *Library and Information Science Research, 12*(4), 341–353.

Wilson, T. D., DePaulo, B. M., Mook, D. G., & Klaaren, K. J. (1993). Scientists' evaluations of research: The biasing effects of the importance of the topic. *Psychological Science, 4*(5), 322–325.

Winn, W. (1993). An account of how readers search for information in diagrams. *Contemporary Educational Psychology, 18*(2), 162–185.

Wyatt, D., Pressley, M., El Dinary, P. B., & Stein, S. (1993). Comprehension strategies, worth and credibility monitoring, and evaluations: Cold and hot cognition when experts read professional articles that are important to them. *Learning and Individual Differences, 5*(1), 49–72.

Yochum, N. (1991). Children's learning from informational text: The relationship between prior knowledge and text structure. *Journal of Reading Behavior, 23*(1), 87–108.

Yussen, S. R., Stright, A. D., & Payne, B. (1993). Where is it? Searching for information in a college textbook. *Contemporary Educational Psychology, 18*(2), 240–257.

8

Design Details for Information Systems

Introduction

It is only now that this discussion can turn to the specific components of information-system design. After examining all of the individual and social factors that can influence information behavior, it is now possible to consider in some detail the characteristics of information systems that will serve to meet users' information needs, while taking into account their goals, the tasks they accomplish, and the resources they bring to those tasks.

This chapter will consider the kinds of information that should be included in an information system. The data-centered, traditional approach to information-system design begins with the question of what should be included in the information system. A collection of data is accumulated, based on criteria such as anticipated use, quality, balance, or completeness. In some situations, the collection may be built "because it's there." Journals are added to the collection because they are being published and data archives because a government agency distributes them. Customer records are assembled because they are available. In the user-centered approach, questions of what should be included in the collection have been left until this point, because some different criteria for collection building can now be established. The questions that leap out of the pages of the discussion thus far are: Do these resources meet information needs? Can people scan this information? Can they evaluate it? Can they learn from it? Are there other sources of information that are more easily evaluated or that contribute more completely to learning?

Similarly, this chapter can finally consider the organization of information. In the data-centered approach, organization comes after acquisition. The basis for organization is typically the data in the collection. Information is organized according to *a priori* principles or according to the characteristics of the collection. Points of intellectual organization and access are derived from the data. Indexing and classification of the data provide the basis for retrieval. The user is nowhere in sight. However, now that the analyses in the preceding chapters have been completed, it is possible to consider questions of organization in a new light. Will this organization allow easy browsing for individuals with minimally verbalized statements of information need? Will these access points be consistent with the vocabulary of users and so be capable of being used? Will this classification allow learning? Are there better approaches to organizing this information to enhance learning?

Finally, this chapter can pay more attention to interfaces. The approach already indicated is to create usable information systems, rather than creating unusable information systems and then trying to remedy the situation by slapping a graphical user interface or some other cognitively correct interface on the front end. Now that user behavior has been examined in more detail, it is possible to see whether there may be interface elements that are better geared to meeting certain kinds of information needs or that are more usable for people with certain levels of learning abilities.

The design implications derived from the discussion in Chapter 7 may be summarized as follows:

General Design Principle

Information systems should minimize the cognitive and group-process loads that users bear in completing an information task.

Specific Design Implications

I. Information systems should facilitate the efficient scanning of presented materials.

   A. Materials should be presented in a way that is consistent with the knowledge that users have of the topic.

   B. Knowledge of the topic that will assist users in scanning should be presented to the user as preparation for scanning.

   C. Materials should be presented in a way that is consistent with the knowledge that users have of the structure of information sources.

   D. Knowledge of information-source structures should accompany the presentation of those sources.

   E. Materials should be presented in a way that is consistent with the task being accomplished by the user.

   F. Materials should be presented in a way that allows users to make best use of their cognitive abilities, particularly perceptual speed and spatial orientation.

II. Information systems should facilitate the effective evaluation of materials presented.

   A. Presentation of materials should highlight data particularly useful in evaluation.

   B. Materials should be presented in a way that allows users to make best use of their cognitive abilities, particularly logical reasoning.

    III. Information systems should facilitate learning from materials presented.

      A. Materials that enhance dual coding should be presented.
      B. Materials should be presented in a way that is consistent with the task being accomplished by the user and with the domain being studied.
      C. Materials should be organized to emphasize associative links that facilitate elaborations.
      D. Materials should be presented in a way that allows users to make best use of their creativity.
      E. Materials should be accompanied by organizing materials that will facilitate learning.
      F. Knowledge of information-source structures should accompany the presentation of those sources.
      G. Information from people and the media should be linked to recorded messages.

    IV. Information systems should facilitate planning for information seeking.

      A. Scripts or heuristics should be presented along with information.

    V. Information systems should facilitate group processes.

      A. Mechanisms that will facilitate group discussion and consensus should be incorporated into information systems.

Chapter 6 sketches some preliminary design features of information systems that respond to different kinds of statements of information need. It is now possible to see how the design principles listed here can fit into the designs already sketched to produce a more realistic view of information systems optimized for meeting user information needs. The first information system, System 1, is designed to address failures of perception.

System 1 characteristics:
- Browsing and navigational systems allow users to access information in a minimally semantic fashion. These systems include classificatory and associative networks and interfaces that facilitate browsing.
- Expert knowledge is encoded as associative networks of images of objects, diagnostic expert systems, or human experts linked to the information system by electronic messaging or by referral.
- Words are defined, perhaps through a dictionary lookup, and the information provided is explained by systems, analogy, or human experts.

System 2 is designed to address the identification of alternatives.

System 2 characteristics:
- Primary access is provided through a body of texts modeled on an encyclopedia, a textbook, or a how-to guide.
- Easy access is provided through an index of structured labels.
- Hierarchical associative networks are used for systematic topic exploration, combined with lateral references to analogous topics to enhance elaboration of understanding.

System 3 is designed to facilitate evaluation of alternatives.

System 3 characteristics:
- A vector-space model accepts verbose and reasonably expert statements of need.
- Primary access is provided through portions of documents assembled to constitute the raw materials of a review article or meta-analysis (for high-demand topics, primary access is provided through review articles).
- The system is linked to human experts who can provide advice.

This chapter now considers each of these design sketches in light of the design implications derived from Chapter 7.

Designing for Scanning

The first of the specific design implications outlined previously is that information systems should facilitate the efficient scanning of presented materials. This section considers how each of the six recommended approaches to designing for scanning may influence the design sketches developed in Chapter 6.

Materials should be presented in a way that is consistent with the knowledge that users have of the topic.

Materials should be presented in a way that is consistent with the task being accomplished by the user.

In general terms, all three systems present materials in a way that is consistent with user's knowledge of the topic of their information search. However, the system designs presented in Chapter 6 are concerned primarily with the quantity of knowledge that users have. To facilitate scanning, it is also important to consider how users structure that knowledge. In System 2, the primary access document is a topical, hierarchical encyclopedia article. In System 3, the primary access document is a collection of document sections presented in calculated order of similarity to the extended statement of information need. If the organization of these primary access documents does not match the organization of knowledge in the user's mind, scanning will be slow and inefficient. An example from the study of history illuminates this point. Suppose a user has searched a label and obtained an encyclopedia article on the history of France. That article may be organized either in narrative order (i.e., presenting events in the order in which they occurred) or in thematic order (i.e., considering the history of ideas, social organization, religion, and international relations separately). If the user's expectation, driven by the way he or she understands history, is for one of these organizations, then the other organization may impede scanning. Similarly, in System 3, the order of calculated similarity to the statement of need may jumble together different themes, particularly once one moves part of the way down the primary access document. For example, there may be a group of documents that partially match the statement of need. However, some of the documents may take an approach to the topic that is different from that taken by others, and this combination of approaches may confuse the issue sufficiently for the users to slow their scanning of the document.

Chapter 6 presents the idea that the information presented by the information system has to be organized in a variety of ways to meet the goals and purposes of the user, to be congruent to the problem situation in which the user finds himself or herself and to accommodate the social constraints on the type of information that is acceptable. Being capable of reorganizing the information quickly and on demand into different structures now can be seen as important to scanning as well. In the case of System 1, this seems reasonably straightforward. The primary documents of retrieval are already presented as associative networks for browsing, and it seems clear that users may browse through that network in many directions, thus (in effect) creating their own organization as they browse. In the case of System 2, multiple organizations have also been specified. Any particular chunk of text can be indexed as an event that occurred at a particular time or as a specific outcome of an economic theory. One can move to that chunk of text either from previous events or from more general discussions of the economic theory. Multiple superimposed hierarchical networks seem to be necessary, in addition to the multiple versions of each chunk of the text considered in Chapter 6. In the case of System 3, some flexible means of clustering documents within the raw materials documents seems to be necessary. Here, it is assumed that users know enough about the domain to pick out particular chunks of text as representing some aspect of the topic (in their own organization of the topic). It seems reasonable to have the user specify several chunks of text as representing the main aspects of the topic and to have the system reorganize the raw materials documents into clusters around those representative chunks. This clustering presumably is done on the basis of similarity measures between documents already calculated by the vector-space-based system. The addition of this simple restructuring mechanism makes System 3 capable of presenting its primary access document in a wide variety of organizations.

> Knowledge of the topic that will assist users in scanning should be presented to the user as preparation for scanning.

The importance of organizational devices in preparing people to scan information is emphasized in Chapter 7. One mechanism that provides preparatory knowledge is a knowledge map of the information about to be presented. The term "knowledge map" is used in education to refer to a reasonably structured way of presenting concepts and the associations between them (Rewey, Dansereau, & Peel, 1991). The term is used here more generically to refer to any knowledge summary that facilitates navigation and scanning.

In System 1, which is essentially a large associative network for browsing, a knowledge map consists of a summary of the network designed to facilitate navigation. The labels associated with the centroids of specified spans of the network are presented so that users are able to understand that, if they browse in a particular direction, they will find information of a particular type. In System 2, which has now been refined to include a number of hierarchical relationships, a network diagram of each hierarchy, perhaps presented as a tree diagram, will be available to the user. So, for example, a user may wish to explore information about agriculture using one of several different hierarchical networks. The information may be organized by produce type (plants and animals, each subdivided by type), by combinations of climate and soil (tropical farming, dry land farming, etc.), or by profitability (cash crops, factory operations, subsistence farming). The choice of organizational structure can be presented to the user with several small tree diagrams. Once a selection is made, the chosen tree diagram will be expanded to show more detail; then the user will begin scanning the primary access document. In System 3, which has now been refined to include the possibility of a wide variety of user-generated structures and substructures, an overall map of the retrieved document sections, perhaps produced by multidimensional scaling based on similarity measures between document sections, is a reasonably simple knowledge map to create and will allow users to obtain a visual perspective on the organization of the raw materials they are about to scan. Of course, if an actual literature review is being employed, the structure of that review can be displayed as an aid to scanning.

> Materials should be presented in a way that is consistent with the knowledge that users have of the structure of information sources.

> Knowledge of information source structures should accompany the presentation of those sources.

In each of the systems sketched in Chapter 6, there is a two-step information interaction envisioned. In System 1, scanning through an associative network of terms or object representations is the first step. Once a term or object representation is found, further information seeking can occur through dictionary lookup or by retrieving the kind of detail found (for example) in a field guide. Similarly, the information system will be able to present an initial representation of experts who can be contacted for help. The second step is to contact them and receive their expert opinions. In System 2, the encyclopedia-like primary access document is keyed to more complete documents through bibliographic links. For example, the encyclopedia article may say, "For more detail, see the textbook by Smith," at which point the user will be able to navigate directly to a representation of (or perhaps the full text of) that text. In System 3, the document pieces are clearly linked to the full documents from which they are drawn, allowing users to move backwards and forwards between the review article and the reviewed materials.

When users move to the second step, they come into contact with a variety of different information resources, each of which has its own structure. To facilitate the scanning of these information sources, structured representations of the sources can be presented as advance organizers. In the case of text, this requires nothing more than presenting a document outline or table of contents. In the case of documents with figural content (graphs, illustrations, etc.), the structure of the many different types of figural content can be made available to the user. For example, a bar chart may be accompanied by an (optional) display of what to expect on the X axis (a quantity or proportion), what to expect on the Y axis (the categories associated with the variable of interest), and so on. Alternatively, if a flow chart is included in the document, it can be keyed to a few brief comments about what a rectangle means or why the network branches at decision boxes. In other cases (for example, with human experts), the information-source structure is a bit more amorphous, and the organizer presented to the user may be more like general advice on how to interact with an expert.

In fact, these advance organizers serve to meet both requirements here. Showing a table of contents permits the knowledge that users already have of information-source structures to be activated and thus facilitates their scanning of the documents. If the users do not have an existing knowledge of the structure of a particular information source, presenting the table of contents gives them enough knowledge of the structure to enable them to scan it more effectively.

> Materials should be presented in a way that allows users to make the best use of their cognitive abilities, particularly perceptual speed and spatial orientation.

Chapter 7 presents the idea that some people are better at scanning than others, because they have different levels of the cognitive abilities associated with scanning. However, this situation is complicated by the fact that people can adopt different scanning strategies that employ different abilities. Information-system design can take advantage of cognitive abilities that are used in scanning in many ways. If people are using top-to-bottom scanning strategies, placing important content at the top of any material presented will take advantage of this strategy and will also facilitate learning because of the primacy effect discussed in the following. If people are using a location-oriented approach (looking for certain types of information in certain locations), the system can facilitate scanning by ensuring that similar details are found in the same place on each screen. A system of indentation, for example, is a simple way to facilitate this kind of scanning. Mnemonic icons or words can be used to flag sections of the document so that readers can scan for the flags associated with the information they wish to locate (Lansdale, Simpson, & Stroud, 1990).

In summary, this section has proposed a combination of user-selected and standard enhancements to the information-system designs previously outlined. Users may select different organizations of the materials presented. They may select outlines or tutorials to help them with the structure of the information sources. They may request that certain sections of documents be flagged for quick reference. All of these user-selected features are based on the understanding that people with different resources (for example, levels of knowledge, ways of organizing that knowledge, or cognitive abilities) will find different design features more conducive to scanning. This idea is in line with the approach to designing for usability presented in Chapter 2. The standard features presented in this section include organizing information in such a way that important details are presented first, indenting the sections of a document consistently and prefacing any presentation of information with a summary or map of that information. These features are seen as so general in their application to making scanning more efficient and effective that they can be hard-wired into the various systems under discussion. Of course, all of these design features are intended as illustrations only. As system designers complete their own detailed analysis of the tasks accomplished by their users and the resources used to accomplish those tasks, they will be able to identify many other system-design features that can be either applied directly to systems or made available as user-selected options.

Designing for Evaluation

The second of the specific design implications outlined previously is that information systems should facilitate the effective evaluation of materials presented. This section considers how two recommended approaches may influence the design sketches developed in Chapter 6.

Presentation of materials should highlight data particularly useful in evaluation.

The discussion of designing for scanning notes that there are a variety of design features that can be used to draw attention to important parts of the material presented to users by information systems. Placing the important information first is one such technique. Others may involve the use of screen position, formatting (such as underlining or color), or mnemonic labels or icons. Because these techniques have already been included in the information systems sketched here, the only question that remains is which parts of the materials presented should be highlighted. In other words, what is important?

The obvious answer to this question is that any component of the information that allows users to judge its value to them is important. Users must be able to judge efficiently and effectively whether any individual chunk of information is worth the extra effort required to consider it in more detail. It is obvious that topic descriptions fall into this category, but only in a rather coarse-grained way. Because of the nature of statements of information need, materials may be on topic without being useful or relevant without being pertinent. Tiefel (1993) describes a front end to an online catalog designed to assist users in completing the evaluation task. The catalog presents screens that encourage users to consider a number of evaluative criteria, such as the date (i.e., recency) of the material, the reputation of the author, the reviews that the material received, and the quality of the journal in which the article was published. These criteria are, however, impoverished compared to the many user-centered criteria that are discussed in Chapter 7. Perhaps the best way to combine Tiefel's approach with a richer set of evaluative criteria is to consider the enhanced indexing and cumulative user-supplied indexing presented in Chapter 6. An example will illuminate how this works. An instructor in a school of business is searching for a case suitable for use in a graduate-level, case-based marketing course that illustrates the importance of directing advertising toward a narrowly defined market niche. A search on System 3 will produce a set of records describing marketing casebooks or (if the system is based on full-text representations) a set of marketing cases. Judging the suitability of these materials will, however, remain a difficult task with a great deal of cognitive load. Searching the document sections themselves or the document representations for terms like "graduate-level," or even "narrow-niche advertising" may not reduce the problem significantly. Neither the documents nor their representations can be expected to contain this kind of verbiage in any consistent manner. Now suppose that the user does a second search on the cumulative user-supplied indexing attached to each record, looking for the detail that is probably not part of the documents or document representations. The evaluative comments (if any were found to match terms like "case," "graduate-level," or "narrow-niche advertising") will appear above each document section, highlighted by color, font, or style. The user will be able to read comments like "detailed case studies, good for use in MBA studies," "brief cases, focused on single issues," or "Case 5 is particularly good for studying market niche analysis." Of course, the longer the materials have been used and evaluated by other users and the more conscientious users have been about entering comments on the materials, the more effective such a system will be.

Although this example focuses on System 3, the use of cumulative user-supplied indexing can be used with equal effect in any of the systems sketched here. One can, for example, use the evaluative comments about human experts supplied as part of System 1 to select a consultant in a specific problem area. Evaluating the documents that are linked to the encyclopedia-like texts in System 2 can be facilitated by the prominent display of user comments.

Materials should be presented in a way that allows users to make the best use of their cognitive abilities, particularly logical reasoning.

Chapter 7 notes that individuals who have higher scores on a cognitive ability called logical reasoning are more selective in their evaluations of documents presented by an information-retrieval system. This ability allows people to link premise with conclusion in a syllogism in an evaluative manner. For example, logical reasoning allows people to conclude from the statements "Socrates is a man" and "All men are mortal" that Socrates is mortal. The information-retrieval syllogism may mean the ability to conclude from the statements "I'm interested in learning about aircraft" and "This document is about aircraft" that I am interested in reading this document. In other words, logical reasoning ability emphasizes an evaluative criterion that consists of a close linkage between the statement of information need and understanding the topic of the information presented by the information system.

Users who do not adopt this close-link evaluative strategy are, in all probability, more likely to assess each document or other information presented by the system on its own merits. This phenomenon is seen quite clearly in the behavior of students using text-retrieval systems who select virtually everything they see (at least up to the point at which they feel they have enough materials), sometimes uttering comments such as, "Oh, that's interesting" or "I'm interested in that, too." There is no intent here to claim that selective behavior is to be preferred over nonselective behavior. Rather, the information system can be tailored for one or the other of these approaches by user-selected design features.

If someone who is usually selective wants to engage in a broader, serendipitous, nonselective information search, that user should select a search that retrieves broadly related materials and a form of information presentation that emphasizes the links between one topic and another. Similarly, someone who is usually nonselective and who wants to engage in a narrow, tightly defined search should select a search that retrieves narrowly related materials and a form of presentation that emphasizes the association of the retrieved materials with the statement of need. These two different approaches can be illustrated best by System 3. The degree of narrowness or breadth in the topic definition can be varied by adjusting the threshold number of document sections that will be displayed. Because the documents are ranked by similarity to the statement of need, selecting more documents for display will mean selecting greater breadth in topic definition. If the user wants to emphasize the association of the retrieved materials with the statement of need, the user may select the usual rank-order presentation, which displays the retrieved document selections in order of their similarity to the statement of need. If the user wants to emphasize the links between topics, the user may select as a means of presentation a knowledge map created by multidimensional scaling of the retrieved documents, using existing document–document similarity measures, through which the user can browse and select documents from many areas.

In System 1, the degree of selectivity of the system can be adjusted by the number of experts selected. This point can be illustrated with an example from the field-guide components of the system. A user can specify browsing only field guides to birds or can add in expert information on other aspects of nature. In the first case, the browse through bird representations will end up with the identification and definition of the type of bird and nothing more. In the second case, the browse can move from the definition of the type of bird to the definition of the type of tree that the bird sits in or the type of bug the bird eats. In System 2, the degree of selectivity of the system can be adjusted by emphasizing either hierarchical or lateral links between the text elements that make up the encyclopedia articles. A highly specific article can be created by following a single hierarchical set of links from top to bottom. A more general article can be created by starting at a reasonably high point in a hierarchy and following lateral links to related topics. In the first case, one may peruse an article on agriculture that begins with the subject of agriculture, then moves on to animal husbandry, cattle ranching, and finally to the prevalence of cow–calf operations in the midwest. In the second case, one may start with agriculture and move to the rural economy, the depopulation of rural areas, increased urbanization, and the development of national transportation grids.

It should be emphasized that none of these user-selectable design features require any additional refinements to the capabilities of the systems. Refining System 2, allowing several overlapping hierarchical structures to facilitate scanning, adds the capability to formulate the different types of encyclopedia articles discussed previously. Suggesting a knowledge map as a scan-enhancing adjunct to the display of information in System 3 adds the capability to move to a less selectivity-oriented display format. It is encouraging to see that the design features that are suggested by the analysis of information tasks and the resources required to complete them are consistent with each other.

Designing for Learning

The third specific design implication outlined previously is that information systems should facilitate learning from materials presented. This section considers how each of the seven recommended approaches may influence the design sketches developed in Chapter 6.

Materials should be presented in a way that is consistent with the task being accomplished by the user and with the domain being studied.

Materials should be accompanied by organizing materials that will facilitate learning.

Knowledge of information source structures should accompany the presentation of those sources.

The implications for system design derived from Chapter 7 and listed here have already been adequately considered in the discussion of information-system features that will facilitate scanning. To reiterate briefly, taking advantage of multiple hierarchical structures and existing similarity measures will allow users to view or create a form of information presentation that matches the way they structure their knowledge of the topic and domain. Outlines and knowledge maps facilitate learning by providing advance organizers. Tables of contents or interpretive instructions that accompany information sources reduce the cognitive load associated with the task of learning. These design features, drawn from considerations of scanning and judging, are also important inputs into designing systems that are usable for learning.

Materials that enhance dual coding should be presented.

Materials should be organized to emphasize associative links that facilitate elaborations.

Materials should be presented in a way that allows users to make the best use of their creativity.

Information from people and the media should be linked to recorded messages.

These four system-design implications powerfully suggest the use of hypermedia system features. Hypermedia systems provide multiple ways of presenting information to enhance dual coding, including personal and electronic sources, and emphasize associative links and creativity. However, Spiro's adaptation of cognitive flexibility theory to the educational environment, discussed in Chapter 7, emphasizes that hypermedia works well in ill-structured domains or topic areas, but may be overkill in well-structured learning situations. This observation leads to the conclusion that hypermedia elements should be user-selectable. In other words, hypermedia elements can be incorporated into the design of these systems (in fact, such elements have already been included to a considerable extent), but they should be designed as options that users can select if they wish.

System 1 is already a hypertext system, with links to human informants. The field guide that is the model for much of System 1 already employs dual representations, ideal for the learning reinforcement of dual coding. If one scans a naturalist's guidebook or a catalog of antiques, one uses images as the primary representation of information. These images are linked to short descriptive texts. So it appears that the only design implications remaining to be added to System 1 are associative networks for elaboration and mechanisms to encourage the use of individual abilities such as creativity. These characteristics seem inappropriate for System 1. This is a system designed to facilitate a specific kind of learning: the identification and definition of previously unknown entities or concepts. Elaboration and creativity seem less crucial in this kind of learning. Therefore, the sketch for System 1 remains unchanged by the implications of designing for learning.

System 2 already has a few hypermedia features included in its design. For example, the basic pattern of information retrieval in this system is to move from an encyclopedia-like article that is capable of several orders of presentation to more detailed documents or document representations. In addition, this system uses lateral network relationships ("see" references) that allow people to make associative elaborations during learning. However, in the sketch of this system, the value of dual coding has not been considered. Dual coding suggests that the encyclopedia must be illustrated with images, graphs, schematic drawings, and so on. This is really not a revolutionary addition to the design; currently available electronic encyclopedias make good use of these types of illustrations, and there seems to be no reason not to follow their lead. Also, although the importance of human informants is acknowledged in Systems 1 and 3, this capability is not a major part of System 2. It now appears that links to the outside should be added to the design, perhaps through electronic messaging, to allow users to extend their exploration of the topic to human informants.

Finally, the discussion turns to individual differences. It is amply clear to any educator that some students are more capable than others of creating their own learning. There are students who will create a synthesis of ideas, who will associate one idea with another, and who will ask wide-ranging and provocative questions. There are other students for whom ideas remain separate, who cannot see the links and associations and who accept what they are given at face value. Popov (1992) spoke of this difference between students as one of differing levels of creativity, and this seems as good a label as any. It seems clear that the creative student will relish System 2 as it has been sketched to date. The richness of multiple representations of information, linked hierarchically for exploration and laterally for elaboration, may seem, however, a confusing jumble to the plodding, linear, uncreative learners. For those who cannot see the connection between agricultural development and the national transportation grid (one example used previously), lateral links may be a feature that is less than useful. At the same time, the very richness of this system may be a distraction to the creative students. They may spin off into lateral connections before obtaining a solid understanding of the foundations of a topic.

These considerations seem to argue for a basic, hierarchical approach to topic exploration as the default presentation of the primary access document. It is possible to change the metaphor and think of this primary access document as a textbook chapter rather than an encyclopedia article. It can be enriched by increasingly accessible lateral links at the user's request [perhaps by adding links such as those explored by Welsh, Murphy, Duffy, & Goodrum (1993)]. In general, the correct design approach seems to be to start simple and allow users to add complexity as they wish.

To conclude this discussion of designing for learning, it is important to note the investigation of Piekara (1990), who found that some kinds of information systems enhance learning, while others produce no learning. This result suggests clearly that information systems designed to facilitate the task of learning should have different features than those that are designed to serve other functions (for example, to provide a convenient form of external memory). Neuman (1993) makes this point in suggesting design characteristics that can transform traditional information access tools into systems that support higher level learning. The features sketched here

are not necessarily typical of many operational information systems, but they provide examples of how systems can be designed to facilitate learning.

Designing for Planning

The fourth specific design implication outlined previously is that information systems should facilitate planning for information seeking. This section considers how one recommended approach may influence the design sketches developed in Chapter 6.

Scripts or heuristics should be presented along with information.

The individual tasks of interacting with an information system, such as scanning, evaluating, and learning, are always part of a larger sequence of tasks that lead
to the successful resolution of information needs. Keeping this larger picture in
mind is important for any user. For example, there may be an appropriate sequence
from System 1 to System 2, and finally to System 3. Within each of the systems,
there may be a sequence of steps as well. For example, in System 2, there will presumably be a point at which the user will benefit from moving away from the
encyclopedia-type articles and instead following up on the full-text articles that are
linked to the encyclopedia-type articles. There will be times when the next appropriate step for a user will be to move away from the information-retrieval system
completely and to accomplish certain other tasks (perhaps, for example, writing
the term paper).

Although these sequences of steps may be familiar to many users, it remains
possible that some users will need help remembering the possibilities facing them.
This is where an information-seeking road map will be of great use. One is reminded of an icon found on the toolbar of certain Microsoft products: a small light-
bulb. This symbol is presumably familiar to most people in western culture as the
cartoon symbol for an idea. As implemented in Microsoft Excel, this icon is linked
to diagnostic information about the processes recently completed by the user, and
clicking on the icon produces an information box that tells the user alternative ways
to accomplish the task just completed. If this idea is taken one step further, and the
task just completed is placed within a sequence dictated by a script or a heuristic,
clicking on the icon will suggest not only alternative ways of completing the current task, but reminders of what to do next. Such a mechanism can be added to all
of the information-system designs sketched thus far. The only real requirement is
that there be a reasonably clear step-wise progression through the information tasks
that can be represented in the road map.

The author remains highly skeptical of claims that an ideal step-by-step approach to information seeking exists, which recognizes that experienced users will
necessarily have developed ways of understanding that will guide their planning for
information seeking. Rather than attempting to define an ideal process, system de-

signers may well investigate and incorporate a number of user scripts and heuristics in building this kind of planning aid. As a result, the system can suggest a number of possible next steps for users, based on the work habits and processes developed by previous users.

Designing for Group Information Tasks

The final specific design implication outlined previously is that information systems should facilitate group processes. This section considers how one recommended approach may influence the design sketches developed in Chapter 6.

> Mechanisms that will facilitate group discussion and consensus should be incorporated into information systems.

The collective process of interacting with information systems requires all of the individual resources and cognitive loads that are associated with information tasks, plus an extensive group-process load associated with the collective scanning of, evaluation of, and learning from materials presented to the group by individual information-seeking and gatekeeping activities. Chapter 6 sketches an information workspace that allows groups to collectively present their information needs to a variety of information resources. The idea is that information retrieved from these resources can appear on the worksheet to be scanned, evaluated, and transferred (where appropriate) to the collective information store. It is now appropriate to consider in more detail exactly how this may happen.

Given the space constraints of the information workspace sketched in Chapter 6, any piece of information has to be presented by an abbreviated record, and even this short representation can remain within the workspace window for only a limited amount of time. As a new information representation appears in the workspace, it must be identified as new, requiring scanning and evaluation. Flagging information as new may be done by ensuring that all new materials are shown in bold type and by designing a flashing icon to appear beside any new materials not scanned and assessed by any group member. Clicking on the flashing icon will activate a window in which the full information is presented, along with a dialog box that allows group members to assess the importance, utility, and relevance of the information and to augment that assessment with their comments. Once this assessment has been made, the flashing icon disappears from the individual member's information workspace, but the document representation remains in the group workspace until all members (or some designated proportion of members) have completed the scan/evaluation task. At this point, the information will be disposed of in one of several ways, depending on the consensus achieved. Resnick, Iacovou, Suchak, Bergstrom, and Riedl (1994) describe a system called GroupLens, which allows members of a group to evaluate information in a collaborative manner similar to that suggested here. Their system has the additional capability to use the collected evaluations to filter incoming information automatically. This facility can be particularly important if there is a great deal of incoming information to evaluate.

The first alternative for disposal of evaluated records is that the new information would be added to the collective information store of the group. The sketch of the group information system has left this information store somewhat undefined. At this point, it may be appropriate to sketch some elements of the implementation of a collective external memory for group processes. As noted in Chapter 6, it is possible to use a standard bibliographic reference file here. If this is done, it seems crucial to have descriptors added to the reference through a consultative process. If this is not done, the "Where did you put it?" question will appear regularly in the group's correspondence. A thematic organization of information elements is also a possibility. The result may resemble a literature review or annotated bibliography in thematic order. There is, however, a great deal more overhead in maintaining such an information store, because it is necessary for the group to agree about where each new piece of information fits into the existing thematic structure. However the collective external memory is organized, the acceptance of a new piece of information into that store must be accompanied by a collective agreement about how to describe the information.

Another possibility for what may happen to information representations from the information workspace is that all (or a sufficiently large proportion) of the group members will regard the information as of no relevance, importance, or usefulness. One is tempted to simply erase the information from the system, but a case may be made for logging the decision in some way so that the collective understanding of the group's problem and focus can be suitably amended. Alternatively, a member may wish to retain the information in his or her individual workspace, and this decision should also be recorded in some way to ensure that the group has a solid idea about each member's interests and preferences.

Finally, it is possible to consider situations in which there is a split decision about any piece of information. In such situations, a second evaluation mechanism may be required to develop a group decision. This second evaluation can consist of the reappearance of the flashing icon and the re-presentation of the information and the evaluation dialog box, this time accompanied by the comments from each of the group members. The second evaluation will be definitive according to a decision rule such as "When in doubt, throw out."

The process of learning from materials is implicit in much of the preceding discussion. The in-depth processing of information required to evaluate it must produce individual learning. In the group context, a discussion of learning must move beyond changes in an individual's knowledge structures to consider the collective knowledge structures. The sketch of a group information system represents the group's collective knowledge structure as a collaboratively maintained statement of task and focus. Learning from materials means a collective change in those statements. It is possible to speculate about a system enhancement that produces a high-level summary of new materials added to the knowledge store, compares this summary with the existing statements of task and focus, and suggests changes to those statements. These suggestions are then considered by the group for incorporation into their collective understanding of what they are doing. Although this hypothetical system enhancement is highly speculative, it fits into developments in systems to support collaborative learning such as the CLARE system presented by Wan and Johnson (1994), in which problem identification and summarization of information are important system components.

The group information system has many features not presented in the design sketches for Systems 1, 2, and 3. It is really an additional system with unique features, providing an additional level of information processing and management. As such, it can be used in conjunction with any information system or device designed to meet individual information needs.

Refocusing Information–System Design

The information transfer cycle, as usually portrayed, begins with the creation of information. Authors of documents, producers of videos, or creators of hypermedia engage in their creative tasks, driven in part by a need to create or perhaps by a need to make money. As a result, a marketplace exists in which information commodities can be purchased or otherwise acquired. Individuals who are engaged in creating information systems approach that marketplace and select from it the information that will be included in their system. Alternatively, the information materials may be generated as a necessary part of or byproduct of doing business. They are therefore available to the system designer without a market mechanism.

Selection is the first stage of creating an information system, and it adds value by drawing attention to the similarities between the items selected for inclusion, thus making retrieval easier. The next stage is the organization of information for access. This organization may be in terms of a classified arrangement for browsing or in terms of enhanced descriptions and indexing for searching. In any case, the organization adds additional value to the information by making it more accessible. Next comes the development of an access system. This access system may be a physical arrangement of documents, a keyword-based retrieval engine, or a query-by-example database system. Again, value is added at this stage, because users now have access systems that work (more or less well) to find specific information. Next, one or more interfaces to the access system are created, enabling users with different problems, tasks, and abilities to use the information system. There is a big jump in the information transfer cycle between these elements of information-system design and actual use of the information. In a sense, this is a kind of leap of faith. System designers (in the usual information transfer cycle) can only have a kind of blind expectation that, after all of the work of selection, organization, access, and interface design, people will actually use the information.

It should be clear from the discussion already presented in this book that the user-centered approach demands a refocusing and reformulation of the information transfer cycle. In a real sense, users do not care about the creation of information. Their attention is directed toward completing the tasks that will allow them to achieve their goals and objectives. In designing information systems, therefore, the information transfer cycle must be entered at a new place. Beginning with information use leads directly to a consideration of designing systems for use. In this way, the value-added processes of selection, organization, access, and interface development can be refocused to deal not with a marketplace of information commodities or a data store, but with a universe of goals, tasks, and resources.

Information Selection

The first system or design element to be considered in detail is the nature of the information included in the system. The usual basis for deciding what information to collect for any information system consists of topic and availability. It should be noted that the term "information collection" is being used here in a broad sense. Whether one is maintaining a collection of documents in a library or providing access to information in remote locations is largely irrelevant to this discussion. The criteria noted previously are complex. When an information designer or an information specialist working on maintaining the system thinks that a particular type of information is on a topic that may be of interest to users, he or she employs classificatory principles without necessarily being aware of what the classification actually is. The designer may be making judgments about relevance, without having the knowledge of individual and social variables that will permit such judgments. He or she may be thinking about intellectual level or other aspects of user-appropriateness, again with only an informal or approximate idea of what the users may need. The question of availability usually encompasses questions of cost as well.

Rather than using these approximate, informal, and casual approaches to information-system design, it is possible for those who collect information to address users directly. Now the questions become "Can our users scan this material?", "Can they evaluate it and learn from it?", and "Is this material directed towards a specific need?" The discussions in this chapter suggest that the answers to these questions are crucially dependent on users' resources for interaction: their knowledge of a topic or domain, their understanding of the conventions of expression in a particular medium, and their cognitive abilities. In specifying the design of the three systems discussed initially in Chapter 6 and refined in this chapter, collecting specific types of information was considered, such as expert resources for problem solving, hierarchically arranged articles for exploration of topics, or hypermedia systems with linked text and images to enhance dual coding. Using the materials found in the marketplace of information commodities was severely limited. Similarly, using customer records or other found materials in an unprocessed form seems inappropriate. The choice of information sources included in any information service ultimately has little to do with the sources themselves. As Palmer

(1991) found, library and document-based activities fail to predict information style. Rather, the use of any information service will depend on individual and social factors. Palmer identifies factors such as enthusiasm, gender, discipline, work role, and organizational role as crucial determinants of information style.

It is possible to draw additional implications for information collection from this discussion. The presence of any particular piece of information in any collection must be far more subject to negotiation than is usual. Information collections should be created to meet specific needs and accomplish specific tasks, to be used by people with specific resources. As any of these user variables changes, so the collection must also change. To put it in an extreme manner, a collection may exist only for a week, then disappear because its users' needs have changed. Materials may be added to or deleted from a collection on a daily or even hourly basis to ensure that the collection is tied closely to the characteristics of a particular user group.

Organization of and Access to Information

Approaches to organizing information have been based to some extent on the same poorly documented understanding of users that drives traditional information-collection activities. Someone deciding to organize a collection of archival documents by the names of the offices or agencies that generated the documents does so, presumably, on the basis that users will be looking for collections of documents generated by specific agencies or offices. It is true that the archivist seldom has any evidence to support that assumption, but the user focus is present, if uninformed. Similarly, a public library may shelve all of its mysteries in one section, organized by author's name, on the understanding that users want to read mysteries as an identifiable genre, and they identify mysteries by the author's name. Again, there is usually only anecdotal evidence to support such assumptions.

Other forms of organization include the description of information, typically by indexing or abstracting. In textbooks that attempt to instruct information professionals in these activities, the first step is usually to identify the important ideas in the information. This kind of instruction, usually not elaborated in any way, is singularly unhelpful. The task of deciding what is important is, as demonstrated previously, a complex one that depends on many individual and social factors. One may suppose, or perhaps more correctly, hope devoutly, that information professionals have a model of the user in mind when they accomplish this task. But these user models are unlikely to be informed by any clear understanding of user goals, purposes, and objectives, or of the tasks that users are trying to accomplish and the resources they bring to the tasks.

Another alternative to organization and description of information is generation of index elements by computer processing of data. Of techniques that represent this approach, the most commonly employed is keyword indexing of text data. This approach ignores users completely by relying on the vocabulary contained in the data to organize the information and provide the basis for retrieval.

There are implications for information organization in the user-centered approach to information-system design. The most obvious implication is the idea of cumulative user-provided indexing introduced in Chapter 6. This approach applies the user's own methods of understanding the information and how that information matches his or her needs to organize information. The second implication is that standardized organizations are destined to fail. It is clearly not possible for any single means of organization to coincide with users' highly varied states of knowledge, cognitive abilities, or social situations. The approach adopted in sketching the designs presented in this book is to allow the organization of information to respond to users' knowledge and correspond to their tasks. Individualizing the organization of information is not an easy task. The approaches taken in the design sketches presented here are rather simplistic: building in a few alternative link structures for a hypertext presentation of encyclopedia-type information. More sophisticated, adaptive information organization can be based on logging navigational patterns, for example. The crucial point is that the organization of information should be as dynamic as the collection itself in order to adapt to information users and their individual needs.

Access mechanisms are usually driven by the decisions made about information collection and organization. The systems sketched in this book demonstrate how access mechanisms can be tailored toward specific types of information needs. This rough demonstration shows how a high degree of user-selected customization can be added to flexible information selection and organization. Similarly, Watters, Shepherd, and Qiu (1994) show how access methods can be customized to fit the user's specific task. The decision as to whether or not to implement a particular design feature, such as an access method, depends on how the feature combines with user characteristics to create a usable system. Although this area requires a great deal of additional research, it seems clear that most information systems, even those designed to deal with specific information problems and a narrowly defined user group, will have to employ several access methods, because users bring different levels of knowledge and abilities to their information tasks.

Interface Selection

Chapter 6 considers briefly the role of interfaces as part of information systems, particularly those aspects that relate to the browsability of systems. This chapter can go into more depth about the aspects of interfaces and how interface design options can interact with human characteristics to enhance system usability. Interface design is the domain of studies of human–computer interaction (HCI), and the literature is truly massive. So great is the concern for creating ergonomically and cognitively sound interfaces that some (e.g., Carroll, 1992) have argued that HCI should provide a basis for the design of usable systems. This approach represents a tendency to lose sight of the substantive issues of system design, while placing too great an emphasis on the cosmetic aspects of design. It is essential to consider the extent to which a system is a successful problem-solving tool before considering whether it has a usable interface.

In the system sketches provided in this book, there are a variety of features that may be regarded as interface features. For example, a highly visual approach to browsing, links to knowledge maps and heuristics for planning, hypertext links from one type of information to another, and so on are included. Clearly, these features fit into the current literature on human–computer interaction. The browsing approaches suggested for Systems 1 and 2 are consistent with interfaces that require little or no query activity on the part of the user, such as query by browsing (Dix & Patrick, 1995) or the answers first, then questions approach noted by Owen (1986). The emphasis on browsing and navigation in retrieval is also consistent with the browsing approach described by Thompson and Croft (1989).

The organization or reorganization of the information to correspond to user knowledge and tasks suggested for Systems 2 and 3 is similar to database interface approaches suggested by Ellis, Finlay, and Pollitt (1995) and Haw, Goble, and Rector (1995). These approaches allow the data-driven design for a database to be masked behind an interface based on user knowledge. As indicated previously, such approaches are typical of interface design and can (at least conceptually) be replaced by systems in which the data structures are user-driven from the beginning.

The approach to knowledge maps as guides to retrieval sketched in this chapter is similar to the interface developed by McMath, Tamaru, and Rada (1989), in which a graphical thesaurus provides the basis for information searching. In general, graphical approaches, such as those discussed by Furnas (1991) and van der Veer (1994), seem applicable to the systems outlined in this book. Similarly, in allowing the presentation of information to be customized to correspond to the user's task and social situation, some of the concerns of Brown and Duguid (1992), who recommend that interface design incorporate an understanding of how information behavior is socially constructed and socially distributed, have been met.

From this brief discussion, it seems clear that many contemporary approaches to interface design have incorporated features that are useful and appropriate in user-centered information systems. They have, in many cases, been proposed for the wrong reasons. Rather than making sensible interface choices to cover over the inadequacies of data-centered structures and capabilities, the choice here has been to propose sensible interface choices because they are consistent with user-centered approaches to the entire system-design process.

Conclusion

The point has already been made several times that the designs sketched in this chapter are general and illustrative. With those qualifications, however, it seems reasonable to assert that they demonstrate how the process of user-centered design can proceed in actual design contexts. The approach of focusing all aspects of the design, creation, and maintenance of information systems on user needs, tasks, and re-sources has led to the derivation of what may be seen as a revolutionary vision of how information systems should look and behave. Information systems designed according to the user-centered approach are likely to be dynamic in a way that has not typically been associated with such systems. This point leads to a consideration of the context in which information systems operate: information services. The next chapter shows how the design of user-centered information systems can lead to a redefinition of the way information systems function.

User-Centered Design: A Practical Guide IV

Note: At the end of each even-numbered chapter of this book, a brief guide to the practical aspects of design is provided. This guide summarizes discussions in preceding chapters as they relate to the practical aspects of conducting user-centered design. Contents that have been added to this version of the guide are shown in boxes.

1. Identify a user population. The first and obvious step in user-centered design is to find a user, or more appropriately, a user population. Sometimes user identification is dictated by the mission of the organization where the designer works. In other cases, users may be selected by the designer. The identification of the user population is such an obvious step that it is sometimes omitted. This omission results in systems that are not particularly usable for any set of users.

The user population may be composed of either individuals or groups or perhaps a combination of both. Because different design decisions will be necessary for groups, they should be identified separately when they occur within the user population.

2. Investigate the information needs of your user group. The users identified in step 1 have a number of information needs. These can be investigated using a wide range of research methods, which are easily accessible in manuals on social science research or market research. The key element of this step is to talk to users and find out what kinds of information they need to resolve problems they encounter. No information system can meet all of the information needs of a user group. Once the full range of information needs has been identified, system designers must select those that their information system will be designed to meet.

User needs can be identified by reference to a problem-solving model. According to this model, information needs can be associated with problem perception, alternative identification, or alternative selection. Each of these classes of information needs will require different approaches to system design. User needs can also be typified by their setting. Information needs can occur in individuals or in groups. Group needs are sufficiently different from individual needs to require different design approaches.

Both individual and social factors influence the information needs that may occur within a user population. Designers should investigate the social and organizational settings in which information needs occur, because these settings may give rise to or constrain the information needs experienced by users. Figure 5 summarizes the design principles that emerge from a consideration of user information needs.

Some information needs arise from failure of perception. Some information needs are associated with a process of exploring a topic area so as to identify alternative courses of action. Some information needs arise from the need to associate alternatives with outcomes.

People can, and frequently do, engage in information avoidance. They interact with their environment by limiting their intake of information, ignoring information if it is associated with negative outcomes, and taking information shortcuts. Organizations are frequently equally irrational in their collection, processing, and use of information.

3. Discover the tasks that users accomplish as they meet these information needs. Again, research methods from social science and market research are useful in this step. The key element is to talk to users and observe them as they work on meeting their information needs. Identify the tasks that users employ as they meet their information needs and how they accomplish these tasks. Note the sequential ordering of the tasks. Try to distinguish between the tasks that are essential and those that are optional. The result will be one or more task models for each information need.

Tasks may be accomplished individually or collectively. Where users are observed to be completing tasks as a group, it is important to consider these group tasks separately from individual tasks in the design of information systems.

Tasks accomplished may be dictated by the social setting in which information seeking occurs. Social and organizational factors must be analyzed carefully, because they may constrain the number of tasks that individuals and groups choose to accomplish. When social factors constrain tasks in this way, information system design can be considerably simpler than when users can select from a broader range of tasks.

Expressing an information need is one key task that users will typically accomplish while meeting information needs. Different types of needs produce different types of need expressions and accordingly place different requirements on information system design.

Scanning the output produced by an information system, evaluating it, learning from it, and planning for additional steps in the retrieval process are important tasks in interacting with an information system. Designing for usability requires that these tasks be made easy for the user.

4. Investigate the resources that users require to complete these tasks. Each task completed by a user who is meeting an information need requires a variety of resources: background knowledge, procedural knowledge, and abilities. List the resources required for each task and identify the level of the resources required. For example, expert knowledge or high levels of verbal ability may be required to complete a task involving vocabulary selection. At the same time, it is important to note the levels of these resources that users possess. Some users, for example, may have less expert topic knowledge or lower levels of verbal abilities, and gaps between resources required and resources possessed are obvious areas of concern. Research methods to investigate the resources possessed by users can be found in any text on psychometrics.

Resources may be individual or collective in nature. Where individual knowledge and ability are concerned, psychometric methods are adequate to identify levels of resources possessed by users. In the case of collective knowledge and ability, however, it is essential to investigate the group processes by which consensus is reached. Collective resources may differ considerably from the sum of the individual resources of group members.

Resources may derive from and be constrained by social factors. Accordingly, it is important to investigate the social and organizational setting in which resources are being applied to the completion of information tasks. These settings may provide additional resources or may constrain how resources are applied to tasks.

Resources particularly important to the expression of information needs are knowledge of the problem situation, linguistic knowledge, knowledge of informants and what information they have, and knowledge of the social constraints that govern the expression of information needs.

Resources particularly important to scanning are abilities such as perceptual speed and reading ability, knowledge of the topic, and knowledge of the ways in which information is presented both textually and in images. Resources used in evaluating materials include abilities such as logical reasoning, as well as knowledge resources that relate to the topic area and the problem under consideration. Resources for learning include learning abilities and styles, as well as knowledge about how information is presented. Particularly important for planning are knowledge structures such as scripts and heuristics.

---

5. Summarize the preceding steps in user models. For each distinct user group to be served by the information system, there will be a number of information needs that the system is designed to meet. For each of these information needs, there will be a number of tasks that must be accomplished. For each of the tasks, there will be a list of resources that are necessary. Integrating these elements together results in a user model that can be used to guide design decisions or that can be implemented as part of the information system to direct how the system will respond to users. For example, user models can form the basis for the preset options for how the information system will work, but users will be able to change the options to make the system conform to their own preferences.

6. Consider each design decision in the light of resource augmentation and enabling. The goal of system design is to allow users to complete the tasks that will meet their information needs. With this in mind, system features that will augment the resources of users when necessary will enable them to complete the tasks. Some of these features will be required by all users, while others will be required by only a portion of the user group. In the latter case, system features are best implemented as user-selectable options. Experimental research to identify interactions between user resources and design options can be used to select system features that should be implemented as user-selectable options.

For those who are trying to perceive a problem, a browse-based system with associative links seems ideal. What is needed is a system that will allow people to enter the system with minimal verbal expression and navigate toward their information need. Linked experts that can provide the identification and diagnosis that people need can supplement such a system.

For those trying to identify alternatives by completing their understanding of a topic, a general-to-specific information system that allows selective exploration of topics in depth, while at the same time providing lateral links to related topics is needed. The electronic encyclopedia, textbook, or selective annotated bibliography may represent the kind of information service that can be useful in this process.

For those trying to select alternatives, in-depth information, arranged in such a way as to permit specific-to-general consideration and evaluation of alternatives, is needed. Advice can be provided by the information system about the consequences of various alternatives. A vector-space retrieval engine adapted to create the raw materials of review articles or meta-analyses may also be appropriate.

Information selected must be appropriate to information needs, particularly as those needs are located within social and organizational contexts. Organization of information must facilitate the scanning, evaluation, and learning processes. Storage and retrieval techniques should permit information to be customized to the specific needs of users. This argues for flexibility in the design of storage and retrieval techniques. User interfaces can assist in expressing information needs, perceiving and scanning information, learning from information, and planning for further information seeking. Particularly important are navigational methods for finding information, help features to explain not only how to find information but how to interpret the information found, and facilities that allow users to select their preferences for how the information system operates.

References

Brown, J. S., & Duguid, P. (1992). Enacting design for the workplace. In P. S. Adler & T. A. Winograd (Eds.), *Usability: Turning technologies into tools* (pp. 164–197). New York: Oxford University Press.

Carroll, J. M. (1992). Creating a design science of human–computer interaction. In A. Benoussan & J.-P. Verjus (Eds.), *Future tendencies in computer science, control and applied mathematics. International conference on the occasion of the 25th anniversary of INRIS* (Lecture Notes in Computer Science 653) (pp. 205–215). Berlin: Springer-Verlag.

Dix, A., & Patrick, A. (1995). Query by browsing. In P. Sawyer (Ed.), *Interfaces to database systems (IDS94): Proceedings of the second international workshop on interfaces to database systems* (pp. 236–248). London: Springer-Verlag.

Ellis, G. P., Finlay, J. E., & Pollitt, A. S. (1995). HIBROWSE for hotels: Bridge the gap between user and system views of a database. In P. Sawyer (Ed.), *Interfaces to database systems (IDS94): Proceedings of the second international workshop on interfaces to database systems* (pp. 49–62). London: Springer-Verlag.

Furnas, G. W. (1991). New graphical reasoning models for understanding graphical interfaces. In S. P. Robertson, G. M. Olson, & J. S. Olson (Eds.), *Human factors in computing systems. Reaching through technology. CHI '91 Conference Proceedings* (pp. 71–78). New York: Association for Computing Machinery.

Haw, D., Goble, C., & Rector, A. (1995). GUIDANCE: Making it easy for the user to be an expert. In P. Sawyer (Ed.), *Interfaces to database systems (IDS94): Proceedings of the second international workshop on interfaces to database systems* (pp. 25–48). London: Springer-Verlag.

Lansdale, M. W., Simpson, M., & Stroud, T. R. (1990). A comparison of words and icons as external memory aids in an information retrieval task. *Behaviour and Information Technology, 9*(2), 111–131.

McMath, C. F., Tamaru, R. S., & Rada, R. (1989). A graphical thesaurus based information retrieval system. *International Journal of Man Machine Studies, 31*(2), 121–147.

Neuman, D. (1993). Designing databases as tools for higher level learning: Insights from instructional systems design. *Educational Technology, Research and Development, 41*(4), 25–46.

Owen, D. (1986). Answers first, then questions. In D. A. Norman & S. W. Draper (Eds.), *User centered system design: New perspectives on human–computer interaction* (pp. 361–375). Hillsdale, NJ: Lawrence Erlbaum.

Palmer, J. (1991). Scientists and information: I. Using cluster analysis to identify information style. *Journal of Documentation, 47*, 105–129.

Piekara, F. H. (1990). Effects of using information systems on retention of information. *Zeitschrift für Psychologie, 198*(4), 443–461.

Popov, A. (1992). Creativity and reading comprehension. *Journal of Creative Behavior, 26*(3), 206–212.

Resnick, P., Iacovou, N., Suchak, M., Bergstrom, P., & Riedl, J. (1994). GroupLens: An open architecture for collaborative filtering of netnews. In R. Furuta & C. Neuwirth (Eds.), *Proceedings of the conference on computer supported cooperative work* (pp. 175–186). New York: ACM.

Rewey, K. L., Dansereau, D. F., & Peel, J. L. (1991). Knowledge maps and information processing strategies. *Contemporary Educational Psychology, 16*(3), 203–214.

Thompson, R. H., & Croft, W. B. (1989). Support for browsing in an intelligent text retrieval system. *International Journal of Man Machine Studies, 30*(6), 639–668.

Tiefel, V. (1993). The gateway to information: The future of information access . . . today. *Library Hi Tech*, *11*(4), 57–65.

van der Veer, G. C. (1994). Mental models of computer systems: Visual languages in the mind. In M. J. Tauber, D. E. Mahling, & F. Arefi (Eds.), *Cognitive aspects of visual languages and visual interfaces* (pp. 3–40). Amsterdam: North-Holland.

Wan, D., & Johnson, P. M. (1994). Computer supported collaborative learning using CLARE: The approach and experimental findings. In R. Furuta & C. Neuwirth (Eds.), *Proceedings of the conference on computer supported cooperative work* (pp. 187–198). New York: ACM.

Watters, C., Shepherd, M. A., & Qiu, L. (1994). Task oriented access to data files: An evaluation. *Journal of the American Society for Information Science*, *45*(4), 251–262.

Welsh, T. M., Murphy, K. P., Duffy, T. M., & Goodrum, D. A. (1993). Accessing elaborations on core information in a hypermedia environment. *Educational Technology Research and Development*, *41*(2), 19–34.

9

Information Services from the User's Perspective

Introduction

The focus of this book up to this point has been on information systems, which have been defined fairly broadly. However, as mentioned in Chapter 1, information systems are typically found in information services. It seems clear that the discussion of how user-centered design can be understood and implemented in information systems has implications for the design and organization of information services. The introductory chapter briefly considers a definition of information services, and it is now time to review and elaborate on that definition.

The distinction between an information system and an information service is a bit fuzzy. It is possible, however, to think of information services as organizations devoted to meeting a specific type of information need or the needs of a specific type of patron. Information services may include many different information systems that perform their function. These information systems may be organized in many different ways, but because they share elements with each other, groups of information systems can be organized together as a service. The shared elements include first of all the users. Because the users are a major defining element in any information system, a group of information systems that shares the same users already shares a great deal of cognitive and social background. Secondly, the information systems in an information service share the human intermediary elements. These intermediaries bring a common approach to all of the information systems that helps to define the systems as being similar in nature. Finally, the information service typically operates in an institutional setting, which adds commonality to the ways the component systems function by providing an overarching purpose and management framework.

An information service is a collection of information systems established to meet the needs of some specified user group. The main justification for a user-centered focus lies in the term "service." The fundamental reason for designing information services with specific user groups in mind is that the raison d'être of information services, as of information systems, is to meet information needs. The people with information needs are the users. A commitment to information service requires that there be a user orientation. Any other orientation is not a service orientation.

The definition of information services used in this chapter, which focuses so narrowly on meeting the needs of a specified user group, is a clear departure from a substantial body of practice in both private- and public-sector information services. Information services are far more likely in the real world to be associated not with user groups, but with information resources or types of information resources. Examples of these types of services include government document libraries, video rental services, and census data archives. If the focus is primarily on materials, this is a warehouse orientation, rather than a service orientation. Other information services may be established on a basis of staff expertise. So, for example, there are travel agencies and directional information desks are found in malls or airports. If the focus is primarily on staff and their capabilities, this is a bureaucratic orientation, rather than a service orientation.

If information services are to be designed with user information needs in mind, then a logical way of organizing them would be to bring together those information systems that meet the needs of the same set of users. It is conceivable, of course, that an information service may choose to assemble a group of systems designed to meet the needs of a variety of different users. This approach is difficult to justify, however, because it makes the central purpose of the service obscure and diffuse. The focus on a single set of users and their needs seems most productive.

The introductory chapter points out that, in an information service constituted on the basis outlined previously, there are two constants: the users and the intermediaries. In all other components, the information systems can vary: the types of information resources, the interfaces, or the modes of data presentation. One way of visualizing the difference between an information system and an information service is to think of an information system as defined by a three-way relationship between the user, the intermediary, and the information device. When several systems are aggregated together into a service, the information devices involved may have many different forms: some may be books, some databases, and some networked electronic resources. The third component of the three-way relationship accordingly becomes blurred and indeterminate. What remains constant is the two-way relationship between users and intermediaries. Therefore, what defines the information service remains the interaction between users and intermediaries. This interaction, and how it can be optimized to meet information needs, is the subject of this chapter.

Partnership Model of Service Interaction

The nature of the activities of information intermediaries has already been sketched in the chapters on information-system design. Intermediaries have the functions of directing users to experts, explaining the information that people find, and advising on the use of information systems. However, the discussion of these intermediary activities does not pay attention to the details of the service interaction between intermediaries and users. To design this service interaction on user-centered design principles requires a focus on how the intermediaries fit in with the users' needs, tasks, and resources. Before beginning this detailed design, however, it is possible to consider service interactions more generally and to outline an approach to user–intermediary interactions.

A range of possible service interactions can be identified, covering a spectrum of service types. Most service interactions are typified by a negotiated balance of control, expertise, and contribution. The first way of defining that spectrum of service types is to consider the degree of control exercised by the intermediary and the user. In certain retail transactions, the customer is always right. A sales clerk merely acts to take the request, provide the merchandise, and accept payment. This is the automat approach to service, represented by vending machines and their human counterparts in other retail settings, such as fast-food organizations.

A diametric opposite of the automat service model can be found in certain kinds of medical practice, in which the customer (in this case, the patient) has little control over the service provided. Perhaps the most extreme case of this type of service, and unfortunately the one with the greatest potential for abuse, occurs when patients are deemed not to be responsible agents. If the patients are diagnosed as senile (as in some nursing home situations), mentally incompetent (as in certain psychiatric hospital situations), or too young to be able to make rational decisions (as in some pediatric or school situations), the service provider has virtually complete control in the treatment intervention. For example, the physician can (within established guidelines) prescribe drugs and have drugs administered without patient consent.

The extremes of the automat and medical models, as with all extremes, are relatively seldom encountered. Most service situations require some degree of shared control. In retail situations, for example, the sales clerk may be called upon to give advice, make suggestions about other possible purchases, or negotiate the price. Here, both the customer and the service provider have some control over the service transaction, and the relative control each has must be negotiated during each transaction. It is possible that advice from a sales clerk may not be entirely welcomed by a customer, particularly if the advice concerns additional purchases that the clerk is recommending. Similarly, having a customer attempt to take control of the cost of products (as in the case of price negotiation) may not be accepted by the service provider.

Similarly, shared control is far more likely in medical transactions where the patient is an active decision maker in the treatment process. This shared control requires patient teaching, through which enough medical information about the disease and treatment options is given to the patient to enable informed decision making. Patients' rights statements, created and maintained by patients' rights organizations, are important evidence of this move toward shared control in the medical context. In mental health situations, it is not uncommon for an ombudsman to be included in the service organization to assist patients in exercising their rights to be involved in their health decisions. There have been enough published cases of institutional abuse of the elderly and the young that society has come to realize that the power of the service provider must be moderated by some level of shared control.

The second way of defining the spectrum of service types is in terms of the expertise possessed by the participants in the service interaction. A high degree of customer control in a retail transaction presumes that customers are fully aware of all of their choices and the consequences of those choices. For example, in a fast-food restaurant, it is appropriate to assume that the customer knows enough about hamburgers or fried chicken to make an informed selection. In the medical situation, however, patient expertise may be far exceeded by the physician's medical knowledge. In fact, it can be argued that the main reason people consult physicians for health service is to take advantage of their high levels of medical knowledge.

As in the case of control, most service transactions can be arrayed along a spectrum of shared expertise. In any particular transaction, there is a negotiation of that expertise that involves some kind of knowledge sharing. It is noted previously that, to enable a certain level of patient control in the medical transaction, patient teaching occurs, to ensure that some medical knowledge is shared. On the other hand, in some transactions the teaching may go the opposite way, and the customer may instruct the service provider. An example of that sort of sharing of knowledge is when a physician takes a patient history or a customer explains to a caterer precisely the kind of party that is being planned.

The third way of defining the spectrum of service types is in terms of the contribution the service provider and the customer make to the transaction. In the extreme form of the medical model, the contribution of the patient etherized upon the table is minimal. The physician performs the diagnosis and treatment, and the patient is largely a passive object. In the extreme automat model, the customer contributes virtually everything; in fact, the contribution of the service provider is easily automated. Most service transactions can be found somewhere between these two extremes. The balance of contribution between the two parties is negotiated for each transaction, although there are stereotyped balances that can be applied with minimal negotiation. In a restaurant, for example, it is an accepted contribution on the part of the customer to taste a dish and send it back to the kitchen if it is not acceptable. In this case, it is not an accepted contribution for the service provider to taste the dish in turn and engage in an argument with the customer about its quality, although even this contribution can be negotiated in certain circumstances. In other situations, the precise nature of the contributions of the service provider and the user have to be negotiated from scratch during each service encounter. Kuhlthau, Spink, and Cool (1992) studied the communication patterns between users and intermediaries in traditional, library-based information seeking. They found that there was ongoing communication between the intermediary and the user about their collective progress in working through the steps or stages in the information-search process. This kind of communication is central to the negotiation of contributions by the partners in information seeking.

Siehl, Bowen, and Pearson (1992) developed a typology of service encounters that has a great deal in common with the preceding discussion. Their spectrum of service ranged from low (fast-food service, for example) to medium (retail service, for example) to high (again, the physician example). For each level of service, they compared language, gestures, emotion, and ritual, or the kinds of symbolic behaviors that establish the nature of the relationship between client and service provider. For example, in low-level service situations, the language is passive and neutral, there are few gestures, the emotions consist of low-level empathy, and the rituals include an avoidance of verbal interaction or eye contact on the part of the service provider. Medium-level service situations employ active and pleasant language, more gestures, emotions that extend to personal caring and empathy, and ritualistic behavior such as small talk, eye contact, and turning toward the customer. In high-level service encounters, the language is active and intimate, there are more gestures, the emotions can extend to compassion and sympathy, and the ritual behavior consists of customer-relevant talk, expressiveness, and a closing of the social space between the customer and the service provider. All of these factors combine to create an appropriate level of psychological involvement between the customer and the service provider, thus facilitating information sharing. This research emphasizes that information sharing is a crucial variable; the more information the service provider needs from the customer and the more intangible the service, the more involvement the customer will expect. It also noted that levels of involvement by the service provider above or below the expected level of involvement will lead to customer dissatisfaction with the service.

The discussion thus far can be summarized by saying that most service interactions are typified by a negotiated balance of control, expertise, and contribution. This type of service interaction can be labeled a partnership, because the two parties to the interaction share control, contribute their own expertise, and make individual contributions toward a goal. In this case, the goal is to solve the problem faced by the user. In other words, the information interaction is one of partnership between a user and an intermediary, in which problem-solving communication systems are used to resolve the information needs of the user.

This view of the information service, then, is one that is defined by a partnership interaction directed toward solving an information-related problem and using information systems in the process. From this formulation, it is possible to develop a few general impressions about the design of information services. An information service should be flexible enough in its organization that users can negotiate with intermediaries the control that each will have at different points in the process, the knowledge that will be shared, and the contribution that each will make. This flexibility is particularly important because each information-related problem can fall anywhere along a wide spectrum of possible levels of involvement.

Kuhlthau (1993) categorizes the possible levels of involvement between users and intermediaries using the following typology.

1. The intermediary as organizer: The role of the intermediary is simply to "stock the shelves" so that users can find information without intermediary intervention.

2. The intermediary as locator: Even with well-organized shelves, it is sometimes difficult for users to find information. The intermediary intervenes to locate single items.

3. The intermediary as identifier: The intermediary selects several information items that may meet the need of the user.

4. The intermediary as advisor: The intermediary suggests some information that is more likely to meet the need than others and gives advice on how to develop the search for information.

5. The intermediary as counselor: The intermediary intervenes thoroughly in the information-search process, including helping the user to construct a search, develop a strategy, and evaluate sources.

These five approaches to involvement between the intermediary and the user are of interest, and without too much imagination it can be seen how different types of services will be identified by the kind of involvement that predominantly identifies them. It is necessary, however, to consider the kinds of partnership between users and intermediaries that are appropriate to different information tasks.

Designing Services

Expressing Statements of Information Need

Chapter 5 discusses in detail the task of expressing an information need in a statement of need. For situations involving failure of perception, the general approach to completing this task is to:

- find an expert,
- approach the expert,
- identify the problem (usually in few words), and
- ask for help.

Chapter 6 begins sketching an information system that will allow these steps to be accomplished and will help a user understand the response received from the expert. It is hard to see a user with this type of information need as being satisfied with an intermediary as organizer or locator. Some higher level of involvement is required. In fact, in most cases it is likely that the high level of involvement associated with an advisor or counselor is most appropriate. The intermediary may have to give counsel in the area of finding and approaching the expert and identifying the problem. There are many information devices that operate through classificatory or associative links that permit users to browse from a starting point to information that may resolve their information need. The important function of the information service may be simply to match the user to an appropriate source. It is important for intermediaries to recognize that browsing is not an inferior approach to information retrieval, but rather is sometimes the only possible or viable approach that will meet an information need. The function of the information service is to direct the apparently inarticulate user to browsable tools and to help him or her navigate the classificatory or associative networks. In fact, the information system identified as System 1 demands a highly active role for an intermediary. The device by itself, with its associated networks of images, lists of expert informants, and dictionary lookup, is probably not usable on its own, but requires the active advice and collaboration of a partner who is an information specialist to produce effective results. In addition, the information system has links to a variety of experts who can help the user diagnose and identify the information needed. As noted previously, most of these experts are human beings, rather than expert systems, and can be accessed through standard communication paths. The intermediary, recognizing that the user may not be able to resolve the information need from the associative network of images contained in System 1, must be able to refer the user to an expert who can provide the needed information. One can conceive of the intermediary as someone who may not be expert in many specialized fields of knowledge, but who has contacts with a constellation of available experts within the community.

In the case of identifying alternatives by slot filling, an information system is sketched that allows users to systematically explore a topic area and to create an elaborated understanding of that topic by following associative links to related topics. It will certainly be possible for users to approach System 2, type in a label, and pursue the hierarchical information network to establish the details of available alternatives. In this interaction, the amount of the intermediary's involvement is likely to be limited to the role of organizer or locator. However, there may be many different versions of the information in the system, created by the combination and recombination of text chunks in order to match users' resources, problem situations, and social constraints. Intermediaries play a role in working with the user to obtain the version of the information that most closely matches the user's situation.

Alternative evaluation is presumed to be accomplished using an information system with the capability to accept a detailed statement of need and to prepare a literature review (or the raw materials for such a review) that allows users to match alternatives with outcomes. Operation of System 3 can occur in an unintermediated environment, but (as in the case of System 2) customizing the information to match the resources, problem situation, and social constraints of the user requires intermediary involvement. Similarly, working with users to help them avoid information they do not want can be an important intermediary role.

Scanning, Evaluating, and Learning from Information

Chapter 7 turns to the additional tasks that users must accomplish: scanning, reviewing and evaluating, learning from the information systems, and planning for ongoing information seeking. There is a role for active intermediation in many of these tasks. Scanning is a task that requires little intervention by an intermediary. If the information systems are designed with the features discussed in this book to facilitate scanning, it will be possible for people to scan most information without assistance. However, evaluation is another matter. Despite the system-design features that may enhance the selectivity of users or that may draw attention to evaluative criteria, evaluation requires a substantial level of cognitive load. Despite the availability of the evaluative comments of previous users captured in cumulative user-supplied indexing, users may still require the active assistance of an information specialist capable of suggesting evaluative criteria and their application.

Of course, learning from information is the objective of the whole exercise and the task that seems to most require the assistance of an intermediary. Perhaps, in this judgment, the author is influenced by his years working as a reference librarian. In that setting, one frequently hears the plaintive question, "But what does it mean?" or "Does that mean that . . .?" Users are trying to learn from information presented, but they are having trouble. Admittedly, sometimes figuring out the meaning of what they have seen is a valuable exercise for users, and the intermediary should not always try to answer these questions. On the other hand, the task of learning carries with it the role of teacher, and it is entirely appropriate for the intermediary to facilitate learning in a way that reduces the frustration and increases the comprehension of users. Sometimes all that is necessary is confirmation that another human being has read the same material and come to the same understanding.

In all of the system designs sketched in this book, there is room for an intermediary as learning facilitator. In System 1, the user may browse to the information that will remedy the failure of perception, but still may need help in interpreting, judging, and learning from the information. In System 2, the user may need assistance in reorganizing the information to meet the task and in interpreting the relevance of associative links. In System 3, the user may need help in synthesizing the information from the literature review into a coherent set of evaluations of alternatives. The presence of an intermediary as an active partner, with involvement at the higher levels of adviser and counselor, seems most appropriate.

Planning for ongoing information seeking is also a task that can benefit from active assistance from a partner. Information intermediaries are exposed to many information-search tactics and strategies as they work with users. The resulting familiarity with scripts and heuristics can be shared with the users as they plan for future information tasks. Again, the higher service levels of adviser and counselor appear to be appropriate for the service interaction in the context of information planning.

This discussion has led to an understanding of user-based information services as highly intermediated, with human experts in partnership with users as they browse, explore, and learn. It must be admitted, however, that there is a contrary tendency found in many information systems and services: the self-service approach, in which intermediaries play the minimal roles of organizer and locator. The government information kiosk in the neighborhood post office, the wealth of information pumped through television programs and other broadcast media, and the widespread accessibility of networked information resources are all examples of this self-service approach. The tendency is to encode the functions assigned to the intermediary in the preceding discussion into the information device itself. So, for example, the information device takes upon itself the functions of explaining "what it means," of maintaining a network of expert contacts to whom users can be referred, and of directing the exploration along productive pathways.

It seems clear that these functions can be performed by a device, but only by making some gross generalizations about users. For example, television information programs assume that the viewer has the vocabulary, knowledge level, interest level, and attention span of an elementary school student. Networked information services seem to assume that information seekers will have the knowledge levels and interests of the people who post the information. The serious, purposive seeker after information will have immense difficulties meeting his or her objectives from devices such as these.

Balancing Devices and Intermediaries

The self-service approach shifts the task of working in partnership with users from one part of the information system to another, from the human intermediary to the information device. There may be good reasons for adopting this approach. For example, human intermediaries cannot usually be delivered to remote locations over telecommunication networks. Systems with humans in the loop have a potential for failure, as witnessed by the number of aircraft accidents attributed to pilot error. On the other hand, the boundary between the human and the device is determined by the relative capabilities of the two types of resources. To continue the example, there are many things that pilots can do that autopilots cannot. Hence, there are pilots in airline cockpits. Avionics have improved continually, and the boundary between the human and the device has shifted accordingly, but the ability to diagnose a problem situation and respond flexibly and quickly to that situation is still the domain of the human component of the system.

Similarly, there are important functions that human intermediaries can accomplish with relative ease that are far beyond the present capabilities of information technology. The ability to interact sensitively and flexibility with a user who is working on a problem is one of them. Most computers cannot even recognize a basketball when it is placed in front of them. It is unlikely that they will be able to recognize a user experiencing failure of perception, and even less likely that they will be able to deal sensitively with both the affective and cognitive contents of a situation. The optimal approach for the present and the foreseeable future will be to establish a partnership in which human intermediaries play an important role, while allowing information technology to do what it does well.

Intermediaries and Group Information Activities

The partnership between individual users and intermediaries may be seen to serve as a model for collective information needs. It is conceptually possible to associate an information specialist with every decision-making group or every group engaged in learning. This approach can be established structurally within academic or research settings by associating a librarian with every research laboratory or research and development (R&D) project. There are, however, a number of reasons for thinking that such an arrangement is unlikely to succeed. Throughout the discussion of collective information needs and the systems that may be put in place to meet those needs, several features have been stressed: the importance of the dynamics occurring within any group in achieving consensus about the purpose and focus of the group, the way this focus evolves over time, and the way this focus can serve as a basis for information seeking. The intermediary is likely to be an interloper and outsider to the group, whose presence distorts the group dynamics.

Within any group, the importance of boundary spanning and gatekeeping has been emphasized, as well as the somewhat anomalous roles sometimes played by gatekeepers. These individuals are, by definition, group members, but they also have the ability to bring information to the group from outside. It seems preferable to see the partnership of the intermediary and the group as operating through relationships between intermediaries and gatekeepers. This arrangement does not disturb the dynamics of the group, but it does allow the expertise of the intermediary to guide the external information seeking that will help the group achieve its purpose. If a group does not have people performing the gatekeeping role, a partnership relationship must be developed between intermediaries and individual group members who at various times seek information for the group. In such situations, group information seeking is not centralized through gatekeepers and may occur in a more spontaneous manner as individual group members engage in problem-solving partnerships with intermediaries.

At the same time, information systems can play an invaluable role in facilitating internal communication and information transfer within the group. One may wonder to what extent a human intermediary can be part of this process. The general principle enunciated previously is to let humans do what they do best and to let technology do the same. Following that principle, it seems unlikely that human intermediaries will be needed in the internal communication and negotiation for consensus that occurs within a group. Rather, the group must establish and follow its own procedures for deciding (for example) whether a particular item of information is relevant to their focus. Communication technology, such as that associated with GDSS and CSCW, can facilitate this process in a way that can be far less obtrusive and intrusive than a human facilitator.

Instruction

The discussion presented thus far in this book has deliberately downplayed one set of individual and social variables that clearly and inevitably influence the information-seeking behavior of individuals: knowledge of information technology. This knowledge is both individual in nature and socially constructed. The knowledge of information technology that an individual brings to an encounter with an information system, or in some cases, the perception or feeling of knowledge of information technology that an individual brings to that encounter, determines in part how information tasks are performed. For example, users with high levels of confidence in their knowledge of information technology may express their statements of information need in a way they believe is likely to be accepted by the information technology or will result in a successful search. Their perceived knowledge of the technology may lead them to select one particular informant over another. Their expertise in using the technology may allow them to scan the information presented by the system more efficiently and evaluate the information more effectively, and may enhance the learning they derive from the information.

At the same time, an understanding of information technology is socially constructed. In an organization, for example, the understanding of information technology as a positive force will be constrained by the organization's culture. Members of two different organizations may have entirely different attitudes about a particular information technology, depending on the collective history of their organization in dealing with such technology. In more general terms, there may be socioeconomic, linguistic, and ethnic differences in social groups that will influence their collective perceptions of information technology. Certainly, there are social factors that influence the prevalence of computer literacy, a foundation element of knowledge of information technology.

The reason that this obviously significant influence on information behavior has been neglected until this point in the discussion can be found in the emphasis on user-centered design that has been adopted in this book. It was considered important to approach information-system design with a clean slate, without being limited by the characteristics of current information systems. To put it another way, knowledge of existing information technology may not help people who want to use the types of systems discussed in this book. If the user's knowledge of standardized methods of information organization are given too much attention, for example, some of the flexible and dynamic means of information organization discussed in Chapter 8 may be seen as less plausible. The fact that users are more or less familiar with the Dewey decimal classification, Standard Query Language (SQL) database query methods, or current generation hypertext systems such as HyperCard should not be allowed to restrict the options considered in developing usable information technology.

Now that the system-design chapters of this book are complete, it is possible to reintroduce the knowledge that users have of information technology and consider how users' knowledge of information systems can be incorporated into information services. The first point to be noted is that the illustrative designs for user-centered information systems include a number of self-guiding or instructional features. The links to information about information structures, for example, or to advice about information plans and heuristics are good examples of system features that reflect and enhance user knowledge of these technologies.

As may be expected, however, the main approach to knowledge of information technology taken in this book is not technology-centered, but user-centered. This approach means that knowledge of information technology is not being presented to users as learning about the system. Rather, knowledge about technology is embedded in the problem-solving process. As a consequence, knowledge about technology is contextualized within a particular user's problem domain, and knowledge of information technology will be subordinated to knowledge of information seeking. Users will not need to know standard techniques such as SQL query formulation, because there will be no such standard techniques in the information systems. Rather, users will need to know how to express their information needs in several different ways, depending on the nature of their needs and the problems they are trying to solve. Again, the users will not need to know standardized knowledge organizations such as a Dewey decimal classification, but they will need to know how to browse through hierarchical networks of various kinds.

It will perhaps be clear now why a discussion of user training has been postponed to the chapter on information services. Because information services focus on the needs of specific groups of users and information intermediaries are engaged in a partnership with users as they engage in problem solving, the instructional role seems most appropriate for information services, rather than for the information devices.

The function of intermediaries, as a result, will be to help people learn information technology as they help them express information needs, evaluate information, and learn. In doing so, the intermediaries will be sensitive to users' goals, purposes, and objectives; the tasks they are completing to accomplish those goals and meet those needs; and the cognitive and social resources they bring to bear on the tasks. This model is entirely individual in focus. The discussion of intermediaries presents their role as one of partnership with individual users. It follows that group instruction is unlikely to constitute a major element of the instructional services of intermediaries.

Instruction in the use of various kinds of information technology has been given a number of unattractive labels, including "bibliographic instruction." The main approach has been analogous to the function performed by interface design: to accommodate users to the poorly designed, data-centered information systems that now exist. A slightly more attractive approach has been given the term "information literacy," although this term is so amorphous in definition as to be virtually devoid of meaning. At its best, the information literacy approach may be seen as the broader approach to user instruction outlined here. For example, Jacobson and Jacobson (1993) examine some of the individual and social resources that people use in information seeking. Mental models (the knowledge structures or metaphors by which people understand the functioning of information systems), situated cognition (an understanding that social variables are crucial in understanding information needs and information seeking), and cognitive flexibility (the understanding that ill-defined problems, such as many information-related problems, require different problem-solving approaches than well-defined problems) are recommended as approaches to be incorporated in instruction. Similarly, Nahl-Jakobovits and Jakobovits (1993) draw attention to the critical-thinking approach emphasized previously as central to the completion of information tasks, the strategy planning considered in Chapter 7, and the learning that is so important to resolving information needs as elements that should be included in instruction.

The instructional role of intermediaries is one that depends on their familiarity not only with information-seeking behavior, but also with information technology. It is a mistake to think of instruction as something separable from the rest of the activities of the information partnership. Rather, intermediaries engage in instruction throughout the information interaction with users and so help to ensure users' success in meeting their information needs.

Contacting Users

Chapter 4 considers the first of many general design principles that can drive the development of information systems and services. That discussion notes that, for every type of information user, the information service has the responsibility to decide whether or not to serve that type of user and how to attract that type of user to the service. Both of these steps are preliminary to meeting the information need. It can be assumed that the first question has been answered in the affirmative. The service has decided to attempt to meet the needs of a particular type of user. It remains to be seen how users may be contacted and attracted to the service.

This discussion has been postponed to this chapter, because attracting users is not really the function of information systems. Rather, the information systems are designed to provide information in response to information needs. At the same time, the definition of information services is that they are focused on specific groups of users and their needs, so it seems appropriate to consider the task of contacting and attracting users as a responsibility of the information service and specifically of the human intermediaries who provide and maintain that service.

Chapter 4 considers the mechanisms that services such as hospital emergency rooms use to sweep the community for those in need and notes that information services need to rely on similar mechanisms. Information services (like health services) rely to a large extent on self-referral: patrons who take the initiative to contact the information service. In health services, however, there are features such as emergency telephone numbers that make self-referral simple and easy and mechanisms such as ambulance services that perform the function of bringing the user into contact with the service. It is not clear that information systems typically have the same features to facilitate contact. In general, self-referral works best when there is a high level of awareness about the service in the community of potential users. In addition, ease of contact will make self-referral more likely, and simplified physical delivery of the service is an additional factor in attracting users. Finally, the health service analogy provides another suggestion to consider. People may be attracted to health services because of a service relationship that has been developed with their physician. They may feel confident in the health care offered by that physician because of a history of interaction with that one service provider.

This analogy has produced four directions for exploration in contacting and attracting users of information services:

- awareness of the service in the community,
- ease of contacting service providers,
- simple mechanisms for service delivery, and
- personal relationships with service providers.

Awareness of a service is achieved primarily by marketing. The next chapter considers marketing as an institutional responsibility. At this point, it is important to point out that it is the responsibility of the information intermediaries to ensure that the service they are offering to the community is well represented in institutional marketing efforts. In some large information organizations, it may be possible for a particular service to maintain its own marketing function. This arrangement is analogous to the separate marketing of a particular product or product line by a multiproduct firm. On the other hand, a good case can be made (particularly in smaller organizations) for an integrated marketing function that has the responsibility to increase the community's awareness of all of the services offered by the organization. In either case, the information intermediaries in any information service bear the primary responsibility for developing a marketing approach that will increase community awareness of the service and develop positive feelings in the community about their service.

The second point is that ease of contact makes contact more likely. In many communities, a single telephone number (typically three digits, designed for ease of recall) makes contact with a service representing a variety of emergency organizations, such as police, fire departments, and ambulance services. Similar ease of contact occurs in the case of retail stores that are physically grouped together in areas that provide convenient vehicular access and ample parking. Some information industries provide for easy contact by establishing physical outlets in every home. Telephone and cable television companies, for example, facilitate contact by ensuring that every home in a community is wired to receive their service. With these different models to draw upon, information intermediaries should be able to select mechanisms that will provide ease of contact. One way of conceptualizing this mechanism is as an information hotline or information home page that places members of the user community in direct contact with a variety of information services.

Simplicity of service delivery is the next point to be considered. Because the key component of information services is the interaction between users and intermediaries, the question of service delivery becomes one of presenting partnership opportunities to members of the user community. There are a variety of models from which to choose. A user may interact with a service provider by visiting the institution or organization in which the service is provided, or the service provider may visit the user in his or her home or office. Telecommunication systems may be used to put the two individuals into contact with each other. Again, it is the responsibility of the information intermediary to establish simple and effective ways of delivering information services, so that barriers are not established between users and the services they need.

Finally, there is the importance of an ongoing, personal relationship between service providers and users. One tends to find this kind of relationship with physicians, insurance agents, and even grocers. The partnership model outlined in this chapter makes it clear that information services are entirely amenable to this aspect of service provision. It is primarily the responsibility of the information intermediary to maintain contact with users, to encourage them to use the service, and to retain the kinds of records of the service interaction that will ensure continuity in the service relationship. At the same time, this kind of personal relationship will ensure that marketing through word of mouth will be an effective tool in identifying new users for the information service.

Conclusion: A User-Centered Approach to Information Services

The outline of a typical user-centered information service can now be sketched. It brings together in one place (physical or virtual) a set of information systems that are designed to meet the specific needs of a defined set of users. For example, it may be designed to meet the information needs of a research lab investigating a particular aspect of chemical structures using scanning tunneling microscopy. Alternatively, it may focus on the needs of fifth grade students studying ancient Egyptian culture and civilization. Each information system that is part of the service will have its information content, organization, access mechanisms, and interfaces tailored to the needs being met. However, because these needs are diverse and evolve as the user's knowledge changes, the systems may be devoted to such different stages of the information process as problem recognition, exploration of alternatives, and evaluation and selection of alternatives.

The people responsible for creating the service and (to a large extent) creating the information systems that are brought together in the service are information intermediaries. These individuals are able to enter into partnerships with individual users to accomplish specific information tasks. They have the additional function of instructing users in their interaction with the information systems and more generally in their approach to information seeking.

The sketch of information-system design leads to the conclusion that information systems will be dynamic, changing rapidly and flexibly to meet the changing needs of users. This dynamism also applies to information services. The microscopy lab will change its focus as it moves from one research project to another. Fifth grade students will move rapidly from studying the civilization of ancient Egypt to learning about current political systems in Europe. Information services undergo rapid transformations in response to these changes. Some information needs may recur in a cyclical fashion. The ancient Egypt information service may be packed away (figuratively), emerging next year to be used by another group of students. Other changes may be less structured, and the information service for the microscopy lab may change from week to week as research projects are begun or completed.

These examples have permitted the interpretation of the place in which the information systems are assembled as a physical space. It is equally possible, however, that the space is a virtual one. In this circumstance, the users of the information service are geographically dispersed, and the information resources (including the intermediaries) can be equally dispersed. The partnership arrangements will be supported by telecommunication, as will the instructional services. An example may be an information service supporting those individuals who provide care for patients with a particular chronic illness. The discussion of health information needs notes that such individuals need information about the disease and its treatment and also about caregiver support. It is entirely possible for information systems, complete with human intermediaries, to be accessible to these users through telecommunication links, and for the information needs to be met as effectively as if the users and systems were in physical contact.

In summary, the user-centered design approach leads to a vision of information services that is intimate and dynamic and that maintains a balance between human insight and technological capability. The discussion now turns to a consideration of the information institutions that will support such services.

References

Jacobson, F. F., & Jacobson, M. J. (1993). Representative cognitive learning theories and BI: A case study of end user searching. *Research Strategies, 11*(3), 124–137.

Kuhlthau, C. C. (1993). *Seeking meaning: A process approach to library and information services.* Norwood, NJ: Ablex.

Kuhlthau, C. C., Spink, A., & Cool, C. (1992). Exploration into stages in the retrieval in the information search process in online information retrieval: Communication between users and intermediaries. In D. Shaw (Ed.), *ASIS '92. Proceedings of the 55th Annual Meeting of the American Society for Information Science* (pp. 67–71). Medford, NJ: Learned Information.

Nahl-Jakobovits, D., & Jakobovits, L. A. (1993). Bibliographic instructional design for information literacy: Integrating affective and cognitive objectives. *Research Strategies, 11*(2), 73–88.

Siehl, C., Bowen, D. E., & Pearson, C. M. (1992). Service encounters as rites of integration: An information processing model. *Organization Science, 3*(4), 537–555.

10

Information Institutions

Introduction

The previous chapter insists that the only reasonable definition of an information service is user-centered, because only users have information needs to be met. This approach is distinguishable from information organizations that are established to make use of specific resources and that may be described based on a warehouse model or a bureaucratic model. In this chapter, the discussion of the nature of information services is extended to consider the role and function of information institutions. Chapter 1 outlines the distinction between information services and information institutions. To recapitulate briefly, information institutions are aggregations of information systems. They act as support structures for information services by marketing the services and obtaining funding, either through price setting or by establishing their services as public goods that can be supported by public or philanthropic funds. They provide a managerial structure that obtains, controls, and accounts for the resources required to operate information services. They control access to the services by attracting users of certain types, preventing access by other user types, or perhaps a combination of both. Information institutions are, therefore, the formal structures within which users, intermediaries, and informants come together in a purposive way to meet information needs.

When the user-centered design of information systems and services was considered, a considerable contrast was found between the results achieved through this approach and those associated with a data-centered approach. The same is true for information institutions. A data-centered approach to information institutions makes data the first organizing feature of the institution. A data archive is a good example of such an institution. Data are stored, possibly for future use or because government regulations require them to be stored. The responsibilities of the institution are to guard the data from unauthorized access and use, to ensure that the storage media remain undamaged, to maintain an accurate catalog of the data, and to obtain and manage the resources required to accomplish these objectives.

By contrast, an information institution designed from a user perspective will focus on optimizing use. User access to the institution will be a major priority. Obtaining and managing the resources to support active and dynamic information services will be the focus of activity in the managerial echelons. The following sections present in detail the kind of institution that may evolve from this approach.

A Market Focus

The first characteristic of user-centered information institutions must necessarily be a narrow and unwavering focus on the market. This statement is another way of presenting the main theme of this book: information systems, services, and institutions must be user centered. However, discussing users as constituting a market introduces a number of nuances into this theme. The marketing approach treats users as a collectivity rather than as individuals meeting their specific needs. This emphasis allows a close focus on similarities between users and the way these similarities create a community of interest. In addition, the marketing approach draws attention to the economic power that is exercised by the community of users. The decisions that users make about how and where they will search for information, when summed across the user community, create a demand that can influence the availability of information services, the form that institutions take, and the way in which value is reflected by prices.

As is the case in so many service organizations or companies, the survival of information institutions depends on attracting a substantial clientele and retaining that customer base over time. There is a close link between the service provided and the institution that provides the service. This point may be illustrated by contrasting goods with services. In the case of a consumer product (for example, soap), the product itself is marketed by the manufacturer. One can purchase the identical product in dozens of different retail outlets. There is little association between the product and the institution that provides the product. In the case of services, on the other hand, the institution that provides the service determines the characteristics of the service, because each institution has a different mix of personnel and technological resources. Hence the marketing of the service and of the institution are closely linked. To put it another way, with information there is no equivalent of the soap manufacturer. The entire burden of marketing falls on the information institution.

In this sense, information institutions resemble other services. Financial planners, accountants, lawyers, and (in many cases) medical practitioners have an overwhelming responsibility to maintain contacts with the larger community from which their customers are drawn and to attract business to their firms. This feature is another point that distinguishes the marketing of services from the marketing of goods. Because of the generic nature of goods (e.g., one box of soap is much like another box of soap), the product can be marketed by large-scale advertising. However, services such as those provided in information institutions are not generic. Each information interaction is uniquely characterized by the needs of the user and the features of the information system (including the characteristics of the human intermediaries involved). Accordingly, marketing of information services is much more local in scale, and information professionals, like other service professionals, have a responsibility for this marketing.

Furthermore, the nature of the information business is determined to a large extent by the customers that information professionals attract. Just as a surgeon may develop a reputation as being highly expert in performing a certain type of operation and accordingly attract to his or her practice patients with a specific disease, so information professionals and information services may develop a reputation for expertise in meeting specific types of information need. A reputation for excellence in a particular domain is a key marketing tool, one that can strongly influence the development of an information institution.

The market focus, then, is a user-centered focus for information institutions. The discussion now turns to a more detailed analysis of some of the implications of this market focus for the planning and development of information institutions.

Identifying Markets

Some information institutions are known as research institutions, because users employ their services to conduct scholarly investigations of various kinds. In another sense, all information institutions must be research institutions. They must conduct ongoing investigations of their own markets to identify them and develop an understanding of their characteristics. For example, in a university library, the identification of the market may seem trivial; surely the faculty and students of the university are the market. Of course, this is entirely too simplistic, first because the list is incomplete, and second because it is too general. There may, in fact, be many other clients of the university library. For example, it is a foolhardy library that turns a wealthy alumnus away from information services or that considers state bureaucrats unworthy clients. The list of potential members of the institution's market can extend to many individuals drawn from international academia and the university's regional and national constituencies.

There are a number of alternative methods by which markets can be identified. In a bureaucratic organization, for example, the market is frequently identified in policy statements of various kinds. These policy statements, developed in a political process, invariably represent a political view of the institution. Those customers who have the most power in the institution are likely to be given greater emphasis in the market profile. One can, for example, see the market for management information systems being defined largely in terms of department heads, vice-presidents, and other senior executives. This bureaucratic approach may be contrasted with the user-centered market approach. Here, it is the nature of the information needs, the tasks that are accomplished in meeting those needs, and the resources that are necessary to accomplish the tasks that characterize the market, rather than the power of any particular group of users within the institution. This approach implies that the responsibility for identifying markets lies with those members of the information institution who are closest to the user community: the intermediaries.

Identifying the market also requires that the members of that market be characterized in some detail. What kinds of information needs do they have? What tasks are they trying to accomplish on a regular basis that relate to those information needs? What resources do they have and what resources do they need to complete those tasks? The entire set of questions considered in this book can be used to characterize the market for an information institution. It may be argued that, if the investigations required for user-centered information-system design are completed rigorously, there will be no need for a separate investigation of markets at the institutional level. It is true that the investigations of users' needs that are associated with system design will contribute substantially to market identification, but these individual investigations are necessarily limited in scope. At the institutional level, the research involved in identifying multiple user needs can be wide-ranging, designed to identify the characteristics of the user community in a broader, more integrated manner.

As if this task were not sufficiently daunting, the market is in constant transition. For example, it is hard to argue that today's undergraduates have the same information needs as those of five years ago. The internationalization of scholarship through networked information resources has brought about a different understanding of the information needs of faculty and of the resources required to meet those needs. Again, it seems clear that the task of identifying transitions and trends in the user community must be the responsibility of the human intermediaries who are in constant contact with users. Through this contact, they will be ideally placed to understand the influences that are molding user needs and to respond not only with changes in information systems and services, but with a transformed information institution that will respond to the evolving user community.

Service Development

It is against this background of in-depth understanding of the continually changing institutional market that service development occurs. It should be emphasized that the process of user-centered information systems and service design that has been the focus of much of this book is precisely the kind of service development presented here. The task of analyzing the needs of specific groups of users and considering the tasks they must accomplish and the resources they need to accomplish these tasks is the first step in service development. Then the resources that users have can be compared with the resources they need. There are knowledge resources that are needed to complete many information tasks. In any user community, users may have different levels of these knowledge resources, depending on their individual backgrounds, their association with different groups within the community, and social norms and standards. Similarly, members of a user community may possess different levels of important skills and abilities. As information institutions serve groups, it becomes important to assess the collective resources for consensus building that are available to these user groups. Through an analysis of the levels of these resources available to members of the user community, information institutions will be able to tailor the information systems and services that are devoted to meeting user information needs. The interaction between user resources and aspects of the service being developed drives the decision making about the aspects to be included in any service. If some members of a user community lack important knowledge resources, systems can be selected and tailored to augment knowledge levels. System features can be selected to ensure that users with all levels of skills and abilities can complete their information tasks. Features of information systems and services can be developed to facilitate group processing of information resources. As a result, collections can be selected and organized, access can be provided, and system and interface features can be selected to assist users in meeting their needs.

O'Leary (1992) chronicles the growth of awareness of this kind of product development in one of the leviathans of the information industry: Dialog. The firm acknowledges the importance of consumer demand and the need to develop services for a wide variety of user groups. As the great, monolithic, one-size-fits-all information providers come up against the needs of real users, they will be forced to take a serious, user-centered approach to product development. It is to be hoped that they will do this, rather than simply trying to develop customized front-ends and interfaces, as suggested in the O'Leary (1992) article.

The active nature of this approach is clear. As Jaffe (1994) suggests, information service providers should not be in a position of simply reacting to user requests. Rather, in a corporate MIS environment, the information-service function should regularly deliver to users some features from which they would benefit, but that they have not yet requested. This advice seems to apply in all information-service development. User-centered proactivity in service innovation has as its main purpose the improvement of information services. However, service providers will also benefit, both in reputation and support, by being active in meeting information needs. Of course, the key to success in private-sector information services is to increase the profitability of the firm. Some managers may see a conflict between profitability and a user-centered approach such as that suggested here. Expending company resources on meeting demands that are not yet recognized or providing services that are not yet requested may seem wasteful. The convincing counterargument is that more effective management and use of information, one of any firm's most important resources, can be achieved by meeting user information needs. This argument suggests that profitability and user-centered approaches go hand in hand and that proactive information service development can be associated with greater efficiency as well as greater effectiveness.

In both public- and private-sector information institutions, there is typically a division in service development between a few information institutions, which do most of the system design and development, and the majority of institutions, which acquire information devices and develop them into systems and services by tailoring them to meet local users' needs. This approach represents an economical way to develop information services, but it means that the needs of local users are considered last in service development, rather than being the initiating and driving force in this process. There are, however, a number of general approaches to information-service development outlined in previous chapters that provide more capabilities for information institutions to give more attention to their users during service development. One recommendation is that there should be a reasonably large number of system features that are available as user-selected options. An information institution can test each of these options against the resources of its own user community and develop preset preferences files that tailor the system to the needs, tasks, and especially the resources of its users. Another suggestion is that information collected for any given system should be subject to continual change, as information specialists and intermediaries work in partnership with users to meet their needs. Through this process of developing information resources to meet narrowly-defined needs, information institutions will be able to engage in user-centered service development. A third recommendation is that cumulative user-supplied indexing should provide one main mechanism for organizing information. If this is done on a consistent basis within each user population, information services will automatically be tailored to meet local needs. There will, no doubt, be a great deal of additional effort required for user-centered service development to succeed at the level of the local institution. The question that must be answered here is whether the additional effort (and cost) of user-centered service development is justifiable. This question can only be answered by the users themselves. There will presumably be a portion of any user community for whom a generic, one-size-fits-all information system will be satisfactory. User-centered service development can only occur if there is another segment of the user community who will demand, and pay for, customized and individualized services. The composition of each user community will determine the extent to which local, specialized service development is justified.

Customer Relations

In service organizations, such as the information institutions discussed here, customer relations are crucial to continued success. The partnership model discussed in Chapter 9 establishes one basis for strong and positive relations between customers and the institution. If an information specialist works closely with a user to meet an information need and that partnership relationship is extended over a period of time as the user addresses a series of information needs, there is great potential for customer loyalty and return business.

It is, however, important to think about the institutional structures that may facilitate the development of strong customer relations so that the information partnership may be successful. Criteria for judging the appropriateness of the institutional structures range from enhanced profitability (in private-sector institutions) to higher levels of customer satisfaction and return business (in all institutions). It seems clear that organizational structures that minimize the potential for conflict or adversarial relations between users and the institution are most likely to be appropriate in facilitating information partnerships. In practical terms, this means avoiding the typical bureaucratic organization, with its emphasis on rules and penalties and its notorious lack of service orientation. In any bureaucratic information institution, the user is at the bottom of the hierarchy in terms of influence and power, and the intermediaries are typically caught between a desire to meet the users' needs and the need to control resources dictated from higher levels in the administrative hierarchy. An organizational structure that will facilitate good customer relations will require the inversion of the hierarchy, with customers and intermediaries having higher levels of power and influence. At the same time, the organization must adopt criteria for success that relate to user satisfaction and return business rather than to control over resources.

In many information institutions, putting the customer first involves placing other priorities at lower levels. It may not be possible to maintain consistent and limited office hours or to limit the costs associated with acquiring and organizing materials. In this regard, it can be noted that the continuing and flexible redefinition and reorganization of information systems to meet the changing needs of users discussed in this book require a great deal of effort from information professionals. Rather than the "mark it and park it" or "if you build it, he will come" self-service orientation of some information institutions, good customer relations require continual attention and effort in defining new information products and working directly with users.

Strategic Planning

The market focus identified previously provides the basis for strategic planning for information institutions. The key question in planning is "How will the market change in the future?" There are, of course, other elements in the environment that planning must consider. For example, planning must consider how technology will change and how the regulatory environment may change. But the key, central issue facing planning for information institutions is the nature of the market and how it will change. In an academic situation, the key to planning for the institution's future is understanding how faculty and student information needs will develop. In a corporate situation, the needs of company executives for information to support decisions must be anticipated, and the needs of workers for information to enrich their jobs and lives must be considered. In an ideal world, the information services of the institution would have information systems in place to meet any new information need and solve any new information problem as soon as that problem was experienced. Strategic planning requires information professionals to be in constant contact with their market, anticipating future developments as they occur.

The first of the areas to be monitored for changes driving the strategic planning process is the nature of the overall activities of individuals who are members of the target market. In an R&D lab, the development of a new project or the acceptance of a new contract may be associated with new information needs. In an educational environment, it may be possible to anticipate the changes in student activities that are associated with curriculum changes. In times of economic contraction, it may be possible to anticipate that individuals in society will need information related to coping with unemployment and job searches. The second of the areas that should be monitored is the methods that people are using in their activities. If the R&D lab is going to be using a new instrument to conduct research, the scientists may need information about using the instrument and interpreting the results obtained from its use. In an educational environment, changing approaches to teaching (for example, adopting resource-based learning) will likely produce information needs related to the method and the results that may be expected. In society as a whole, the increased use of automation of various kinds is likely to generate a series of information needs that relate to technology training.

The information institution planner must also be aware of changes in the composition of the target market. Large-scale demographic trends are usually easy to detect, but subtle changes can influence the nature of information needs and how they are addressed within the user community. Changes in ethnic and cultural composition of the user community may bring about different social constraints on approaches to information. Changes in the background of members of the user community may reflect widespread changes in education, and such changes will affect the knowledge resources that users bring to information seeking. Even changes in the average age of the members of the user community may have an impact on their cognitive abilities and also on their performance of information-related tasks.

Information needs that arise in groups are also subject to change. To plan for future developments in these information needs, information professionals must investigate the overall activities of groups in the target market, the methods used in those activities, and the composition of groups in the target market. In addition, planning for information institutions must consider the internal dynamics of groups that are so central to their understanding of information needs and their seeking for and use of information. Changes in how group members interact with each other can be crucial indicators of changes in information seeking. To detect such changes and incorporate them into planning for information services, information professionals must be well informed about and sensitive to group processes within their target market.

The Short-Range Focus

Strategic planning normally considers a multiyear period in order to provide a long-range plan for the information institution. In organizations or firms for which changes in technology or other resources are the main determinants of long-term changes, this makes sense. Installation of a new technology base or retooling to take into account a new approach to production are appropriately multiyear processes. This seems less likely with the kinds of information institutions considered here. The technology of information systems, as emphasized throughout, should be dynamic and flexible. It is true that certain elements of the technology may be less flexible than others. Hardware, for example, may be more difficult to change than software, and software may take more work to adapt it to changing information tasks than data. However, it is essential that the combination of hardware, software, data, and human intermediaries be flexible enough that information professionals can rapidly create new combinations of these basic elements to respond to changes in information needs and tasks. Because the principal focus in strategic planning is on changes in user communities, it seems appropriate to respond in the short term rather than over a multiyear period.

This approach to strategic planning, accordingly, emphasizes short-term, dynamic responses to changes in an information community. With such an emphasis, there is always the possibility that medium- or long-range continuity will be ignored. However, long-term continuity can be ensured by focusing on an enduring user community. The mission of an information institution must be stated in terms of this enduring community. For example, the mission of an academic institution is to meet the information needs of faculty and students; the mission of an MIS department is to meet the information needs of executives of the firm. These mission statements are essentially useless for planning, because the composition of the enduring community and its information needs and activities change substantially in the short term. To decide about information systems and services that are to be provided, information professionals must consider the characteristics of current users and how those characteristics may change in the near future. The overall mission of the information institution ensures long-range continuity, but realistic planning takes place in the short term.

The long-term perspective may also be included within a short-term planning perspective because there is frequently a cyclical or repetitive nature in information needs. For example, after a period of contracting economic conditions during which job information is a major concern, there may come a period of economic expansion in which the need for job information is replaced by other concerns, perhaps how to manage personal finances. Information services must respond to short-term shifts in information needs by providing information on personal finances while recognizing that, in the long term, the need for job information may return. The short-term shifts in emphasis may simply require increasing the accessibility and salience of an information system that has been less used for a period and ensuring that the body of knowledge represented in the information system corresponds to the information needs of current users.

This is a lesson that software producers have learned, according to Sengstack (1994). In a profile of a firm called Creative Multimedia, the point is emphasized: license content rather than producing it from scratch, put it in a format that is exciting and simple to use, and put it on the market quickly. Although the approach of this firm is, necessarily, product-centered, it can be generalized to service provision. In the information-service industry, fast-response planning seems an important route to success.

Technology and People

In developing plans for the types of information systems and services discussed in this book, an information institution will be able to employ a variety of resources. These resources can be used in any combination, and plans for information systems can emphasize one or another type of resource. For example, it is possible to emphasize high levels of technology and low levels of human resources. Alternatively, technology may be de-emphasized, with more emphasis placed on human resources. To illustrate this point, two libraries can be contrasted. The first is the typical academic library, where large investments are made in a variety of information technologies, such as books, specialized buildings, computers, and electronic data resources. However, this type of library has typically minimized human resources whenever possible, for example, by accepting standardized ways of organizing and providing access to information. Use of these standardized approaches means that the library staff minimally processes information resources to make information available for users. Such minimal processing is associated with basic levels of access, because standardized methods of organization and access cannot take into account the special needs of a user community and accordingly cannot provide more sophisticated information access to members of the community.

The other library is a special library serving a small group of managers or researchers, where typically, large collections are not the objective. Enough technology is used to establish a basis for information access, but a larger proportion of human resources is devoted to meeting information needs. For example, trained intermediaries may establish links to the wide range of networked information resources, establish quality filters to help users evaluate information, or summarize and report on trends that are visible in the information.

Of course, both of these libraries are stereotypes, designed to illustrate the range of options available to information agencies. Based on the discussion in this book, however, it seems clear that user-centered information systems and services will require an approach to strategic planning that places a high level of emphasis on human rather than technological resources. The main factors that support such an emphasis are the short-term planning cycle, the flexibility and adaptability of information systems, and the need for intermediaries to work in close partnership with users. These components of the user-centered program for information services require that human resources be deployed to create and adapt information systems when necessary, to maintain contact with the user community in order to plan for future information systems, and to work with people in using the information systems and services. The balance of technological and human resources must be adjusted to assure that intermediaries are in place to engage in these activities.

The examples used previously were drawn from libraries, just one particular type of information institution, but the same options face any information institution. In the MIS department of a large firm, the same choice exists between high-technology solutions and approaches that rely more on human expertise. Each institution must employ a balance of resources that will allow it to provide flexible and adaptive services to its users. In an MIS department, this may mean that certain types of information systems can be developed using a high-tech approach. For example, accounting information, provided in standard forms to respond to standard queries, may need little intermediation. On the other hand, technology scans that will support R&D or environmental scanning that will support strategic planning in the firm may require the flexibility and expertise that is associated with human information professionals.

Because information institutions will be likely to develop information systems that employ different combinations of resources, there will always be some institutions engaged in the ongoing development of information technology. At the same time, information institutions must experiment with new ways of using human resources in information systems. This balance between new information technology and personnel development is important. Unfortunately, in current information institutions, there is sometimes a temptation to regard research and development of information systems from the perspective of technological development alone. Incorporating the user-centered approach will mean that planning for information systems and services will include a larger emphasis on the productive deployment of human resources in meeting information needs.

Interinstitution Integration

Another aspect of the planning environment is that information institutions coexist in the same service space. In many communities, there are a large number of institutions to which citizens can turn for information: newspapers and other forms of broadcast media, libraries, information brokers, database services, and so on. There are indications that the boundaries between these institutions are becoming more permeable. Newspapers are sponsoring telephone information services through which users can find (sometimes on a fee-for-service basis) current sports scores or answers to health questions. Rather than being available only once or twice a day at set times, newspaper information has adapted to 24–hour availability. Similarly, libraries are engaging in multitype cooperation, recognizing that the resources of special libraries (such as hospital libraries), academic libraries, and public libraries can be important to meet the information needs of their users. Both of these developments, which are only examples of a wide range of interinstitution cooperation, are consistent with the user-centered approach. In both cases, limitations inherent in data-centered approaches are overcome in order to meet user needs more effectively. When information institutions are planned on the basis of the nature of the information they contain or the types of technology they use, services are inevitably fragmented. User needs cross the boundaries between information types and technological approaches. Accordingly, the user-centered focus is likely to bring together a wide variety of existing information institutions in new relationships designed and planned around the information needs of users.

As information professionals turn to the task of strategic planning, they are likely to consider ways in which institutions that were formerly based on a particular type of data, medium, or bureaucratic organization can be reorganized in cooperative ways into user-centered institutions. The task of planning and developing user-centered institutions is a daunting one. Existing patterns of funding, for example, may act as a barrier to interinstitution cooperation. Information resources that belong to a private-sector company may be inaccessible to individuals who are not employed by that company. Similarly, information institutions developed with tax revenues from one community may not be accessible to citizens of another community. Fortunately, both technological and human solutions exist that can overcome the barriers posed by existing institutional boundaries. One of the more exciting technological developments has been the emergence of networked electronic information resources, with standardized approaches to navigation, presentation of data, and data sharing. Through such mechanisms, users may obtain access to the information resources of corporations, public libraries, research institutions, and government agencies. There are obvious limits to the ability of this technology to transcend institutional boundaries, but it is encouraging to see the development of mechanisms such as this, with the potential to overcome barriers between users and information. At the same time, the human solution should not be ignored. Institutional boundaries are frequently ignored when one information professional approaches another, asking for help in meeting a user's information needs. This sometimes requires the subversion of institutional regulations, or rather the subordination of such regulations to a higher ethic of service provision. The outcome is that information professionals can work to transcend institutional boundaries, working in tandem with technological solutions to accomplish interinstitution cooperation.

There is another set of considerations that leads to an emphasis on interinstitution integration. Serious attention to a market focus in creating information institutions means that there will be instances in which a user approaches the wrong institution for service. Despite the best efforts of marketing and promotion, people will end up in the wrong place or will bring inappropriate expectations to an institution. Consider a young family looking for a nice family restaurant walking into a hypothetical Café de Paris. One look at the menu, the decor, or the clientele produces the observation, "Boy, are we in the wrong place," followed by a rapid retreat. In this example, presumably, no harm has been done, but the family is still hungry and in need of advice in their search for a place to eat.

Perhaps a friendly waiter will advise them that there is a nice family restaurant just down the block. In an information environment, there should be enough interinstitution integration that the next stop made by a user after entering an inappropriate institution is, in fact, an appropriate institution. It is even possible, although perhaps not likely, that a user will obtain access to the appropriate institution and its services by telecommunication from the first (inappropriate) institution. In the library world, networks have been developed to facilitate the sharing of resources and the implementation of technological change. Gradually, these networks have become more inclusive of different types of libraries. These networks have come to fill the role of the friendly waiter. A user entering a public library with a request for highly technical information will be directed to a special or academic library with more appropriate information systems. An expansion of this approach to interinstitution networking to include all information institutions seems to be required to ensure that users are directed to the institutions best equipped to meet their information needs.

Value and Pricing

In all information institutions, users pay for the services offered. One of the profound differences between the types of information institutions relates to the question of how they pay for the systems and services. They can do so either directly or indirectly, in a variable or fixed manner. For example, direct variable payments may be made to information brokers or pay-per-view television. In these cases, each additional use of information incurs an additional cost. Direct fixed payments include subscriptions to newspapers or journals or paying a fixed monthly amount for access to cable television. In these cases, the payment remains the same regardless of how much or how little of the information resource is actually used.

Indirect payments for information occur whenever there is an intervening body between the user and the service provider. Almost all such indirect payment schemes rely on fixed-cost models. One example is the public (tax-supported) information institution. The payment from the user to the information institution is indirect, because there is an intervening agency: the municipality or state that collects the taxes. In most cases, users pay a certain amount per year and have unlimited use of the information resource. Other examples include state-supported museums and federally supported clearinghouses such as the ERIC clearinghouse on education. A similar indirect fixed-fee payment occurs when a student pays his or her tuition. In this case, the intervening agency is the university, and the fixed fee entitles the student to open access to the information resources of the university. Indirect, fixed-fee payment schemes have the additional characteristic that nonusers pay as much as users for the service.

Tax-supported public information institutions are sometimes considered to be instances of public goods. Public goods are goods that are seen to be necessary or important to society as a whole, but which individual consumers would be unwilling or unable to purchase. The typical example of public goods is the armed forces. A country may decide that an aircraft carrier is a good thing to have, but there is no way that individual consumers can (or will) elect to purchase one. Accordingly, funds are collected from taxpayers to purchase the aircraft carrier. It is possible that some large elements of information infrastructure, such as national libraries or national telecommunications networks, may be properly considered to be public goods. It is, however, difficult to support the idea that most information services are public goods. Individuals elect to purchase information services such as newspapers or books, to subscribe to online services, and to make room in their budgets for cable television. Individual consumers purchase specialized information such as tax advice or medical consultation. In the marketplace, it seems clear that the majority of information services are far closer to private goods such as food and shelter than they are to public goods.

Sponsored information is a somewhat different type of indirect user-pay scheme. In sponsored information, a company or agency purchases information and distributes it free to users. One example may be a religious organization that distributes its proselytizing and catechetical literature free to anyone who asks for it. Sometimes governments sponsor the free distribution of information. This may be propaganda, health education materials, or reports of the activities of government agencies. In both of these examples, the sponsoring agencies have a mission. In the case of the religious organization, the mission is to attract people to a particular set of beliefs. In the second case, the government has a mission to present a set of beliefs, to encourage healthful practices, or to inform its citizenry about government activities (whether they want to be informed or not). These kinds of free information are based on indirect user payment, because readers who are convinced by the proselytizing literature may contribute money to the religious organization. Similarly, people who are convinced by the government's message may be more willing to be taxed.

Another case of sponsorship is the commercial sponsorship of information through advertising. A series of messages extolling the virtues of some product is incorporated into the information device or system. This may be in the form of television advertising or display ads in newspapers and magazines. The interaction between the information and the advertising is complex; the information exists to hold the attention of the users so they will pay attention to the advertising. In addition, the information acts as a means of molding feelings and opinions. Positive feelings and attitudes about the information may spill over into positive feelings and attitudes about the advertised product. This kind of sponsored information may also be considered a case of indirect payment, because individuals who purchase the products or services that are advertised pay for the information at the same time.

Hybrid systems abound. Some public libraries are primarily tax-supported institutions, but incorporate direct payment for certain services. For example, they may have an information brokerage as part of their organizational structure, operating a commercial information service within the boundaries of a tax-supported institution. Few newspapers or magazines are totally supported by advertising sponsorship, but must charge subscribers some amount.

There are many widely varied approaches to payment for the information provided by information institutions. It is now important to consider whether there is one approach that is more compatible with the user-centered approach to developing information institutions. An approach to funding that emphasizes the importance of users and enhances the important interaction between users and intermediaries seems to be most appropriate.

Private or Public?

The user-centered approach to information services may initially be seen to be neutral with regard to the economic issues outlined in the preceding paragraphs. There is reason, however, to focus on the user–intermediary relationship when considering who will pay for information services. The preceding discussion indicates the importance of the intermediary in making information systems responsive to individual users and in developing the helping and training relationship that is central to the success of information services. A case can be made that a financial relationship brings the intermediary and the user closer together. If the intermediary's continuing income depends on success in meeting users' information needs, thus ensuring repeat business, the intermediary may provide a higher quality of service to users than if he or she has no financial motivation to provide good service. Similarly, users tend to be more critical of the service obtained from an information system or service if they are actually paying for the service, demanding a higher quality service in a fee-for-service environment than in a bureaucratic environment, where people are conditioned to expect mediocre service. On the other hand, a financial relationship may in some cases prevent the establishment of a good working relationship between information users and intermediaries. The pressure to obtain extra income may lead intermediaries to spend less time with users so they can provide services to (and obtain fees from) more users. Similarly, in a fee-for-service relationship, the user may feel a certain level of suspicion that the intermediary is more interested in the money than in the service being provided.

Institutions that are funded through fixed-price arrangements such as taxes or through sponsorship have the common disadvantage that their funding systems can constitute barriers in the relationship between the user and the information system or service. In tax-supported information institutions, users may perceive the information service as of little value, because it is (apparently) free. As a result, user expectations of the kind of service they will receive may be set at a low level. Alternatively, tax-supported information institutions can be seen as a kind of social service that caters to the indigent. Again, this perception can reduce user expectations for service. It seems likely that when users have low expectations of the services they will receive, intermediaries and other information professionals will be less motivated to provide higher levels of quality in their interactions with patrons. In addition, in institutions based on fixed fees, the incremental income from each subsequent use of the information service by a customer decreases. A family that pays $100 in taxes for public library use and uses it only once a year pays $100 for that single use. If the family uses the library 100 times, they pay only $1 per use, an amount that hardly supports the costs incurred by the library in providing the service. This reasoning may lead some institutions to discourage repeat use of their services. In this way, fixed-fee funding can inhibit a service orientation.

Sponsored information places other barriers between the user and the information service. Because of the complex relationship between the advertisement and the information, the information can be selected, or even transformed, in such a way as to make it appealing rather than accurate, or entertaining rather than informative. A comparison of public television with network television or of popular magazines with scholarly journals makes this comparison clear. In providing information services in a sponsored information institution, intermediaries may find themselves torn between helping the user to meet information needs and helping the sponsor to achieve financial or ideological goals.

These considerations lead to the suggestion that information institutions may function best from the user-centered perspective when the positive elements of direct user-pay funding are preserved and the negative elements of this approach to payment are minimized. It seems clear that the user-centered approach to information systems and services can work in any information institution, but information professionals may wish to think about the following rhetorical point: If the information they are providing is valuable, people should be willing to pay for it. If the information they are providing is not valuable, then they should not be providing it.

If a private-sector, fee-for-service model of funding information institutions is adopted, it will be possible to establish financial relationships between users and intermediaries, leading to the positive effects cited previously. Intermediaries will be attentive to providing high-quality service, and users will demand that kind of service. There are, of course, many cogent arguments against the fee-for-service approach suggested here. Line (1995) summarizes these arguments clearly and succinctly. At the same time, it is important to minimize the temptation for intermediaries to achieve high volume through lower levels of attention to each user and to minimize the suspicion that users may have that they may be ripped off by the intermediary. These negative effects can be minimized through adding a written estimate to the service negotiation that occurs in the user–intermediary interaction, as outlined in Chapter 9. In this estimate, an intermediary will contract with a user to provide a certain level of service for a specified fee. Users who are dissatisfied with the estimate received from one service provider can obtain competitive estimates from others. This will help to keep intermediaries honest, and at the same time, will allow users a certain level of confidence that they are not being taken advantage of by service providers.

There have been suggestions in the literature about making information institutions client-centered. In libraries, this phrase is associated with the suggestions of Martell (1983) about the organization of academic libraries. Most of these suggestions focus on groups of users or populations of users. Martell's suggestion for academic libraries is associated with the proliferation of branch libraries dedicated to providing services to groups such as physics students and faculty. The approach to user-centered organization outlined here moves beyond this concern with groups and populations and focuses on the relationship between individual users and intermediaries. Establishing a modified fee-for-service payment mechanism is one way of making information services focus more closely on the individual user.

Payment for Service: Implications for Salaries

Information intermediaries have been given a lot of responsibility in this book. The user-centered perspective demands that there be someone who is in contact with the user, to assess needs, observe tasks, and test the interaction between resources and system design features. At the same time, the user-centered approach implies a partnership between information professionals and users. All of the elements of the job description for information professionals developed here combine to create a challenging, important job. It seems true, however, that the remuneration currently received by information intermediaries is among the lowest received by information professionals. Reference librarians, particularly those who work with lower-status user groups such as children, fall behind systems librarians and managerial staff in salary. Similarly, client-relations personnel in a database management firm or service providers in an MIS department may be paid less than programmers and other technical staff. It can be argued that the data-centered or bureaucratic approaches are more likely to be influential in determining salaries than the user-centered approach.

If the fee-for-service payment approach outlined previously is adopted more broadly by information institutions, it will constitute a more user-centered approach to salary determination, and information intermediaries will be in a position to increase their salaries substantially. They will assume the position of professionals, operating in a service environment. Like dentists in private practice, lawyers in law offices, and architects who deal directly with clients, information professionals who work directly with users will tend to receive the highest salaries in the information institution. These ideas suggest that intermediaries should be responsible for establishing fees for their services and other workers in the institution should be paid on contract by the intermediaries. If, for example, an intermediary makes use of a computer programmer in developing a new information device as part of an ongoing information service, that programmer should be paid by the intermediary just as a dental technician is paid by a dentist. One may well wonder whether managerial staff in some information institutions would continue to be paid such high salaries under this kind of arrangement.

Payment for Service: Implications for Service Promotion

Before leaving the economics of information institutions, the question of promotion of services can be considered briefly. Information services are not renowned for their marketing. Only a small proportion of the advertising that appears in the marketplace is for information institutions. In many cases, there is a feeling that promotion of a service such as legal or medical services (both of which have important information-service components) is somehow unethical or inappropriate, and this stigma may carry over to information institutions. In addition, the predominance of the data-centered or bureaucratic approaches to information institutions may explain the lack of promotion and advertising. In the data-centered approach, the majority of the managerial attention is paid to the collection and preservation of data. If the data is present, users will inevitably come to make use of it, according to this ideology. In fact, managers who operate institutions with this focus typically avoid promotion because it may bring too many users to disturb the fine collection of data that is their primary focus. Similarly, a bureaucratic organization does not need to advertise for customers. Here, the primary focus is on the organization itself and its continued functioning. Only enough marketing is done to justify the bureaucracy to its funding agency. The user-centered approach seems to argue for a more aggressive approach to promotion. If users are important and the service provided to them is important, it follows that users should be attracted to the information institution. Particularly if the economic basis of the institution is fee-for-service (as suggested previously), it makes sense to attract customers.

The most important aspect of promotion for an information organization is the competence of the information professional. Another aspect of the important role of the intermediary is to ensure that existing customers return and that they pass the word to new customers that the information systems and services are effective and worth the money they cost. The role of the information professional in promoting information services can be compared to that of an accountant in private practice. The accountant has a responsibility to remain active in the business community, to make contact with potential clients through social gatherings of various kinds, and to ensure that the accounting practice is well known to the community of actual and potential users. Similarly, the good service provided by the accountant will be communicated from existing clients to the community at large through that most effective of advertising media, word of mouth. The information professional has a personal responsibility to engage in precisely this kind of promotion of the information service and the information institution within which it is found.

However, as Shermach (1994) indicates, intermediary relationships are not enough. It is important to have a general marketing plan that, after identifying the users who occupy the market, presents services to them in such a way as to be attractive and inviting. The example cited is a company called Delphi Internet Services, which chooses to market existing internet services to a particular market group: affluent youth who have never used interactive services. In the (somewhat grating) language of the marketer, they describe their marketing plan as reflecting the way people live and work, "showing consumers that high tech can be fun and exciting" (p. 19). Similarly, a marketing campaign for Bell-South Telecommunication begins by acknowledging the fear of information technology that consumers have and approaching consumers with attractive lifestyle changes that may overcome that fear.

Following the implications of the user-centered approach has led to a view of information institutions that may be somewhat surprising to those who are familiar only with traditional institutions based on data-centered approaches and organized along bureaucratic lines. Transforming a public library, an MIS department, or a database vendor into an information brokerage may seem a dramatic and somewhat fanciful suggestion. On the other hand, it seems clear that such an approach will produce a qualitatively different relationship between intermediaries and users, thus transforming both the quality of service and the internal structure of the institution. Although it is true that user-centered information-system development can occur in any kind of organization, managers of information institutions may wish to consider organizational options such as fee-for-service or voucher systems that will enhance the responsiveness of their institutions to users' needs.

Resource Management

One of the responsibilities of any organization is to manage resources in such a way as to obtain the best possible result from each unit of input. In hierarchically structured organizations, resources are managed through control. Higher levels in the organization control the resources available to lower levels, thus providing at least the illusion of careful resource management. The user-centered institutions discussed in this chapter seem to require some alternative approach to resource management. Because the user-centered organization focuses on the rapidly changing information needs of user groups and continually reorganizes resources into systems and services to meet those needs, it has no stable basis upon which the hierarchical control of resources can be established. Furthermore, the ideas developed in this chapter imply that information intermediaries should provide the primary basis for organization and funding of services. This suggestion means that the usual hierarchical pyramid is turned on its head, and the resulting flat organization is not suitable for hierarchical and authoritarian control of resources.

These considerations suggest that alternative means of managing resources in information organizations should be examined. Resource management is necessary, and if it cannot be achieved through hierarchical control, it is important to explore alternative mechanisms for achieving it.

Personnel for Service

One of the advantages of a hierarchical organization is that everyone (except the person at the top of the pyramid) has a supervisor. In the organization sketched in this chapter, users are essentially at the top of the pyramid. Each user or user group works with one or more information intermediary. This intermediary develops and adapts systems, pulls together services that will meet the users' information needs, and works directly with the users as they employ information systems. However, users are not in a position to supervise information intermediaries in any traditional sense. They are not able to train the information staff to ensure that they have the skills needed for their jobs. They are unable to conduct formal personnel evaluations or ensure that the intermediaries' skills remain up-to-date and they employ those skills appropriately in assisting users.

Because the intermediaries play such a key role in the user-centered information institution, it is important that some alternative means be devised of providing the personnel functions that would be accomplished by supervision in the hierarchical organization. Three approaches seem to recommend themselves: peer evaluation, maintenance of professional standards through licensing, and market forces. In the user-centered institution, absolving users of the responsibility for formal evaluation means that the only other viable observers of performance are peers: colleagues who work together in an information service. Peer evaluation is well understood in most academic environments, and it seems likely that it can be adopted to any information institution. This conclusion is particularly true if information intermediaries act as professionals, maintaining not only close relationships with users, but also collegial connections with other intermediaries. In such a situation, intermediaries may refer users to other information professionals for consultation concerning information needs in specialized areas. Referral relationships of this sort allow information professionals to work together and to establish a basis upon which they can evaluate each other's effectiveness in meeting information needs.

Peer standards regarding functions such as training can also be important, particularly if they are incorporated into formal requirements for maintaining one's license to practice as an information professional. Even without licensing arrangements, however, peer standards can be influential in controlling personnel resources. If the intermediaries working in an information service believe that one of their colleagues is not meeting their collective standards for service provision, effective pressure can be brought to bear on that individual to obtain appropriate training or to adjust his or her attitudes about service provision.

However, the ultimate sanction that enforces management of personnel resources may well be the market. In any information service, there will be some intermediaries who perform better than others. There is no particular mystery about this: users soon recognize those who design usable information systems, give reliable advice, have expertise that matches users' needs, and work well in partnership with individual users or user groups. The idea of making the information professionals the basis for the funding of the information institution, if taken to its logical conclusion, means giving information professionals the responsibility for their own salaries. They will ensure that their salaries remain high by attracting customers and maintaining good ongoing relationships with them. Under these conditions, some information professionals will inevitably earn more than others. Those individuals who do not do a good job will find themselves receiving less than the average salary and may elect to choose another career.

Another way of expressing the importance of the market in managing personnel resources is to note that there will be a variety of information institutions in any market. In one institution (perhaps the discount information supermarket), expectations for service levels will be low, while in another (perhaps the upscale information boutique), expectations will be high. Information professionals whose approaches to service provision do not meet with user expectations in any given institution may find it necessary to migrate to a different institution, where there will be a better fit between user expectations and their approach to service provision.

Organizational Structure

The preceding discussion has many implications for the organizational structure of information institutions. It has been clear to many authors that the hierarchical or bureaucratic structure is inappropriate for a user-centered institution. For example, Kochen and Deutsch (1977) note that it is important to shift the locus of decision making to the lowest level possible in an information organization. This discussion goes a step beyond the conclusions of previous authors by suggesting that, if the people who have direct contact with users are the ones who are best suited to be making decisions about service, higher levels of the hierarchy can be eliminated or at least subordinated to the intermediaries. This approach turns the hierarchy into a flat, collegial organization.

Within the flat, collegial organization, there is a constantly shifting network of alliances as intermediaries working with certain users or groups of users develop new information systems and aggregate them into information services. These systems and services are direct responses to user information needs, and in this sense, the organizational structure of the information institution matches the market structure. It is interesting to note that this approach was one of the innovations at Mead Data Central (Griffith, 1994). The company shifted from a product-driven corporate structure to one that reflected the marketplace. This structure meant creating four market groups: legal, business, government, and international. Within each market group, the organization was flat enough to allow units to be devoted to specific groups of users. This approach is exactly the kind of organizational structure advocated here, and it is tempting to think that this approach to the marketplace may have made the firm a more attractive acquisition in the period following the publication of Griffith's article.

The implementation of a flat, collegial organizational structure for information institutions seems a reasonable recommendation for small institutions, where there are only a few resources to manage and accordingly no need for an extensive hierarchical structure. The adoption of such an approach in larger institutions, such as research libraries, database vendors, and government clearinghouses, may seem more problematic. Particularly of concern may be the lack of unified direction over the activities of the institution: an important aspect of control over the resources of the institution. Without some central authority structure to develop and promulgate a common mission and ideology for the institution, information services may be fragmented, and there may be a corresponding fragmentation of the mission of the institution. Service providers are frequently so bound up in their daily work that they are too busy to concern themselves with questions of mission or ideology. Gaps in services and inconsistencies in the activities of service providers may result. What seems to be needed is an approach to control that will coordinate the overall activities of the institution without requiring a hierarchical structure.

Several managerial approaches can provide for control over the overall mission of the institution, including ensuring that the efforts of all staff are coordinated, services are provided consistently, and a commonly espoused mission and ideology exist. These techniques, all of which center on communication between information providers, can work even in a large, flat organization. An institution does not require a large departmental hierarchy to ensure that all service providers have the opportunity to share with each other their approaches to developing information systems and services, their problems in working with users, and their ideals of service. Techniques of electronic communication seem to have particular merit in this regard. Electronic bulletin boards, discussion groups, and e-mail have the potential to facilitate intrainstitutional communication and thus lead to a spontaneous sense of mission rather than a mission dictated from the top of a hierarchy. It is entirely appropriate for an information organization to use communication technology for purposes of maintaining internal coordination and control over its operations, in addition to using it for service provision.

Program Budgets

The final aspect of resource management relates to financial resources. If the institution adopts the fee-for-service approach suggested previously, then the income of any information service will depend on how many users it attracts and serves and how well these users are able (and willing) to pay for the information they receive. Planning for expenditures on resources will be part of the responsi bilities of the information professionals who are engaged in providing the service. They may, for example, develop the fee structure for any system or service to include a percentage that can be applied to resource acquisition.

It is, however, possible to develop user-centered budgets in a more traditional funding environment by using program budgeting. This technique brings together the costs anticipated for meeting the needs of any particular user group. This assessment of user-centered costs can then lead to a request for funding from whatever resources are available to the institution. Every information service, defined (as throughout this book) as a collection of information systems dedicated to meeting the needs of a user population, can serve as a program in a program budgeting system. The budget process requires the information service to plan for one year of service and to anticipate the costs associated with providing service to its users for that year. It also requires the information service to justify the importance of the information service to users and to think through the most cost-effective ways of providing information services that will meet the information needs of its users. This chapter has emphasized throughout the dynamic nature of information systems and services and the importance of retaining a high level of flexibility so that information services can respond immediately to changes in user needs. The imposition of an annual cycle of financial planning can limit the ability of information services to respond as quickly as possible to changes in the user population. On the other hand, an annual process of financial planning provides an indispensable element of resource management, and it seems clear that information professionals must take the responsibility for ensuring that effective financial management is in place. This approach to financial management is one way to ensure that an information organization will survive as a viable institution. It seems appropriate to give up some degree of flexibility to obtain a stable and effective institutional infrastructure that will support information services on an ongoing basis.

Conclusions

This chapter has sketched some of the attributes of user-centered information institutions. Building and maintaining such an institution is essentially in the hands of information professionals. Inverting the bureaucratic hierarchy and placing managerial control in the hands of service providers will transform information institutions in the same way that focusing on users will transform information systems and services. This discussion has followed some of the implications of this transformation for the economics of information institutions. In a sense, the idea of implanting the fee-for-service approach in information institutions is a logical one, and a case can be made that such an approach will lead to a positive change in the attitudes that users and information professionals have about information service. It would be a mistake, however, to focus too much on the economic aspects of user-centered information institutions. It is quite possible to effect the transformation described in this chapter within the framework of more traditional approaches to funding information services.

Dramatic changes are occurring in the information and communication sector. New enterprises are coming into existence, and existing companies are merging to create communication giants. Some of this architectural change in the information industry is being driven by technological innovation, some by changes in national information policy, and some by a realization that there have been profound changes in how people live and work. These widespread changes in the information industry create an environment that encourages change in information organizations. The user-centered and market-driven approach recommended here can lead to viable, productive, and profitable information institutions in the future.

User-Centered Design: A Practical Guide V

Note: At the end of each even-numbered chapter of this book, a brief guide to the practical aspects of design is provided. This guide summarizes discussions in preceding chapters as they relate to the practical aspects of conducting user-centered design. Contents that have been added to this version of the guide are shown in boxes.

1. Identify a user population. The first and obvious step in user-centered design is to find a user, or more appropriately, a user population. Sometimes user identification is dictated by the mission of the organization where the designer works. In other cases, users may be selected by the designer. The identification of the user population is such an obvious step that it is sometimes omitted. This omission results in systems that are not particularly usable for any set of users.

The user population may be composed of either individuals or groups or perhaps a combination of both. Because different design decisions will be necessary for groups, they should be identified separately when they occur within the user population.

> Marketing considerations suggest that user populations identified for service by information systems will be increasingly narrow and focused in nature. This will facilitate the development of systems with features that are customized to meeting the information needs of one narrowly defined population, rather than large and diffuse user populations.

2. Investigate the information needs of your user group. The users identified in step 1 have a number of information needs. These can be investigated using a wide range of research methods, which are easily accessible in manuals on social science research or market research. The key element of this step is to talk to users and find out what kinds of information they need to resolve problems they encounter. No information system can meet all of the information needs of a user group. Once the full range of information needs has been identified, system designers must select those that their information system will be designed to meet.

User needs can be identified by reference to a problem-solving model. According to this model, information needs can be associated with problem perception, alternative identification, or alternative selection. Each of these classes of information needs will require different approaches to system design. User needs can also be typified by their setting. Information needs can occur in individuals or in groups. Group needs are sufficiently different from individual needs to require different design approaches.

Both individual and social factors influence the information needs that may occur within a user population. Designers should investigate the social and organizational settings in which information needs occur, because these settings may give rise to or constrain the information needs experienced by users. Figure 5 summarizes the design principles that emerge from a consideration of user information needs.

Some information needs arise from failure of perception. Some information needs are associated with a process of exploring a topic area so as to identify alternative courses of action. Some information needs arise from the need to associate alternatives with outcomes.

People can, and frequently do, engage in information avoidance. They interact with their environment by limiting their intake of information, ignoring information if it is associated with negative outcomes, and taking information shortcuts. Organizations are frequently equally irrational in their collection, processing, and use of information.

3. Discover the tasks that users accomplish as they meet these information needs. Again, research methods from social science and market research are useful in this step. The key element is to talk to users and observe them as they work on meeting their information needs. Identify the tasks that users employ as they meet their information needs and how they accomplish these tasks. Note the sequential ordering of the tasks. Try to distinguish between the tasks that are essential and those that are optional. The result will be one or more task models for each information need.

Tasks may be accomplished individually or collectively. Where users are observed to be completing tasks as a group, it is important to consider these group tasks separately from individual tasks in the design of information systems.

Tasks accomplished may be dictated by the social setting in which information seeking occurs. Social and organizational factors must be analyzed carefully, because they may constrain the number of tasks that individuals and groups choose to accomplish. When social factors constrain tasks in this way, information system design can be considerably simpler than when users can select from a broader range of tasks.

Expressing an information need is one key task that users will typically accomplish while meeting information needs. Different types of needs produce different types of need expressions and accordingly place different requirements on information system design.

Scanning the output produced by an information system, evaluating it, learning from it, and planning for additional steps in the retrieval process are important tasks in interacting with an information system. Designing for usability requires that these tasks be made easy for the user.

4. Investigate the resources that users require to complete these tasks. Each task completed by a user who is meeting an information need requires a variety of resources: background knowledge, procedural knowledge, and abilities. List the resources required for each task and identify the level of the resources required. For example, expert knowledge or high levels of verbal ability may be required to complete a task involving vocabulary selection. At the same time, it is important to note the levels of these resources that users possess. Some users, for example, may have less expert topic knowledge or lower levels of verbal abilities, and gaps between resources required and resources possessed are obvious areas of concern. Research methods to investigate the resources possessed by users can be found in any text on psychometrics.

Resources may be individual or collective in nature. Where individual knowledge and ability are concerned, psychometric methods are adequate to identify levels of resources possessed by users. In the case of collective knowledge and ability, however, it is essential to investigate the group processes by which consensus is reached. Collective resources may differ considerably from the sum of the individual resources of group members.

Resources may derive from and be constrained by social factors. Accordingly, it is important to investigate the social and organizational setting in which resources are being applied to the completion of information tasks. These settings may provide additional resources or may constrain how resources are applied to tasks.

Resources particularly important to the expression of information needs are knowledge of the problem situation, linguistic knowledge, knowledge of informants and what information they have, and knowledge of the social constraints that govern the expression of information needs.

Resources particularly important to scanning are abilities such as perceptual speed and reading ability, knowledge of the topic, and knowledge of the ways in which information is presented both textually and in images. Resources used in evaluating materials include abilities such as logical reasoning, as well as knowledge resources that relate to the topic area and the problem under consideration. Resources for learning include learning abilities and styles, as well as knowledge about how information is presented. Particularly important for planning are knowledge structures such as scripts and heuristics.

> Resources available to users include not only those they possess as individuals or groups and those that are added to the information device during the design process, but also those that are brought to the information interaction by intermediaries. Designers must consider these intermediary resources and make decisions about the boundary between the device and the intermediary when they create information systems.

5. Summarize the preceding steps in user models. For each distinct user group to be served by the information system, there will be a number of information needs that the system is designed to meet. For each of these information needs, there will be a number of tasks that must be accomplished. For each of the tasks, there will be a list of resources that are necessary. Integrating these elements together results in a user model that can be used to guide design decisions or that can be implemented as part of the information system to direct how the system will respond to users. For example, user models can form the basis for the preset options for how the information system will work, but users will be able to change the options to make the system conform to their own preferences.

6. Consider each design decision in the light of resource augmentation and enabling. The goal of system design is to allow users to complete the tasks that will meet their information needs. With this in mind, system features that will augment the resources of users when necessary will enable them to complete the tasks. Some of these features will be required by all users, while others will be required by only a portion of the user group. In the latter case, system features are best implemented as user-selectable options. Experimental research to identify interactions between user resources and design options can be used to select systems features that should be implemented as user-selectable options.

For those who are trying to perceive a problem, a browse-based system with associative links seems ideal. What is needed is a system that will allow people to enter the system with minimal verbal expression and navigate toward their information need. Linked experts that can provide the identification and diagnosis that people need can supplement such a system.

For those trying to identify alternatives by completing their understanding of a topic, a general-to-specific information system that allows selective exploration of topics in depth, while at the same time providing lateral links to related topics is needed. The electronic encyclopedia, textbook, or selective annotated bibliography may represent the kind of information service that can be useful in this process.

For those trying to select alternatives, in–depth information, arranged in such a way as to permit specific-to-general consideration and evaluation of alternatives, is needed. Advice can be provided by the information system about the consequences of various alternatives. A vector space retrieval engine adapted to create the raw materials of review articles or meta-analyses may also be appropriate.

Information selected must be appropriate to information needs, particularly as those needs are located within social and organizational contexts. Organization of information must facilitate the scanning, evaluation, and learning processes. Storage and retrieval techniques should permit information to be customized to the specific needs of users. This argues for flexibility in the design of storage and retrieval techniques. User interfaces can assist in expressing information needs, perceiving and scanning information, learning from information, and planning for further information seeking. Particularly important are navigational methods for finding information, help features to explain not only how to find information but how to interpret the information found, and facilities that allow users to select their preferences for how the information system operates.

References

Griffith, C. (1994). Mead Data Central's Rod Everhart: One year later. *Information Today, 11*(5), 21–22.

Jaffe, B. D. (1994). In absence of competition, a philosophy of proactivity will improve IS. *InfoWorld, 16*(45), 63.

Kochen, M., & Deutsch, K. W. (1977). Delegation and control in organizations with varying degrees of decentralization. *Behavioral Science, 22*(4), 258–269.

Line, M. B. (1995). Who pays for information? And why should they? In A. H. Helal & J. W. Weiss (Eds.), *Information superhighway: The role of libraries, information scientists and intermediaries* (pp. 262–275). Essen, Germany: Universitatsbibliothek Essen.

Martell, C. R. (1983). *The client-centered academic library: An organizational model.* Westport, CT: Greenwood Press.

O'Leary, M. (1992). Dialog targets end users. *Link-Up, 9*(5), 9.

Sengstack, J. (1994). Business profile: Creative Multimedia. *CD-ROM Professional, 7*(5), 59–69.

Shermach, K. (1994). Marketing's task: Make ride on the info highway a pleasant one. *Marketing News, 28*(6), 1.

11

Conclusion

User-Centered Design and Evaluation

Introduction

This book has considered a series of arguments that suggest that user-centered approaches create more usable information systems, more flexible and responsive information services, and more effective information institutions. All of these propositions have implicit evaluative content. The goal of developing information systems that are more usable than existing systems presupposes that there are ways of evaluating the usability of the systems. The idea of developing more flexible and responsive information services implies that there are ways of assessing how information services are adapting to user demands. To meet the objective of developing information institutions that support information systems and services more effectively, it seems clear that mechanisms to gauge how well the information institutions are attaining that objective are necessary.

Although the issue of evaluation has been implicit in much of the discussion throughout this book, evaluation criteria and methods have not been discussed in detail. This omission was quite deliberate. There was a real concern that a consideration of evaluative issues would interrupt and obscure the focus on the design of information systems and services. There are a number of reasons for this concern. The first is that information-science research has been dominated to a significant extent by evaluative methods and the results of evaluations. As Saracevic (1995) points out, evaluation research has been central to the development of information systems and services. The seminal investigations that establish the tone for a great deal of information science research include the Cranfield tests (Cleverdon, 1966), Lancaster's evaluation of Medlars (Lancaster, 1968), and (more recently) the Text Retrieval Conference (TREC) investigations (Harman, 1995). Similarly, among the research studies that have had the greatest impact on library-science research are Crowley and Childers's (1971) development of unobtrusive testing of reference services.

The centrality of evaluation in library and information science has had unintended consequences. The most important of these is that a cyclical design–

evaluation process has become the accepted approach to creating information systems and services. Designers of information systems create a base system, then rely on repeated evaluations of its functioning to gradually improve its performance. This reliance on a cyclical evaluation and redesign approach can work, but the success of the approach depends critically on the quality of the base system. If the base system is not carefully crafted, incremental improvements may be incapable of transforming it into a usable, functioning information system. In this sense, an emphasis on evaluation can be the enemy of good design. The earlier chapters of this book focused on principles of good design rather than on evaluative techniques, precisely because design principles have not always received the attention they deserve in library and information science research.

Another unintended consequence of the emphasis on evaluation in information science has been to shift the focus on quality to a post hoc process. In other words, efforts to build high-quality information systems and services occur after the design has been completed. What this means is that a continuity of effort must be maintained through the design, evaluation, and redesign processes. Unfortunately, there are numerous examples of designs, particularly of experimental systems, that are never completed by a thorough evaluation. There are a number of reasons for this. Some design efforts are rushed into production without evaluation in order to meet user demands. More frequently, designers complete the initial task of creating a base system, then move on to further design tasks. After all, design is their job. It is what demands their efforts and holds their interest. The evaluation of systems is left to researchers who may not have been involved in the design, and who have little interest in redesign and no vested interest in creating high-quality information systems. As a result, evaluation can be neglected, and the results achieved by these evaluations that occur can be perceived as irrelevant to the design community and consequently overlooked by designers. The continuity of effort demanded by the design–evaluation–redesign cycle frequently does not occur.

What seems to be needed is an integrated approach to design and evaluation. If the design principles outlined in this book are successful in creating improved systems, services, and institutions, only evaluation will demonstrate that success. At the same time, if user-centered design is employed, the amount of evaluation and incremental improvement required to generate successful and effective systems, services, and institutions will be minimized. Another way of looking at the suggestions made in this book is to think of a shift in the timing of research. Evaluation, as a post hoc process, takes place at the end of the design process, but the user-centered approach suggested here requires that research into user needs, tasks, and resources occurs before the design can begin. This conclusion means that the bulk of the research effort will be shifted from the end of the design process to the beginning. There are a number of important implications that arise from this shift in the timing of research. First, studies of user needs, tasks, and resources can occur in a system-independent manner. This type of research is to be contrasted with evaluation, which is always evaluation of a given system. System-independent investigations have the potential to discover new ways of creating usable systems and flexible services, because they are not constrained by the limitations of existing systems and services. The second implication of shifting from evaluative studies to studies of the user population is that user studies can create a systematic and cumulative understanding. One of the problems with evaluation research is that it is notoriously difficult to generalize from one evaluation to another. As a result, a systematic body of knowledge about information systems is not developed, and every system must be independently evaluated. However, investigations of the effects of different levels of knowledge resources on the expression of information needs or of the effects of different levels of cognitive abilities on scanning text produce results that are likely to be stable and that can be generalized to a wide variety of information-seeking situations. The result is a cumulative and increasing body of knowledge about information users that can be used in many design projects.

There is, however, another aspect of the interrelationship between design and evaluation that must be stressed. New design principles seem likely to require new evaluation criteria and methods. In the past, design efforts have been data-centered, and evaluation has assessed the effectiveness and efficiency of data retrieval. In some cases, design has been device-centered, and evaluation has focused on the performance of the information storage and retrieval device. However, as designers move toward user-centered design, it seems clear that existing approaches to evaluation will be perceived as inadequate. The emphasis on data retrieval and device performance must be augmented by user-centered evaluation. The remainder of this chapter considers how user-centered evaluation can supplement existing evaluation criteria and methods.

Evaluating Information Systems

As indicated previously, most evaluations of information systems have focused on data retrieval and system performance. The most important measures of data retrieval have been precision and recall, and it is interesting to note that in the most thorough approach to evaluation of the 1990s, the TREC initiatives, measures of system quality remained precision and recall, with the addition of related measures such as precision and fallout, and average precision taken at various recall levels (Harman, 1995; Sparck Jones, 1995). The fact that recall and precision are based on assessments of relevance has not changed from Cranfield to TREC, nor has the predominant technique of ignoring user judgments of relevance in favor of expert judgments. Chapter 7 describes the transition from this traditional approach to relevance toward an emphasis on user-centered relevance criteria. The first step in moving toward user-centered evaluation of information systems is surely to replace artificial relevance judgments with those of real people with real information needs. This first step is just the beginning of the transformation that user-centered evaluation demands.

Measures of device performance have included speed of retrieval, usually measured through response time, and internal measures of efficiency, or the number of times a device reads information from a storage device, such as a hard disk or a CD-ROM. Response time has a certain attraction as a user-centered evaluation criterion, since many users find slow responses frustrating, but elapsed time is not the best way to measure how users will react to an information system. It seems clear that time is relative in the minds of users. They will wait happily for good results, provided the results come within a period of time bracketing their expectations of a reasonable time period. On the other hand, users will be likely to consider even a short time waiting for useless information to be far too long.

The development of evaluation criteria and techniques that place users at the center of the evaluation process can begin by adding usability to criteria such as retrieval effectiveness and device performance. Chapter 2 discusses the deficiencies of many current approaches to usability testing. Frequently, usability assessment is left until the end of the design process, where it is least able to influence that process. As a result, it is done hurriedly, using such shortcuts as cognitive walkthroughs. However, if usability is built into the information system by design, it seems clear that it can be an important addition to standard evaluative measures. The procedures suggested in the chapters of this book may be adapted to provide new approaches to the evaluation of usability.

The design process can be summarized briefly. The designers of the information system identify the users of the system in advance. They conduct detailed investigations of the information needs that these users experience, the tasks they accomplish in meeting those needs, and the resources they employ in completing the tasks. Then, for all design options, the designers consider how their design features interact with the resources that users bring to information tasks. Where research indicates that it is appropriate to do so, one design option will be selected for inclusion in the information system, because it augments user resources that are necessary to complete information tasks. In other cases, more than one design option will be built into the system as a user-selectable feature. In these cases, users will be able to select the configuration of the information system that provides them with the most appropriate resource mix, so that they can complete their information tasks and so meet their information needs.

The discussion now turns to the evaluation process. Usability can be assessed by sampling active users of the information system. For this sample of system users, interview, survey, and focus group techniques can be used to ascertain the nature of the information needs experienced by those users. These information needs may be identical to those discovered during the design stage, but it is more likely that the information needs of the user population will have changed to some extent between the design and evaluation processes. The tasks that users accomplish to meet their information needs can be similarly assessed. Once again, there may be some level of evolution in the nature of information tasks over time, and continued evaluation will show how these tasks change as new users with new information problems begin to interact with the system. Finally, the resources that users bring to the information tasks can be assessed through testing.

Thus far, the evaluation component mimics the design component. One can consider this kind of evaluation to be an extended and ongoing design process. This understanding may in fact provide a fruitful reconceptualization of evaluating information systems. Having completed the analysis of needs, tasks, and resources of a user sample, the usability assessment turns to the ways that this sample of users interacts with the information system. Detailed transaction logs will reveal, for example, which system features are selected for use from among the user-selectable design options. These transaction logs will also reveal the extent to which the information system is able to augment the individual and socially provided resources of users to allow them to complete their information tasks.

Of course, transaction logs are unobtrusive but indirect indicators of usability. The best evidence for system usability will come from user reactions to the system. This consideration leads to the rather slippery domain of user satisfaction. User satisfaction with information systems, as assessed through a variety of survey instruments, has been rightly denigrated as providing little solid evaluative information. User satisfaction depends critically on the expectations the users bring to the encounter. These expectations may be so low that virtually any response from an information system will be considered satisfactory. It seems likely, however, that the principal fault with user satisfaction measures is not with the criterion, but rather with how data have been collected. Using more in-depth approaches to data gathering, including interviews and systematic observation, it should be possible to determine whether users from the sample have satisfied their information needs, whether they found the information tasks easy to accomplish, and whether they found the information system pleasant to use. Detailed measures of user-centered relevance of information provided by the system can supplement results from interviews and observation. The result will be a balanced assessment of information-system usability that can be applied to the ongoing task of information-system redesign and improvement.

The preceding discussion relates chiefly to large-scale bibliographic or text-retrieval systems. Evaluation of other types of information systems, including large-scale corporate databases, has followed similar patterns and achieved similar results. In these systems, however, there are frequently two levels of users. In a credit-card processing center, for example, the ultimate user may be the customer making a telephone call to find out how his or her credit limit can possibly have been exceeded. The other user is the employee who is talking to the customer and trying to get the information system to divulge the relevant details. User-centered evaluation in this situation is complex, because it requires data collection from both the customer and the employee. Contacting the customer to judge user satisfaction is an approach that is frequently adopted, but employee satisfaction with system performance is just as important.

Another approach to assessing the performance of information systems and the effectiveness of data retrieval provides an additional example of how evaluation can be transformed by a user-centered approach. In pioneering studies, Crowley and Childers (1971) introduce the techniques of unobtrusive evaluation to the domain of library information systems and services. In this study, the user is represented by a surrogate, a trained proxy who approaches an information system or service and asks a factual question. The performance measure is usually the accuracy of the response received, aggregated across a number of queries posed in a similar manner to the same information system or service. More recent elaborations have studied other aspects of the information interaction, such as the setting in which information services are provided (see, for example, Durrance, 1989). However, for the most part, unobtrusive testing has been used to assess the performance of the human component of these systems and services, the information intermediary or reference librarian. In some cases, the performance of individual librarians (measured by the accuracy and completeness of their responses to factual questions) has been the focus. It is clear from the large body of documented research that unobtrusive testing remains centered not on the user, but on the information service and its constituent information systems.

It is not difficult to see how unobtrusive testing can be transformed into a test of information-system usability, in addition to its focus on information-system performance. Instead of having the control over extraneous variables and relative ease of research administration that comes from using surrogates or proxies, one should use real users who have real information needs in assessing information services and systems in these tests. Instead of artificially created factual questions, the information interactions should center on genuine expressions of information need. To implement unobtrusive testing with real users, researchers will have to work for some time with people who may be expected to experience information needs. This advance preparation sets the stage for observing the information interaction through the users' eyes. When the inevitable happens and an information need occurs, the researcher will be able to meet with the user and collect data about how well the information tasks were accomplished, how well the information system augmented individual resources, and how effectively the information provided by the information system or service met the information need.

Evaluating Information Services

In information services (as opposed to information systems) evaluative techniques have not been as thoroughly developed. In part, this is because of the em-

phasis in library and information science on evaluating systems as part of an iterative design approach. Information services, not usually considered suitable objects
for iterative design, seem to have been evaluated on a rather ad hoc basis, but the
information partnership between user and intermediary that is at the heart of the
information service seems an obvious focus for evaluation. It is not yet clear if
there have been any attempts by researchers or practitioners to evaluate the effectiveness and success of information partnerships.

The information partnership as outlined in Chapter 9 is a crucial part of the
functioning of the information service. Through this partnership, assistance and
instruction are offered to the user. Negotiations about the objective of the information interaction and the sharing of effort between intermediaries and users occur in this partnership. The relationship between the partners is cemented by these
negotiations and by the sharing of information about the problem being jointly
addressed in the information interaction. In short, this is a complex service relationship that can succeed in many ways, but can also fail. It seems clear that any approach to usability assessment for information systems must be focused on the information partnership.

It is not difficult to piece together the details of a research design that can accomplish this kind of usability assessment. It is possible to take a hint from the survey approach to evaluating library reference department transactions developed by
Bunge and Murfin (Bunge, 1985; Murfin & Gugelchuk, 1987). In this technique,
librarians and patrons both complete a brief survey that asks about the information
interaction. In the analysis, the responses of the two respondents are compared to
obtain a more complete picture of how the interaction succeeded and where it
failed. Although the survey technique is probably inadequate for gathering the kind
of detailed data that allows an in-depth assessment of the information partnership,
the idea of obtaining separate assessments from each partner has a great deal to recommend it. Accordingly, researchers can establish a mechanism through which selected users and their information intermediary partners will be interviewed at various times. If the information interaction extends over a period of weeks or months,
this evaluation can occur while the partnership is developing and evolving. If the
information interaction is rather brief, there can be an exit interview with both
parties that will assess the success of the interaction.

In the interviews, researchers will be able to investigate the nature of the negotiations that established the objectives and divided the labor of the information
interaction and then question the extent of information sharing, including the assistance, advice, and instruction offered by the information intermediary. The success of each of these mechanisms for building and maintaining an effective partnership can then be compared with the outcome of the process as perceived by each
of the parties. Particularly important, of course, is the perspective of the user. One
principal focus of the investigation must be to consider how pleasant and productive the information interaction was for the user, including the extent to which
the user perceives that his or her information need has been met.

Evaluating Information Institutions

The evaluation of an information institution may seem at first sight to be an inappropriate candidate for the user-centered approach. Institutions are typically evaluated on how well they meet their stated objectives and fulfill their mission. As indicated in Chapter 10, the mission of an information institution is simply to provide a management infrastructure that will support the provision of information services, and at the same time, be flexible enough to allow its component information systems and services to adapt to changing user needs.

In any private-sector information institution, the ultimate test of the institution's effectiveness is its bottom line. If the institution provides a business environment that allows information systems and services to deliver valuable and valued information to users, then users will be willing to pay for that information. To the extent that users are satisfied customers, they will return to the information institution repeatedly to resolve their information needs. The firm will develop a reputation for delivering high-quality information services at fair prices and will flourish. Here, the bottom line is truly a summative measure of the effectiveness of the information institution. Of course, there are many examples of firms that have made a great deal of money in the short run by selling shoddy products to unsuspecting customers, but these firms cannot maintain their sharp business practices in the long run. Consumers will ultimately learn their lesson, and profits will fall. In private-sector information institutions, there are many ways to make money, but all of them involve matching the quality and value of the information provided with the price of the service, thus ensuring customer satisfaction. In a sense, the accountant's bottom line, net income, is a truly user-centered measure of the effectiveness of information institutions, because it is the users who purchase the information services and so establish the income figures that ultimately result in the net income of the firm.

Taking a parallel approach to assessing the quality of information institutions in the not-for-profit sector is impossible. There seems to be no single measure that can be used to assess how well libraries and related institutions are functioning. In such institutions, expenditures rise to consume available funds, and there is no clear link between funding received and the success of the institution in providing an infrastructure that will support quality information services. The absence of such a link between funding and institutional success may be seen as another argument in favor of the fee-for-service approach to funding information institutions, recommended in Chapter 10. In the absence of bottom-line measures, however, information institutions can employ more qualitative approaches to evaluation.

There are a variety of approaches to assessing quality in information institutions. The objectives of these institutions, as outlined in Chapter 10, include providing a managerial infrastructure that will support flexibility and quality in service provision, marketing information services to the target audience, and cooperating with other institutions and agencies to ensure that effective information systems and services are made available to all users. Each of these objectives can be compared with institutional performance to create user-based evaluation mechanisms. Once again, a sample of the user population is the starting point. Details of information interactions with information systems and services within an institution will provide ways of assessing the quality of the institution. Users may, for example, reveal details of how long they had to wait to obtain an appointment with their information specialist. This variable indicates the institution's effectiveness in performing its management function of ensuring adequate staff to meet demand. User input can also be obtained on how the information systems and services of the institution anticipate emerging needs. These information needs, associated with changes in the user community or in the bodies of knowledge of interest to the user community, can be resolved easily if the information institution has adequate flexibility in its management of information resources. So, for example, a new information system can be put in place to anticipate user needs for information about current trends in science or current events in world politics. If users experience gaps in the availability of information systems in these emerging areas, this experience suggests that the information institution is not sufficiently flexible in its resource management.

The marketing function of an information institution can also be assessed through interaction with users. The effectiveness of marketing campaigns in terms of product and brand-name recognition, customer loyalty, and attitudes about the product are frequently measured in the corporate sector using focus groups. This technique can be easily adapted to assessing an information institution's effectiveness in attracting patrons to its information services. The objective of attracting patrons can be further elaborated by considering that only some of the members of the community at large should be attracted to any given information institution. Other members of the community should be dissuaded from making use of the information systems and services of the institution. No information agency can be expected to meet all of the information needs of all possible members of that community. Focus groups representative of all components of the community at large will reveal the marketing campaign's effectiveness in attracting appropriate patrons, while making it clear to others that it may be better to employ the services of other institutions.

The quality of the institution while cooperating with other information agencies can also be assessed through a user's eyes. As noted previously, no institution can be expected to be all things to all members of the user community. Chapter 10 sketches the details of a referral network that ensures that users are placed in contact with appropriate information institutions quickly and efficiently. This discussion recognizes that it can be exceedingly frustrating for people to be referred from one service to another repeatedly, without receiving the needed information from any service. Simply asking a sample of users about their experience with referrals from one institution to another will provide clear evidence of the effectiveness of any information institution in performing this referral function.

The general approach to evaluation at the institutional level proposed here is to consider each of the information institution's objectives in turn and to ask users about their experiences with institutions in ways that will reveal the institution's effectiveness. At the same time, the outcome of evaluating the quality of information systems and services will provide an indirect assessment of the institutions in which those systems and services are housed. The result will be a balanced and thorough evaluation of information institutions that can supplement traditional economic (bottom-line) measures in the private sector and can stand alone in the evaluation of not-for-profit organizations.

Conclusion

These approaches to evaluation have provided an opportunity to draw together the many themes of this book. Just as user-centered evaluation is seen as transforming the evaluation of information systems, services, and institutions, user-centered approaches have the potential to transform the entire information industry. The approaches to the design and implementation of information systems that occupy the largest part of this book are revolutionary in the sense that they refocus the priorities of system designers. Similarly, the ways that information systems are combined into services and ultimately into institutions can be dramatically reshaped by focusing on the needs that users have, the tasks they accomplish in meeting those needs, and the resources they employ in accomplishing those tasks.

The user-centered approach advocated in this book has solid underpinnings in theory and research, and at the same time, represents the practical experience of information professionals engaged in developing information services, of business people establishing and refining information enterprises, and of scholars studying the information sector. In closing a discussion that has moved from the inner workings of the human mind to the political realities of the workplace, it seems appropriate to reflect back to the words of Norman (1986), who proposes that the business of system design is to create systems that are pleasant to use. Although this objective may seem a bit quixotic, the approaches outlined in this book may provide one way to approach the design of pleasant information systems and information systems, services, and institutions that will really work to meet the needs of users.

The greatest cause for optimism about the future of user-based design in the information sector is the dynamism of the information industry, driven partly by technological change and partly by organizational restructuring. One outcome of this dynamism is the widespread availability of a substantial amount of electronic information in many different media and formats. Concurrent with this development is the widespread distribution of multimedia authoring packages based on Hyper Text Markup Language (HTML) and its successors. In this environment, the design and implementation of information systems is no longer in the hands of a few specialists. Rather, every information professional can create small-scale information systems focused on specialized information needs.

Out of the chaos that typifies the World Wide Web today, a number of user-centered information-system features are developing, including navigational approaches to finding information, facilities for incorporating user comments into the information structure, and a highly competitive environment for search engines that may enhance the effectiveness of search systems. At the same time, there is some reason to hope that the diverse activities of many research and development laboratories that are subsumed under the label Digital Libraries will do more than simply generate large batches of digital data. There are some intentions in these research projects to understand user needs and tasks and to take this understanding into account in information-system design. Although there may be some legitimate question about the seriousness of these intentions, and the extent to which the user-centered aspects of Digital Library projects really influence the design process, there are opportunities for user-centered design in these projects that can revolutionize access methods and systems.

Within the ferment and dynamism displayed by the information industry, the user-centered approach advocated in this book can provide a constant direction. Despite changes in data, technology, and infrastructure, the real information needs of real people provide a uniform purpose and guide for information-system design and implementation. The user-centered approach is, therefore, more than a revolutionary basis for creating information systems, services, and institutions. It represents a constant criterion for success in the information industry.

References

Bunge, C. A. (1985). Factors related to reference question answering success: The development of a data-gathering form. *RQ, 24*, 482–486.

Cleverdon, C. W. (1966). *Factors determining the performance of indexing systems.* Cranfield, UK: Cranfield College of Aeronautics.

Crowley, T., & Childers, T. (1971). *Information service in public libraries: Two studies.* Metuchen, NJ: Scarecrow.

Durrance, J. C. (1989). Reference success: Does the 55 percent rule tell the whole story? *Library Journal, 114*(April 15), 31–36.

Harman, D. (1995). Overview of the second text retrieval conference (TREC-2). *Information Processing & Management, 31*(3), 271–289.

Lancaster, F. W. (1968). *Evaluation of the operating efficiency of MEDLARS: Final report.* Washington, DC: National Library of Medicine.

Murfin, M. E., & Gugelchuk, G. M. (1987). Development and testing of a reference transaction assessment instrument. *College and Research Libraries, 48*, 314–338.

Norman, D. A. (1986). Cognitive engineering. In D. A. Norman & S. W. Draper (Eds.), *User centered system design: New perspectives on human–computer interaction* (pp. 31–61). Hillsdale, NJ: Lawrence Erlbaum Assoc.

Saracevic, T. (1995). Evaluation of evaluation in information retrieval. In E. A. Fox, P. Ingwersen, & R. Fidel (Eds.), *SIGIR '95: Proceedings of the 18th international ACM SIGIR conference on research and development in information retrieval* (pp. 138–146). New York: ACM.

Sparck Jones, K. (1995). Reflections on TREC. *Information Processing & Management, 31*(3), 291–314.

Index

A

Abilities, cognitive, *see* Cognitive, abilities
Access to information, *see* Information, access
Action–consequence links, 72, 77, 83, 87–88
Advance organizers, 161, 203, 224
Affordances, 163
Alternatives
   evaluation, *see* Selection of, alternatives
   identification, *see* Identification of, alternatives
   selection, *see* Selection of, alternatives
Analogy, 165, 203
Anomalous state of knowledge, 60
ASK, *see* Anomalous state of knowledge
ATM, *see* Automated teller machine
Automated teller machine, 66
   comparison with OPAC, xi
Automaticity, 63–64, 79, 86

B

Blunting, 12, 90, 119–120
Body of knowledge, 4, 7, 36, 115, 133, 140
Boundary spanning, 147–149, 178
Bounded rationality, 118–121, 175
Browsing, 159–163, 166, 238
Budgeting, *see* Program budgeting

C

Classification, 159–161
Cognitive
   abilities, 40, 224
   engineering, 16, 127
   load, 209–210, 212
   model, 58–73
   styles, 40
Collection of information, *see* Information, collection
Collective
   information needs, *see* Social cognition model
   knowledge, *see* Group, knowledge

Communication models, 5
Comprehension, 191, 201
Computer-Supported Cooperative Work, 113, 177, 255
Consequences of actions, *see* Action–consequence links
Consumer information needs, 94–96
CSCW, *see* Computer-Supported Cooperative Work
Customizing information systems, *see* Information, systems, customizing

D

Data-centered design, 14–17, 111–112
Decision making, 100–102
   group, *see* Group, decision making
Design
   data-centered, *see* Data-centered design
   for
      failures of perception, *see* Failures of perception, design implications
      identification of alternatives, *see* Identification of alternatives, design implications
      information evaluation, *see* Evaluation of, information, design implications
      knowledge resources, *see* Knowledge, resources, design implications
      learning, *see* Learning, design implications
      planning, *see* Planning, design implications
      scanning information, *see* Scanning information, design implications
      selection of alternatives, *see* selection of, alternatives, design implications
   of information services, *see* Information, service, design implications
   user-centered, *see* User-centered design
Development of information services, *see* Information, service, development
Display formats, 194–195, 200, 204, 224

Documents, electronic, *see* Electronic documents
Dual coding, 204

E

Economics of information institutions, *see* Infor-
  mation, institution, economics
Electronic documents, 199–200, 205–206
Enabling states, 44, 152
Engineering, cognitive, *see* Cognitive, engineering
Evaluation
  gulf, *see* Gulf of, evaluation
  of
    information, 197–200, 210, 252
      design implications, 219, 225–228
      institutions, *see* Information, institution,
        evaluation
      services, *see* Information, service,
        evaluation
      systems, *see* Information, systems,
        evaluation
Execution, gulf, *see* Gulf of, execution
Expert, 131–136,163–164, 174–175
Explanation, 164–165

F

Failures of perception, 56, 65–69, 75–76,
  79–82, 110–114
  design implications, 158–167
Fee-for-service, 272, 276–278
Formats, display, *see* Display formats

G

Gaps in knowledge, *see* Knowledge, gaps
Gatekeeper, 148–149, 177–181, 254
GDSS, *see* Group Decision Support Systems
Goals, 192
Gratification, *see* Process gratification
Group
  decision making, 102
  information systems, *see* Information systems,
    group
  knowledge, 79–82, 86–87
  learning, 78, 211
Group Decision Support Systems, 102, 113, 177,
  255
Gulf of
  evaluation, 127, 189
  execution, 127

H

Health information needs, 90–94
Hypertext, 196, 229

I

Icons, 162–163
Identification of alternatives, 62, 69–71, 77,
  82–83, 87, 114–116, 136–138
  design implications, 167–172
Indexing, user-supplied, *see* User-supplied
  indexing
Individual differences, 39–41, 193, 198, 202,
  227
Informant, defined, 5
Information
  access, 236–237
  agency, *see* Information, institution
  as
    knowledge, 3–4, 115, 170
    process, 3–5, 14, 115
    thing, 2, 5, 14
  avoidance, *see* Blunting
  collection, 235–236
  defined, 2–3
  device, 18
    defined, 4
  institution, 120–121
    defined, 19–21
    economics, 274–280
    evaluation, 297–299
    management, 280–284
    marketing, 263–268
    planning, 268–274
  interaction, 246–250
  needs, *see* Needs analysis
    collective, *see* Social cognition model
    consumer, *see* Consumer information needs
    health, *see* Health information needs
    individual, *see* Cognitive, model
    managers, *see* Managers, information needs
    newcomers, *see* Newcomers, information
      needs
    political, *see* Political information needs
  organization, 238
  seeking, 26, 88
  service
    defined, 19–21, 245–246
    design implications, 250–255
    development, 265–267
    evaluation, 292–295

marketing, 111–113, 116–117, 120–121, 257–259, 279–280
  policy, 110–111, 115–116, 117, 120
  source selection, 140–143, 156–157
  structures, 114–116
  systems
    customizing, 47–48
    defined, 5, 19
    evaluation, 292–295
    group, 176–181, 232–234
  tasks, *see* Task analysis
  technology, 255–257
Institution, information, *see* Information, institution
Instruction, 255–257
Interfaces, 161–163, 237–238
Intermediaries, 5, 144–145, 246–250, 281–282
Intersubjectivity, 67, 81–82

K

Knowledge
  body of, *see* Body of knowledge
  collective, *see* Group, knowledge
  defined, 2–3
  disavowal, 102
  gaps, 62–73
  group, *see* Group, knowledge
  map, 221, 236
  resources, 35–39, 128–130, 135, 137–139, 143–144, 146–149, 192–194
    design implications, 152–156
  sharing, 249
  structures, 61–66, 69, 71, 200

L

Learning, 200–208, 252
  design implications, 228–231
  group, *see* Group, learning
Load, cognitive, *see* Cognitive, load

M

Management
  information systems, 12, 112
  of information institutions, *see* Information, institution, management
Managers, information needs, 100–102
Marketing of

information institutions, *see* Information, institution, marketing
information services, *see* Information, service, marketing
Medical information needs, *see* Health information needs
Mental models, 146, 161–162
Metacognition, 37, 212
Models
  mental, *see* Mental models
  of information needs
    cognitive, *see* Cognitive, model
    organizational, *see* Organizational model
    social, *see* Social model
    social cognition, *see* Social cognition model
Monitoring, 90–91

N

Needs analysis, 24, 26–29, 55–107
Newcomers, information needs, 27, 98–99

O

Online public access catalog, comparison with ATM, xi
OPAC, *see* Online public access catalog
Organization of information, *see* Information, organization
Organizational model, 58, 85–88
Organizers, advance, *see* Advance organizers

P

Partnership model, 246–251, 253–254, 260, 267–268
Perception
  failures, *see* Failures of perception
  problem, *see* Problem, perception
Person-in-situation model, 88–90
Persuasion, 80
Planning, 208–209, 252
  design implications, 231–232
  information institutions, *see* Information, institution, planning
Political information needs, 96–98
Problem
  perception, 62
  solving, 11–14, 18, 79–80, 91–92
Process gratification, 97
Program budgeting, 283–284

Q ————————————————

Questions, 129–131, 135–138

R ————————————————

Relevance, 197
Resource analysis, 24, 35–41

S ————————————————

Scanning information, 190–197, 210, 252–253
   design implications, 221–225
Schema theory, 69
Selection of
   alternatives, 71–73, 77–78, 83–84, 87–88,
      109, 116–118, 138–140
     design implications, 172–176
   information sources, *see* Information, source
     selection
Shared control, 247
Slot filling, *see* Identification of alternatives
Social cognition model, 57–58, 78–84
Social model, 57, 73–78
Socialization, 76
Statement of information need
   defined, 126
   group, 145–150
   individual, 127–145

Stereotypes, 42
Styles, cognitive, *see* Cognitive, styles
System
   1, 166–167, 220, 250–251
   2, 167–172, 221, 251
   3, 172–176, 221, 251

T ————————————————

Task analysis, 24, 29–35, 189–190

U ————————————————

Usability, 24, 45–48
   testing, 26, 45–47
User
   models, 24, 41–43
   studies, 59–61, 119
User-based customizing, *see* Information, systems,
   customizing
User-centered design, 16–19, 126–127
   comparison with
     bureaucracy, 2
     data-centered design, 14–19, 119–121
   model, 24
User-supplied indexing, 154–155, 157–158,
   166, 170–171, 173–174, 226–228, 252,
   267

Library and Information Science

(Continued from page ii)

Lois Swan Jones and Sarah Scott Gibson
Art Libraries and Information Services

Nancy Jones Pruett
Scientific and Technical Libraries: Functions and Management
ume 1 and Volume 2

Peter Judge and Brenda Gerrie
Small Bibliographic Databases

Dorothy B. Lilley and Ronald W. Trice
A History of Information Sciences 1945–1985

Elaine Svenonius
The Conceptual Foundations of Descriptive Cataloging

Robert M. Losee, Jr.
The Science of Information: Measurement and Applications

Irene P. Godden
Library Technical Services: Operations and Management,
Second Edition

Donald H. Kraft and Bert R. Boyce
Operations Research for Libraries and Information Agencies:
Techniques for the Evaluation of Management Decision Alternatives

James Cabeceiras
The Multimedia Library: Materials Selection and Use, Second
Edition

Charles T. Meadow
Text Information Retrieval Systems

Robert M. Losee, Jr. and Karen A. Worley
Research and Evaluation for Information Professionals

Carmel Maguire, Edward J. Kazlauskas, and Anthony D. Weir
Information Services for Innovative Organizations

Karen Markey Drabenstott and Diane Vizine-Goetz
Using Subject Headings for Online Retrieval

Bert R. Boyce, Charles T. Meadow, and Donald H. Kraft
Measurement in Information Science

John V. Richardson Jr.
Knowledge-Based Systems for General Reference Work

John Tague-Sutcliffe
Measuring Information

Bryce L. Allen
Information Tasks: Toward a User-Centered Approach to
Information Systems